THE BIBLE
THROUGH
THE AGES

THE BIBLE THROUGH THE AGES

The Reader's Digest Association, Inc., Pleasantville, New York/Montreal

Address any comments about
THE BIBLE THROUGH THE AGES to
    Editor, U.S. General Books
    c/o Customer Service
    Reader's Digest
    Pleasantville, NY 10570.

To order additional copies of
THE BIBLE THROUGH THE AGES,
call 1-800-846-2100.

*The illustration on the title page
of this book shows scribes copying
sacred Scripture in the garden
of a Benedictine monastery. It is
taken from an illumination in a
14th-century manuscript.*

Library of Congress Cataloging in Publication Data
The Bible through the ages.
        p.   cm.
     At head of title: Reader's digest.
     Includes index.
     ISBN 0-89577-872-6
     1. Bible—History.   2. Bible—Introductions.   I. Reader's digest.
     BS445.B457 1996
     220 '.09—dc20   96-11548

THE BIBLE THROUGH THE AGES

Staff

EDITORIAL

Project Editor
Robert V. Huber

Senior Associate Editors
Kathryn Bonomi
Judith Cressy

ART

Project Art Editors
Sandra Berinstein
Henrietta Stern

Senior Art Associate
Joan Gramatte

Associate Art Editors
Bruce R. McKillip
Susan Welt

RESEARCH

Project Research Editor
Kathleen Derzipilski

Senior Research Editor
Eileen Einfrank

Research Editors
Susan Biederman
Sandra Streepey

Research Associate
Deirdre van Dyk

Picture Research Associate
Yvonne Silver

Picture Research Assistant
Richard Seidel

PRODUCTION

Assistant Production Supervisor
Mike Gallo

Quality Control Manager
Ann Kennedy Harris

Contributors

Consultants
See page 6.

Writers
Celine M. Allen
Sean Dolan
Robin M. Jensen
Robert Kiener
Stephen M. Miller
Polly Morrice
Ora Horn Prouser
Thomas L. Robinson
Diane M. Sharon
Henry Wiencek
Joanne Wosahla

Researchers
Sally Dorst
Paula Phelps

Picture Research Editors
Alice Lundoff
Joan Scafarello

Picture Researchers
Joyce Deyo
Ede Rothaus

Editorial Assistant
Claudia Kaplan

Timeline Designers
Reineck & Reineck

Copy Editor
Susan Converse Winslow

Indexer
Marion Lerner-Levine

READER'S DIGEST GENERAL BOOKS

**Editor-in-Chief,
Books and Home Entertainment**
Barbara J. Morgan

Editor, U.S. General Books
David Palmer

Executive Editor
Gayla Visalli

Art Director
Joel Musler

Editorial Director
Jane Polley

Research Director
Laurel A. Gilbride

BOARD OF CONSULTANTS

The editors, researchers, and designers of THE BIBLE THROUGH THE AGES were privileged to work with some of the most distinguished scholars of our time. The names of these consultants and a brief sampling of their accomplishments follow.

Bruce Metzger, the overall consultant for THE BIBLE THROUGH THE AGES, has lectured at leading institutions around the world and has been a member of the faculty at Princeton Theological Seminary since 1940 (emeritus since 1984). He is the author, editor, or co-editor of a large number of books, including *The Oxford Annotated Bible with the Apocrypha* and *The New Oxford Annotated Bible with the Apocrypha, The Canon of the New Testament, An Introduction to the Apocrypha, The Reader's Digest Bible, The Oxford Companion to the Bible, Breaking the Code—Understanding the Book of Revelation,* and *New Testament Studies.* In addition, he has contributed to most of the major biblical journals.

Demetrios J. Constantelos is Charles Cooper Townsend Sr. Distinguished Professor of History and Religious Studies at the Richard Stockton College of New Jersey. He is author or editor of numerous articles and books, including *Understanding the Greek Orthodox Church.* He is a member of the Revised Standard Version Bible Committee of the National Council of the Churches of Christ in the U.S.A. and the Anglican–Eastern Orthodox Theological Consultation.

James M. Connolly is a former professor of liturgy at St. Joseph's Seminary in Dunwoodie, Yonkers, New York, and the Redemptorist Seminary in Esopus, New York. He is the author of *Human History and the Word of God.*

Armand Dasseville, O.F.M.,Cap., has devoted his life to teaching and writing about Francis of Assisi and related topics. He has worked extensively with Secular (Third Order) Franciscans.

Mindell Dubansky is the head of the Preservation/Conservation Unit of the Thomas J. Watson Library at the Metropolitan Museum of Art in New York City. She has written about and taught bookbinding and papermaking.

H. George Fletcher is the Astor Curator of Printed Books and Bindings at the Pierpont Morgan Library in New York City. He is an accomplished lecturer and has written extensively on early printing, including *Gutenberg and the Genesis of Printing* (the catalog for one of the many exhibitions he has mounted).

David Noel Freedman has been a lecturer and professor of Hebrew and the Old Testament at museums, seminaries, and universities since 1946. He is a professor and holds an endowed chair in Hebrew biblical studies at the University of California in San Diego, and is editor in chief of the Anchor Bible Project. His numerous books include *Archaeology of the Bible: Book by Book.*

David F. Graf, a historian who specializes in the Roman Near East, is a professor of history at the University of Miami. He was an associate editor on the *Anchor Bible Dictionary.*

David Hall is professor of American religious history at the Harvard Divinity School. He is the author of *Worlds of Wonder, Days of Judgment: Popular Religious Belief in Early New England.*

Robin M. Jensen is professor of the history of Christianity at Andover Newton Theological School in Massachusetts. She lectures and writes on political themes in early Christian art. She has also written pieces for the revised *Encyclopedia of Early Christianity.*

David Marcus is professor of Bible at the Jewish Theological Seminary of America in New York City and chair of the Hebrew Bible seminar of Columbia University. He has written *From Balaam to Jonah: Anti-Prophetic Satire in the Hebrew Bible* and *Jephthah and His Vow.*

Eugene Nida, a linguist, minister, and author, was the executive secretary of translations of the American Bible Society from 1943 to 1980 and the coordinator of research in translations of the United Bible Societies from 1970 to 1980. He continues to serve as consultant of translations for the American Bible Society and the United Bible Societies. Among his many books are *God's Word in Man's Language* and Translator's Handbooks of various Books of the Bible. He is the co-editor of the *Greek-English Lexicon of the New Testament.*

Thomas L. Robinson is a former professor of biblical studies at Union Theological Seminary in New York City and Harvard Divinity School. He wrote *The Bible Timeline,* co-authored *A Guide to Greek Syntax,* and was script consultant to *A.D.,* a television miniseries.

Jonathan D. Sarna is the Joseph H. and Belle R. Braun Professor of American Jewish History at Brandeis University in Waltham, Massachusetts. He is co-author of "Jewish Bible Scholarship and Translations in the United States" in *The Bible and Bibles in America* and author of "When Jews Were Bible Experts," in *Moment* magazine.

Frederick H. Shriver is professor of church history at the General Theological Seminary in New York City. He has lectured and written numerous articles and reviews on the Reformation, particularly the English Reformation.

William M. Voelkle is Curator of Medieval and Renaissance Manuscripts at the Pierpont Morgan Library in New York City. He has written *Masterpieces of Medieval Painting: The Art of Illumination, Italian Manuscript Painting 1300–1500,* and numerous articles related to medieval manuscripts and illumination.

Bruce Zuckerman directs the Archaeological Research Collection and West Semitic Research Project at the University of Southern California's School of Religion. He is also senior editor and publisher of *Maarav, A Journal for the Study of the Northwest Semitic Languages and Literatures.* He co-edited the *Facsimile Edition of the Leningrad Codex,* and his writings include *Job the Silent: A Study in Historical Counterpoint.* He has taught Aramaic, Dead Sea Scroll Epigraphy, Ugaritic, and Syriac.

Table of Contents

The Bible Through the Ages

❧ PART ONE ❧

The Oral Tradition

14

❧ PART TWO ❧

The Written Word

52

❧ PART THREE ❧

Words of a New Faith

130

☙ PART FOUR ❧

Copying the Word

216

The Printed Word

288

Introduction

THE HISTORY OF THE BIBLE STARTED THOUSANDS OF YEARS AGO, CONTINUED THROUGH THE AGES, AND IS HEADED FOR THE FUTURE.

Most books, no matter how influential they come to be, are written by a single individual or a group of individuals working together over a brief period of time—generally no more than a few years. The Bible, however, the greatest of all books, was written by a wide variety of authors, most of them unknown to us, over a period of more than 1,200 years. But it was not written as a single work. It is, in fact, a collection of sacred books, including volumes of law, history, poetry, wisdom, and prophecy.

The Bible Through the Ages The history of the Bible did not end with the writing of the last of its books. Once the books of both the Old and New Testament were written, someone had to determine whether or not they were divinely inspired and so qualified as sacred Scripture. The final canon of the New Testament was not set until the late fourth century. Later the sacred texts had to be copied and recopied, and great care had to be taken to establish texts that were free from scribal error and to translate those texts into languages that everyone could understand.

In the beginning, biblical truths were passed on by word of mouth. Later they were written on scrolls and still later in books

---

*A*bove, Jerome distributes copies of the Vulgate, his Latin translation of the Bible, in a miniature from the ninth-century Vivian Bible. (Copies of the book are shown in storage sheds on the sides of the panel.)

THE HEBREW SCRIPTURES (24 BOOKS)

THE LAW:

Genesis	Numbers
Exodus	Deuteronomy
Leviticus	

THE PROPHETS:

Former Prophets:	Latter Prophets:
Joshua	Isaiah
Judges	Jeremiah
Samuel	Ezekiel
Kings	The Twelve

(The Book of the Twelve includes: Hosea, Joel, Amos, Obadiah, Jonah, Micah, Nahum, Habakkuk, Zephaniah, Haggai, Zechariah, and Malachi.)

THE WRITINGS:

Psalms	Lamentations
Job	Esther
Proverbs	Daniel
Ruth	Ezra-Nehemiah
Song of Solomon	Chronicles
Ecclesiastes	

Amos

11

THE ROMAN CATHOLIC OLD TESTAMENT (46 BOOKS)

THE PENTATEUCH

Genesis	*Numbers*
Exodus	*Deuteronomy*
Leviticus	

Joshua	*Ruth*
Judges	

THE HISTORICAL BOOKS

1 Samuel (1 Kingdoms in Greek)
2 Samuel (2 Kingdoms in Greek)
1 Kings (3 Kingdoms in Greek)
2 Kings (4 Kingdoms in Greek)
1 Chronicles (1 Paralipomenon in Greek)
2 Chronicles (2 Paralipomenon in Greek)
Ezra (2 Esdras in Greek)
Nehemiah (continuation of 2 Esdras in Greek)
Tobit
Judith
Esther (with Greek additions)
1, 2 Maccabees

THE WISDOM BOOKS

Job	*Song of Songs*
Psalms	*Wisdom*
Proverbs	*Sirach*
Ecclesiastes	

THE PROPHETIC BOOKS

Isaiah
Jeremiah
Lamentations
Baruch (including the Letter of Jeremiah)
Ezekiel
Daniel (including the Prayer of Azariah and the Song of the Three Jews, Susanna, and Bel and the Dragon)

Hosea	*Nahum*
Joel	*Habakkuk*
Amos	*Zephaniah*
Obadiah	*Haggai*
Jonah	*Zechariah*
Micah	*Malachi*

of parchment, papyrus, and finally paper. In the Middle Ages Bibles were highly decorated and illustrated by hand. With the invention of printing, missionaries were able to carry Bibles to the far parts of the earth. Today the Bible can be sent electronically on the Internet. THE BIBLE THROUGH THE AGES sketches the first 4,000 years in the story of the Bible and points to its continuing history in future millennia.

Noah

Books of the Bible The number of the authoritative books in the Bible varies in different religious traditions. The Samaritans recognize only Genesis, Exodus, Leviticus, Numbers, and Deuteronomy. These 5 along with 19 others make up the Hebrew Scriptures of the Jews. The authoritative version of these books, known as the Masoretic text, is arranged in three groupings: the Law, the Prophets, and the Writings. The Law comprises the 5 books accepted by the Samaritans. The Prophets includes the Former Prophets and the Latter Prophets. The Writings includes all the remaining books. Thus the Hebrew canon comprises 24 books, as shown in the chart on the preceding page.

Historically, Protestant churches have regarded the Hebrew canon as their Old Testament, though differently ordered and with several books divided, making a total of 39 books. (Samuel, Kings, Ezra-Nehemiah, and Chronicles are divided into two books each, and The Twelve is broken into 12 separate books.) With the addition of another 27 books, called the New Testament, the Bible used by Protestants contains 66 books.

The Roman Catholic Church accepts an enlarged Old Testament comprising additional books and parts of books that are found in the Septuagint—the Greek translation of the Hebrew Scriptures that was widely used in the early church. Manuscripts of the Septuagint contain books that are not part of the Protestant canon, though they are sometimes printed as the Apocrypha.

Eastern and Ethiopian Bibles The Eastern churches accept all the books in the canon of the Roman Catholic Church, plus a few other books. The Greek Orthodox canon includes 1 Esdras, the Prayer of Manasseh, 3 Maccabees, and Psalm 151. (It also renames some of the books, as shown in the chart at left.) The Slavonic canon adds 2 Esdras as well, but designates 1 and 2 Esdras as 2 and 3 Esdras. Other Eastern churches have 4 Maccabees as well.

All of the books in the Eastern, Protestant, and Catholic canons are available in English translation in the New Revised Standard Version of the Bible (NRSV), which also identifies the several churches that accept them. Consequently, biblical citations in this book, THE BIBLE THROUGH THE AGES, are taken from the NRSV, which was first published in 1990.

The Ethiopian Church, in which the concept of canonicity is regarded more loosely than it is by most other churches, has two main forms of the Bible canon. In both forms the books total 81 in number, but the "broader canon" reckons 46 books to the Old Testament and 35 to the New Testament, while the "narrower canon" reckons 54 books to the Old Testament and the familiar 27 to the New Testament. Books not recognized as authoritative by churches include *1 Enoch, Jubilees,* the Epistles of Clement, and *The Shepherd of Hermas.*

Unity of the Scriptures The most remarkable feature of the Bible is its unity. The books were written over a period of at least 1,200 years by a large number of diverse authors in several languages (Hebrew and Aramaic for the Old Testament and Greek for the New Testament). Yet all bear witness fundamentally to the same understanding of the nature of God as (1) a God who acts, (2) a God who redeems, and (3) a God who gives hope.

The unity of the Scriptures can also be described in terms of the gospel (or good news) of Christ. Thus, the Old Testament can be regarded as the preparation for the gospel of Christ; the four Gospels set forth the manifestation of the gospel of Christ; the Acts of the Apostles narrates the early propagation of the gospel of Christ, from Jerusalem to Rome; the epistles provide the explanation of the gospel of Christ as relating to problems that confronted various congregations and individuals in the early church; and, finally, the Book of Revelation discloses the consummation of the gospel of Christ.

Critical Study of the Bible At times reverence for the Bible has been carried to such a point that any critical study of its books was frowned upon. But when it is found that some traditional views of the authorship and the date of certain books have been ill-grounded, it is not irreverent to seek for another interpretation that will do full justice to the facts of Scripture.

By such methods several traditional opinions have been virtually overthrown; for example, the Pentateuch is no longer attributed to the personal authorship of Moses but ascribed to a much later period in the history of Israel (probably the ninth through the fifth century B.C.). In the New Testament the differences in historical value between the Gospel According to John and the other three, synoptic, Gospels are generally acknowledged. It is now recognized that reverent and critical study of the language of the Bible, its thought, and its background can only lead to a fuller understanding of its essential message.

By the end of 1995 the entire Bible had been translated into 349 different languages, the complete New Testament into 841 languages, and at least one book of the Bible into 2,123 languages and dialects. As a result, at least 80 percent of the people of the world have some part of the Bible in their mother tongue.

—BRUCE M. METZGER

THE PROTESTANT OLD TESTAMENT (39 BOOKS)

THE HISTORICAL BOOKS:

Genesis	*Ruth*
Exodus	*1, 2 Samuel*
Leviticus	*1, 2 Kings*
Numbers	*1, 2 Chronicles*
Deuteronomy	*Ezra*
Joshua	*Nehemiah*
Judges	*Esther*

THE POETICAL BOOKS:

Job	*Ecclesiastes*
Psalms	*Song of Solomon*
Proverbs	

THE PROPHETIC BOOKS:

Isaiah	*Jonah*
Jeremiah	*Micah*
Lamentations	*Nahum*
Ezekiel	*Habakkuk*
Daniel	*Zephaniah*
Hosea	*Haggai*
Joel	*Zechariah*
Amos	*Malachi*
Obadiah	

Matthew

THE NEW TESTAMENT (27 BOOKS)

The Gospel According to Matthew
The Gospel According to Mark
The Gospel According to Luke
The Gospel According to John
The Acts of the Apostles

Romans	*Titus*
1, 2 Corinthians	*Philemon*
Galatians	*Hebrews*
Ephesians	*James*
Philippians	*1, 2 Peter*
Colossians	*1, 2, 3 John*
1, 2 Thessalonians	*Jude*
1, 2 Timothy	*Revelation*

The Oral Tradition

Almost everyone knows the stories recounted in the Books of Genesis and Exodus. They are among the best-known in the world. But as often as they are heard or read they continue to enthrall, teach, and edify. Tales of Abraham's journey, Lot's wife, Joseph's dreams, and others endured for centuries before being written down. They were treasured and passed along as part of an oral tradition that was common to cultures throughout the ancient Near East. For the Hebrews, the oral tradition was a way of recording their history and faith. It continued long after the Bible as we know it was written down.

"Paradise" by Flemish painter Jan Brueghel the younger

From the Settling of the Nile Valley to the Anointing of King Saul

PART ONE TIMELINE (The dates below are based on scholarly speculation and are approximate.)

4000 B.C.   3000 B.C.   2000 B.C.   1010 B.C.   1 B.C. | A.D. 1   A.D. 1000   A.D. 2000

4000–3400

BIBLE LANDS

4000 Settlement begins in the Nile Valley.

3761 Jewish calendar begins.

3500 Mesopotamian city-states such as Sumer, appear.

Sumerian worshiper figure

ASIA & AUSTRALIA

EUROPE

AMERICAS

AFRICA

3800 Nubia—the land called Cush in the Bible—arises.

Nubian incense burner

3400–3100

3400 Great flood covers Ur.

3300 A pictographic writing system is used in Sumer.

Stone tablet engraved with pictographs

3200 Early Bronze Age begins.

3200 Hieroglyphic writing is developed.

Egyptian hieroglyphs

3000 Earliest known ceramic pottery in Americas is made in Ecuador.

3000 Cattle overgrazing causes expansion of the Sahara.

Nubian bowl with cattle decoration

3100–2600

3100 Pharaoh Menes creates a united Egypt out of diverse tribes, with Memphis as its capital.

2700 Earliest known written story, the *Epic of Gilgamesh*, contains a Babylonian flood saga similar to the one in Genesis.

Legendary hero-king, Gilgamesh

2700 Chinese develop acupuncture and herbal medicine.

Medicinal ginseng root

2600–2350

Pyramids of Giza

2550 Pharaoh Khufu (Cheops) builds the Great Pyramid at Giza.

2500 Egyptians use papyrus as writing material.

Papyrus reeds

2500 Semitic people, including ancestors of the Patriarchs, move into the Fertile Crescent.

2600 Silkworms are cultivated in China.

2500 Peruvian craftsmen create decorative objects in gold.

2475 Corn (maize) is domesticated.

2350–1950

2350 Sargon the Great creates first empire in Mesopotamia.

King Sargon of Akkad

2160 Tower of Babel is built, probably patterned after a ziggurat, the stepped temple of Mesopotamia.

2000 Age of the Patriarchs begins.

2000 Bronze-working is widespread in China.

Bronze ritual vessel

2200 Minoan culture rises on Crete.

2000 Stonehenge in England is a center of religious worship.

Stonehenge

2000 East African cattle farmers carve bowls out of stone.

AMERICAS · EUROPE · ASIA · AFRICA · BIBLE LANDS · AUSTRALIA

1950–1600	1600–1400	1400–1292	1292–1190	1190–1010

1728 Hammurabi gives code of laws to the Babylonians.

1700 Hyksos, nomads from Syria and Palestine, invade Egypt and introduce the horse and chariot.

Stele inscribed with Code of Hammurabi

1600 Israelites migrate into Egypt to escape famine.

Egyptian mourners at a funeral about 1400 B.C.

1580 Egyptian funerary texts are codified in the Book of the Dead.

1500 Canaanites create the first alphabet.

1400 Hittites smelt and forge iron.

1366 Pharaoh Amenhotep IV (Akhenaton) introduces the worship of one god.

Akhenaton

1300 Phoenicia develops sea trade.

1292 Rameses II, pharaoh of the Exodus, begins his monumental building program.

1275 Moses leads Israelites out of Egypt.

Moses and the tablets of Law

1190 Egypt is invaded by the Sea Peoples.

1184 Trojan War ends with the sack of Troy.

1020 Saul is chosen first king of Israel.

1876 Chinese record first known eclipse.

1500 Indo-Europeans settle India and introduce Hinduism there.

Inscribed seal from Indus Valley

1200 Chinese create a writing system based on 2,000 pictographs.

Chinese pictographs engraved on tortoise shell

1950 Palaces and cities are built on Crete in Golden Age of Minoan civilization.

Double ax, a Minoan religious symbol

1600 Mycenaean warriors settle in Greece and soon control Aegean.

Figure of a warrior from an inlaid Mycenaean dagger

1200 Olmec culture, considered by many to be the "mother culture" of Mexico, rises.

57-inch tall Olmec basalt head

The World of the Patriarchs

THE LAND, LAWS, AND CUSTOMS OF THE ANCIENT NEAR EAST PROVIDE THE CONTEXT FOR THE EVENTS IN THE BOOK OF GENESIS.

The land that Abraham and his family traveled was the great arch known as the Fertile Crescent, which skirted the upper reaches of the Arabian and Syrian deserts. It was a land of arid vistas and rocky hills interrupted with green pastures, planted fields along the flood plains of rivers, and cities busy with the activities of merchants, craftsmen, and builders.

On the eastern side of the Fertile Crescent were the Tigris and Euphrates rivers, Mesopotamia, and the city of Ur, where Abraham was born. To the west was Egypt in the valley of the Nile River. Mesopotamia and Egypt were the homes of the Near East's earliest major civilizations. In time, the land between them, Canaan, also became important. With no major rivers running through Canaan, water and fertile ground were in short supply, but the land was of great value because the trade routes running through it linked Mesopotamia and Egypt. Consequently, a steady flow of traders and travelers brought the people of Canaan and its towns of Shechem, Hebron, Beer-sheba, and others into contact with the civilizations to their east and west.

Civilizations in the Fertile Crescent By the Age of the Patriarchs—sometime between 2000 and 1500 B.C.—the history of the Fertile Crescent was already long and complex. People had inhabited Meso-

Patriarchal clans such as Abraham's were actually extended families who traveled together. Family members shared the tasks of producing what they needed to live, but they also traded sheep and goat products for urban goods. Canaanite craftsmen are known to have been exceptional potters. They also wove fabrics and worked in bronze.

potamia from the earliest times, and large-scale settlement had begun there about 3500 B.C. with the arrival of the Sumerians. These ingenious people, who are thought to have come from central Asia, developed the first major civilization in the Near East. They devised irrigation systems that allowed them to cultivate grain and other crops in an arid climate, they invented one of the first forms of writing—cuneiform—and they may also have invented the wheel. Although there was no rock to be quarried along the flood plains of their rivers, the Sumerians became masterful architects, building massive pyramidlike ziggurats for worship, and city walls for defense, using bricks they had made from mud or from clay and bitumen.

Within 500 years Sumerian cities such as Kish, Erech, Nippur, and Ur functioned as independent states. But these powerful city-states fought for supremacy among themselves and against outsiders, ultimately losing their collective power. Around the time of Abraham—the 19th century B.C.—control of the region had passed completely from the Sumerians into the hands of a Semitic people known as Amorites, who ruled as the first Babylonian dynasty.

Civilization in the Nile Valley followed close behind that of Sumer and in many ways paralleled it. The Egyptians developed an extensive agriculture, devised a system of writing based on hieroglyphics, and were highly inventive builders and engineers. They too constructed buildings and walls of mud brick; but with sandstone, limestone, and other rock available to them as well, the Egyptians became the first architects of monumental stone structures—including the pyramids and other royal tombs. Geographically isolated in the ancient Near East, Egypt did not suffer the constant problem of invasion and attack experienced by the Sumerians. Nevertheless, about 3100 B.C., kingdoms established on the Nile in Upper and Lower Egypt merged into a single, unified, political state that would remain an entity—though its power waxed and waned—throughout the Old Testament period.

Life Outside the Cities There were cities, tiny villages, and vast stretches of unsettled land in the Fertile Crescent. Populations in the region varied in their ethnic makeup and language, and they changed constantly as new groups of people arrived

PATRIARCHAL CLANS IN THE FERTILE CRESCENT

Semitic people from Arabia first appeared in the Fertile Crescent about 2500 B.C. Some made permanent settlements there, but others spent their lives moving throughout the region as seminomadic clans. Indications about how these people looked, dressed, and equipped themselves come from a mural painted on the walls of a second-millennium B.C. Egyptian tomb (detail above). In it the women are pictured in bright-colored tunics and soft boots, and the men are shown wearing beards, loincloths, and sandals. The entourage includes children and donkeys; an assortment of tools, weapons, and musical instruments; and a supply of trade goods.

The villages of Sumer may well have resembled this marsh settlement located where the Tigris and Euphrates converge in what is now Iraq. The houses are made of reeds, and boats are the main means of transportation.

and settled. It was a complex world that Abraham walked into when he left his home in Ur. Obeying God's call to travel to Canaan (and briefly to Egypt), he would never return to his birthplace. Like other seminomadic clans, Abraham and his family probably lived outside the main cities, but although they traveled with their livestock, they were identified with specific areas—planting and harvesting crops and sometimes staying at a site for a year or more at a time.

A Sense of Permanence Clans traveled on foot and by donkey (camels were not domesticated until about 1200 B.C.), and the need to stay close to water restricted the distances they were able to travel at any given time. The tents that families used as dwellings were well suited to a seminomadic life—sizable enough for comfort yet easily transportable, offering shade and protection wherever they were set up. The clans were often well known to the townspeople at their various sites and frequently conducted business with local rulers and merchants. Many of the families owned slaves and vast amounts of property. Abraham bought land to use as a family burial ground, and Jacob bought land in Shechem. Given the importance of land in the patriarchal narratives and covenants with God, it is clear that Abraham's family had a strong sense of permanence in Canaan.

Although seminomadic clans probably had to cooperate at least nominally with local ordinances, their own internal laws were very much those of an extended family with a patriarchal leader. A combination father and governor, whose rule was undisputed until his death, the patriarch had many roles to fulfill. He was responsible for making sure that his family had a safe place to live and enough to eat. It was he who contracted for grazing and watering rights with local rulers each time the family settled, and he who set the terms for trading the clan's goat and sheep products for goods such as fabric, pottery, or bronze tools made by urban craftsmen. But locating sites and doing business were only part of it. Patriarchs such as Abraham were also responsible for making sure that family customs were properly observed.

Kinship and Marriage Among the customs maintained by the patriarch were securing a wife and inheritance for sons, and a husband and dowry for daughters. Sons traditionally remained connected to their father's home as adults, while daughters left when they married and became part of their inlaws' households. The bond between daughters and fathers-in-law was a strong one.

The most acceptable marital contracts were those made with other members of the extended family—an arrangement that secured loyalty and continuity. Thus Abraham married his half-sister, Sarah, and searched for a wife for his son, Isaac, among his own kin. Jacob married two of his cousins, who happened to be sisters. Many such marital customs would be forbidden when Mosaic Law was introduced. Meanwhile, it was not unknown in the patriarchal age for a man to marry two women, either of his own volition or because his first wife could not produce the desired heirs. Once a woman married, she was expected to produce an heir for her husband.

The Role of the Heir The son designated as the heir of a patriarch inherited his role as leader and a major share of his property, as well as his responsibilities. Having an heir was so important that a wife

might engage a slave to conceive her husband's child if she could not do so herself. Sarah made just such an arrangement with her servant, Hagar, although she would later resent the child of that union when her own son, Isaac, was born. Evidently in such cases the title of heir did not automatically go to the child of the marriage, or to the firstborn, since Sarah had to fight with Abraham to take any and all inheritance away from Hagar's son and secure it for her own. But God blessed Sarah's determination, letting it be known that Isaac was to be the sole inheritor of the covenant. "Do not be distressed because of the boy and because of your slave woman," God said to Abraham; "whatever Sarah says to you, do as she tells you for it is through Isaac that offspring shall be named for you [Genesis 21:12]."

There was one other factor that was just as important as inheritance to a son's success in achieving the highest position in his clan: the patriarchal blessing. Although this would seem to be the birthright of the eldest son, the Old Testament indicates the possibility of exceptions to that tradition when Rebekah cleverly secures Isaac's blessing for her younger son, Jacob. Although her actions might be seen as devious, it appeared to be God's will that she succeed. Trickery or no, Isaac's blessing fell to his younger son, and once a patriarchal blessing was bestowed, it could not be revoked. ❖

EVERYDAY LIFE IN SUMER

The Sumerians were extraordinarily inventive and their creativity extended to making both religious and household objects. An inscription on the seated figure (left), which was found at the Temple of Ishtar, identifies it as a singer named Ur-Nanshe. The stone toy or votive object (below left), made as a hedgehog on a wheeled cart, measures less than three inches long. A detail from a frieze depicting milking scenes (above), shows men pouring milk through a funnel into a jar. The hammered bronze kettle (above right) was a luxury item. Ordinary people would have used vessels made of pottery or leather in their homes.

21

Abraham and His God

THE CONCEPT OF A SINGLE, ALL-POWERFUL GOD DEVELOPED IN THE MIDST OF BELIEF IN MULTIPLE DEITIES OF EVERY DESCRIPTION.

Whan Abraham heeded God's call and left his home for Canaan, he set out on a journey of faith as well as a trek across the land. But even though this was a pilgrimage in response to God's promise of a great nation, the journey cannot have been easy. Abraham and his clan were covering unfamiliar terrain that was alternately baffling and awe-inspiring, inhospitable and rewarding. Though their travels brought them into contact with intensely religious cultures, Abraham's personal relationship with God was different from anything he found in his travels or had known in Ur.

A Land of Many Gods Little is known about Abraham's early beliefs, but as a man who belonged to the culture of the Fertile Crescent, the Patriarch originally may have worshiped many gods. Joshua hinted at those beliefs when he asked the people of Canaan to "put away the gods that your ancestors served beyond the River [Euphrates] and in Egypt [Joshua 24:14]."

By Abraham's time—about the 19th century B.C.—religious practices of the newly established Babylonians in Mesopotamia were already ancient, since they were built on those of the earlier Sumerian civilization. Such borrowing from other religions was common. When invaders conquered a people they often took over the existing gods and goddesses, renamed them, and added them to their own pantheon. Thus the Sumerian moon god, Nanna, the fertility goddess, Inanna, and the sun god, Utu, among many others, kept their important positions when the Babylonians took power, and were renamed, respectively, Sin, Ishtar, and Shamash. Over time, some of the lists of gods kept by cultures in Mesopotamia included the names of thousands of deities, old and new.

This map depicts Abraham's journey from Babylonia to Egypt. The Patriarch was exposed to many religions and pagan gods (shown in gold) during his travels. Virtually all the people of the Fertile Crescent worshiped multiple deities, including the people of Canaan, where Abraham made his home.

PADDAN-ARAM

Haran

Halab
Ebla

Hamath

Mari

Nineveh

Asshur

M E S O P O T A M I A

Tigris River

Euphrates River

A K K A D

Eshnunna

Sippar

Babylon
(Sumer)

B A B Y L O N I A

Lagash

Erech

Larsa

Euphrates River

Ur

LOWER SEA
(PERSIAN
GULF)

Laish

Hazor

U P P E R   S E A
(MEDITERRANEAN SEA)

C A N A A N

Shechem

Bethel

Jericho

Salem
(Jerusalem)

Mamre
Hebron

Gerar

Beer-sheba

Sodom &
Gomorrah

Zoar

The Babylonians' religion was far-reaching. Not only did it elicit a good measure of respect for the deities, it also provided guidance and rules to live by. In fact, the Babylonians developed a solid body of laws that codified acceptable behavior and detailed such things as responsibilities in marriage as well as the rights of concubines and heirs. But they were just as aware of the need to provide answers to the great mysteries of life as to the mundane questions. They did so through a rich and lively literature that explained such things as the creation of the world, the origins of Babylonia, and the forces of nature.

Virtually all peoples in the Fertile Crescent had reason to fear nature, since they continually dealt with the difficulties of irrigating arid land and coping with seasonal floods and droughts that wiped out crops and whole populations. Not surprisingly, their beliefs were based on nature worship, with a god or goddess representing each element and sometimes particular rivers, hills, and trees.

A Hierarchy of Worship The gods were assigned differing ranks, depending on their influence and importance. At the top of the Babylonian hierarchy were deities representing heaven, air, water,

23

and earth. Among the Semitic Canaanites, the chief god, El, was followed in the hierarchy by Baal and Astarte, who were linked to the forces of nature and, like nature itself, had the power to create and destroy. Egypt's many gods included Horus, who ruled the sky, Ra, the sun, Thoth, the moon, and Geb, the earth.

In Egypt and Mesopotamia, and to a lesser extent in Canaan, where towns were smaller, there were also gods that represented each city. In addition, every craft and industry had its own protective god, and individual homes had altars for worshiping household gods, who were rather low in the hierarchy. The more areas of specialization a culture had, the more gods were included in its pantheon.

None of this could be of much use to seminomadic clans like Abraham's. In their society, the patriarch was the only one who had a

There was a solitary quality in the faith of Abraham. Not only was the Patriarch alone in his personal relationship with God, but his methods of worship differed from those of the people around him. His communications with God did not rely on priests, elaborate temples, or idols. They may even have taken place with the simplicity shown in this 19th-century painting, "God Renews His Promise to Abraham," by James Tissot.

leading role within the clan's daily round of herding, planting, preparing food, and looking after children. They did not need the protection of the gods of potters, metalsmiths, scribes, and merchants. Nor could they depend on the protection of gods associated with particular landmarks and towns, since they continually traveled with their flocks. The patriarchs' way of life may have had much to do with their recognition of a single God who would be with them wherever they went and who would be the patron deity of the clan rather than one associated with things and specific places.

Accepting a belief in only one God did not necessarily happen all at once; it had to be learned. There are occasional references to other deities in the patriarchal narratives. When God tells Jacob to settle in Bethel, Jacob says to his household, "Put away the foreign gods that are among you, and purify yourselves [Genesis 35:2]." But when Jacob gathers those foreign gods and hides them under an oak near Shechem, his actions indicate the abandonment of pagan practices.

The relationship that the Patriarchs had with their God was also a departure from those between other societies and their deities. Only powerful rulers and priests were privileged to communicate with the important gods in Egypt, Canaan, and Mesopotamia. The patriarchal clans had no priests. They communicated with their God directly, just as ordinary Babylonian believers did with their household deities. God in turn revealed himself and his purposes through them. When God decided to punish the people of Sodom for their wickedness by destroying the city, for instance, he talked with Abraham about his plan. Abraham not only answered but challenged God, arguing that there were people such as his nephew Lot in Sodom who deserved to be saved. God listened to the argument and agreed that he would not destroy the city if even 10 good people could be found. This was truly a new kind of relationship between man and his God.

The Face of God There were also great differences in how people saw their gods. In many religions of the Fertile Crescent, a symbolic face and form was assigned to each of the various deities. These images were reproduced as idols made in every material from precious metals to pottery. In most cases the gods depicted resemble humans, but some are partly or entirely animalistic in appearance.

In Egypt believers associated each of their deities with an animal: Horus with the falcon, Thoth with the ibis, and Ptah with the bull, for

Stone altars, like this Canaanite altar at Megiddo, were commonly built on high ground, to bring sacrificial offerings closer to God. The Patriarchs built altars and sanctuaries throughout Canaan, at places where God made himself known to them.

instance. Egyptian deities might be represented in either their human or animal forms. Mesopotamian gods were usually depicted as humans, athough some were linked with animals. Ea, who was the guardian of wisdom and fresh water, was associated with a fish. The symbol of Nergal, god of the netherworld, is a mace with a lion's head.

Not only were the gods thought to resemble human beings, they also represented both the best and worst of human behavior. They were capricious—alternately benign and malicious—and were believed to engage in periodic drinking bouts, carousing in the heavens while ignoring their subjects on earth.

The figures above right are family deities. The household gods that Rachel stole from her father and hid in her saddle may have resembled these lesser Canaanite gods. The god Baal (above) was often depicted wearing a crown with a single point to represent fertility. Baal was considered the lord of heaven and earth by the Canaanites.

This view was nothing like the concept of God that was developing among the patriarchal families. Their God was not associated with any one element or force but was all things. He could not be symbolized by an animal or a sun and was never pictured with a human face or form. In fact, he was the one powerful God of the ancient Near East who was never pictured at all. In one sense he was unknowable, yet at the same time his followers spoke to him directly—not through an image. Neither did Abraham and his descendants see God as a capricious force who ignored his people. He was always there, everywhere. If he grew angry and punished individuals or societies—as he ultimately did at Sodom—his actions were seen as just.

Ways of Worship God continually made it clear to Abraham that the way to please him was to turn away from evil and lead a good life. Certainly it had to be easier to know what sort of behavior was acceptable to God if he could be depended on to be reasonable and fair. In any case, the rituals of faith that developed with the Patriarchs were far simpler than those of the religions around them.

The Egyptians, Babylonians, and Canaanites alike built elaborate complexes of temples and related buildings that were set off from the rest of the community by a high wall. Important Babylonian temples were generally set on top of ziggurats, stepped towers that soared as high as 300 feet. Canaanite and Egyptian temples were often built as pillared halls. Only priests were allowed to enter these sacred places and tend the deity who was believed to dwell there. Inside, they would regularly feed, clothe, and bathe a statue of the god, which they believed to be alive. During festivals—which could last for days—the statues were removed from the temples and carried out into the courtyard or streets in special processions that allowed ordinary people the chance to honor the great gods.

The Rituals of Belief The deities seemed to have voracious appetites for the offerings of food and sacrificial gifts that were made to please or appease them. The burning of offerings and other sacrificial rituals were usually carried out at an altar or sanctuary at a site associated with the god. This might be one of the grand temples, but it just as easily could be a hill or man-made mound that brought the offering closer to the god. There was often a measure of sympathetic magic in these rituals: for instance, the Babylonians believed that by pouring water they could encourage a god to bring rain, and the Canaanites believed that reciting spells would kill their enemies.

The Patriarchs' religious practices resembled those of their neighbors in some ways, but there were important differences, such as putting aside magical rituals and the worship of idols. They acknowledged God by making offerings of food and drink and animal sacrifice, but according to some interpreters, God made it clear that he did not want human sacrifice from them when he spared Isaac's life. The altars and sanctuaries that the Patriarchs built were simple too—a circle of stones, perhaps, built up near a site where God had made his presence known to them. There was a sanctuary at Shechem and others at Bethel, Mamre, and Beer-sheba. Some of these were the same sites that the Canaanites used for their rituals, but the Patriarchs raised their own simple stone altars and worshiped only one God—the God of Abraham, Isaac, and Jacob. ❖

The golden bull with the face of a bearded man (below) is typically associated with the Mesopotamian sun god Shamash. He was seen not only as a beneficent god but as a god who had high moral standards. One prayer to Shamash said in part, "Whatever has breath, you shepherd equally; you are their keeper, above and below."

Storytelling and the Oral Tradition

THE CUSTOM OF COMMITTING TALES TO MEMORY AND RECALLING THEM ALOUD KEPT HISTORY ALIVE FOR COUNTLESS GENERATIONS.

Although tales of the Creation, of the Flood, and of the Patriarchs and their families started circulating almost as long ago as the events themselves, scribes probably did not begin to write down the lore of the Hebrews—the descendants of Abraham—until King David's reign in the 10th century B.C. By then, many of the tales recorded were already centuries old, but they had been preserved and passed along through a much respected tradition—storytelling.

The tradition of storytelling was shared by all the peoples of the ancient Near East. Tales traveled throughout cities, villages, and desert camps from the Euphrates to the Nile. The same story might become part of the lore of many different peoples or it might be unique to a single tribe. The key to preserving all these tales was the storyteller. For while parents surely told their children of long-remembered events—perhaps of Abraham, the Exodus, or of divine guidance in the wilderness—there were also gifted individuals who performed that role for their community. It might be a shepherd who was admired for his anecdotal expertise and who told his tales to his extended family in an open field, or perhaps it was a celebrated artist who recited by request at festive gatherings—but the storyteller's job was more than simply entertainment. His stories preserved the identity and collective memory of his people.

Storytelling Skills Until writing became common, memory was invaluable, since without it, ideas were lost forever. Thus the capacity for total recall was formidable among the ancients: a great storyteller might memorize an epic of some 30,000 lines of poetry as part of his repertoire. The ability to memorize through constant repetition was a skill that was admired among the people of the Near East, including the Hebrews.

Learning by repetition was almost as important to the people who listened to the stories as it was to the performer. They expected familiar tales to be told the same way each time they heard them. Rarely would listeners let the storyteller invent something new. Although he might add embellishments or weave in variations as his listeners responded to his story, the basic form and meaning of a tale could not be touched. It belonged to the people. The fixed story line helped them maintain links with the past and keep history rooted in the things they knew to be true.

Forms of Tradition Nevertheless, the oral tradition lent itself to a great diversity of forms. Genealogies served as historical records, proverbs provided memorable nuggets of instruction or codified acceptable behavior, and prophecies forecast the possibilities and dangers of the future. Poetry was common in all cultures with an oral tradition: the rhythmic cadences of songs, psalms, hymns, and laments served as an aid to memory—both for the storyteller and his audience. In addition, many types of stories were told as pure narrative. Gripping tales of the temptation of Adam and Eve in the garden, of Noah and the ark, of Jacob's wooing of Rachel, of Joseph sold into slavery, and of Moses and the Exodus fascinated listeners for ages before the stories were written down.

Stories of Faith For the Hebrews, two powerful forces gave authority to the voice of the storyteller: he spoke for their history, and he told the story of God's dealings with Israel. While the storyteller might incorporate details from material that was shared by other cultures— the story of Joseph and Potiphar's wife, for instance, was known to the Egyptians in a somewhat different form—his tales inevitably reflected the Hebrews' faith in a single God, and God's special relationship with them. As these tales were gathered, put in order, and written down over the course of five centuries—beginning about 1000 B.C.—they formed the basis of the Bible and a record of who the Hebrews were and where they had come from.

For hundreds of years after scribes first began recording their stories, the spoken word remained a powerful force among the Hebrews. Memory was still the storehouse of tradition, and the oral tradition would continue side by side with the written, finding its most heartfelt expression in religious ritual. As long as memory preserved the faith, it could never be destroyed. ❖

*S*haring traditional stories of faith has always been a cherished part of Jewish life. In ancient times, such tales might be recalled at a gathering of the family in the open air (left). Present-day Jews continue the tradition at the Passover seder. Celebrated (above) by a family in Iran, this ritual meal always includes a reading from a book called the Haggadah, which tells the Passover story.

Stories in the Oral Tradition

TALES THAT RECORDED THE DEEDS OF RULERS, EXPLAINED HISTORIC EVENTS, OR TAUGHT MORAL LESSONS OFTEN HAD AN ENTHRALLING QUALITY THAT MADE THEM MEMORABLE.

There were many types of tales told in the ancient Near East. Some were based on the doings of historical figures—kings, queens, and heroes—whose adventures were often spiced in the telling with magical events, mythic beasts, and superhuman deeds. Other stories, such as those that would become part of the Old Testament, were about ordinary people. Their concerns about raising children, increasing their flocks, and tending their wells were identical to those of the people who listened to the tales, yet these individuals also wrestled with a force that was larger than life, trying to follow the will of God or avoid it.

There were also stories that explained the hows and whys of fundamental events and beliefs—the Creation of the world, the concept of paradise, and the Deluge, among others. Different versions of these tales appeared in the oral traditions of people throughout the region. Though some may have sprung up independently, others probably derived from a single source and spread by word of mouth.

One of the great centers of culture at the time of the Patriarchs was Babylonia, whose oral tradition was widely influential. Themes from Babylonian tales resurfaced in stories told by the Hittites and Canaanites, as well as the Hebrews. Travel was a way of life for many people in the ancient world, and good stories traveled with them.

Creation Stories A poem called *Enuma Elish* is thought of as a Babylonian Genesis. But though it and the Bible story tell how the world was created out of chaos, they also differ dramatically. Starting at the beginning of time when the universe was nothing but water, the Babylonian tale explains how two powerful oceans—Apsu and Tiamat—joined forces as husband and wife to create the gods who would represent the physical features of the world. The first to appear were two gods named Lachmu and Lachamu, who represented silt. Next came the horizons, Anshar and Kishar, then Anu, the sky, and Anu's child, Ea, who was earth.

According to the tale, more gods would be created and battles would be fought among them before the world would look as it does, before the Tigris and Euphrates would flow where they do in Mesopotamia, and before Babylon could be established there. *Enuma Elish* was traditionally told on the fourth day of each New Year's celebration.

Flood Stories Traces of a deluge dating to about 3400 B.C. have been found in Mesopotamia, and some believe that it may be the basis for the story of the Flood in Genesis. Not surprisingly, there were also several Babylonian accounts of a flood that were passed along in the oral tradition. The most famous of these is told in an epic known as *Gilgamesh*—a poem so long that it requires an afternoon to recite. In one part of it, the hero-king Gilgamesh wants eternal life and goes in search of Utnapishtim—the only person in the world who has ever achieved it. When the two men meet, Utnapishtim says that he cannot help the young hero, but he does tell the story of how he won eternal life after surviving a great flood.

When he was king of the city of Shuruppak, he explains, the gods decided to destroy humanity because man was making too much noise. But the god Ea warned Utnapishtim and instructed him to build a great ship. After doing as he was told, Utnapishtim went on board with his family, his silver and gold, and representatives of all species of animals. Then a storm arose with such force that "the gods cowered like dogs" and the mountains were soon covered by water. After seven days it stopped, and when the land was dry enough Utnapishtim made an offering, sending it to heaven with sweet-scented smoke. The gods grudgingly granted him eternal life but did not allow him and his family to repopulate the earth as God did Noah. ❖

A Tale Within a Tale

Utnapishtim, who appears in the *Epic of Gilgamesh*, is called the Babylonian Noah. His tale of a flood—part of which appears below—is often compared to the Deluge described in Genesis.

When the seventh day arrived,
The flood-carrying south-storm subsided in the battle,
Which it had fought like an army.
The sea grew quiet, the tempest was still, the flood ceased.
I looked at the weather: stillness had set in,
And all of mankind had returned to clay.
The landscape was as level as a flat roof.
I opened a hatch, and light fell upon my face.
Bowing low, I sat and wept,
Tears running down on my face.
I looked about for coast lines in the expanse of the sea:
In each of fourteen regions
There emerged a region-mountain.
On Mount Nisir the ship came to a halt.
Mount Nisir held the ship fast,
Allowing no motion,
One day, a second day, Mount Nisir held the ship fast,
Allowing no motion,
A third day, a fourth day, Mount Nisir held the ship fast,
Allowing no motion,
A fifth, and a sixth day, Mount Nisir held the ship fast,
Allowing no motion.

When the seventh day arrived,
I sent forth and set free a dove.
The dove went forth, but came back;
Since no resting-place for it was visible, she turned round.
Then I sent forth and set free a swallow.
The swallow went forth, but came back;
Since no resting-place for it was visible, she turned round.
Then I sent forth and set free a raven.
The raven went forth and, seeing that the waters had diminished,
He eats, circles, caws, and turns not round.
Then I let out all to the four winds
And I offered a sacrifice.

No one knows for sure, but Gilgamesh (left) might have been an actual king about 2700 B.C. His adventures were circulated as individual stories long before they were recorded as a single epic. The tales were so popular that many copies were made—tablets of which (above left) continue to be dug from Mesopotamian sites.

31

Monumental works, such as the Rock of Behistun, left, often featured cuneiform writing cut into stone. More often cuneiform was impressed in clay tablets, bottom, some of which had their own clay envelopes, below.

The Birth of Writing

CUNEIFORM IS THE EARLIEST KNOWN SYSTEM OF WRITING. TRANSLATING IT OPENED THE DOOR TO A GREATER UNDERSTANDING OF MESOPOTAMIAN CULTURES AND BIBLICAL HISTORY.

Much of what is known about the laws and lifestyles of people from the time of the Old Testament comes from ancient texts—some more than 5,000 years old. The texts, which appear on clay tablets, stone monuments, statues, and even buildings, were inscribed in cuneiform, the earliest and once the most widespread form of writing in the Fertile Crescent.

For a long time, many scholars believed that these inscriptions were mere decoration. But by the mid-19th century, researchers had set to work seriously deciphering cuneiform script and in the process, discovering and reconstructing the languages of Mesopotamia. Among those who made major contributions toward revealing the secrets of cuneiform was Sir Henry Rawlinson, an intrepid English military man, classical scholar, and student of languages.

As a young officer stationed in Persia (modern Iran) in the 1830's and 1840's, Rawlinson became so intrigued with cuneiform that he risked his life to study it. The object of his obsession was the Rock of Behistun, a sacred site located on a 4,000-foot-high peak in the Zagros Mountains.

Heroic scenes and inscriptions on the rock date from about 500 B.C. and celebrate the deeds of Darius I, who ruled the Persian Empire. What fascinated Rawlinson, however, was that the rock's 10 columns of cuneiform writing—which cover a span

Writing in the Near East is thought to have evolved in the fourth millennium as a means of keeping accounts. Shaped-clay tokens, like those below, represented merchandise exchanged in a trade. The tokens were kept safe by sealing them into a clay pouch, or bulla, above right. A record was sometimes kept on the outside of the pouch by impressing the tokens in the surface.

some 60 feet wide and 22 feet high—represented three ancient languages of the region: Old Persian, Elamite, and Akkadian.

The writing was inscribed at a height of more than 300 feet on the rock's face, but Rawlinson was undaunted. He copied some of the text while standing on a ladder perched precariously on an 18-inch ledge, "steadying the body against the rock with the left arm," he wrote, "while the left hand holds the notebook and the right hand is employed with the pencil."

Rawlinson remained at his task until he had copied the entire inscription. By 1847 he had translated the Old Persian cuneiform, and by 1850 he had done the same with the other two languages on the rock. Understanding what was written on the Rock of Behistun was only a beginning. The ultimate deciphering of cuneiform required decades of work and the contributions of many scholars. But it is largely due to Rawlinson's efforts that cuneiform can be read today.

What scholars discovered in deciphering this ancient writing and tracing it back to its earliest forms, was that each cuneiform figure began as a symbol that represented a word or an idea. By the time that Darius I commissioned the inscriptions on the Rock of Behistun, those symbols had become highly stylized, the result of nearly 3,000 years of evolution.

THE DEVELOPMENT OF CUNEIFORM

In its original form, writing was inscribed in vertical columns and it was pictographic—each picture represented a word. Later, when larger clay tablets—which could not be held in the hand—were used as a writing surface, inscriptions were made horizontally, and the symbols were turned 90 degrees to the left. Pressing the symbols in clay with a wedge-shaped reed made the writing true cuneiform and further stylized the pictures. Some 2,400 years after its start, cuneiform writing bore only the slightest resemblance to its early pictorial forms.

The Beginning of Writing Cuneiform is thought to have emerged in Sumer, developing out of an early form of record keeping. Records were kept with clay tokens that served as a sort of receipt for items exchanged in a trade. The shape of the tokens indicated whether the goods were oxen, sheep, jars of oil and grain, or slaves. Markings on the clay indicated how many items each token represented. By the fourth millennium, this means of keeping accounts was taken one step further. The tokens were sealed into hollow clay pouches called bullae, which were then dried and baked to make a permanent record of the transaction. At a later time, the tokens were pressed into the outer surface of the bullae before baking so that the record could be read without breaking the pottery. It did not take long for people to realize that this system was redundant.

	ORIGINAL PICTOGRAPH	PICTOGRAPH ROTATED 90°	EARLY BABYLONIAN	ASSYRIAN
OX				
ORCHARD				
TO GO				
TO DRINK				

33

A record could be kept simply by making a series of marks on a slab of clay. It was the first step toward writing,

While it was easy to represent an ox or another physical object with a picture, it was much harder to communicate actions, ideas, and sequential thoughts. That task pushed writing to the next step. People realized that if a circle could represent the sun, the same drawing might convey ideas such as heat, light, day, or even indications of time such as "on the day that." Similarly, a picture of a leg might easily refer to actions such as walking and running,

The Sound of Symbols At some point, Sumerian cuneiform included about 2,000 symbols, but they were not enough to express all the words in the language or the grammatical features necessary for expression. The next step was the development of a phonetic system that used the symbols for their sounds, as when a picture of a bee followed by a picture of a leaf forms the word *belief.* With this system, a symbol could have a meaning of its own, or it could be part of thousands of other words. That meant that fewer symbols (about 600) were necessary and that the same symbol-sounds could be combined to form words in other languages. Cuneiform was adopted by the Hittites, Hurrians, and Elamites and remained in use by the Persians until the first century A.D.

As the language developed, the look of cuneiform also went through many changes. At first the symbols were made as simple line drawings in the soft clay with a wooden or reed stylus. The pictorial quality was gradually lost, however, as the symbols were drawn with ever shorter, quicker, strokes. Eventually, scribes realized that pressing the marks into the clay was much faster than drawing each line. The distinctive wedge-shaped mark that resulted when a trimmed reed was pressed into the clay prompted modern scholars to name the writing cuneiform: *cuneus* is Latin for wedge.

Scribes and Archives Pressing the marks in clay may have made cuneiform quicker to execute, but it by no means made it easy. Cuneiform was difficult to learn and cumbersome to practice. Ordinary people never had the opportunity or any call to learn to read or write cuneiform. For the most part, those were skills mastered only by professional scribes, whose talents were put to many purposes. They copied ancient stories, such as those of Gilgamesh, and recorded recent events, such as the deeds of Darius I. They made maps and kept records of crops, weather,

Ashurbanipal, surrounded by cuneiform, above, was a seventh-century B.C. Assyrian king and one of the first known book collectors. His archives at Nineveh have been invaluable to biblical scholars.

inventories, and trade. Scribes transcribed bodies of laws, beliefs, religious practices, prayers, and poetry. They recorded details of diplomatic events, personalities, speeches, battles, natural disasters, and even menus and recipes. Virtually all aspects of life were captured on clay tablets in cuneiform's distinctive symbols. Many of these tablets were stored as official records in palaces and temples. Others were gathered in royal and priestly libraries.

For biblical scholars, one of the most important ancient archives for cultural history was that of Ashurbanipal, who ruled Assyria in the seventh century B.C. and prided himself on his literacy. In his palace at Nineveh he collected more than 1,500 cuneiform texts, some from the earliest times. Much modern understanding of the environment of the ancient Fertile Crescent comes from studies of some 20,000 cuneiform texts assembled at the Royal Archives at Mari—an important crossroads city. And many aspects of law and diplomacy in Egypt, Canaan, and Mesopotamia come from archives at Nuzi, on the Tigris River, at Tell el-Amarna, on the Nile, and from Ras-Shamra on the Mediterranean Coast. Because of their extraordinary richness, these tablets help furnish the background for many details and events in the Old Testament. ❖

Tablets of writing were carefully maintained in archives. Scribes, below left, often copied information from small tablets onto larger index tablets for reference. Once the clay tablets had been baked, they could be stored on archive shelves, below. The clay tablets used for cuneiform were usually no larger than 12 by 8 inches, but they could convey a lot of information. The one at far right includes a map and an inscription.

The settlement of Goshen and the Hyksos capital of Avaris are thought to have been neighbors on the Nile Delta in northern Egypt. As shown by this present-day scene, the area is highly fertile and suitable for farming and tending flocks.

The Egyptian Sojourn

THOUGH THE STORY OF JOSEPH GIVES CLUES THAT DATE ITS EVENTS, THE TALE ITSELF WAS PROBABLY WRITTEN DOWN CENTURIES LATER.

One of the most dramatic narratives in Genesis is the tale of Joseph. The story's fascination has as much to do with the way that it is told as it does with the events of Joseph's life. For while the earlier stories of Genesis read as though they were selected from a vast and ancient oral tradition, Joseph's story seems to have been written down all of a piece.

The tale reads like a short but complete novel. Joseph is adored by his father, Jacob, but despised by his jealous older brothers, whose treachery leads to his exile in Egypt. Instead of being lost to slavery, however, Joseph gains favor by his intelligence and his talent as an interpreter of dreams. He rises to a position of power second only to that of the pharaoh himself. The story reaches a climax when Joseph once again meets with his brothers and arranges a reunion with his father. The story comes full cycle when Joseph dies in Egypt and is finally taken home to Canaan to be buried.

Foreign Rule in Egypt It is thought that the story of Joseph might have been written near the time of King Solomon, about the 10th century B.C., by which time the patronage of the court made the creation of new literary works possible. The period described in the story, however, is much earlier. The events of Joseph's life in Egypt seem to date somewhere between 1710 and 1570 B.C., when Asian invaders—arriving from the north through Syria and Palestine—controlled Egypt from their capital on the Nile at Avaris. The Egyptians referred to these foreigners as the Hyksos, which means "rulers of foreign lands." As foreigners themselves, many believe, the Hyksos were probably more tolerant of immigrants than Egyptian rulers might have been. It is unlikely that Joseph could have achieved power and position in Egypt without the presence of foreign rule. Not surprisingly, the area called Goshen—a region on the Nile Delta where Hebrews are believed to have lived during that period—was in the immediate area of the Hyksos capital. During the period of Hyksos rule, and for a long while afterwards—or until about 1300 B.C.—there were great migrations of people in and out of Egypt owing to drought and famine and the slave trade. The approximate dates of 1710 to 1300 B.C. correspond with the Old Testament statement that Abraham's descendants sojourned in Egypt for 400 years.

Joseph gained audience with the pharaoh, as shown below in a scene from Gustave Doré's 1866 illustrated Bible, because of his extraordinary ability to interpret dreams. Among the Egyptians, dream interpretation was recognized as a profession. For the Hebrews, however, God was considered the revealer of dreams.

Arrival of the Chariot More than just the tolerance of immigrants suggests the Hyksos period as that of Joseph's time in Egypt. There are other clues as well. For instance, when the Hyksos won supremacy on the Nile, they introduced new military methods into Egypt, the most significant of which were the horse and chariot. It was not until after the arrival of the Hyksos that scenes of travel, battle, and hunting by chariot begin to appear in paintings and relief carvings on Egyptian walls. And it is in the story of

Joseph that these chariots and horses appear for the first time in the Bible. "Removing his signet ring from his hand, Pharaoh put it on Joseph's hand; he arrayed him in garments of fine linen, and put a gold chain around his neck. He had him ride in the chariot of his second-in-command [Genesis 41:42–43]."

Cultural Influence When Joseph's brothers arrived in Egypt they did not recognize him in his role as the pharaoh's overseer, dressed in Egyptian clothing and pretending to need a translator to talk to them. Joseph had been accepted by the Egyptians, although they never really recognized Hebrews as part of their culture. We learn in one scene when Joseph's brothers are at his house that "he [Joseph] said, 'Serve the meal.' They served him by himself, and them by themselves, and the Egyptians who ate with him by themselves, because the Egyptians could not eat with the Hebrews [Genesis 43:31–32]." In general, despite their centuries in Egypt, the Hebrews seemed to be influenced only minimally by the surrounding culture. Even over the course of four centuries, they kept their customs. At least in part, this continual separation of cultures may have been due to the fact that Hebrews living in Goshen under the Hyksos were among their own people, with little need to interact in Egyptian life. Later, in bondage in Egypt, the choice was not theirs.

Stories and Dreams Although Egyptian culture probably had only a minimal impact on Hebrew life, it shows up in subtle ways in the story of Joseph, generally in the amount of emphasis given to certain parts of the story. One of the best known tales within the larger story, for instance, takes place when Joseph first arrives in Egypt and is sold to Potiphar. Ultimately, in that household, Joseph has to rebuff the advances of Potiphar's wife, who "cast her eyes on him," and is thrown in prison when she claims that he tried to "lie with her." In Egyptian

*E*gyptian burial customs were copied by other cultures. The Egyptian-style casket, above, was made for a Phoenician king. Both Jacob and Joseph were embalmed in the Egyptian manner, and Joseph was put in a casket to await his future burial in Canaan.

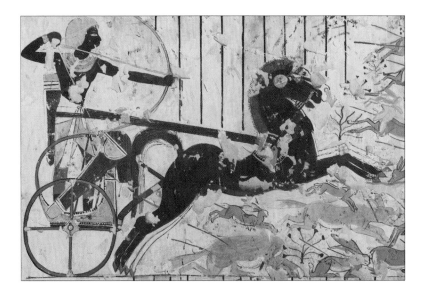

*M*any scholars believe that the chariot was developed in Asia about 2000 B.C. and that horses were ridden there perhaps 2,000 years earlier. Asian Hyksos introduced the horse and chariot to Egypt about 1710 B.C. as a vehicle for war. But as seen in this detail from a 15th-century B.C. Egyptian mural, it was used for hunting as well.

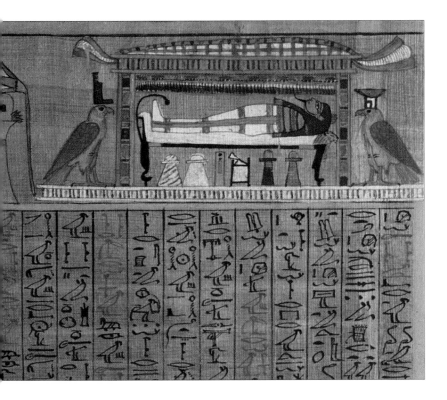

literature at that time there was an older story known as the Tale of Two Brothers. In the first part of this story, the two brothers—Anubis, who was married, and Bata, who was not—share a house. One day when Anubis is not home, his wife tries to seduce Bata but is rejected. Fearing what will happen if her husband discovers the truth, the wife slanders Bata, and he is forced to flee for his life. The inclusion of the story of Joseph and Potiphar's wife in the Genesis story is another example attesting to the cultural authenticity of the biblical narrative.

The emphasis placed on dreams in the Joseph story is also interesting in the light of its time and setting. Dreams are mentioned earlier in Genesis, but whether those of Jacob or Laban, they are straightforward and easily understood. The dreams in the Joseph story, by contrast, are complex and symbolic. Each time Joseph interprets a dream, his life changes. Interpreting his own dreams as a boy leads to his expulsion from Canaan. Providing that service in Egypt for the chief baker and cupbearer gets Joseph out of prison, and interpreting dreams for the pharaoh wins Joseph his position of power.

The Hebrews believed that dreams are meaningful, but dreams did not play as large a role in their society as they did in that of their neighbors. Both the Egyptians and the Assyrians had books devoted to dream interpretation, and they made use of dream interpreters. There was no such profession among the Hebrews. The only men in the Bible who specialize in those skills are Joseph and, later, Daniel—both of whom perfect their talents in the service of foreign rulers. ❖

THE EGYPTIAN BOOK OF THE DEAD

The ancient Egyptians took great care burying their dead with the things they would need in the afterlife. From as early as 2400 B.C. these burial gifts included hieroglyphic inscriptions on the inside of tombs. The inscriptions were spells meant to protect the dead as they made the passage from this world to the next.

By the 16th century, during Hyksos rule, spells were also placed inside coffins. They were written on sheets of papyrus 12 to 18 inches high, left, that were glued together to form scrolls that measured up to 90 feet in length. Painted illustrations appeared only on scrolls made for particularly wealthy or prestigious persons.

Egyptians called these manuscripts "spells for coming forth by day," though they are known today by a name given them in the 19th century: the Book of the Dead. No two scrolls are identical, though all have the same general purpose: helping the *ba*, or soul, on its way. For instance, the *ba* had to face many ordeals, including hideous monsters and powerful inquisitors. But by knowing these creatures' names—which were provided on the scrolls—the *ba* could get by them safely and ultimately reach an afterlife of eternal joy.

Papyrus: Egypt's Gift to Writers

PAPYRUS NO LONGER GROWS WILD IN EGYPT, BUT FOR SOME 5,000 YEARS, IT WAS PLENTIFUL ENOUGH TO PROVIDE SCRIBES WITH A DEPENDABLE SUPPLY OF WRITING MATERIAL.

Egyptian scribes sat cross-legged; their kilts, pulled tight across the lap, formed a flat surface for a writing palette and papyrus.

Thousands of years ago, the papyrus plant, a type of reed, grew in abundance in the marshes of the Nile Delta. By the fourth millennium B.C., Egyptians had learned to transform the 10- to 15-foot stalks of the plant into thin sheets that made a fine writing surface. Sheets were joined to form long strips for lengthy manuscripts and were rolled up as scrolls for storage.

As the first lightweight, inexpensive, durable writing material, papyrus gained an importance in the history of the Bible that can hardly be overestimated. Many of the oldest surviving biblical documents, including some of the Dead Sea Scrolls, were written on papyrus. Furthermore, it is from this reed that we derive the words *paper* and *Bible*: The Greeks called papyrus rolls *biblia*, which referred to the ancient Phoenician city of Byblos, an important seaport for the export of papyrus. In time, the word came to denote manuscripts and books, thus resulting in the word *Bible*, a term for "The Book." ❖

A wall relief from the third millennium B.C., left, depicts Egyptians harvesting reeds. The surface of the papyrus sheet, far left, shows how it was made of crosswise layers of fibers. The papyrus plant itself is shown above.

THE MAKING OF PAPYRUS

Ancient Egyptians harvested the papyrus plant and turned it into writing material using the following steps:

1 The stem of the harvested reed was divided into sections, usually between 12 and 18 inches long. The green outer rind was stripped off, exposing the soft white inner pith. While still fresh, the pith was cut lengthwise into strips.

2 The strips were moistened with water until the pith softened to produce a natural gummy substance. Then the strips were laid out vertically on a hard surface with their edges touching or slightly overlapping. A second layer of strips was arranged horizontally over the first and covered with a cloth to absorb excess water. The gummy surfaces of the strips acted as a binding agent between the layers.

3 In order to consolidate the two layers, the papyrus strips were pounded with a wooden mallet for an hour or more, until the fibers broke down and matted together. Then the sheet was placed under a heavy weight and left to dry in the sun. The bonding of the two layers of fibers made the papyrus strong enough to use as a writing surface.

4 The dry sheet was trimmed, and its surface was smoothed with pumice and burnished with a shell, stone, or piece of ivory. The side with horizontal fibers was more carefully polished than the other. This was the side usually selected for writing, although many papyrus documents were written on both sides.

The resulting creamy white sheets were attached end to end with flour paste to make long lengths that were then rolled up as scrolls. The papyrus was rolled so that the vertical fibers—which had more give—were on the outside. To aid in unrolling the scroll, dowels made of wood or stone were attached to the ends.

Scribes worked with special tools including the palette and double inkwell (for red and black ink), above, and a set of pens and penholder, top. The flowing script on the above manuscript came into use after Egyptians had learned to make papyrus.

Moses in Egypt

MOSES WAS RAISED IN THE HOME OF AN EGYPTIAN PRINCESS, BUT HE WAS ALWAYS AWARE OF THE PLIGHT OF HIS PEOPLE, AND HE NEVER LOST HIS FAITH IN GOD'S POWER TO RESCUE THEM FROM BONDAGE.

In 1570 B.C., after 140 years of foreign domination, Egyptian warriors finally succeeded in driving their oppressors, the Hyksos, out of Egypt. For a long while afterward, Egyptian rulers would have nothing to do with the Delta region of the Nile, where the Hyksos had built their capital. The Hebrew settlements there continued to prosper as they had before. But by the end of the 14th century B.C., that situation began to change, eventually leading to the state of Hebrew bondage that existed when Moses came of age.

The Bible does not name the pharaoh who ruled Egypt at the time of the Exodus, an omission that some think may reflect the writers' lack of regard for Egyptian authority. Many scholars believe, however, that the pharaoh in question was Rameses II, who moved the seat of government from Thebes in Upper Egypt to the Delta. In making the move, Rameses launched a vigorous building program on a monumental scale. His plans required unlimited materials for making bricks and a ready source of slave labor. Delta mud and Nile water served the first requirement admirably. The Hebrew population, whose prosperity offended the pharaoh, served the second: he could get the buildings he wanted and at the same time saddle the male Hebrew population with heavy labor.

The Hebrews in bondage worked under a daily quota system that was inhuman in its demands. One scroll from the reign of Rameses II mentions 40 men, each of whose quota was 2,000 bricks a day. And an earlier record written on the wall of a tomb describes the Egyptian attitude toward their foreign slaves. "He [the brickmaker] is dirtier than vines or pigs from treading under his mud. . . . He is simply wretched through and through." Men were beaten if they did not meet their quotas, but the pharaoh's cruelty

The stylized painting above characterizes the disparity between Egyptian taskmasters and their foreign slaves. The scene recalls one in Exodus when Moses attacks and kills an Egyptian officer whom he found mistreating a Hebrew slave.

did not have the desired effect. "The more they were oppressed, the more they multiplied and spread, so that the Egyptians came to dread the Israelites [Exodus 1:12]." The situation drove the pharaoh to even harsher methods of reproach, and he twice demanded the lives of all male Hebrew babies.

The Childhood of Moses It was the second of these demands—death by drowning in the Nile—that first caused Moses to be singled out. Rescued as an infant, he was raised within the pharaoh's own household. Ironically, his knowledge of the Egyptian court later contributed to making Moses a formidable opponent of the pharaoh in power at the time of the Exodus.

Although Moses was raised apart from the Hebrew community, he nevertheless remained aware of how his people were treated. "One day, after Moses had grown up, he went out to his people and saw their forced labor. He saw an Egyptian beating a Hebrew, one of his kinsfolk. He looked this way and that, and seeing no one he killed the Egyptian and hid him in the sand [Exodus 2:11–12]." Despite Moses' privileged upbringing, he championed the oppressed instinctively. It was an instinct that would later allow him to overcome his reluctance to lead and to become a great leader.

Moses and His God Following the Egyptian's death, Moses fled Egypt and went to live in the land of Midian (northwestern Arabia). It was there that he received his first revelation, when God spoke to him from the burning bush. From that point on, for the rest of his life, Moses' relationship with God was unique. God had guided Abraham's tribe through their travels, but he now spoke almost exclusively to Moses. Moses was the intermediary, relating God's word to the Hebrews, interceding with God on their behalf. It would not be until the revelation at Mount Sinai that the people heard from God themselves.

Scholars have questioned whether there was any sort of parallel between Moses' faith in a single God and that of the pharaoh Akhenaton, who ruled Egypt briefly between 1375 and 1358 B.C. Akhenaton,

The Egyptian brickyard above may well resemble those in the time of Moses. The Hebrews made their bricks out of black mud and chopped straw called teben. *A single building project could require more than 20 million bricks.*

This mural from an Egyptian tomb shows slaves at work. From the left they are drawing water; mixing water and clay with wooden tools; forming bricks in molds; drying them in the sun; carrying bricks, mortar, and stone blocks to a site; and setting them into place.

who is known as the heretic king, went against Egypt's long-established tradition of worshiping multiple deities and put all his faith in the god Aton, the sun disc. (A comparison of hymns appears on page 45.) But Akhenaton's beliefs were never brought to the people. Egypt quickly returned to its old beliefs, destroying Akhenaton's temples after his death. If Moses actually did live in the late 14th century B.C., it is possible he might have heard about Akhenaton, but it is doubtful that the heretic pharaoh had any real influence on the Hebrews' faith.

Birth of a Nation The relationship between God and Moses and the Israelites grew out of God's saving acts—the 10 plagues that were brought upon the Egyptians. Because of them, important changes had taken place. The Egyptians had learned to fear God's power and to recognize that they had no choice but to free the Israelites. The Israelites had developed an awareness of and an appreciation for God's power. And Moses had become a mature and confident leader, capable of guiding the Israelite people through the trying times ahead.

The special relationship between God and the nation of Israel grew out of the Exodus itself. In fact, the narrative of the Exodus can be read as the story of the birth of a nation. Out of the chaos of their lives in Egypt, God brought the Israelites together as a people. No obstacle, not even the sea, would stop him from fulfilling his covenant with them—his promise of leading them to a good and broad land. "The Song of Miriam," which is thought to have been written by someone who witnessed the passage through the Red Sea, celebrates the event. "Sing to the Lord, for he has triumphed gloriously; horse and rider he has thrown into the sea [Exodus 15:21]."

As the sea closed on the Egyptians who followed close behind them, the Israelites were literally and symbolically cut off from their old life of oppression. They were free to create a new nation, and they were bound together in their faith in a kind and powerful God. ❖

*M*any scholars believe that the period of bondage in Egypt dates from the 19th dynasty, which began in 1307 B.C. The most prodigious builder of monuments and abuser of slaves during that period was Rameses II, who is thought to be the pharaoh of the Exodus. His portrait, below, is one of many sculptures he had made in his likeness; it was created as part of his temple complex at Luxor, shown at bottom.

From Israel and Egypt:
Songs of Praise and of Faith in a Single God

Psalm 104, the "Hymn to God the Creator," is often compared to Akhenaton's "Hymn to the Sun Disc." Verses 19 through 28 of the psalm appear at left, below. Sections of Akhenaton's hymn appear at right: their sequence has been rearranged to correspond with the sequencing of the psalm.

*You have made the moon
to mark the seasons;
the sun knows its time
for setting.
You make darkness
and it is night, when all the
animals of the forest come
creeping out.*

*The young lions roar
for their prey,
seeking their food from God.
When the sun rises, they
withdraw and lie down in
their dens. People go out to
their work and to their labor
until the evening.*

*O LORD, how manifold
are your works!
In wisdom you have made
them all; the earth is full
of your creatures.*

*Yonder is the sea, great
and wide, creeping things
innumerable are there,
living things
both small and great.
There go the ships,
and Leviathan that you
formed to sport in it.*

*These all look to you to
give them their food
in due season;
When you give to them,
they gather it up;
when you open your hand,
they are filled
with good things.*

*A*khenaton and his wife, Nefertiti,
carved into the limestone tablet above, are
shown worshiping the sun disc, Aton, which
they recognized as the sole god.

*To maintain all that thou hast
created, thou makest seasons:
winter to cool them, and the hot
that they might taste thee.
When thou settest in the
western horizon, the land is in
darkness in the manner of
death. . . .*

*Every lion is come from
his den, all creeping things
sting, darkness dominates. . . .
When day dawns, shining
on the horizon, thou gleamest
as the Sun Disc in the day.
The whole earth
goes about its tasks. . . .*

*How manifold
is what thou hast made,
and difficult to discern.
O thou sole god beside whom
there is no other!*

*Thou madest the earth
according to thy desire. . . .
All things that fly and alight,
they live when thou shinest
on them. Ships go downstream
and upstream likewise, every
road is open at thy rising:
the fish in the river dart
about before thee, thy rays are
within the ocean. . . .*

*The earth came forth upon thy
hand as thou madest them,
thou shinest and they live, thou
settest and they die.
Thou thyself art a lifetime and
through thee do they live.*

Moses and the Law

THE INSTRUCTIONS THAT MOSES RECEIVED ON THE MOUNTAINTOP WERE MORE THAN RULES TO LIVE BY. THEY WERE THE DEFINITION OF ISRAEL AS A NATION.

The image of Moses on Mount Sinai receiving the Ten Commandments from God stands out as one of the most vivid scenes in the Bible. Amid thunder and lightning, smoke and fire, we are told, God appeared to Moses and engraved two stone tablets for him to deliver to the Hebrews waiting for him below.

Moses spent 40 days on Mount Sinai receiving God's revelation, and to his followers this seemed an inordinate amount of time. As they waited, their initial awe at witnessing God's presence on the mountain turned to impatience. Ultimately believing that Moses—their link to God—would never return, they decided they needed a new god to lead them and they created a pagan idol, a golden calf.

When Moses came down from the mountain carrying the tablets with the Decalogue, or Ten Commandments, in his hands, he saw the golden calf and shattered the tablets in anger. He destroyed the idol, and when those responsible for its manufacture were punished, he returned to the mountain to plead with God on behalf of the people. God agreed to renew the covenant and to give Moses the Decalogue again, but Moses had to inscribe the laws himself. This time, the people received the Commandments with due respect.

The Nature of the Tablets Scholars have questioned what the two sets of tablets might have looked like, since the great stone slabs typically depicted in paintings would be far too heavy for a man to carry down the side of a mountain. Some researchers have suggested that the tablets might have been made of clay, like

Returning from the mountain to discover a scene of pagan revelry, "Moses' anger burned hot, and he threw the tablets from his hands [Exodus 32:19]." French illustrator Gustave Doré captured this dramatic scene for an 1865 Bible.

those commonly used for cuneiform writing, but the Bible is clear that the material was stone. One possibility is that the laws were written on limestone, which can be flaked into relatively thin, flat sheets. Small pieces or flakes of limestone were used like paper in the ancient Near East. Large pieces are known to have been used by students as copybooks. Often, both sides of a limestone flake were flat enough to use as a writing surface. Writing could be done either with pen or brush and ink, or by incising the stone with a sharp point.

A Body of Laws The Ten Commandments given to Moses are the cornerstone of biblical law, but there are many other laws in the Bible. More than 600 laws are presented in the Pentateuch, the first five books of the Bible, and collectively both the laws and the books are referred to as the Torah (a word whose meaning is actually closer to "instruction" than "law").

Most of the laws in the Torah fall into one of two types, casuistic or apodictic. Casuistic, or case, laws govern situations in everyday life. They do not constitute a theory of justice but rather describe what should be done in a specific case. "When you buy a male Hebrew slave, he shall serve six years, but in the seventh he shall go out a free person without debt [Exodus 21:2]." Apodictic, or categorical, laws give absolute commandments to do or not to do something. The most familiar examples of apoditic laws are in the Decalogue. "You shall not murder. You shall not commit adultery. You shall not steal [Exodus 20:13-15]." The two forms of laws seem to be randomly interspersed throughout the Torah.

Most of the laws in the Torah are found in four major codes. The Covenant Code, or Book of the Covenant, found in Exodus is, in a sense, a constitution for the nation of Israel, instructing the people how to live as subjects under God and forming a framework for the entire life of the community. It covers both secular and religious laws, including laws defining crimes against people and property, the rights of slaves, judicial proceedings, and worship. The Deuteronomic Code, found in the Book of Deuteronomy, contains regulations for the centralization of worship and laws that define the roles of prophecy, kingship, and holy war. The Holiness Code, presented in Leviticus 18–26, includes many laws regarding worship and morality and stresses the importance of holiness in the people and the priesthood. The word *holiness* in this case refers to the Israelites' distinct moral and religious tenets and includes such subjects as the proper procedures for sacrifice, sexual practices, and celebrating holidays. Other laws, sometimes referred to collectively as the Priestly Code, are scattered throughout the Books of Exodus, Leviticus, and Numbers.

The Near Eastern Context The Hebrews were not the first to invent a legal system; theirs was only one of many in the ancient Near East. In fact, the legal systems of some of the surrounding cultures were already centuries old when Moses climbed Mount Sinai to receive the

The document above, known as the Nash Papyrus, dates from about 150 B.C. Written in Hebrew, the text includes the Ten Commandments as well as the words of Moses from a portion of Deuteronomy 6:4-5. It reads in part, "Hear, O Israel: The Lord is our God, the Lord alone."

Mount Sinai, which is called Mount Horeb in Exodus 33:6, may be part of the arid mountain range at right. Parts of the Sinai wilderness, such as this, are so dry they can barely support life.

Hammurabi's Code is inscribed in cuneiform on the diorite stele above. Together, the code's 282 civil and criminal laws make up the most complete and perfectly preserved collection of Babylonian laws known.

Ten Commandments. The most famous of these ancient codes, the Code of Hammurabi, which dates from the 18th century B.C., was one of many that derived from Sumerian laws of the third millennium B.C. King Hammurabi, who was one of the founders of the Babylonian Empire, had his code inscribed on a stone stele that stands more than seven feet tall and was installed in the great temple of Babylon. At the top of the stone, a relief carving shows Shamash, the god of justice, seated before Hammurabi while he gives the king the authority to enact and enforce laws. Below the picture, an inscription nearly 300 paragraphs long contains a body of laws on various subjects, including matters of public order, property rights, economic transactions, injuries and damages, and slavery. In the prologue and epilogue to the code, Hammurabi describes the role of the king as one who establishes laws and promotes justice to ensure the welfare of the people and the success of the government and the empire.

Israel's Unique Laws Although biblical laws shared elements with the law codes of the surrounding cultures, they differed in significant ways. For instance, in most of the ancient Near Eastern cultures the king devised, proclaimed, and instituted laws, as Hammurabi had done. However, God himself was considered the author of the biblical laws, and Moses merely played the role of an intermediary, receiving the laws from God. Other legal collections in the region were restricted to secular law, making no reference to religion. Biblical laws interweave matters of worship and religion with the secular, making it clear that all are part of God's domain. Since God had created a holy nation, it was not possible to follow his laws without being aware of one's own ethical responsibilities.

Class distinction was a matter of great importance in most of the ancient Near East. Law codes favored the powerful members of society, and penalties were applied according to the social status of the

48

In Jewish tradition, when Moses received the Torah on Mount Sinai, he also was given a body of authoritative commentary, or guidelines, for interpreting the laws. For while God decreed that no work be done on the Sabbath, for instance, he did not specify which tasks *could* be done. Those judgments would be made by religious sages from Joshua to the teachers and scholars of postbiblical times.

For hundreds of years, the commentary—known as oral law—and the scholarly interpretations were not set down in writing. Yet the commentary helped to keep the Torah a vital part of people's lives since laws could be adapted to change. For example, those laws governing sacrifice in the Temple could be reinterpreted even after the Temple was destroyed.

The Torah, therefore, remained as it was when Moses received it, while the body of oral law grew as new social and political problems arose. By about A.D. 200, the body of commentary had become overwhelming, and scholars began to systemize the material and write it down. The result was the Mishnah, the first codification of oral law and one of the most important documents in Judaism after the Bible itself.

offender and the victim. For example, Hammurabi's Code explains that "If an upper-class man has destroyed the eye of a member of the aristocracy, they shall destroy his eye. . . . If he has destroyed the eye of a commoner . . . he shall pay one mina of silver." In other cases, vicarious punishment was prescribed. As Hammurabi's Code details, "If a builder constructed a house for an upper-class man, but did not make the work strong, with the result that the house which he built collapsed and . . . caused the death of a son of the owner of the house, they shall put the son of that builder to death."

In contrast, biblical laws ban vicarious punishment and make it clear that—except for slaves—all who commit crimes receive the same punishment, regardless of status. In addition, they show great concern for the protection of the weak and disadvantaged and include specific laws to protect the poor, strangers, widows, and orphans. "You shall not strip your vineyard bare, or gather the fallen grapes . . . you shall leave them for the poor and the alien [Leviticus 19:10]."

The Torah Precisely how the Torah was compiled is not known. Although we are told that Moses was the author of the laws, scribes may have assisted him in recording, collecting, and arranging them into codes. Moses did not himself fashion the finished codes. Until the conquest of Canaan, the laws may have been entrusted to priests at various sanctuaries. The priests would have had the responsibility of preserving the Torah and instructing the Hebrews orally until the laws could be written down in the form we have them today. ❖

Champions of the Promised Land

A SONG IN JUDGES RECALLS THE STRUGGLE FOR ISRAEL AND IS AMONG THE EARLIEST KNOWN BIBLICAL WORKS WRITTEN IN THE NEW LAND.

The Book of Deuteronomy ends in sadness with the death of Moses, though grief is soon offset by the arrival of the Israelites in the Promised Land. Moses had chosen his faithful assistant Joshua as his successor, and in time, through clever military strategy and the help of God, Joshua led the people to conquer a fair amount of Canaan.

The Israelite settlement grew up as a loose conglomerate of 12 tribes, each with its own allotment of land. For more than 300 years, beginning with Joshua's death about 1375 B.C., the tribes had no single leader or central government, yet when they confronted foreign oppression they banded together to fight. The Bible describes a cyclical pattern to the life of the community during this transitional time known as the period of the Judges: The people would ignore their responsibilities to God and God would punish them by sending an oppressor. Then the people would cry out to be saved, and God would raise up a leader, or judge, to free the people from oppression. Years of peace would follow before the next crisis.

One of the Judges was a woman, a prophetess named Deborah. At a time when the Israelites were being oppressed by the Canaanites, Deborah called on the Israelite general Barak to fight them off, prophesying victory. Barak agreed to do as Deborah asked as long as she would join him, and so she did. Their successful battle was crowned when the Canaanite general Sisera was killed by an Israelite sympathizer, a tent-dwelling Kenite woman named Jael.

The story is told in prose in Judges 4 and in verse in the Song of Deborah in Judges 5. Elements of the song's language exhibit linguistic traits of very early Hebrew, and it is believed to be one of the oldest pieces of writing in the Bible.

Deborah's song stresses God's revelatory power, emphasizing that Israel's victory was due to a combination of the people's strength and the forces of nature—all under God's direction. The recovery of significant amounts of ancient Canaanite literature has shed light on many aspects of biblical literature, in particular, early Israelite poetry. ❖

Deborah often sat under a palm, where "the Israelites came up to her for judgment [Judges 4:5]."

The earliest known nonbiblical record of a nation of Israel appears on the stele of Merneptah, above. It commemorates a 13th-century B.C. Egyptian raid against Canaan.

Excerpts From the Song of Deborah

Deborah's prophecy of victory was fulfilled when, under Barak's command, "all the army of Sisera fell by the sword [Judges 4: 16]." Sisera, who had fled the battle, met his own fate in the tent of Jael and Heber. Excerpts from the ancient victory hymn (Judges 5) follow.

*In the days of Shamgar son of Anath,
in the days of Jael, caravans ceased and travelers
kept to the byways. The peasantry prospered
in Israel, they grew fat on plunder, because you
arose, Deborah, arose as a mother in Israel. . . .*

*Tell of it, you who ride on white donkeys, you
who sit on rich carpets and you who walk by the way.
To the sound of musicians at the watering places,
there they repeat the triumphs of the Lord,
the triumphs of his peasantry in Israel. . . .*

*Awake, awake, Deborah! Awake, Awake,
utter a song! Arise, Barak, lead away your captives,
O son of Abinoam. Then down marched
the remnant of the noble; the people of the Lord
marched down for him against the mighty. . . .*

*The kings came, they fought; then fought
the kings of Canaan, at Taanach, by the waters
of Megiddo; they got no spoils of silver.*

*The stars fought from heaven, from
their courses they fought against Sisera. . . .
March on, my soul, with might! . . .*

*Most blessed of women be Jael,
the wife of Heber the Kenite,
of tent-dwelling women most blessed.
He asked water and she gave him milk,
she brought him curds in a lordly bowl.*

*She put her hand to the tent peg
and her right hand to the workmen's mallet;
she struck Sisera a blow, she crushed his head,
she shattered and pierced his temple.
He sank, he fell, he lay still at her feet;
at her feet he sank, he fell;
where he sank, there he fell dead. . . .*

*So perish all your enemies, O Lord!
But may your friends be like the
sun as it rises in its might.*

*In this detail from a 13th-century manuscript, Jael gives Sisera refreshment in a bowl,
kills him with a tent peg in his sleep, and shows General Barak what she has done.*

The Written Word

The Israelites are thought to have begun writing down their oral literature and history during the reign of David in the 10th century B.C. However, they paid far greater attention to the written word after the fall of Jerusalem to the Babylonians in the 6th century B.C. Realizing they were at risk of losing touch with their oral history, traditions, and developing faith, the Israelites put everything in writing. Some of those records came to be recognized as holy and are known today as the books of the Hebrew Bible—the Old Testament.

Ancient Hebrew inscribed on stone

From the Kingship of David Through the Rule of the Hasmonean Dynasty

PART TWO TIMELINE (Many of the dates below are based on scholarly speculation and are approximate.)

4000 B.C.   3000 B.C.   2000 B.C.   1010 B.C.   65 B.C.   A.D. 1   A.D. 1000   A.D. 2000

	1010–960	960–800	800–650	650–560	560–500
BIBLE LANDS	**1004** David is made king and begins to unite tribes as kingdom of Israel.	**952** Solomon dedicates the Temple in Jerusalem. **922** Israel is divided into the Southern Kingdom of Judah and the Northern Kingdom of Israel. **853** Assyrian Empire launches its first attack against Israel.	**800** Phoenicians develop multi-oared longboats and dominate Mediterranean trade routes. **722** Israel's capital falls to Assyria.	**621** A book of the Law is discovered in the Jerusalem Temple. **586** King Nebuchadnezzar II of Babylonia destroys Jerusalem and the Temple.	**539** Cyrus II of Persia conquers Babylonia, later decrees Hebrew exiles can return to Jerusalem. **516** The Second Temple is completed in Jerusalem.
	King David		*Phoenician warship*	*Confucius*	*The Cyrus Cylinder*
ASIA & AUSTRALIA	**1000** Chinese develop refrigeration using blocks of winter ice.			**600** The Upanishads, texts proclaiming the doctrine of the transmigration of souls, are written in India.	**551** Chinese philosopher Confucius is born. **521** In India the Buddha preaches his first sermon.
EUROPE			**800** Homer composes the *Iliad* and the *Odyssey*. **776** First recorded Olympic games are held in Greece. **753** According to legend, Rome is founded by King Romulus.		**550** Greeks develop red-figured vase-painting. **509** Roman republic is founded under Brutus and Collatinus.
		Romulus and Remus fed by a she-wolf	*Discus thrower*	*Red-figured vase*	
AMERICAS	**1000** Woodland culture of eastern North America cultivates crops.		**800** Adena people of the Ohio River area build earth burial mounds. **800** Olmecs in Mexico build ceremonial centers at La Venta.	**650** Paracas culture flourishes in Peru, producing textiles.	
AFRICA		**814** Phoenicians found Carthage on North African coast.	**716** Ethiopia begins 50-year rule of Egypt.		**525** Egypt is conquered by the Persians, who rule for more than a century.
			Olmec carved jade figure	*Persian archer*	

500–400	400–325	325–200	200–150	150–65

458 Ezra returns from Babylonia with a scroll of the Torah.

445 Nehemiah begins to rebuild Jerusalem.

Nehemiah

500 Iron smelting is developed in China.

500 Mayan culture flourishes in Guatemala.

Mayan pottery vessel

500 Darius I builds a canal between the Nile and the Gulf of Suez to connect the Mediterranean and Red Seas.

332 Alexander the Great conquers the Persian Empire.

Alexander the Great

387 Plato founds the Academy at Athens, which later becomes the world's first university.

432 The Parthenon is consecrated to the Greek goddess Athena.

The Parthenon

400 Hohokam people develop irrigation canals in the Sonoran Desert area of Arizona.

323 Ptolemy I gains control of Palestine and Egypt following Alexander's death.

Coin with the earliest known image of a menorah

250 Parchment is produced at Pergamum in Asia Minor.

214 Shih Huang Ti, the first emperor of the united China, starts building the Great Wall.

Great Wall of China

312 Rome begins a highway system with the construction of the Via Appia.

218 Carthaginian general Hannibal crosses the Alps and invades Italy.

300 Mogollons dig pit houses in their mountain villages in Arizona.

294 Alexandria's library is established, and the city becomes a center of scholarship.

250 The Septuagint is produced in Alexandria.

200 Ptolomies are defeated by the Seleucids of Syria, who take control of Palestine.

167 Judas Maccabeus leads rebellion against Antiochus IV, who defiled the Temple.

164 The Temple is rededicated, a ceremony henceforth celebrated as Hanukkah.

200 Rosetta Stone is carved in three languages. Its discovery helps modern scholars translate hieroglyphics.

Rosetta Stone

Dead Sea Scroll

140 Essenes found a community at Qumran near the Dead Sea.

134 The Hasmonean Dynasty begins its 71- year reign over an independent Jewish kingdom.

146 Rome is victorious in the Macedonian and Punic Wars, becoming the major power in the Mediterranean.

150 Earliest settlers arrive at Teotihuacán in Mexico.

100 Monumental burial mounds made in the Ohio and Mississippi River regions by people of the Hopewell culture.

A Mighty Kingdom

THE ESTABLISHMENT OF A MONARCHY AND CENTER OF GOVERNMENT IN ISRAEL PROMPTED THE CREATION OF A NATIONAL LITERATURE.

The stone fragment, right, discovered in 1993 in the ruins of the ancient town of Tel Dan in northern Israel, bears the earliest known reference, outside the Bible, to the House of David. Once part of a large monument, the fragment is thought to date from the ninth century B.C. The House of David is mentioned in the ninth line of the inscription, which seems to commemorate a battle.

Rich, colorful prose chronicles the exciting story of the rise of kings in Israel—from the anointing of Saul, through the ascent of David, to the selection of Solomon. As told in 1 and 2 Samuel and 1 Kings, the dramatic episodes demonstrate that history is not a collection of random events but the unfolding of God's plan. With the creation of a mighty kingdom, the sufferings in Egypt, the wanderings in the wilderness, and the uneven nature of leadership in the days of the Judges reached a purposeful end. When the prophet Samuel anointed Saul as their first king, some Israelites resisted, acknowledging God alone as their king, but they slowly came to accept a temporal ruler as the will of God.

Beginning about 1020 B.C., Saul mobilized the Israelite tribes to offset Philistine military threats. In doing so, he laid the groundwork for King David, who forged the contentious confederation of tribes into a strong, centrally controlled state. During his reign, which began about 1010 B.C., he subdued the Philistines and transformed Israel into one of the strongest nations between the Nile and the Euphrates. David was promised by God that his house, or family, would endure forever. He was succeeded by his son Solomon, who governed from 961 to 922 B.C. Solomon vastly increased the wealth and power of the nation and erected the Temple in Jerusalem, which would not only be the dwelling place of God but the symbol of the unshakable union between faith and state.

David is the subject of some of the best-known stories in the Old Testament. Here he is shown bearing the head of Goliath and leading King Saul, in a detail from a 13th-century illuminated Bible.

Monarchy and the Bible The writing of the Bible most probably was begun in this atmosphere of burgeoning nationhood. Many scholars believe that King David created the post of court recorder, whose job it was to write and circulate official decrees, and that of court scribe, who was in charge of correspondence with foreign rulers. But David and, later, Solomon also assembled a group of scribes whose task was to collect and record the Israelites' oral histories and to begin refining them into what would become a great national epic.

The story of David's rise to power and Solomon's accession is described in what is called the court history of David, which includes 2 Samuel 9–20 and 1 Kings 1–2. This record is among the most dramatic and finely crafted narratives in the Old Testament. The writing is so vivid—full of conversation and anecdote—that scholars believe it must have been composed by someone who was an eyewitness to the events. Some scholars think that the account of David's rise from humble origins as a shepherd boy is a somewhat romanticized history that may have been composed to deflect opposition to his rule.

The Lively Arts Histories and official documents were not the only sorts of writing stimulated by the monarchy. David himself was a musician and writer. When King Saul was tormented with depression, David played his lyre to drive the evil spirits away from the older man. And one of the earliest poems in the Bible is David's lamentation at the death of King Saul and his son. "Saul and Jonathan, beloved and lovely!" he wrote. "In life and death they were not divided; they were swifter than eagles, they were stronger than lions [2 Samuel 1:23]."

The early books of the Bible include references to music and singing, such as Miriam's and Deborah's songs of victory. But with the establishment of the royal court, it seems, there was far more music, much of it officially sanctioned. David, in fact, may have formed the first guild of musicians, which later became part of the court's trappings of power.

Musicians performed at feasts and religious festivals. Kings were crowned to the sound of blaring trumpets or pipes or to the singing of enthronement psalms. David also commissioned the writing of songs and hymns for his court's official worship of God. These songs would constitute much of the Book of Psalms. "Sing to God," we are told, "sing praises to his name; lift up a song to him who rides upon the clouds [Psalm 68:4]." ❖

Women welcome the triumphant David and Saul in a scene described in I Samuel 18:6-7. "The women came out of all the towns of Israel, singing and dancing, to meet King Saul, with tambourines, with songs of joy, and with musical instruments." This detail is part of the ilumination shown on the facing page.

Poetry in the Old Testament

POETRY AND SONG WERE IMPORTANT LITERARY FORMS IN EARLY ISRAEL, AS THEY WERE IN THE SURROUNDING STATES. SIX BOOKS OF THE OLD TESTAMENT ARE COMPOSED ALMOST ENTIRELY OF POETRY.

Even as writing is thought to have gained prominence during King David's reign in the 11th century B.C., the oral tradition remained important. More than a third of the Old Testament was written as poetry that was meant to be sung or recited. Included are whole books: the Song of Solomon, Lamentations, Ecclesiastes, Proverbs, Job, and Psalms, as well as portions of the Prophets and individual songs in other books. The importance of poetry and song as a means of storytelling and record keeping can only be guessed at. However, the earliest known pieces of writing in the Bible are all songs or fragments of songs. Among them are Miriam's song in Exodus 15:21, the Song of Deborah from Judges 5:1-31, and David's elegy over Saul and Jonathan in 2 Samuel 1:19-27. ❖

The great variety and sheer amount of poetry in the Old Testament suggest its importance in Israelite society, where poems were often sung. This colorful illustration is a detail from the opening page of the Song of Solomon in the Rothschild Mahzor, a Hebrew prayer book that dates from 1492.

Poetry of Love and Sadness

The Song of Solomon—also called the Song of Songs—was written as a dialogue of love. No one knows for sure when it was composed, but it is possible that some of the verses were wedding songs. Solomon's association with the song comes from the attribution in 1:1 and the mention of his name in 3:9 and 11, and 8:11-12. The excerpt, below left, is from 2:12-14. Collections of Egyptian love poems that date from 1300 B.C. or earlier, share some similarities with the verses in the Song of Solomon. They too were meant to be sung to music. As in the Song of Solomon, the lovers often refer to each other as "my brother" and "my sister." An excerpt from one of the songs is given below right.

Song of Solomon

*The flowers appear on the earth; the time
of singing has come, and the
voice of the turtledove is heard in our land.
The fig tree puts forth its figs, and the vines
are in blossom; they give forth fragrance.
Arise, my love, my fair one, and come away.
O my dove; in the clefts of the rock,
in the covert of the cliff, let me see your face,
let me hear your voice; for your voice is sweet,
and your face is lovely.*

Egyptian Love Poem

*The voice of the swallow speaks and says:
"The land has brightened—What is thy road?"
Thou shalt not, O bird, disturb me!
I have found my brother in his bed,
and my heart is still more glad,
[When he] said to me: "I shall not go afar off.
My hand is in thy hand. I shall stroll about,
And I shall be with thee in every pleasant place."
He makes me the foremost of maidens:
He injures not my heart.*

The poignant psalms in Lamentations commemorate the destruction of Jerusalem in 587 B.C. It is not known whether they were composed by a single author or were a collaborative effort by several writers. Verses from Lamentations were recited on days of fasting or mourning. The excerpts, below left, are from 1:1, 2:21, and 4:2–3. About 2100 B.C., the Mesopotamian city of Ur was destroyed by invading armies, and some time later a collection of 11 songs lamenting the destruction was written down. Three of the verses from the fifth song appear below right.

Lamentations

*How lonely sits the city that once was full of people!
How like a widow she has become, she that was
great among the nations! She that was a princess
among the provinces has become a vassal.*

*The young and the old are lying on the
ground in the streets; my young women
and my young men have fallen by the sword;
in the day of your anger you have killed them,
slaughtering without mercy.*

*The precious children of Zion, worth
their weight in fine gold—how they are reckoned
as earthen pots, the work of a potter's hands!
Even the jackals offer the breast and nurse
their young, but my people has become cruel,
like the ostriches in the wilderness.*

A Lamentation Over the Destruction of Ur

*The [good] storm was carried off from the city;
that city into ruins, O Father Nanna, that city into
ruins was made. . . . Its people, not potsherds,
filled its sides; its walls were breached, the people groan.*

*In its palaces, where the festivities of the land took
place, the people lay in heaps. . . . Its dead bodies,
like fat placed in the sun, of themselves melted away.
Its men who were brought to an end by the axe
were not covered with head bandages.*

*The judgment of the land perished; the people groan.
The counsel of the land was dissipated; the people groan.
The mother left her daughter; the people groan.
The father turned away from his son; the people groan.
In the city the wife was abandoned, the child was
abandoned, the possessions were scattered about.*

A mosaic pavement uncovered during excavations of the sixth-century synagogue in ancient Gaza shows David (identified in the inscription above him) playing the lyre as various animals listen.

David and the Psalms

THE HYMNAL OF ANCIENT ISRAEL, TRADITIONALLY ASCRIBED TO KING DAVID HIMSELF, IS THE MAJESTIC EXPRESSION OF A PEOPLE'S FAITH IN THEIR GOD.

The Book of Psalms has been called a perfect union of poetry and religion. Though most of the psalms were written to accompany Temple rituals, their themes mirror those of all great poetry: love and death, hope and despair, alienation and community, the sacred and the profane. The spontaneity and simplicity of the psalms appeal directly to the human heart. Their imagery is concrete—God is a shepherd, the sun, a rock, a dwelling place—and their emotions are intense.

Poems to Be Sung In Hebrew the Book of Psalms is called the *Tehillim*, which means "praises," and, indeed, many of the psalms extol the glory of God and his creation. Others record the words chanted by worshipers during Temple liturgies, festivals, pilgrimages, royal coronations and weddings, and at the time of the renewal of the covenant. Some psalms are communal or personal expressions of thanksgiving, lament, or moral dilemma.

The Greek root of the word *psalms* derives from *psalmos*, meaning the "twanging of strings," a reference to the stringed instrument played along with the poems as they were sung. That they were intended to be sung is evident from the cues and other musical directions the psalms supply for the choirmaster, instrumentalists, and singers. In addition, a number of psalms repeat similar or contrasting statements in successive lines. This parallel structure corresponds to the ancient Hebrew singing style in which two groups of voices alternately answered each other.

David and His Lyre King David was the most beloved and celebrated singer and musician of Bible times, credited in the Second Book of Samuel as the composer of a moving elegy and hymns of thanksgiving and praise (2 Samuel 1:17–27; 22; 23:1–7). It was David, according to later tradition, who established liturgical music in the Temple and determined the role of the Levitical singers.

By the second century A.D., a tradition had taken hold that David was the author of all the psalms and that variations in their tone and substance marked the changing circumstances of his life: for instance, a celebratory psalm reflected a moment of personal triumph, and a lament, a time of distress. Nearly half of the psalms bear the Hebrew designation "le-David," a term that had long been translated as "by David." But "le-David" can also be interpreted to mean "concerning David," "dedicated to David," or "in the style of David"; moreover, biblical scholars now believe the attribution to David was appended to the psalms long after they were composed.

In the mid-19th century, scholars seriously questioned David's authorship, and by the turn of the 20th century, some went so far as to assert that many of the psalms were written, not in the Davidic era but some 500 years later, after the Babylonian Exile. This extreme position has since been challenged in light of recent archeological discoveries of other ancient Near Eastern writings. These literary works— which include examples of Canaanite, Babylonian, Assyrian, and Egyptian writings—display striking similarities to the Hebrew psalms. Current thinking holds that the Israelites adopted the poetic form of the psalms and some aspects of their vocabulary and use in worship from neighboring cultures.

Scholars now date Psalms 29 and 68 as being among the earliest writings in the Bible. Many believe that most of the psalms probably originated before the Babylonian Exile but that a majority of these were later altered to fit political and religious circumstances. Doubtless a variety of authors, most of them unknown, assembled the 150 psalms included in the Bible over the course of many centuries.

The psalms have been treasured over the years by Jews and Christians alike. Composers from Johann Sebastian Bach to Leonard Bernstein have written music for them, and a version set to English melodies was the first book ever published in the American colonies. Though the psalms reflect the unique story of the Hebrew people and their relationship with God, the epic spiritual journey they describe— man's desire to be in touch with the divine—is a universal one. ❖

The early Christians adapted the Book of Psalms for their own religious services. The front cover of the eighth-century Dagulfe Psalter is carved in ivory with two scenes from the life of King David.

The Temple and Worship

SOLOMON ERECTED A GREAT TEMPLE IN JERUSALEM SO THAT GOD MIGHT "DWELL AMONG THE CHILDREN OF ISRAEL [1 KINGS 6:13]."

Amid a vast throng of Israelites, a procession reverently carried the Ark of the Covenant from the tabernacle provided by David to the Temple built by Solomon. The priests placed the Ark within the Holy of Holies. As they emerged, "a cloud filled the house of the Lord [1 Kings 8:10]," signaling the presence of the divinity. Solomon spoke to those assembled: if there was famine, plague, war, or any other calamity, the Israelites should "stretch out their hands toward this house [1 Kings 8:38]."

From that autumn of perhaps 952 B.C. forward, the Temple became the center of Israelite worship. Congregants gathered in the Temple courtyard to sacrifice, pray, and offer thanksgiving and praise to God. Within the sanctuary the priestly descendants of the tribe of

AUTUMN FESTIVAL

Solomon's Temple was dedicated during the autumn new year celebration. Every year thereafter the Israelites expressed their thanks for the return of the Ark of the Covenant, which remained in the Holy of Holies flanked by lionlike cherubs (inset above left). The priests performed purification rites before the molten sea, a bronze basin supported by oxen, and they offered sacrifices (inset far right). The worshipers praised God: "The voice of the Lord causes the oaks to whirl . . . and in his temple all say, 'Glory!' [Psalm 29:9]."

Levi tended their duties as guardians of the house of the Lord. The high priest alone entered the Holy of Holies, where the Ark of the Covenant, recovered by King David from the Philistines, resided.

Praising God in His Sanctuary In Exodus God commands his people: "Three times in the year you shall hold a festival for me. You shall observe the festival of unleavened bread [Passover]. . . . You shall observe the festival of harvest [Shavuot]. . . . You shall observe the festival of ingathering [Sukkot] at the end of the year, when you gather in . . . the fruit of your labor [Exodus 23:14–16]." Pilgrims from the entire region came to the Temple to observe these and other festivals, occasions when work was forbidden and worshipers were to "blow the trumpets over your burnt offerings and over your sacrifices [Numbers 10:10]."

Feast days were celebrated with sumptuous meals, dancing, and the singing of psalms. And many of the psalms that come down to us, though most were recorded after the dissolution of the monarchy, retain the essence of songs or ritual dating from Solomon's time. Psalm 68, for example, suggests the character of the early celebrations: "Your solemn processions are seen, O God, . . . the

This ivory pomegranate is probably the only surviving holy object from the Temple of Solomon. It may have topped a priest's scepter or been used as a Temple ornament.

singers in front, the musicians last, between them girls playing tambourines [Psalm 68:24–25]." As pilgrims mounted the steps leading to the Temple courtyard they probably chanted songs of ascent, examples of which occur in Psalms 120–134: "To you I lift up my eyes, O you who are enthroned in the heavens [Psalm 123:1]!" To gain admission at the gates, worshipers first had to demonstrate their moral purity by engaging in a question-and-answer ritual such as that contained in Psalm 15. The psalm opens with the congregant asking, "O Lord, who may abide in your tent"; to which the priest answers, "Those who walk blamelessly, and do what is right." The singers of Psalm 118 joyously enter the Temple grounds: "The Lord is God, and he has given us light. Bind the festal procession with branches, up to the horns of the altar [Psalm 118:27]."

The Tribe of Levi The priesthood was sanctioned after the revelation at Mount Sinai when God singled out the House of Levi to be his priestly servants in reward for standing by Moses at the time of the golden calf episode. The Levites were made responsible for the Ark of the Covenant and the tabernacle. Aaron and his sons were anointed with the oil used to dedicate the tabernacle and they offered the first sacrifice before it.

With the establishment of the monarchy, the priesthood came to play a central role in the life of Israel. The Pentateuch (the first five books of the Bible) describes three types of clerics. In descending order of importance they are the high priest; the regular priests; and the Levites, musicians in the Temple services. Under David, the Levitical priests, to whom some of the psalms are attributed, enjoyed an exalted status.

The priest (*kohen* in Hebrew) acted as a mediator, representative of the Hebrews to God and God's representative to them. His chief duty was to perform sacrifice. He sprinkled the blood and burned portions of the sacrificed animal and ensured that the offering was in no way defiled. Priests were also subject to strict laws of purity. The priest who defiled himself was barred from Temple service until he underwent a cleansing ritual.

Priests as Teachers In addition to presiding over the sacrifice, priests functioned as agents of divine communication and imparters of the torah, or instruction: "They teach Jacob your ordinances, and Israel your law [Deuteronomy 33:10]." They exercised their oracular powers by casting sacred lots called the Urim and Thummim to advise the people on cultic customs and practices and to ascertain the wisdom of actions such as going into battle.

The priest's role as teacher included interpreting the law, ruling on matters such as proper worship, assessing impurity, and providing moral guidance. The priestly torah would ultimately become the writ-

In this 18th-century engraving King David consults the high priest, who throws the Urim and Thummim. These lots, most likely in the form of pebbles, dice, or small sticks, were used to divine the future.

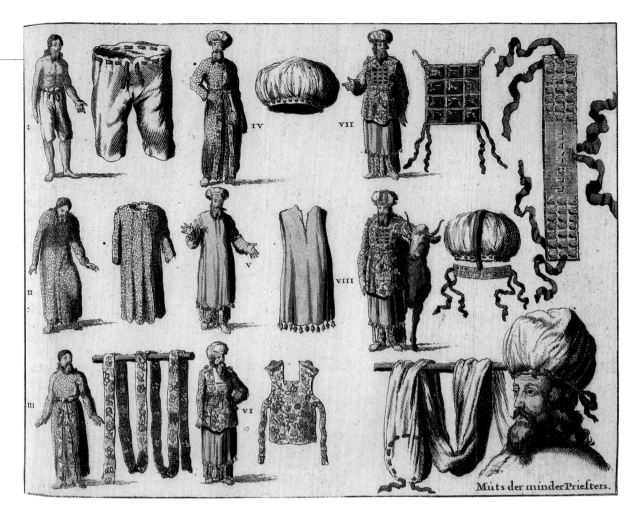

Muts der minder Priesters.

ten Torah, the body of laws contained in the Pentateuch. Other priestly duties included maintaining the Temple grounds and raising funds for its upkeep, adjudicating disputes, and purifying those afflicted with leprosy and other diseases.

After the Monarchy In the time of King Josiah (the seventh century B.C.), when worship at other sanctuaries and holy places was forbidden, most of the priests were required to serve at the Temple in Jerusalem. Thus effective control of the Temple cult was placed entirely in the hands of the priests in Jerusalem. Consequently priests who were cut off from the Temple had to find other employment and it is thought that most of those priests became teachers.

When the Temple was rebuilt after the Babylonian Captivity, the priestly status of the family of Aaron was reasserted—only Aaron's descendants could become priests. Levites from other branches of the family served as assistants to the Aaronic priests and were instrumental in maintaining the Temple and Hebrew teachings. Nearly five centuries later the Temple was rebuilt on a grand scale by Herod the Great. Herod's structure was destroyed by the Romans in A.D. 70, bringing Temple worship and sacrifice to an end. But the story of the Temple survived intact, thanks to the Levites who oversaw the writing of the history recounted in 1 and 2 Chronicles. ❖

This 18th-century Dutch text shows the layers of vestments worn by the high priest as they are described in Exodus 28. Over the tunic (V) and an apron called the ephod (VI) rested a breastpiece (VII) studded with 12 precious stones and inscribed with the names of the sons of Israel. The Urim and Thummin were kept inside the breastpiece to be "on Aaron's heart when he goes in before the Lord [Exodus 28: 30]."

Words of Wisdom

WISDOM WAS MAINTAINED BY TEACHERS IN ISRAEL AND PRESERVED FOR FUTURE GENERATIONS IN THE OLD TESTAMENT.

Many accomplishments were recognized as wise in the Old Testament, from the skills of craftsmen to the industriousness of insects. Individuals known particularly for their wisdom included prophets, priests, and professional sages. The sages, whose role may have evolved from that of court scribe in King David's time, are believed to have been responsible for an important body of Old Testament writing known as wisdom literature, including the Books of Proverbs, Ecclesiastes, and Job. King Solomon's traditional association with this material as the author of Proverbs and Ecclesiastes is probably due to his legendary judgment and skill at solving problems, his prayer for wisdom found in 1 Kings 3: 6-9, and the claim in Ecclesiastes 1:1 that the book's author is a son of David.

Proverbs and Ecclesiastes Many of the proverbs in the Bible probably existed orally long before they were ever written down. Their rhythmical style makes them easy to remember, and the lessons they teach make wisdom accessible to everyone. The proverbs stress the virtues of common sense, practical experience, and ethical standards while making it clear that to be wise means recognizing God as the source of all wisdom. The message is essentially optimistic: a wise and virtuous life brings its own rewards.

A much more philosophical message is revealed in Ecclesiastes, a sober reflection on the meaning of life. The author of Ecclesiastes, which dates from about 300 B.C., is the most pessimistic of observers, but in spite of seeing all of life as vanity, he still maintains his reverence for God.

Book of Job The deeply moving Book of Job is a powerful exploration of the meaning of suffering—and of life itself—and of God's relationship to man. The enduring appeal of the book can be attributed to the poignancy of the drama, the beauty of its language, and the depth of its theology.

The story concerns a pious man whose faith is sorely tested. Job is "blameless and upright, one who feared God and turned away from evil [Job 1:1]." When God praises him in the heavenly council, Satan—one of the members of God's court—questions Job's piety, saying that if he were tested, his faith would crumble. God allows Satan

In 1 Kings 4 we learn that Solomon was wiser than anyone else and that he composed 3,000 proverbs. In this detail from a 13th-century Hebrew Bible and prayer book, the wise king is shown reading the Torah.

Words of Wisdom from Israel and Egypt

The stress on wisdom in the Old Testament reflects a long-standing concern shared by cultures throughout the ancient Near East. There are marked similarities, for instance, between some of the advice offered in Proverbs and that offered in a collection of wise sayings known as *The Teachings of Amen-em-ope*, a sage who taught in Egypt sometime between 1200 and 1000 B.C. The excerpts below compare verses from Proverbs 22: 17-21, 22:22-27, and 25: 21-22 with verses from chapters 1 and 2 of Amen-em-ope's teachings.

Wisdom from Proverbs

*Incline your ear and hear my words, and apply
your mind to my teaching; for it will be
pleasant if you keep them within you,
if all of them are ready on your lips.
So that your trust may be in the Lord,
I have made them known
to you today—yes to you.
Have I not written for you thirty
sayings of admonition and
knowledge, to show you what
is right and true,
so that you may give
a true answer to
those who sent you?*

*Do not rob the poor because
they are poor, or crush
the afflicted at the gate;
for the Lord pleads their cause
and despoils of life those
who despoil them.
Make no friends with those
given to anger, and do not associate
with hotheads, or you may learn their
ways and entangle yourself in a snare.
Do not be one of those who give pledges,
who become surety for debts.
If you have nothing with which to pay,
why should your bed be taken from under you?*

*If your enemies are hungry,
give them bread to eat; and if they are thirsty,
give them water to drink;
for you will heap coals of fire on their heads,
and the Lord will reward you.*

Wisdom from Amen-em-ope

*Listen to what I say, learn my words by heart.
Prosperity comes to those who keep my words in
their hearts. Poverty comes to those
who discard them!
Enshrine my words in your souls,
Lock them away in your hearts.
When the words of fools
blow like a storm,
The words of the wise
will hold like an anchor.
Live your lives with my words
in your heart,
and you will live your
lives with success.*

*Do not steal from the poor,
nor cheat the cripple.
Do not abuse the elderly, nor
refuse to let the aged
speak. Do not conspire to
defraud anyone yourself,
nor encourage anyone else's fraud.
Do not sue those who wrong you,
nor testify against them in court.
Injustice can turn on fools quicker than
floods eroding the bank of a canal,
north winds bearing down on a boat, storms
forming, thunderbolts cracking, crocodiles striking.
Fools cry out. They shout to the gods for help.*

*Do not treat fools the way fools treat you, Pull
the fool up out of high water, give the fool your hand.
Leave the punishment of the fool to the gods.
Feed them until they are full,
give them your bread until they are ashamed.*

In the 12th-century window, above, Solomon makes his judgment establishing the true mother of a child.

to test Job, who quickly loses his livestock and servants. Then all 10 of Job's children are killed and the man himself is afflicted with bodily sores. In his pain Job cries out, "Why did I not die at birth, come forth from the womb and expire [Job 3:11]?" His three friends, as well as Elihu, a young bystander, confront him in his agony. Echoing the Hebrew belief in divine retribution, they tell Job that he must be guilty of some transgression in order to deserve such a fate. The innocent Job denies any relationship between his conduct and his dire circumstances, and in so doing, he flatly rejects the traditional biblical doctrine that evil begets suffering. Job asks the profoundest questions about life (What is the meaning of suffering? How can God countenance evil in the world?) and refuses to accept easy answers.

The Lord then responds to Job "out of the whirlwind [Job 38:1]" and, in a series of probing questions, draws Job deeper into the mystery of his creation, until Job finally experiences a transcendent meeting with the divine. "Now my eye sees you [Job 42:5]," Job declares, and, his faith reaffirmed, he accepts that the workings of God are unfathomable. In an epilogue to the book, God rewards Job with a new family and twice his previous wealth.

Job quickly learns from a series of messengers that he has lost all his considerable wealth and that all of his children and servants have been killed. His impassioned reply to God is "'Naked I came from my mother's womb, and naked shall I return there; the Lord gave, and the Lord has taken away; blessed be the name of the Lord' [Job 2:21]." In this detail from a 16th-century stained glass window in Mariawald, Germany, we see Chaldean soldiers slaughtering Job's herdsmen, as reported by one of the messengers.

Writing of the Book of Job Tales of Job-like men reach far back into antiquity and are recounted in a number of ancient Egyptian and Mesopotamian works, although the name *Job* is used in none of these works. The story that comes closest to the biblical Book of Job is "Man and His God"—often referred to as the Sumerian Job. This poem, dating from before 2000 B.C., tells of an innocent man who, like Job, is stricken with misfortune, prays for relief, is finally delivered from his woes, and praises his god. It is likely that there was also an ancient Hebrew story of Job that had been recited orally for centuries before ever being written down. Scholars believe that Ezekiel, who referred to Job as a righteous man in Ezekiel 14:14 and 14:20—at the beginning of the Babylonian Exile—probably knew of Job from that Hebrew tale.

The Book of Job is a long poem framed by a prose prologue and epilogue. Nothing certain is known about the author, but judging from the deep piety of the work and the great depth and complexity of its thought and language, the anonymous author must have been profoundly religious and highly intelligent.

Some scholars believe that the author of Job took the ancient Hebrew tale and shaped it into a prose prologue and epilogue, which he then used as a setting for his long poetic piece. The nature of Job, they claim, differs in the prose and verse segments. In the prologue, Job patiently endures all his sufferings. In the verse section, he is a rebel, refusing to accept the traditional counsels of his friends and challenging God personally. Although the date of the writing is widely debated, many scholars believe that the bulk of it was composed during the years of the Babylonian Captivity. The Israelites, deprived of their property and the land God had granted them, found it hard to retain their faith in God's covenant with them and, like Job, were called upon to move from despair to an enduring and trusting faith. It is generally believed that the hymn on the inaccessibility of wisdom (chapter 28) and the discourses of Elihu (chapters 32 to 37) were added later, possibly between 400 and 200 B.C. Both passages seem to intrude on the rest of the text and not be a part of it. In addition, Elihu's discourses merely seem to repeat in other words the views of Job's three friends, and Elihu is not mentioned in the epilogue with the rest of the characters.

Other Wisdom Literature Wisdom can also be found in a number of the psalms and sporadically in other parts of the Old Testament—for example, in the familiar story of Solomon's judgment on which of two women is the mother of a child (1 Kings 3:16–28). It is also found in the apocryphal books of the Bible, most notably Ecclesiasticus and the *Wisdom of Solomon.*

Ecclesiasticus was written about 180 B.C. by the sage, scribe, and teacher "Jesus the son of Sirach, son of Eleazar of Jerusalem, who out of his heart poured forth wisdom [Sirach 50:27]." It is also referred to as Sirach or the Wisdom of Sirach to keep it from being confused with the Book of Ecclesiastes. Ben Sira (Hebrew for "Son of Sirach") wrote in Hebrew, but sometime after 132 B.C. his work was translated by his grandson into Greek. The Hebrew text was lost in the early centuries A.D., but in the 20th century about two-thirds of it was found surviving in ancient manuscripts in a Cairo synagogue. Sirach's work resembles Proverbs in tone and content, but rather than setting apart the individual proverbs, Sirach wove them into poetic passages.

Stripped of everything and plagued with "loathsome sores . . . from the sole of his foot to the crown of his head [Job 2:7]," Job refuses to "'curse God, and die' [Job 2:9]" as his wife urges. Instead, he sits in the ashes, while three friends remain silently with him for seven days, as depicted in this miniature from a 12th-century French Bible.

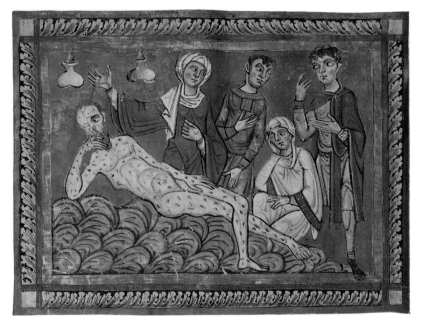

The *Wisdom of Solomon* (or Book of Wisdom) was written in Greek, possibly in Alexandria, Egypt, and dates long after the time of Solomon, probably from the first century B.C. The work personifies Wisdom as the savior of Israel's ancestors and speaks of God's power and mercy and his gift of immortality to the righteous. Its message is that to know God is to know righteousness. ❖

Language of the Old Testament

THE MASTERFUL EPIC OF THE ISRAELITES IS WRITTEN IN CONCISE, POWERFUL PROSE AND A SCRIPT DEVOID OF VOWELS.

L ittle is known for certain about the original language of the desert tribes, whether the Israelites had always spoken Hebrew, as the Bible leads us to believe, or if perhaps they spoke a dialect of Old Aramaic, as some scholars have sumised. By the sixth century B.C., the language of the Persian Empire, Aramaic (like Hebrew, a Semitic language), had become the principal spoken language of the Near East. The Israelites' medium of literature and the sacred Scriptures, however, continued to be Hebrew. The Old Testament is written almost entirely in Hebrew, with the exception of some chapters composed in Aramaic and the occasional intrusion of a word or phrase in another language. Aramaic appears in portions of Daniel—concerning legends set in the Babylonian and Persian courts (Daniel: 2:4–7:28)—and in Ezra 4:8–6:18 and 7:12–26, which relate stories of the Persian kings Artaxerxes and Darius I. Aramaic words and phrases crop up in other texts as well, such as Jeremiah10:11. In Genesis 31:47, the pile of stones signifying the covenant made between Jacob and Laban is named in Hebrew by Jacob and in Aramaic by Laban. Both words, *Galeed* and *Jegar-sahadutha* respectively, mean "the heap of witness." The Hebrew of some of the later books of the Bible (Ezra, Nehemiah, and 1 and 2 Chronicles) is heavily influenced by Aramaic vocabulary and syntax. Greek words appear in Daniel, and isolated Persian words in both Daniel and the Book of Esther.

Hebrew Script Apart from a few brief inscriptions recovered by archeologists, the Bible is our only source for classical Hebrew of the third century B.C. Classical Hebrew was written from right to left using a "square" script similar to modern written Hebrew (see chart); however, its 22 characters consisted solely of consonants. An English

Early Hebrew	Modern Hebrew	Transliteration
	א	ꞌ
	ב	B
	ג	G
	ד	D
	ה	H
	ו	W
	ז	Z
	ח	Ḥ/KH
	ט	Ṭ
	י	Y
	כ	K
	ל	L
	מ	M
	נ	N
	ס	S
	ע	ꜥ
	פ	P
	צ	TS
	ק	Q
	ר	R
	שׁ	SH
	ת	T

This chart shows early Hebrew script of the 10th to the 4th centuries B.C., whose alphabet is chiefly known through a document called the Gezer calendar (letters not used in the calendar are indicated by blank spaces in the first column); modern written Hebrew, whose "square" shape derives from 3rd-century B.C. classical Hebrew; and a transliteration.

The 10th-century B.C. Gezer calendar of agricultural cycles is believed by some to have been written as a schoolboy exercise.

equivalent to this consonantal system would be to write "once upon a time" as NC PN TM. Words thus depleted of their vowels can suggest multiple meanings—in this case the phrase might also be read "nice pen, Tom"—a construction that would certainly confound the present-day reader. As the system common to all Semitic languages, however, the vowel-less alphabet probably created few problems of interpretation for the Israelites. Even modern translators of biblical Hebrew seldom disagree on interpretation because context makes the meaning of particular passages apparent.

The Bible's Vigorous Language Though the writing of the Hebrew Bible spanned hundreds of years, its grammar and its vocabulary of some 7,000 discreet words remain remarkably consistent throughout. One reason for this stability is that Hebrew was the language of literature and, therefore, not subject to the kind of external pressures that exert change on spoken languages. Biblical Hebrew is vibrant: the mode of expression exhibits, as one scholar has put it, a "vigorous terseness and power of condensation." Abstract ideas are rendered in powerful concrete images. For example, when translated literally the Hebrew word describing the notion "stubborn" becomes "hard of neck," and "miserable" becomes "bitter of soul."

The Hebrew Bible inevitably loses some of the force of its prose in translation, as can be illustrated by comparing a passage from Jeremiah 4:19 in various English editions of the Bible: "My bowels, my bowels!" the passage reads in the King James version; "Oh, the writhing of my bowels!" in the New English Bible; and "My anguish, my anguish!" in the New Revised Standard Version. The King James and New English Bible translations are the most faithful to the passage's literal meaning, but the Revised may come closer to the intended meaning, for in the ancient concept of the body the emotions were located in the bowels. Thus Jeremiah cries out a visceral expression of anguish, in much the same way a lovesick person today might lament, "Oh, my heart!" ❖

A fine example of modern Hebrew calligraphy, hand lettered in ink and gouache on vellum, adorns an 18th-century Viennese prayer book.

The Divided Kingdom

THE KINGDOM RULED BY SAUL, DAVID, AND SOLOMON LASTED LITTLE MORE THAN 100 YEARS BEFORE IT WAS DIVIDED INTO TWO KINGDOMS, WITH SEPARATE MONARCHIES AND DIVERGENT HISTORIES.

Through sheer force of leadership, King David brought a disparate group of tribes together as a single kingdom. By the time of his son King Solomon's death, however, about 922 B.C., ancient tribal enmities—combined with fresh resentments over Solomon's governing policies—led to the kingdom's splitting into two separate kingdoms.

Rehoboam, Solomon's son and heir, was recognized as ruler in Jerusalem and the Southern Kingdom. In the North, where Solomon's taxes and forced labor policies had been particularly harsh, elders demanded that Rehoboam abandon his father's heavy-handed ways. The new king refused. "My father disciplined you with whips," he told them, "but I will discipline you with scorpions [1 Kings 12:14]." Faced with such arrogance, the Northern leaders seceded and anointed their own king, Jeroboam.

Two Kingdoms Jeroboam's Northern Kingdom retained the name of Israel, and the town of Shechem was made its first capital. Jerusalem remained the capital of the Southern Kingdom, which was called Judah. Of the two, Israel was the stronger and richer. It had access to the sea. Its population was larger, its army more powerful, and its resources more bountiful. Yet for all the Northern Kingdom's advantages, its history would be marked by political chaos: 19 monarchs from 9 dynasties ruled; 7 kings were assassinated.

Israel endured for two centuries. Judah—whose strengths were its religious continuity and political stability—lasted nearly 150 years longer. Judah was ruled continually throughout its history by kings of the Davidic dynasty and thereby confirmed the promises made by God that David and his family would rule permanently over Judah. Moreover, there was only one Temple—God's earthly dwelling place, which housed the Ark of the Covenant—and it was in Jerusalem. Because it was the most prestigious place of worship, the Temple was

At Solomon's death, Israel included all of the area outlined in red and purple, above, but the nation was soon divided into two independent kingdoms. The Northern Kingdom of Israel fell to Assyria in 722 B.C. Assyria also attacked towns in Judah, but Judah did not fall. The Siloam tunnel, above left, which still stands in Jerusalem, was built by the Judean King Hezekiah in the eighth century B.C. to insure that the city's water supply could not be cut off by the Assyrian army.

central to the religious life of the Israelites. Jeroboam in the North, fearing that his subjects would stream across the border into Judah for religious festivals, refurbished old shrines in the towns of Dan and Beth-El, chose new priests, established new festivals, and appropriated local religious symbols. As substitution for the golden cherubs that flanked the Ark of the Covenant in Jerusalem and served as the throne of God, Jeroboam used a golden calf at each of his shrines as a pedestal for God.

Calves or young bulls, such as this 12th-century B.C. bronze figure from Samaria, were used as religious symbols and objects of worship throughout the Near East and were associated with the Canaanite God El.

Without their central place of worship, many Israelites were persuaded to shift their allegiance to pagan gods. This change met with vehement opposition by the religious faithful in the Northern Kingdom, among whom was the prophet Elijah.

A Prophet of the North There is no book of Elijah in the Bible, but the prophet was one of the most important figures in the Northern Kingdom's history. More is known of his works than his words because of the beautifully told stories of his life and deeds in 1 and 2 Kings. Elijah, whose very name means "my God is Yahweh," spent much of his ministry prophesying against the worship of pagan gods. One such

The stories of Elijah's life are marked by miracles and wondrous happenings. One of the best-known is depicted on this 16th-century German stained-glass window. In the story, a poor widow befriends Elijah. When the widow's child falls ill and dies, Elijah summons his faith and calls upon God, who allows the child to be restored to life.

incident occurred when Elijah was a young man. King Ahab, who by then ruled the Northern Kingdom, built a temple to the Canaanite god Baal to please his wife, Jezebel. You and your father's house have troubled Israel, Elijah ultimately told the king, "because you have forsaken the commandments of the Lord and followed the Baals [1 Kings 18:18.]" He then challenged 450 prophets of Baal to a contest of strength on Mount Carmel to prove whose God was more powerful.

On the mountain, Elijah called on God, who sent fire to consume a sacrifice that had been thoroughly doused with water and who allowed him to slay all of the pagan prophets. When it was time for Elijah to die, he was carried off in a chariot of fire, and his mantle of authority fell on the prophet Elisha. Many miracle stories were also told about Elisha, such as his healing of an Aramaean general named Naaman who was afflicted with leprosy.

Jezebel is thrown from a window to her death in this detail from a 19th-century engraving by Gustave Doré. The incident is dramatically described in 2 Kings 9:30–33.

A Book of Laws The Southern Kingdom had its own religious problems as, in time, people grew away from their tradition of worship and sacrifice in the Temple and instead began to worship at other altars and were even known to honor a pagan god in the Jewish Temple. In the year 621 B.C., during the reign of King Josiah, word circulated that a priest named Hilkiah had discovered an old law book in the Temple. When Josiah read the book and realized how God's laws had been ignored, he launched a series of sweeping reforms. He reinstated the old religious practices and festivals, destroyed the pagan shrines, and finally assembled the people of Judah to listen to the laws and to renew their ancient covenant with God.

While confronting the prophets of Baal, Elijah asked for a sign that he had done God's will. As shown in this illustration from the 15th-century Nuremberg Bible, God then sent a fire from heaven to ignite a burnt offering that had been doused with water. (1 Kings 18:38)

It is possible that Josiah's influential law book was an early version of the Book of Deuteronomy, in which Moses in his farewell address instructs the people on the code they should live by. The theme of the book is the reaffirmation of the special covenant between God and his people, and one of the basic laws governing that relationship is that all worship must be centralized in one place.

Deuteronomy is written in the same style as the early historical books of the Bible—Joshua, Judges, I and 2 Samuel, and I and 2 Kings, which in the traditional division of the Hebrew Bible are called the Former Prophets. The language in these books is similar and a continuous story is told, from the death of Moses to the devastation of Judah by Babylonia. The entire history of that period is told from a religious perspective—events are narrated and kings are rated according to how faithful they are to the laws of Deuteronomy.

A Biblical Record In I and 2 Kings, the Deuteronomist historian (as the anonymous writers of the historical books are collectively known) points to the dividing of the kingdom as evidence of the rebelliousness of the covenant people. Subsequently, the "good" kings are those descended from David, who maintain Jerusalem as the one center of worship. The Northern kings, having their own center of worship, are inevitably found wanting. There is an undeniable Southern bias in this history; and the historian points to the Assyrian conquest of Israel in 722 as confirmation of the Northern Kingdom's evil ways. Dispersed by the Assyrians, the people of the North eventually lose their identity and are assimilated by other cultures. They are popularly known as the 10 lost tribes of Israel. Judah also suffers exile—at the hands of the Babylonians—but the Judeans are able to maintain their identity and traditions until they can return and rebuild Jerusalem. The historian points to their survival as evidence that they were more faithful to the covenant.

Another version of the history of the divided kingdom is found in 1 and 2 Chronicles and is part of the history that also includes Ezra and Nehemiah. Written after the Jews returned home from captivity in Babylonia, 1 and 2 Chronicles are mainly concerned with the religious life of the restored nation. The history recounted in the Books of Chronicles does not pay much attention to—and in fact largely ignores—the history of the once-powerful Northern Kingdom. ❖

*F*igures from a ninth-century B.C. obelisk show King Jehu of Israel paying tribute to the king of Assyria to elicit his aid. In the next century Assyria destroyed Israel.

Who Were the Prophets?

THE PROPHETS OF ISRAEL AND JUDAH DELIVERED THE WORD OF GOD TO THE PEOPLE IN ORDER TO SHAPE THEIR FUTURE BY REFORMING THEIR PRESENT.

Throughout the early books of the Old Testament there are prophets of great faith. Abraham and Moses, in particular, are revered as prophets who worked to carry out God's will and convey his covenants. Moses' prophetic vision allowed him to lead the people toward the creation of a kingdom of Israel. By the end of the 11th century B.C., when Saul was anointed Israel's first king, prophecy had achieved a recognized role in Israel.

There were various types of prophets. Prophets known as seers maintained religious shrines and made predictions for those who visited them. One such prophet was Samuel, who said to Saul, "'I am the seer; go up before me to the shrine, for today you shall eat with me, and in the morning I will let you go and will tell you all that is on your mind' [1 Samuel 9:

19]." Often seers lived and traveled in groups and prophesied from the depths of ecstatic trances, sometimes to the accompaniment of musical instruments. For example, when Saul was on the road to Gibeah, "a band of prophets met him; and the spirit of God possessed him, and he fell into a prophetic frenzy along with them [1 Samuel 10:10.]"

After Samuel became the selector and anointer of kings, some prophets joined the court and began to act as counselors. Samuel himself advised Saul. Nathan advised David. Over time the prophets' role of counselor developed, and prophets became important court functionaries. The prophets also served as guardians of the covenant. If the king broke the covenant, as we know from the cases of David and Bathsheba and Ahab and Naboth, there

Micah predicted the destruction of Jerusalem and the Temple and the restoration of the Davidic kingdom. He is portrayed above in a detail from the 15th-century Ghent Altarpiece by Jan van Eyck.

This 14th-century medallion portrait of Malachi, the last of the Twelve, shown with his scroll, was painted by Giotto in the Scrovegni chapel in Padua, Italy.

An angel carries Habakkuk by his hair in this seventh-century Greek limestone bas-relief. The incident is from Bel and the Dragon, part of the Greek version of the Book of Daniel.

Zechariah is carved in limestone in this depiction of the prophet from the 15th-century Abbey of Champmol near Dijon, France.

was a Nathan or an Elijah to criticize him.

The Classical Era of Prophecy

In the traditional division of the Hebrew Bible, the early historical books—Joshua, Judges, Samuel, and Kings—are called the Former Prophets. The books collectively known as the Latter Prophets—Isaiah, Jeremiah, Ezekiel, and the Twelve—contain the pronouncements of those prophets who received the prophetic call after the kingdom was divided. It was with the Latter Prophets that what is thought of as the classical era of Israelite prophecy began.

In all, the writings of the Latter Prophets span about 400 years—from the eighth through the fifth centuries B.C.—beginning just before the Northern Kingdom fell to Assyrian armies. By the time of the Assyrian assault, the prophet Hosea complained that the population of the Northern Kingdom had turned from God and adopted the gods and worship practices of their Canaanite neighbors. Also in Judah, worship was at times corrupted by Assyrian influences, and people were forgetting the Mosaic Law. As often as the people forgot God's covenant the prophets were there to remind them, to reason with them, and to plead with them to avoid the future disaster that would surely come if they did not change their current way of life.

Who Were They?

The Latter Prophets to whom relatively long books are attributed are referred to as the Major Prophets. They are Isaiah, Jeremiah, and Ezekiel. The others, known collectively as the Twelve, are called the Minor Prophets, because of the brevity of their books. They are Hosea, Joel, Amos, Obadiah, Jonah, Micah, Nahum, Habakkuk, Zephaniah, Haggai, Zechariah, and Malachi.

The prophets came from many different walks of life. Isaiah is thought to have been of Jerusalem's upper classes, but Amos was from a tiny Judean village and referred to himself as "a herdsman and a dresser of sycamore trees [Amos 7:14]." What united these men was that each had been

77

called to carry God's message. Their pronouncements often began with the words, "Thus says the Lord." The calling was a responsibility that few could have wished on themselves, since it compelled them to speak harsh truths to common people and powerful rulers alike about their flagging faith and the likely consequences of their moral and religious negligence. No one wanted to listen. In fact some of the prophets were thrown out of courts and places of worship, scorned, and even threatened with death. Nevertheless, the prophets continued to offer the Israelites hope and to assure them that if they mended their ways they could save their nation from destruction.

The Role of Prophecy in Exile After the fall of Jerusalem in 587 B.C., when the Israelites were taken into exile in Babylonia, they remembered the words of the prophets. From as early as the eighth century

The prophet Amos is shown at right in a carving from a 16th-century German choir stall. His book is the earliest collection of prophetic writings in the Bible.

Voices of the Twelve

The activities of the Minor Prophets spanned at least four centuries. Their method of writing ranged from poetry to woeful lamentations to the Lord and from dialogues between prophet and God to heartfelt pleas to the people. What the prophets shared was that they all felt compelled by God to deliver his message.

Hosea *prophesied in his native Northern Kingdom in the mid-eighth century B.C. He compared God's relationship with Israel to that of a man who loves and forgives his unfaithful wife. "I will take you for my wife in faithfulness; and you shall know the Lord [Hosea 2:20]."*

Joel *is thought to have lived in Judea in the early fifth century B.C. He is known for his prophecy of locusts. "Like blackness spread upon the mountains a great and powerful army comes; their like has never been from of old, nor will be again after them in ages to come [Joel 2:2]."*

Amos *was from Judah, but he prophesied in Israel in the mid-eighth century B.C. He denounced Israel for its unethical conduct. "For I know how many are your transgressions, and how great are your sins—you who afflict the righteous, who take a bribe, and push aside the needy in the gate [Amos 5:12]."*

Obadiah *may have lived in the late sixth century B.C. His book is an oracle against Edom. "On the day that you stood aside, on the day that strangers carried off his wealth, and foreigners entered his gates and cast lots for Jerusalem, you too were like one of them [Obadiah 1:11]."*

Jonah *may have prophesied in postexilic Israel sometime in the late fifth century B.C. His is the only book of the Twelve to consist mainly of a prose narrative. In it, Jonah's oracle against Nineveh is the shortest oracle in the Old Testament. "Forty days more, and Nineveh shall be overthrown [Jonah 3:4]!"*

Micah *lived in the late eighth century B.C. His prophecy of Jerusalem's destruction was recalled 100 years later by Jeremiah. "'Zion shall be plowed as a field; Jerusalem shall become a heap of ruins, and the mountain of the house a wooded height' [Jeremiah 26:18]."*

The prophet Obadiah, who prophesied against the Edomites in 5th-century Judah, is pictured on this 16th-century panel from a French church.

the prophets had warned first of the Northern Kingdom's impending fall and then of the fall of the Southern Kingdom of Judah. Even though the words had gone unheeded, they were put into writing. Collecting and recording prophecy served several purposes. Not only was it a means of preserving the political history that led up to the Exile, but the words of the prophets would also prove instrumental in encouraging the faith of the Israelites in exile.

In some cases, prophets may have recorded their own words. More often, however, their pronouncements were probably inscribed by disciples (called, as a guild, the sons of the prophets) or by other scribes, just as the words of the prophet Jeremiah were written down by his scribe, Baruch. Sometimes prophetic wisdom was recorded only after having been passed along orally for many years.

During the Exile, the prophets continued their work. Isaiah and Ezekiel prophesied that the Israelites would be restored from exile to their home in Judah. Their words came true. And on their return to Jerusalem, other prophets, such as Haggai and Zechariah, were instrumental in encouraging the people to rebuild the Temple and in rekindling the people's faith. ❖

Nahum prophesied in the late seventh century B.C. His words celebrate the fall of the Assyrian Empire as the Lord's judgment against a cruel nation. "Your shepherds are asleep, O king of Assyria; your nobles slumber. . . . There is no assuaging your hurt, your wound is mortal. All who hear the news about you clap their hands over you. For who has ever escaped your endless cruelty [Nahum 3:18-19]?"

Habakkuk is believed to have prophesied during the reign of Jehoiakim, in the late seventh and early sixth century B.C. His prophecies all concern Babylonia, which would one day be destroyed. "Because you have plundered many nations, all that survive of the peoples shall plunder you—because of human bloodshed, and violence to the earth, to cities and all who live in them [Habakkuk 2:8]."

Zephaniah, who prophesied in the late seventh century B.C., is known for his oracle on the Day of the Lord. "The sound of the day of the Lord is bitter, the warrior cries aloud there. That day will be a day of wrath, a day of distress and anguish, a day of ruin and devastation, a day of darkness and gloom, a day of clouds and thick darkness, a day of trumpet blast and battle cry against the fortified cities and against the lofty battlements [Zephaniah 1:14–16]."

Haggai encouraged the rebuilding of the Temple in the sixth century B.C., when the Jews returned from exile in Babylonia. "Go up to the hills and bring wood and build the house, so that I may take pleasure in it and be honored, says the Lord. You have looked for much, and, lo, it came to little; and when you brought it home, I blew it away. Why? says the Lord of hosts. Because my house lies in ruins [Haggai 1:8-9]."

Zechariah's prophecies date from the last decades of the sixth century B.C., when he too was instrumental in rebuilding the Temple. The Word of God came to him in a series of visions. "Therefore, thus says the Lord, I have returned to Jerusalem with compassion; my house shall be built in it . . . and the measuring line shall be stretched out over Jerusalem. . . . My cities shall again overflow with prosperity; the Lord will again comfort Zion and again choose Jerusalem [Zechariah 1:16-17]."

Malachi perhaps lived in the fifth century B.C. and was the last of the prophets. His writing focuses mainly on the theme of faithfulness to God's covenant and laws. "For I the Lord do not change; therefore you, O children of Jacob, have not perished. Ever since the days of your ancestors you have turned aside from my statutes and have not kept them. Return to me, and I will return to you, says the Lord of hosts. But you say, 'How shall we return?' [Malachi 3:6-7]."

The Oracles of Isaiah

THE GREAT PROPHET'S BOOK, WRITTEN ACROSS SEVERAL CENTURIES, BEGINS WITH EXHORTATIONS AND ENDS WITH HOPE.

The prophet Isaiah, while still young, receives inspiration directly from the hand of God, at right, in an illustration from a ninth-century Greek psalter.

Isaiah is known to some as the evangelical prophet who promised the coming of a messiah. He is also called Judah's greatest prophet. Though he spent much of his life immersed in political problems—at a time when the Northern Kingdom was falling to the Assyrians—Isaiah's message is timeless. To Judah, beset by enemies, he counseled faith, exhorting his listeners to know God's ways. And he revealed the ways in which God works in human affairs, reminding us that justice results from righteous behavior.

Isaiah delivered his prophetic messages in the last four decades of the eighth century B.C., during the reigns of four kings: Uzziah, Jotham, Ahaz, and Hezekiah. He is thought to have been well educated and wellborn himself, as indicated by the richness of his vocabulary and by his evident access to Judah's royal court.

The Isaiah scroll shown below is one of 19 copies of the Book of Isaiah that were discovered among the Dead Sea Scrolls and is one of 2 that were found in nearly complete condition. It dates from about 100 B.C.

A Man of God Yet for all Isaiah's worldliness and culture, he was wholly a man of God, who from the first embraced his calling with ardor. While in the Temple one day about 742 B.C., Isaiah had a vision of God on his throne attended by six-winged seraphim. Overwhelmed by his unworthiness to participate in such divine council, he cried out in despair, but he was cleansed of any guilt when a seraph placed a glowing coal upon his lips. The Lord asked, "Whom shall I send, and who will go for us?" And Isaiah answered, "Here am I; send me [Isaiah 6:8]!" His fervor never waned, even when, as God foretold, his message was ignored "until cities lie waste without inhabitant, and houses without people, and the land is utterly desolate [Isaiah 6:11]."

Isaiah carried out his prophetic mission against the backdrop of Judah's worsening political crisis and Assyrian threat. An impassioned orator, he repeatedly and eloquently warned Judah's kings against their expedient but shortsighted strategies of placating Assyria with tribute or seeking alliances with Egypt. Only God could save the nation, Isaiah prophesied; national salvation lay not in politics or diplomacy. Rather, it lay in restoring the people's relationship with God through a renewed commitment to social justice and to the faith that they had avowed in their covenant with God

More Than One Isaiah Isaiah's warnings, which were revealed to him as oracles, went unheeded by his fellow Judeans, but his words were written down, perhaps by his own disciples or scribes. They are recorded as chapters 1 through 39 of the Book of Isaiah. Nearly all of the writing from those chapters, known as First Isaiah, is thought to

In Isaiah's vision in the Temple, God was attended by seraphim. "Each had six wings: with two they covered their faces, and with two they covered their feet, and with two they flew [Isaiah 6:2]." The vision is shown below in a detail from a 12th-century illumination.

have originated during the prophet's time. However, most scholars believe that the remaining 27 chapters of the book—which at 66 chapters is the longest book of the Bible—date from a much later period, probably the sixth century B.C. Because no one knows who actually wrote these sections, chapters 40 through 55 are often referred to as Second (or Deutero) Isaiah, and chapters 56 through 66 as Third Isaiah.

The latter part of the book prophesies Babylon's fall to the armies of Cyrus of Persia in 539 B.C., the end of the Exile, and the subsequent restoration of the nation of Israel. "Comfort, O comfort my people, says your God," chapter 40 begins. "Speak tenderly to Jerusalem and cry to her that she has served her term, that her penalty is paid, that she has received from the Lord's hand double for all her sins [Isaiah 40:1-2]."

Although Second and Third Isaiah were not joined to the first part of the book until long after First Isaiah was written, they seem to complete the prophet's message: the judgments end in deliverance, the promises reach fulfillment, the suffering gives way to salvation. Moreover, the warnings that went unheeded early in the book are ultimately appreciated. Isaiah's words of hope and faith give the book its timeless power. Generations have turned to it for wisdom and have found it there. "Nation shall not lift up sword against nation," he said, "neither shall they learn war any more [Isaiah 2:4]." ❖

Baruch and Jeremiah

IN A TIME OF IMPENDING DISASTER, TWO MEN PLACED THEIR
LIVES IN JEOPARDY TO PROCLAIM THE INSPIRED WORD OF GOD.

Most of the scribes who wrote down sacred Scripture remain largely unknown. Not so Baruch. The man to whom the prophet Jeremiah dictated his powerful oracles is very much a part of the story told in the Book of Jeremiah. Baruch was well educated and came from a prominent scribal family in Jerusalem. He could have had a prosperous career (his brother was a minister in the royal court), but he chose instead to follow Jeremiah, who prophesied that Judah would be destroyed if the people did not return to the ways of the covenant. Baruch did not follow the prophet without some regret, however. In 605 B.C., when he saw what Jeremiah's prophecies would mean, he wrote, "Woe is me! The Lord has added sorrow to my pain; I am weary with my groaning, and I find no rest [Jeremiah 45:3]." Speaking through Jeremiah, God answered him, "And you, do you seek great things for yourself? Do not seek them; for I am going to bring disaster upon all flesh, . . . but I will give you your life as a prize of war in every place to which you may go [Jeremiah 45:5]."

Jeremiah's Prophecies The prophet himself was of a priestly family that may have traced its history back to Abiathar, King David's chief priest. Called by God while he was still a boy of 12 or 13 to become a prophet, Jeremiah reluctantly took up his ministry as a young man. Working in the tradition of earlier prophets, he was an impassioned speaker who proclaimed oracles that he received directly from God. The word of God was like a burning fire within him. "I am weary with holding it in," he confessed, "and I cannot [Jeremiah 20:9]." His calling brought him nothing but anguish. His message to follow the Law or face destruction was harsh, and everyone turned against him—the king, political officials, the priests and other prophets, even his family and friends. At various times he was beaten, imprisoned, subjected to

Jeremiah prophesied in Judah for some 40 years, beginning about 622 B.C. From the time that Baruch joined him about 604 B.C., Jeremiah dictated the prophecies he received from God directly to his friend and scribe. Baruch himself wrote an account of their lives that details the anguish that Jeremiah suffered. These writings show the process of the Bible's composition: the conversion of the prophetic word into the text of sacred Scripture.

public ridicule, and left in an empty cistern to die. In the depths of despair, Jeremiah felt betrayed even by God and lost faith that God would rescue him from his enemies.

Jeremiah's prophecies terrified all who heard them. To many of his listeners, the words of a true prophet were sacred, charged with the awesome power to alter the course of history. King Jehoiakim attempted to protect himself from the truth of Jeremiah's utterances by forbidding the prophet to speak on the Temple grounds.

Writing It Down The prophet would not be silenced. He dictated to Baruch all the words God had spoken to him and he sent the scribe to the Temple to read them aloud. Officials seized Baruch's scroll and read it to the enraged and frightened king. Jehoiakim cut it up, threw it piece by piece into a fire, and ordered the arrest of the prophet and his scribe. No flames could put an end to the fearful oracles, however. God told Jeremiah to get another scroll and write on it the words that were on the first. It is that scroll that forms the nucleus of the Book of Jeremiah.

When the prophecy of Judah's ruin came to pass and Jerusalem fell to the Babylonians, Jeremiah preached hope for the future. In time, however, he and Baruch were forced to flee to Egypt. In exile, Jeremiah continued to urge faithfulness to God but to no avail. The Bible says nothing of his death.

Scholars believe that the Book of Jeremiah was compiled from smaller collections of oracles, some of which may have been dictated by Jeremiah to his scribe. The bulk of the narrative in chapters 26 to 45 is generally believed to have been written by Baruch himself. ❖

THE SEAL OF JEREMIAH'S SCRIBE

In 1975 some fascinating artifacts began to surface in Arab antiquities shops in Israel. They were Hebrew bullae—clay impressions of seals once used to validate official documents. The bullae were scorched and baked—indicating that their storage site had been burned, possibly in the fire that engulfed Jerusalem and destroyed Solomon's Temple in 586 B.C.

Experts were able to link two of the bullae to people mentioned in the Bible. One carried the seal impression of Jerahmeel, King Jehoiakim's son, who had been sent to arrest Jeremiah and Baruch. The other, shown above, is inscribed with the words, "Belonging to Baruch son of Neriah the scribe."

Thus, after 26 centuries, the modern world had uncovered tangible links to one of the Bible's most dramatic chapters.

These fragments, found among the Dead Sea Scrolls, are part of chapter 48 of the Book of Jeremiah.

The Writing Craft

SCRIBES PERFORMED IMPORTANT ROLES IN ANCIENT ISRAEL. SOME WERE INDEPENDENT PROFESSIONALS WHO WROTE DOCUMENTS AND LETTERS FOR THE PUBLIC; OTHERS WERE GOVERNMENT OFFICIALS. AMONG THEM THEY LEFT A FASCINATING AND VARIED ASSORTMENT OF WRITINGS.

Very little is known about literacy in Israel during the time of the monarchy and the divided kingdom. But whether or not most people could read or write anything beyond their own names, they might have needed to draft a letter or a legal document from time to time. On such occasions they could hire a scribe to do the writing for them.

Most scribes led careers as public letter writers or as personal secretaries to wealthy men. Others—at least by Solomon's time—held prominent positions within the government. As the Bible verifies, "King Solomon was king over all Israel, and these were his high officials: Azariah son of Zadok was the priest; Elihoreph and

Ahijah sons of Shisha were secretaries; Jehoshaphat son of Ahilud was recorder [1 Kings 4:1-3]." Royal scribes performed the duties of secretaries of state, conducting official correspondence with other nations and maintaining national records.

Scribes occupied special quarters in the palace and in the Temple, where their duties included assisting priests with revenues. "Whenever they saw there was a great deal of money in the chest, the king's secretary and the high priest went up, counted the money that was found in the house of the Lord, and tied it up in bags. They would give the money that was weighed out into the hands of the workers who had the oversight of the house of the Lord [2 Kings 12:10-11]."

The scribe Ezra is depicted reading from a scroll in a detail from a third-century A.D. mural in the Dura-Europus synagogue in present-day Syria. Below him is a portion of a first-century B.C. copy of the Book of Leviticus inscribed on leather. A scribe would read a scroll by holding it in his left hand and unrolling it slowly to the right.

The silver talisman, far left, which dates from about 700 B.C., is inscribed in archaic Hebrew with a version of the priestly benediction of Numbers 6:24-26. To its right is a papyrus from the mid-seventh century B.C. showing Hebrew script of the First Temple period.

Although scribes were officially associated with the Temple, their role is not thought to have been linked with that of the priesthood while Israel and Judah existed as kingdoms. However, scribes were closely associated with the prophets and in many cases may have been responsible for interpreting their words and writing their books. During and after the Exile, when preserving and copying Scripture took on enormous importance, the role of the scribe began to overlap with that of priest and Levite. And by the second century B.C., most scribes were also priests.

Training and Tools of the Trade Throughout the period of the monarchy and the divided kingdom, the office of scribe was generally an inherited position. There is little evidence that scribal schools existed in Israel as they did in Egypt and Babylonia. Training in the skills of the scribal trade was passed along in familylike guilds.

A scribe could be spotted easily by his distinctive clothing and equipment. Ezekiel describes the appearance of one professional in an oracle. "Among them was a man clothed in linen, with a writing case at his side [Ezekiel 9:2]." Inside the writing case a scribe would keep his tools: a reed pen that was either frayed at the end to create a brush or trimmed to form a nib; a metal stylus, perhaps, for scratching writing onto hard surfaces; a knife for cutting papyrus sheets and excising mistakes; and an inkwell in which he would mix his dry ink with water. Black ink was made from powdered carbon and vegetable gum, red ink from iron oxide and gum. The writing produced with these simple inks has held up remarkably well over the centuries.

A Choice of Writing Surfaces To judge by the number and variety of writing examples that have been excavated throughout the region, the people of ancient Israel required writing skills for many purposes,

The pottery fragment, or ostracon, shown above is one of 21 that were excavated at the ancient town of Lachish and that bear inscriptions relating to Judah's fall to the Babylonians in 586.

and scribes were by no means rare. The materials they used as writing surfaces varied widely. Scribes scratched records onto stone or wrote on stone that had been coated with plaster. Similarly they inscribed text on wooden slabs that had been coated with wax or stucco. They also wrote on clay pots and frequently used pottery shards, known as ostraca, as scrap paper. There are even examples of writing inscribed on thin sheets of copper and silver.

One of the most common materials used for writing in early Israel was papyrus, which was imported from Egypt. Although no one knows exactly when scrolls became a customary form for long documents in Israel, the first scrolls mentioned in the Bible—Jeremiah 36:2 and Ezekiel 3:1—are made of papyrus. Relatively few ancient Israelite papyri have survived, however, since the material, made from the pith of the papyrus plant, gradually disintegrated in Israel's climate. What have survived more successfully are documents on tanned leather, which also found wide use as a writing surface. Individual trimmed skins were stitched together to create scrolls.

Pergamum's Alternative Sometime before the fifth century B.C., people began developing a new writing material—parchment. As thin and light-colored as papyrus but as durable as tanned leather, parchment is a finely processed animal skin. Its name derives from Pergamum, an ancient city near the western coast of present-day Turkey, which became its chief center of manufacture. By the second century B.C., parchment was in widespread use, and in time it replaced papyrus altogether. Although parchment could be made of virtually any skin—including goat, deer, rabbit, and squirrel—the finest parchment, known as vellum, was made of calfskin. More flexible than papyrus and more easily folded, parchment would allow for the eventual scribal transition from writing on scrolls to writing in books. ❖

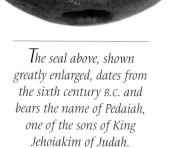

The seal above, shown greatly enlarged, dates from the sixth century B.C. and bears the name of Pedaiah, one of the sons of King Jehoiakim of Judah.

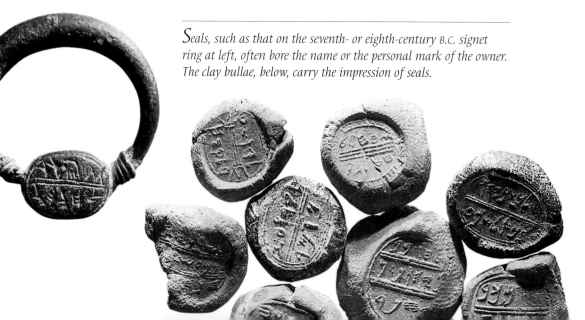

Seals, such as that on the seventh- or eighth-century B.C. signet ring at left, often bore the name or the personal mark of the owner. The clay bullae, below, carry the impression of seals.

THE MAKING OF PARCHMENT

Parchment was the writing surface of choice between the time that papyrus supplies began to dwindle in the second century B.C. and paper came into widespread use in the late Middle Ages. The parchment maker was known as a *percamenarius.* The steps for making parchment follow.

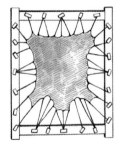

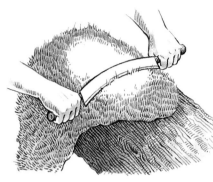

1 The flayed skin of an animal—such as a calf, goat, or sheep—is first carefully washed and then soaked in a vat of clean water for approximately 24 hours.

2 To loosen the hair on the hide, the skin is then placed in a vat containing a solution of lime and water for anywhere from 8 to 16 days (depending on the air temperature) and stirred several times a day with a wooden paddle or pole.

3 The slippery skins are taken out of the vat and draped hair side out over an angled beam or log. The parchment maker stands behind the high end of the beam and scrapes downward, pushing the hair off the skin with the blunt edge of a curved, two-handled knife. This surface is called the grain side of the parchment. The skin is turned over and any residue of flesh is removed from the underside. Then the skin is soaked in fresh water for two days to remove the lime.

4 The skin is stretched with cords onto a wooden frame fitted with adjustable pegs. The pegs are turned to pull the skin tight. To avoid cutting slits into the skin, which would expand into holes as the skin tightens and dries, small pebbles are folded into the edge of the skin to form knobs that are used to help in attaching the skin to the frame.

5 While keeping the skin wet, the parchment maker begins the crucial process of scraping both surfaces of the skin, right, using a *lunellum,* a knife with a deeply curved blade. The taut skin is then allowed to dry on the frame. Direct sunlight quickens the process and shrinks the hide tighter.

6 When dry, the drum-tight skin is scraped again to the desired thinness. The grain side particularly requires shaving to remove its natural shine, which is not acceptable for a writing surface. Finally, the parchment is removed from the frame and rolled up until needed. Before use, the parchment is buffed with pumice to whiten the surface.

On the parchment below, writing from the seventh century overrides a manuscript written in the fourth century. Manuscript pages that are scraped down and used again are called palimpsests.

The lion, a symbol of strength, was used in numerous places to adorn the tiled walls of the palace complex in Babylon. Under Nebuchadnezzar II Babylonia reached the height of its power in the sixth century B.C.

The Babylonian Captivity

IN EXILE AFTER THE DESTRUCTION OF THE TEMPLE, ISRAELITES RE-EXAMINED THEIR FAITH AND RECORDED THEIR HISTORY AND LAWS.

From 605 B.C. through the last 18 years of its existence as a kingdom, Judah was a vassal state of the mighty empire of Babylonia. King Jehoiakim endured the situation for three years before rebelling. Babylonia's King Nebuchadnezzar bided his time before taking punitive action against Jehoiakim, and by the time he launched his attack, Jehoiakim had died. Babylonia's subsequent siege of Jerusalem led to the deportation of the political and religious elite—including King Jehoiachin, Jehoiakim's son and successor—who were taken into exile in Babylonia in 596 B.C.

When Jerusalem once more rebelled, Nebuchadnezzar attacked again in 586 B.C. This time the effect was devastating. The Temple was burned to the ground and Jerusalem was completely destroyed, as were many of the surrounding towns. One of the last holdouts

The cuneiform tablet at right is a Babylonian chronicle of the years 605 to 594 B.C. The events recorded on it include the siege and capture of Jerusalem and the subsequent removal of Judeans into exile.

against the onslaught was the town of Lachish. In the 1930's, 21 pottery shards inscribed with fragments of background material from that period were excavated in Lachish.

Many Israelites were exiled following the conquest, although the actual numbers are not known. In fact, the Bible reveals few details about the Exile, which did not end until Cyrus of Persia conquered Babylon in 539 B.C. However, it is thought that the exiles were treated well and could function relatively freely in their own communities wherever they settled in Babylonia.

Collecting and Writing Texts Without the Temple, the Israelites could not worship as they had, and yet the years of exile were immensely important to the development of their faith. Very likely it was a time when many biblical texts were collected, put into written form, and edited. The words of the prophets whose pre-exilic warnings had proven true are believed to have been written down during this period, as were the books that tell of Israel's history—from Joshua to 2 Kings. The psalms were probably collected at this time as well, and the Book of Lamentations was compiled as a poignant description of the destruction of Jerusalem and the fall of the Temple.

Similarly, much of the final framing of the Pentateuch is thought to have been carried out during or shortly after the Babylonian conquest. The points of view of the exiles are reflected in some of the major themes of its five books. For example, the Pentateuch emphasizes God's fidelity to his covenant with the Israelites—a serious concern of the exiles, since they wanted to believe that God would take them back and that their covenant with him would be preserved. Similarly, in the Book of Deuteronomy, the followers of Moses are poised just outside the Promised Land when they learn why they are being given the land and what they must do to retain it. In this way they are shown that Israel's relationship with God began outside the boundaries of the country— another important concern of people who needed to see their God as a universal God who was with them outside of the Temple and the land.

The Judean town of Lachish was among the last strongholds to fall to the Babylonians in 586 B.C. In this bas-relief Lachish's courageous archers and warriors are shown fending off an earlier armed attack by the Assyrians at the time of Sennacherib.

The focus on the writings allowed the Israelites to retain their faith, recognize the laws they must live by, and learn the lessons their history taught. Their written records would remain central to their community and faith when they returned to Jerusalem and rebuilt the Temple. ❖

Ezekiel: The Voice of Exile

EZEKIEL'S PROPHETIC WORDS TO THE ISRAELITES BEGAN IMMEDIATELY WITH HIS DEPORTATION TO BABYLONIA IN 597 B.C. AND CONTINUED EVEN AFTER THE FALL OF JERUSALEM IN 586 B.C.

From the very start, Ezekiel's prophetic work was distinctive. As described in the opening chapter of the book, Ezekiel was a priest who prophesied while in exile in Babylonia. The detailed account of his calling is remarkable for its vividness and its extraordinary portrayal of God's throne. Ezekiel was in his fifth year of exile, about the year 593 B.C., when he had a vision in which he saw four cherubim—each with four wings and four faces: one face was human, the others were those of a lion, an ox, and an eagle. With these creatures were four wheels that moved in all of the four cardinal directions and made a chariot for God's throne. Above them all appeared "the likeness of the glory of the Lord [Ezekiel 1:28]."

Ezekiel's Role God spoke to Ezekiel, directing him to be a prophet to his rebellious people. Then God instructed him to eat a papyrus scroll that was inscribed with words of lamentation, mourning, and woe. By eating the scroll (which he claimed was sweet as honey), Ezekiel symbolically agreed to speak the words of the Lord.

During the next 20 years or more, the course of Ezekiel's ministry was marked by powerful visions and symbolic acts. His visions and the language he used to describe them are often credited with influencing later apocalyptic writing—notably, the Book of Revelation. Comparison is frequently made, for instance, between the visions of the new Jerusalem detailed in the two books. In both Ezekiel 48:30-35 and Revelation 21:12-14 the city is described as a cube with exits through 12 gates—3 each to the north, south, east, and west—that are named for the 12 tribes of Israel.

Two Halves of the Book The Book of Ezekiel can be divided in half: Chapters 1 to 24 contain the oracles of warning Ezekiel made before the fall of Jerusalem. The remaining 24 chapters of the book contain oracles made after the city fell. In the first half of the book Ezekiel used strong language to condemn the Israelites for their rebelliousness against God and to warn them of the coming disaster. For example, he said, "I will put an end to the arrogance of the strong, and their holy places shall be profaned. When anguish comes, they will seek peace, but there shall be none [Ezekiel 7:24-25]."

Ezekiel also used elaborate symbolism to make Judah's situation clear to his listeners. In one instance, he spoke of God instructing him to lie on his left side for 390 days, symbolizing the years of punishment due the Northern Kingdom of Israel. Then he was to lie on his right side for 40 days, to symbolize the years of pun-

---

While Ezekiel rests by the River Chebar he has his first vision. In it he sees winged creatures and the throne-chariot of God. The illustration above decorates a letter E from the Book of Ezekiel in the 12th-century Winchester Bible.

ishment that lay ahead for the Southern Kingdom of Judah (Ezekiel 4:4-6).

Following God's commands, Ezekiel frequently used himself as a character in his portrayals and acted out scenes before his neighbors. On one occasion he shaved his head and beard and burned the hairs in order to warn people of the fire going out upon the whole House of Israel (Ezekiel 5:1-4). In another instance, he ate his bread in trembling and drank his water in fear and anxiety to show how the inhabitants of Jerusalem would eat and drink in a similar manner because of the future desolation of the land (Ezekiel 12:17-20). As a consequence of his actions, Ezekiel has a reputation as one of the oddest and most extreme personalities in the Old Testament.

A New Message After the fall of Jerusalem, Ezekiel's message had a different focus. Chapters 25 to 32 of the Book of Ezekiel include his pronouncements of doom for the nations that had inflicted pain on Judah, and in the last 16 chapters are his promises to the exiles that they will return to Jerusalem. The book closes with Ezekiel's elaborate account of what the rebuilt city and Temple would look like. It is significant that Ezekiel, like the prophet Isaiah before him, prophesied the coming of a messiah king, who would be of the House of David. "I will save my flock," the Lord said. "I will set up over them one shepherd, my servant David, and he shall feed them: he shall feed them and be their shepherd [Ezekiel 34:22-23]."

Concern for God's Reputation Throughout the book, Ezekiel's involvement with Israel's theological struggles is evident. He insisted that God had not deserted the Israelites; it was the Israelites who had deserted him by breaking their part of the covenant. The breach ought to have been followed by repentance, reconciliation, and restoration. But God could not rely on the people to repent, and he was concerned with the injury to his own reputation. "It is not for your sake, O house of Israel, that I am about to act, but for the sake of my holy name, which you have profaned among the nations [Ezekiel 36:22]." He would give them a new heart. "A new heart I will give you, and a new spirit I will put within you; and I will remove from your body the heart of stone and give you a heart of flesh [Ezekiel 36:26]." Contrition and repentance would come later: "And you shall know that I am the Lord, when I deal with you for my name's sake, not according to your evil ways, or corrupt deeds, O house of Israel, says the Lord God [Ezekiel 20:44]." ❖

In one of Ezekiel's oracles, God takes the prophet to a field covered with dried bones that symbolized Israel. When instructed to do so, Ezekiel prophesied to the bones, and their bodies were made whole and lived again. The vision was pictured in a third-century A.D. mural, above, in the synagogue of Dura-Europus, an ancient Syrian city.

Shaping the Pentateuch

OVER THE PAST 200 YEARS SCHOLARS HAVE COME TO BELIEVE THAT THE FIVE BOOKS OF MOSES WERE NOT WRITTEN BY MOSES AT ALL BUT ARE A SKILLFULLY EDITED COMPILATION OF FOUR SEPARATE SOURCES.

God creates Eve from Adam's rib in this detail from a 16th-century Italian Bible illumination. The artist followed Genesis 2:7-25, in which man is created first, then the plants and animals, and then woman. But in Genesis 1:11-27, God creates the plants and animals and then man and woman together. Such discrepancies in the Pentateuch caused some readers to question the idea that Moses was its sole author.

According to tradition, Moses was not only the central figure in the first five books of the Bible but their sole author as well. In fact, the tradition of Moses' authorship was so solidly a part of the Judeo-Christian heritage that it stood unchallenged until the 17th century, and the Pentateuch is commonly known as the Five Books of Moses.

Since ancient times, however, individuals have encountered problems with this tradition. As early as the third century, scholars noted peculiarities in the text. Events in the stories of the Creation and the Flood, for example, are presented twice with conflicting details. Moses goes to the tent of meeting (Exodus 33:7) before it is built (Exodus 35:10–11), and at the end of Deuteronomy, Moses' own death and burial are described, bringing his authorship of that passage into doubt. Early scholars explained these inconsistencies with elaborate theories, sometimes imagining missing narrative details, and attributed Moses' knowledge of future events, such as the details of his own death, to his prophetic powers. In the following centuries, scholars theorized that later editors had added material to Moses' text but they maintained that Moses was the principal author of the Pentateuch.

Finally, in the 17th century, the English philosopher Thomas Hobbes stated outright that Moses probably did not write most of the Pentateuch. He was soon echoed by others, who supported their views with an increasingly large body of evidence, including the text's repeated use of the term "to this day," obviously referring to a time well after that of the events being described.

The Documentary Hypothesis Later in the 17th century, the French theologian Richard Simon suggested that the core of the Pentateuch was Mosaic but that prophets, acting as scribes, had added other old texts to it, working under the guidance of the Holy Spirit. In the 18th century, scholars built on Simon's theory by studying stories that are told twice in the Pentateuch. As the scholars examined these pairs, known as doublets,

Mystery of the Doublets

The term *doublet* is used for stories that are told twice in the Pentateuch. Sometimes the two versions are separated, as in the account of God's giving Jacob the name *Israel* (Genesis 32:24–32 and 35:9–15). Often they are interwoven, as in the story of the Flood. Part of the Flood account (Genesis 7) is printed below with the versions pulled apart. Obvious differences between the versions are the numbers of animals and the fact that God is referred to as Yahweh (translated here as "the Lord") in one version but as God in the other.

From the older version, now called J

7 Then the Lord said to Noah, "Go into the ark, you and all your household, for I have seen that you alone are righteous before me in this generation. ²Take with you seven pairs of all clean animals, the male and its mate; and a pair of the animals that are not clean, the male and its mate; ³and seven pairs of the birds of the air also, male and female, to keep their kind alive on the face of all the earth. ⁴For in seven days I will send rain on the earth for forty days and forty nights; and every living thing that I have made I will blot out from the face of the ground." ⁵And Noah did all that the Lord had commanded him. . . .

⁷And Noah with his sons and his wife and his sons' wives went into the ark to escape the waters of the flood. . . .

¹⁰And after seven days the waters of the flood came on the earth. . . .

¹²The rain fell on the earth forty days and forty nights. . . .

¹⁶ᵇand the Lord shut him in. ¹⁷The flood continued forty days on the earth; and the waters increased, and bore up the ark, and it rose high above the earth. ¹⁸The waters swelled and increased greatly on the earth; and the ark floated on the face of the waters. ¹⁹The waters swelled so mightily on the earth that all the high mountains under the whole heaven were covered; ²⁰the waters swelled above the mountains, covering them fifteen cubits deep. . . .

²²everything on dry land in whose nostrils was the breath of life died. ²³He blotted out every living thing that was on the face of the ground, human beings and animals and creeping things and birds of the air; they were blotted out from the earth. Only Noah was left, and those that were with him in the ark.

From the later version, now called P

7 . . . ⁶Noah was six hundred years old when the flood of waters came on the earth. . . .

⁸Of clean animals, and of animals that are not clean, and of birds, and of everything that creeps on the ground, ⁹two and two, male and female, went into the ark with Noah, as God had commanded Noah. . . .

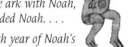

¹¹In the six hundredth year of Noah's life, in the second month, on the seventeenth day of the month, on that day all the fountains of the great deep burst forth, and the windows of the heavens were opened. . . .

¹³On the very same day Noah with his sons, Shem and Ham and Japheth, and Noah's wife and the three wives of his sons entered the ark, ¹⁴they and every wild animal of every kind, and all domestic animals of every kind, and every creeping thing that creeps on the earth, and every bird of every kind—every bird, every winged creature. ¹⁵They went into the ark with Noah, two and two of all flesh in which there was the breath of life. ¹⁶ᵃAnd those that entered, male and female of all flesh, went in as God had commanded him; . . .

²¹And all flesh died that moved on the earth, birds, domestic animals, wild animals, all swarming creatures that swarm on the earth, and all human beings; . . .

²⁴And the waters swelled on the earth for one hundred fifty days.

Noah and some of the animals from the ark are shown in these details from a 10th-century illumination.

they discovered that in one version of each story, the deity is referred to as Yahweh and in the other version, as God. In addition, stories using the name *Yahweh* share characteristics of language and point of view that stories using the word *God* do not. Such differences led to the belief that two separate sources had been combined. Early in the 19th century it was shown that there are triplets, as well as doublets, in the text, indicating three sources. Shortly thereafter it was demonstrated that the language in Deuteronomy differs significantly from that of the preceding four books, and a theory of four sources evolved. The German theologian Julius Wellhausen summed up the work of earlier scholars, established the order in which the sources were probably written, and won widespread acceptance for the theory.

Called the Documentary Hypothesis, the theory, which is today the prevailing view, holds that the Pentateuch is the result of the artful weaving of four sources that were written over the course of five centuries. Scholars have tagged the sources J, E, D, and P and have come to some solid conclusions about them, including the following.

The J Source The oldest of the sources is the J, or Yahwist, account—the "J" being derived from the German spelling of Yahweh (*Jahveh*). The Yahwist author gathered traditional Canaanite and Israelite stories and imaginatively strung them into a lively epic. He writes in an engaging style, sketching characters quickly and making effective use of details. The story of the Tower of Babel is an example of his work.

Of all the sources, J gives the simplest portrayal of God. In J Yahweh is not primarily a supernatural figure who works his will through miracles but rather a powerful humanlike figure, a loyal protector who works through people. For example, through Moses, God subverts the threat posed by Egypt and secures Israel's future by means of the covenant at Sinai.

J was probably written in the 10th century B.C. during the reign of David or Solomon, and it validates the Davidic royal line as the realization of God's promise for Israel—all the tribes are joined in peace under one king. Although it has been suggested that J might have been written by a woman, the author was probably a male scribe from the Southern tribe of Judah. J stresses stories and traditions of the Southern tribes and the role of Abraham, who lived in Hebron, one of the most important cities of Judah and the first capital under David.

The E Source The E account, which was probably written during the period of the divided kingdom, some two centuries later than the J account, exhibits a definite bias toward the Northern Kingdom and so

This illuminated capital J represents the J source of the Pentateuch. The illustration shows Adam and Eve tasting the forbidden fruit in the Garden of Eden. The story of the fall of man, found in chapter 3 of Genesis, is exclusive to J.

An angel comes to the aid of Hagar and her son, Ishmael, who are in danger of perishing in the desert. The boy survives and grows up in the wilderness. The story (Genesis 21:8-21) is found only in the E source.

was probably written there, although nothing definite is known about the author. It is called E because the text refers to God as *Elohim* (Hebrew for "God") until the name *Yahweh* is revealed to Moses at the burning bush. (In J God is called Yahweh from beginning to end.) E emphasizes the covenant and focuses on the leadership of the prophets, especially Moses, in contrast to J, which stresses the monarchy.

The writing style and theology of E are more elaborate and sophisticated than those of J. God often appears miraculously in dreams or through an angel, and the history itself is more detailed and logical.

Moses was not to enter the Promised Land to which he had been leading the Israelites for 40 years. But on the eve of his death, he gathered his people around him to give a final address, as told in the D source of the Pentateuch.

The D Source The D material, which is found primarily in Deuteronomy, is probably the book of laws discovered by the high priest Hilkiah in the Temple at Jerusalem in 621 B.C. Cast in the form of a farewell speech by Moses to the Israelites on the eve of their entry into Canaan, it contains a summary of what has happened to the Israelites since leaving Mount Sinai and a discourse on the Law. It ends with a description of the death and burial of Moses.

Deuteronomy is written in a lofty style and one of its major themes is the centralization of worship. It mandates that worship be conducted at only one sanctuary. Although it never names the sanctuary, the Temple in Jerusalem was later recognized as the official place of worship, where all sacrifice must be made by consecrated priests.

The P Source The P, or Priestly, source has been variously dated from before, during, or shortly after the Babylonian Exile. Like Deuteronomy, it is largely concerned with cultic law and purity. In P the consecrated priest plays the central role in the lives of the people, and he, rather than the prophets of J and E, is their link with God. This is clearly borne out in the texts. For example, in the J account of the Flood, Noah takes on board seven pairs each of all clean animals and birds but only two pairs of each unclean species; after the Flood he offers God sacrifices of each of the kinds of clean creatures. In P Noah takes only one pair of each creature, both clean and unclean, and there is no mention of a sacrifice being made.

In P there are no dreams, angels, or prophets, as there are in J and E. The P account is much flatter and more pedantic than the other narratives. The style of the text is more monotonous and detailed and often includes genealogical lists and numbers.

In P the priest, working within prescribed rules of proper sacrifice, is the only intermediary with God. The text includes detailed descriptions of clerical garments and sacrificial ritual.

The author of P was probably a priest descended from Aaron, for his text focuses on Aaron's role. According to P, Aaron is not only Moses' brother but his older brother, the firstborn son. It is Aaron and his sons who make the first sacrifice in P, while in J and E earlier offerings are made by Cain, Abel, and Abraham. The word *prophet* occurs only once in P and refers to Aaron, thus setting up Aaron and his heirs as the only priests divinely sanctioned to offer sacrifice.

Piecing It Together In the Pentateuch as we know it today, three of the four sources, J, E, and P, are so closely knit together that none of them could stand on its own if separated from the others. The question of how, when, and by whom the various sources were combined is a matter of debate. The prevailing theory is that the sources were integrated in stages over a period of several centuries by a number of redactors—scholarly editors who reworked the older writings to meet the needs and theological perspectives of their times.

In the first stage of redaction, the E document was probably carried south to Jerusalem at the time of the Assyrian conquest of the Northern Kingdom, where it was eventually merged with the J text—probably about 650 B.C. Somewhere about 550 B.C. a redactor or, more likely, a school of redactors added the D material to the combined E and J. Because D describes the death of Moses, it was placed—with few, if any additions—at the end of the earlier material, where it remains, as the Book of Deuteronomy. The redactors of D were probably also responsible for the final editing of the entire Deuteronomical History—the books of Deuteronomy, Joshua, Judges, 1 and 2 Samuel, and 1 and 2 Kings.

Some time later yet another redactor or group of redactors incorporated all the earlier material within the framework of P. Some scholars believe that P was originally a separate work. Others believe that it was written specifically to supplement the already combined texts of J, E, and D. In either case, the date of the synthesis has been widely debated. Many scholars believe that it was redacted in the mid-fifth or early fourth century B.C., during the postexilic period, by Ezra or one or more of the other powerful Aaronid priests. At this time these priests were recasting the history of the Jews to conform to new laws and customs surrounding the creation of the Second Temple in Jerusalem.

Art of the Redactor At every stage of integrating the J, E, and P strands, the redactor had to weave together such disparate material that the process appears to be more an act of alchemy than a task of editing. However, a few of the techniques used are obvious. When faced with reconciling two versions of the same story, the redactor did one of four things. He eliminated one version, as in the case of E's story of Abraham's migration to Canaan (alluded to in Genesis 20:13); he combined two versions by interweaving their verses, as in the J and E versions of the Creation and the Flood; he used one version and

¹⁸For the Lord had closed fast all the wombs of the house of Abimelech because of Sarah, Abraham's wife.

21 The Lord dealt with Sarah as he had said, and the Lord did for Sarah as he had promised. ²Sarah conceived and bore Abraham a son in his old age, at the time of which God had spoken to him. ³Abraham gave the name Isaac to his son whom Sarah bore him. ⁴And Abraham circumcised his son Isaac when he was eight days old, as God had commanded him. ⁵Abraham was a hundred years old when his son Isaac was born to him. ⁶Now Sarah said, "God has brought laughter for me; everyone who hears will laugh with me." ⁷And she said, "Who would ever have said to Abraham that Sarah would nurse children? Yet I have borne him a son in his old age."

⁸The child grew, and was weaned; and Abraham made a great feast on the day that Isaac was weaned. ⁹But Sarah saw the son of Hagar the Egyptian, whom she had borne to Abraham, playing with her son Isaac. ¹⁰So she said to Abraham, "Cast out this slave woman with her son; for the son of this slave woman shall not inherit along with my son Isaac." ¹¹The matter was very distressing to Abraham on account of his son.

A TAPESTRY OF WORDS

The artistry of the redactors of the Pentateuch can be seen in these passages from Genesis. Above, three versions of the story of Isaac's birth are woven together, with the J, E, and P sources keyed by color. In the passage from Genesis 37, opposite, J and E are intertwined, but not quite seamlessly. In verse 28 both the Midianites and the Ishmaelites are said to take Joseph into slavery. In verses 21–22 it is Reuben who tries to save Joseph's life, but in verses 26–27, it is Judah who persuades his brothers not to kill Joseph.

filled it out with details from the other, notably in the story of Joseph; or he reproduced both stories in their entirety, treating them as separate events, as in the two stories of Hagar's being sent away by Abraham. In order to make the text flow more smoothly when combining passages, the redactors made use of three highly effective techniques.

The first technique was to repeat a line in order to insert a new text into an existing one. For instance, in Exodus 6:12 Moses asks God: "How then shall Pharaoh listen to me, poor speaker that I am?" At this point the redactor added a section on genealogy; then, to return to the flow of the original text, he echoed the question. Moses asks: "Since I am a poor speaker, why would Pharaoh listen to me [Exodus 6:30]?" and the original text proceeds as if it had never been disturbed.

The second technique was to add short reconciling phrases to the text to smooth over inconsistencies. These generally consist of several words or even a sentence or so but also consist of as little as a single word, such as adding the word *again* to justify the repetition of an event.

The third technique used by the redactors was to create a frame or chronological structure for the diverse material. The redactor who merged P with the other texts evidently built a frame from two independent Priestly documents. As a means of organizing the stories in Genesis, he cut up one of these documents, the Book of Generations, or list of begats, and interspersed its parts throughout Genesis, thereby connecting the various stories into one genealogical tale. He made similar use of the List of Stations, a Priestly catalogue of the stops the Israelites made during their 40 years in the wilderness. Skillfully woven into the text, the list creates a structure for the wilderness stories and gives shape to a series of otherwise unrelated episodes.

Respect for the Text The repetitions and inconsistencies that remain in the Pentateuch are attributable to the redactors' respect for Scripture. These editors were loathe to delete material from the original texts they were working with, even to reshape the material to reflect current ideas, and they did so as little as possible. Studying the methods of the Pentateuch's redactors reveals the titanic struggle of the human intellect to comprehend, organize, and convey the divine message. ❖

37 . . . ¹⁷Joseph went after his brothers, and found them at Dothan. ¹⁸They saw him from a distance, and before he came near to them, they conspired to kill him. ¹⁹They said to one another, "Here comes this dreamer. ²⁰Come now, let us kill him and throw him into one of the pits; then we shall say that a wild animal has devoured him, and we shall see what will become of his dreams." ²¹But when Reuben heard it, he delivered him out of their hands, saying, "Let us not take his life." ²²Reuben said to them, "Shed no blood; throw him into this pit here in the wilderness, but lay no hand on him"— that he might rescue him out of their hand and restore him to his father. ²³So when Joseph came to his brothers, they stripped him of his robe, the long robe with sleeves that he wore; ²⁴and they took him and threw him into a pit. The pit was empty; there was no water in it.

²⁵Then they sat down to eat; and looking up they saw a caravan of Ishmaelites coming from Gilead, with their camels carrying gum, balm, and resin, on their way to carry it down to Egypt. ²⁶Then Judah said to his brothers, "What profit is it if we kill our brother and conceal his blood? ²⁷Come, let us sell him to the Ishmaelites, and not lay our hands on him, for he is our brother, our own flesh." And his brothers agreed. ²⁸When some Midianite traders passed by, they drew Joseph up, lifting him out of the pit, and sold him to the Ishmaelites for twenty pieces of silver. And they took Joseph to Egypt.

Ezra: The Second Lawgiver

A LEARNED PRIEST, DEVOUT JEW, AND FIERY SPEAKER, EZRA RETURNED FROM EXILE IN BABYLON TO JERUSALEM, WHERE HE ASSERTED THE IDENTITY OF THE JEWISH PEOPLE AND REESTABLISHED MOSAIC LAW.

According to the book that bears his name, Ezra was a priest and scribe, "a scholar of the text of the commandments of the Lord and his statutes for Israel [Ezra 7:11]." He held a high position in the Persian court, apparently responsible for overseeing the conduct of the Jews.

Although Ezra had grown up among the Jewish exiles in Babylon, he followed closely the affairs of those who had returned to their homeland. Distressed by reports of moral disintegration in Jerusalem, Ezra won permission from the king to go there to institute broad reforms. Artaxerxes issued a royal warrant, giving Ezra the right to instruct Jews on the law and in religious and official matters. The king further decreed, "All who will not obey the law of your God and the law of the king, let judgment be strictly executed on them, whether for death or for banishment or for confiscation of their goods or for imprisonment [Ezra 7: 26]."

Armed with these impressive powers—and transporting a treasure in silver and gold—Ezra and

some 1,500 families from 12 clans left Babylon for Jerusalem. The long trek began "in the seventh year of King Artaxerxes [Ezra 7:7]," a reference that dates the mission either to 458 B.C., during the reign of Artaxerxes I, or else to 397 B.C., in Artaxerxes II's time. Even though the travelers would doubtless encounter many dangers on the road to Jerusalem, Ezra did not ask for an armed guard for fear that the request might imply he lacked trust in God's protection. Four months later the party safely reached Jerusalem.

The treasure was deposited with the priests in the newly rebuilt Temple, and the returned exiles offered sacrifice. Then Ezra presented his royal warrant to the local authorities, and some officials approached him with the grievous report of widespread intermarriage among Jews and foreigners. Some of the worst offenders were highly placed officials and nobles. "Thus the holy seed has mixed itself with the peoples of the lands [Ezra 9:2]." Distraught at hearing this news, Ezra tore his garments and pulled hair from his head and beard. That evening he prayed

---

Ezra was many things to many people, from the scribe and lawgiver of Ezra-Nehemiah to the prophet of 2 Esdras, to a king, as in this 15th-century painting by the Spaniard Pedro Berruguete.

A French illumination of the 15th century shows Nehemiah, governor of Judah during the reign of Artaxerxes I, praying to God upon learning that Jerusalem's gates had been destroyed by fire. Nehemiah swiftly set about rebuilding the walls of Jerusalem.

THE DECREE OF CYRUS

In 539 B.C. King Cyrus II of Persia had conquered Babylon, defeating King Nabonidus without a struggle. One of Cyrus' first deeds as leader of the empire had been to issue a decree: he would allow all peoples exiled in Babylon, including Jews, to resettle in their homelands and restore their houses of worship. In the years that followed, the exiled Jews slowly returned to Jerusalem in groups. Among the last to return were Ezra—with the support of King Artaxerxes—and Nehemiah.

The portion of Cyrus' decree pertaining to the release of the Jews is recorded in Ezra 1:2–4 and 6:3–5. The decree is also commemorated on a 10-inch-long clay artifact known as the Cyrus Cylinder (shown below) that dates from 538 B.C. and was found at the site of ancient Babylon in 1879. An inscription written in Akkadian, the official language of Persia, encircles the cylinder and reads in part, "I resettled all the gods of Sumer and Akkad, which Nabonidus had moved to Babylon, unharmed in their former places to make them happy . . . and I endeavored to repair their dwelling places."

on behalf of the people: "for our iniquities have risen higher than our heads, and our guilt has mounted up to the heavens [Ezra 9:6]."

Determined to restore the Jews' religious and ethnic identity, Ezra ordered all the men of the region to attend a meeting at the Temple compound. Amid a driving rain, he accused the assembly of treason and ordered those among them who had married non-Jewish women to dissolve that union. He appointed a commission to investigate the mixed marriages, and after three months the people gave a solemn undertaking to divorce their wives—a testament to Ezra's persuasiveness and prestige.

Reading the Law Several months later, during the festival of thanksgiving known as the Feast of Booths, Ezra enthralled the people by reading aloud the Mosaic Law, probably a version of the Pentateuch collated during the Exile. The account of the reading in Nehemiah 8:1–12 is the earliest mention in the Bible of a copy of the Torah residing in Jerusalem. Over the next eight days Ezra continued to read and interpret the Torah while attending Levite priests translated the original Hebrew Scripture into the more familiar Aramaic. Many among Ezra's audience had never before heard the Law or had long forgotten it, and they wept with emotion. Ezra told them not to mourn but to rejoice, "for this day is holy to our Lord [Nehemiah 8:10]."

Ezra emphasized the importance of the Torah and affirmed the identity of his people. No longer defined by nationality alone, Jews belonged to a community bound by strict adherence to the Law. ❖

The Chronicler

LITTLE IS KNOWN ABOUT THE WRITER CALLED THE CHRONICLER, WHO
REEXAMINED THE HISTORY OF THE JEWS IN THE LIGHT OF HIS OWN
TIME—AFTER THE EXILE AND DURING THE RESTORATION OF ISRAEL.

Many Bible experts hold that one person wrote both 1 and 2 Chronicles (one book in the Hebrew Bible) and Ezra and Nehemiah (also originally a single book). These books share similarities of outlook, style, language, and theme. In addition, the last two verses of 2 Chronicles are repeated in the opening verses of Ezra, perhaps an example of a "catch line," a device used by scribes to guide readers from one scroll to the next.

Some scholars believe that the Chronicler was Ezra himself. Others claim that he was a Jerusalem Levite and Temple administrator who wrote about 400 B.C.

Annals of Israel The story told by the Chronicler is massive in scope, stretching from the beginning of the world to the rebuilding of Jerusalem following the Babylonian Exile. The period from the birth of Adam to the advent of King Saul is covered rapidly in the first nine chapters of 1 Chronicles through the use of genealogies and lists. A description of David's reign follows, notable for the writer's exaltation of David as head of a divinely authorized monarchy. In 2 Chronicles the reader is taken from Solomon's kingdom through the Exile and up to King Cyrus of Persia's decree allowing the Jews to return to their homeland. The inhabitants of the North, and all others who rejected the sole legitimacy of the Temple in Jerusalem, are criticized by the Chronicler.

With Ezra-Nehemiah the Chronicler provides an account of Israel's restoration after the Exile. He describes the enormous task of rebuilding the Temple and the city of Jerusalem, praising those who enacted religious reforms and condemning religious failures.

This 14th-century miniature from a French manuscript portrays part of the lineage of the 12 tribes of Israel as it is set out in 1 Chronicles 1—from Adam to Noah to Abraham (large figures) through their descendants (seated below).

Rich ornamentation and delicate representations of a peacock, the sun, the moon, and coats of arms frame the last page of Ezra-Nehemiah in this 15th-century Hebrew Bible of the Portuguese school.

In retelling the early history of the Jews in 1 and 2 Chronicles, the writer borrowed heavily from other biblical books—especially 1 Samuel 31 to 2 Kings 25—sometimes quoting verbatim. The Chronicles cite some 20 sources by name, such as the "records of the seer Samuel [1 Chronicles 29:29]" and "the history of the prophet Nathan [2 Chronicles 9:29]." But whether these refer to parts of the Hebrew Bible or to other works is hard to determine. For the story of Ezra-Nehemiah, the Chronicler had access to an apparently authentic memoir by Nehemiah (written in the first person) and perhaps also to a memoir by Ezra.

You Will Be Established Despite his numerous source citations, the Chronicler often confuses his chronology. For example, he places events that occurred during the reign of the Persian ruler Darius after stories about Darius' successors Xerxes and Artaxerxes. The Chronicler also glosses over the failings of Israelite heroes and leaders; for example, he avoids all mention of King David's sinful behavior, which is reported so candidly in 2 Samuel.

Some Bible scholars attribute any discrepancies in the Chronicler's texts to the meddling of later scribes or editors. But it is clear that the Chronicler is not a historian in the modern sense—he is, rather, a theologian addressing his kinsmen at a particular moment in time. The Chronicler wrote his books in the hopeful climate of the restored Israel. He drew lessons from an eventful past in order to guide the community to a virtuous, peaceful future. The duty of the subjects in this ideal kingdom is to obey God's will and his law. Disobey God, as did Saul, and you face disaster and ruin. As the ruler Jehoshaphat proclaimed, "Listen to me, O Judah and inhabitants of Jerusalem! Believe in the Lord your God and you will be established; believe his prophets [2 Chronicles 20:20]." ❖

Implements of the Tabernacle, the foundation and rebuilding of which were of central concern to the Chronicler, are shown in this 14th-century German Bible.

Tales That Inspire

THE BOOKS OF RUTH, JONAH, AND ESTHER ARE BELOVED AS
GREAT DRAMATIC TALES AND ARE TURNED TO REPEATEDLY FOR THEIR
VALUE AS GREAT WORLD LITERATURE.

Ruth was gleaning grain when the owner of the field, Boaz, asked his servant who she was. The scene is shown above in an 1866 illustration by Gustave Doré. Both Ruth and Boaz are exemplary for their goodness. In time they marry: their son is King David's grandfather.

The Books of Ruth, Jonah, and Esther are among the shortest books in the Old Testament, but they include some of its most memorable tales. While interpretations of the books' meanings and origins vary, the satisfaction that readers derive from these stories remains consistent. Each of the books is full of action as the characters confront the ways of people foreign to them.

The Good Daughter-in-Law "Where you go, I will go; where you lodge, I will lodge; your people shall be my people, and your God my God [Ruth 1:16]." With those words Ruth, the Moabite widow, embraced the God of Israel, leaving her own land and accompanying Naomi home to Judah.

The story of Ruth is set "in the days when the judges ruled [Ruth 1:1]," and so in most Bibles the book is placed between Judges and Samuel. Scholars, however, are divided on the book's date. Some place it between the 10th and 8th centuries B.C., others in the 4th century B.C. If the later date is correct, the story may have been intended as a plea for religious and ethnic tolerance at a time when—having newly rebuilt Jerusalem—a strong movement arose among Jews against marriage with outsiders. In fact, Ezra and Nehemiah preached against mixed marriages. Seen from this point of view the story of Ruth offers debate. Its writer uses the historical setting to make the point that, though foreign, Ruth is blessed by God and through her marriage helps to found the royal line of David.

The Reluctant Prophet Jonah is considered a prophet, but he is the most reluctant of them all. He deems the people of Nineveh unworthy and does everything in his power to avoid bringing God's word to them. The story is thought to have been written in the fifth or fourth century B.C. Its message, according to some scholars, is that God's power and love are universal and extend to Ninevites as well as Israelites. Other scholars interpret the message of the book as one of repentance: Israel should be as willing to repent as Nineveh was. Repentance is possible for all people.

Jonah's oracle is the briefest prophetic denunciation on record, "Forty days more, and Nineveh shall be overthrown [Jonah 3:4]." Yet it produced the greatest response of all the Old Testament oracles. Not

only did the people of Nineveh fast and cover themselves with sackcloth, but they cried mightily to God. Never before had a prophet been so successful and produced so immediate an effect.

The Courageous Wife The Book of Esther tells of a young Jewish woman who confronts her husband, the king of Persia, and thereby helps to avert the annihilation of the Jews in Persia. It is one of only two Old Testament books that never mention God. (The other is the Song of Solomon.)

The story is thought to be a novella grounded in history. Its plot is filled with ironic reversals. The villainous courtier Haman plans to harm Esther's cousin, Mordecai, who has saved the king's life. When the king asks Haman's advice on how to honor a man, Haman responds, believing himself to be the recipient of the honors. But Mordecai receives the honors recommended by Haman, Haman is hanged on the gallows he erected for Mordecai, and Mordecai takes Haman's place in the king's court.

The events of the tale provide justification for a non-Mosaic festival of deliverance—Purim. In the Hebrew Bible, the Book of Esther is grouped with the Writings and is one of five books read aloud in the synagogue each year. In other Bibles, Esther is placed among the historical books. ❖

Sailors bound for Tarshish throw Jonah into the sea in this detail from a fourth-century ivory chest. Jonah is swallowed by a great fish, which vomits him out on dry land three days later. His attempt to escape God's will has been defeated, and he goes to the hated Nineveh.

The Making of the Septuagint

BY TRANSLATING THE PENTATEUCH INTO GREEK, THE JEWS LIVING IN ALEXANDRIA, WHOSE COMMAND OF THE HEBREW LANGUAGE HAD DIMINISHED, GAINED ACCESS TO THE WORDS OF SCRIPTURE.

The robust cultural life of the city of Alexandria is displayed in a relief of about 225 to 200 B.C. that shows, at top, Zeus and the personification of Memory; below them, the nine Muses, Apollo, and a poet; and, in the lowest register, Homer seated before personifications of his works.

Situated on the Mediterranean coast at the edge of the Nile Delta, Alexandria, Egypt, was a trade hub that connected the West to the East and reached into the interior of Africa. Alexander the Great founded the city in 332 B.C. after defeating the Persians and conquering Egypt. When his empire was divided after his death, his general Ptolemy took Egypt, making Alexandria his capital.

Near the city's eastern harbor, Ptolemy created a magnificent center of learning, known as the Museum, which boasted a library, an observatory, botanical and zoological gardens, and a research institute. In the halls of the Museum the greatest minds of the age gathered, among them Euclid, the "father of geometry," and Archimedes, the inventor and mathematician. Scholars delivered lectures, wrote books, conducted experiments, and copied and edited the great works of classical literature. Under Ptolemy's son, Ptolemy II, who ruled from 285 to 246 B.C., Alexandria grew into a major scholarly center, and the book collection expanded accordingly. Some scholars estimate that the libraries of the Museum contained some 400,000 volumes by the time of Ptolemy III.

Perhaps the highest literary achievement to come out of Ptolemaic Alexandria was the translation of the Pentateuch from Hebrew into Greek. Its impetus came not from the illustrious Museum scholars but from the local Jewish community.

A sizable population of Jews lived in Alexandria by the third century B.C. Some had arrived as captives and were later freed. Their numbers increased as Jews from other parts of the Diaspora migrated to the city, attracted by the relative freedoms and autonomy granted them by the Ptolemaic rulers. Several Alexandrine Jews rose to high positions in the military and in the government. The Jews of Alexandria cleaved strongly to their faith and, unlike their kinsmen of Judea, even made efforts to propagate their beliefs. But like most Jews of the

In an 11th-century Byzantine miniature King Ptolemy II commands his court scribe to request help from the high priest Eleazar in obtaining expert translators.

Diaspora, those living in Alexandria had come under the influence of the pervasive Greek culture and had adopted the Greek language. Eventually members of the community lost their command of Hebrew altogether and so were unable to comprehend their own Scriptures when they were read aloud in the synagogue. Thus Alexandrine Jews required a Greek translation of their Bible.

Translation by the 72 Elders The earliest record of the events surrounding the translation of the Pentateuch into Greek is contained in the Letter of Aristeas, which purports to be written by a member of the Ptolemaic court. The legend described in the letter begins with the great king Ptolemy II and his ambition to collect "as far as he possibly could, all the books in the world." When told by his librarian Demetrius that a Greek translation of the Pentateuch would

Continued on page 108

Alexandria's Museum library is a beehive of activity in this 19th-century engraving, as librarians stack armfuls of scrolls and scholars pore over manuscripts.

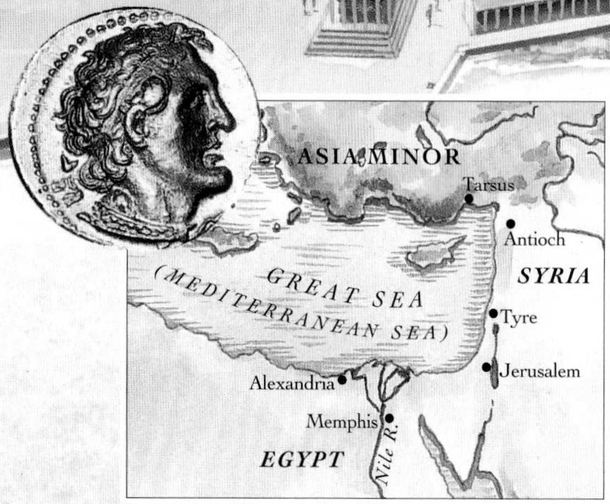

The rapid expansion of Alexandria's great library by Ptolemy II, who is shown on the coin at left, made the city the crossroads of learning in the Mediterranean world (inset map).

ALEXANDRIA

Alexandria became important to the history of the Bible when, during the reign of Ptolemy II (285–246 B.C.), the first five books of the Hebrew Bible were translated into Greek. A colorful legend grew up around the effort, based on an account in the Letter of Aristeas.

Aristeas describes a conversation between Ptolemy II and the librarian Demetrius, who tells the king: "The laws of the Jews are worth transcribing and deserve a place in your library, [but] they need to be translated, for in the country of the Jews they use a peculiar alphabet."

The letter goes on to describe how the high priest in Jerusalem chose 72 scribes as translators. The men were taken to Pharos, shown at right, an island in Alexandria's harbor that was connected to the mainland by a causeway. There, in the shadow of the 400-foot-tall lighthouse—one of the Seven Wonders of the World—the scribes began the translation: "So they set to work comparing their several results and making them agree, and whatever they agreed upon was suitably copied out under the direction of Demetrius. . . . And it so chanced that the work of translation was completed in seventy-two days, just as if this had been arranged of set purpose."

The Septuagint translation was a milestone for Jews who lived outside of Judea and did not read Hebrew, helping them to keep their religious traditions alive. It also opened the Bible to the non-Jewish world.

make a valuable addition to his burgeoning library, Ptolemy set in motion an extraordinary plan to obtain it.

First, the king set free more than 100,000 Jews who had been captured during his father's campaigns in Judea. In return, the high priest sent 72 Judean translators to Alexandria, 6 scholars from each of the 12 tribes of Israel. Thus the translation came to be known as the Septuagint, or the LXX, from the Latin for "seventy," which was roughly the number of translators engaged in the endeavor.

After a week of feasting followed by three days of rest, the translators were led to their quarters—a comfortably appointed compound on the island of Pharos in the harbor. In these congenial surroundings, the group set to work and, according to Aristeas, completed their task in 72 days. When Demetrius assembled the Jewish community for a public reading of the Septuagint, the listeners praised the translation and heaped their gratitude upon Demetrius for bringing it to fruition.

Other retellings of the Septuagint story—in works by Aristobolus, Philo, and Josephus and in rabbinic writings—provide further elabora-

Before the start of their arduous task, the 72 elders were treated to a sumptuous banquet by their host, as shown in this 11th-century Byzantine illumination.

tions on the tale related in the Letter of Aristeas. Later tradition says, for instance, that the 72 scribes worked separately or in pairs and miraculously produced the same translation, word for word, proving that the group was divinely inspired. And among early Christians, who used the Septuagint translation in their own church services, as prominent a figure as Irenaeus, bishop of Lyons, affirmed that "the Scriptures had been translated by the inspiration of God."

Scholars now believe that the Letter of Aristeas was written, not during Ptolemy II's time but in the second or first century B.C.

Although doubt has been cast on its accuracy, the letter probably contains at least elements of truth. Indeed, it is entirely possible that the Greek translation of the Pentateuch received the encouragement, if not the official sanction, of Ptolemy II. Nevertheless, it is likely that translators from the local Jewish community were employed for the job, not 72 scribes imported from Jerusalem.

Translating the Other Books

The term *Septuagint* originally referred only to the third-century B.C. translation of the Pentateuch; but over the next two centuries, other books of Scripture were translated in Alexandria, and gradually "Septuagint" came to signify the Greek translation of the entire Hebrew Bible.

The differing circumstances under which the later translations were produced led to a lack of uniformity and wide variations in the quality of the texts. The prose style, for example, ranges from the wooden language characteristic of the Book of Ecclesiastes, which is slavishly faithful to the Hebrew of the original, to the freer renderings of Proverbs and Job.

Surviving Septuagint translations dating from the time of the early church show that some later translators took great liberties with the Hebrew canon. The classification of books as belonging to the Law, Prophets, and Writings was disregarded in favor of groupings of law, history, poetry, and prophecy. Noncanonical works entered the translation, and, eventually, the Septuagint came to include all of the books or portions of books that now belong to the Apocrypha of the Protestant Bible and that are included in the canons of the Roman Catholic, Greek, and Slavonic Bibles.

Interestingly, much of the Septuagint text diverges significantly from the authoritative Hebrew text that has come down to us. For example, the Septuagint version of the Book of Jeremiah appears rearranged when compared to the Hebrew text; the Book of Job is shorter; Esther and Daniel, longer. Some discrepancies suggest that the Greek translation reflects a version of the Hebrew text dated earlier than the received, or standard, text. The fact that some of the Dead Sea Scroll manuscripts agree more closely with the Septuagint than with the received text supports such a conclusion.

With the creation of the Septuagint, the Jews living in Alexandria and the inhabitants of the entire Hellenistic world had access to the Hebrew Scriptures in the common language of their time. ❖

Today scholars believe that Jews from Alexandria, not Jerusalem, produced the Septuagint. Their theory is supported by the fact that the translation is in a Greek dialect that was common in Egypt but not in Palestine. These fragments from Deuteronomy, which are written in Greek, date from the second century A.D.

The Samaritan Pentateuch

THE SAMARITANS CALL THEMSELVES THE SHAMERIM, OR "GUARDIANS," OF THE LAW, BECAUSE THEY HAVE IN THEIR KEEPING A RARELY SEEN TORAH SCROLL.

Modern-day Samaritans assemble on the heights of Mount Gerizim to celebrate the eve of Passover. One of the key differences between the Samaritan Pentateuch and the authoritative Hebrew text is the Samaritan designation of Mount Gerizim as God's chosen holy site.

Today, the word *Samaritan* is defined either as an inhabitant of Samaria or as a person willing to help someone in trouble. The latter connotation derives from Jesus' parable of the Good Samaritan, of course. But for the Jews of Bible times, "Samaritan" was nearly synonymous with pariah, as illustrated in John 4:9, where a Samaritan woman expresses surprise when Jesus asks her to draw some water from a well for him.

The animosity between the Samaritans and the Jews ran deep, rooted in each group's belief that it alone was the true guardian of the Torah and the rightful heir to the traditions and legacy of Moses.

The Samaritans claimed ancestry from the 10 "lost" tribes of the Northern Kingdom, who were carried off to exile in the eighth century B.C. But the Jews tended to regard them as descendants of the pagan peoples sent to repopulate the Northern Kingdom after the conquest. Today, the Samaritans number fewer than 600, divided into two communities living in the town of Nablus (the ancient city of Shechem) on the West Bank and in Holon, south of Tel Aviv.

Samaritan Scriptures Most modern scholars consider the Samaritans a sect that broke off from the main body of Judaism between the fifth and second centuries B.C. These dates are based in part on the fact that the five books of the Pentateuch constitute the entirety of the Samaritan canon: Samaritans recognize neither the books of the Prophets nor the Writings, both of which were admitted to the canon in the centuries following the return from the Babylonian Exile.

Comparisons of the Samaritan Pentateuch and other early copies of the Hebrew Scriptures shed light on the history of the Bible. The Samaritan Pentateuch corresponds in many respects to the Masoretic text, the traditional Hebrew text of the Bible that was passed down through the centuries and copied by scribes between the 6th and 10th centuries A.D. In some 6,000 instances, however, the Samaritan text departs from the Masoretic. Moreover, about 1,900 variants in the Samaritan text correlate with the 3rd-century B.C. Greek Septuagint translation of the Pentateuch. Some scholars have concluded, therefore, that the Samaritan and Septuagint texts reflect versions of the Scriptures that predate the authoritative Hebrew text.

Abisha Scroll Samaritan claims for the overriding authority of their Scripture are based largely on a document called the Abisha Scroll. According to Samaritan belief, the scroll is the oldest copy of the Torah in existence, written by Abisha, the great grandson of Moses' brother Aaron, just 13 years after the Israelite conquest of Canaan. Abisha's authorship is said to be verified by an encoded message, or *tashqil,* embedded in the scroll's text of the Book of Deuteronomy. Such *tashqils,* read vertically down the center of the page, appear frequently on Samaritan scrolls and provide information about the author's identity and the circumstances of composition. "I am Abisha," begins the Abisha scroll *tashqil.* "I wrote this holy book in the door of the tent of meeting on Mount Gerizim in the thirteenth year of the dominion of the children of Israel over the land of Canaan."

Many scholars question the claims for the scroll's antiquity. Some of the few who have examined it firsthand report it is a patchwork of torn and restored texts copied in different hands over many centuries. The style of the *tashqil's* lettering dates from the 12th century A.D., and references to the scroll in Samaritan histories occur only from the 14th century on. But the Abisha Scroll remains important as one of the oldest copies of the Samaritan Pentateuch and a primary document attesting to the historical origins of the biblical texts. ❖

The sacred Abisha Scroll is rarely made available for examination by the public. A 14th-century Samaritan record relates that as a priest carried the scroll on Mount Gerizim an earthquake struck, shaking the scroll from its case. The wind lofted it into the air and it fell tattered to the ground.

Defining Daniel

TO HELP ENCOURAGE FAITH IN A TIME OF TRIBULATION, THE AUTHOR OF THE BOOK OF DANIEL ALLOWED HIS HERO TO TRIUMPH OVER DIFFICULT PLIGHTS AND TO ENVISION A REWARDING FUTURE.

Gentle-looking lions lick Daniel's hands and knees in this 12th-century stone relief carving at Worms Cathedral in Germany. When Daniel emerged from the lions' den, "No kind of harm was found on him, because he had trusted in his God [Daniel 6:23]."

Within the tales told in the Book of Daniel there are many knotty questions. The book presents scholars with quandaries regarding its authorship and date along with complications regarding interpretation.

One question concerns the two languages of Daniel. The opening (chapter 1 and the start of chapter 2) and the closing (chapters 8 through 12) were written in Hebrew, but the intervening chapters were written in Aramaic. Some scholars have suggested that Daniel may originally have been written in Aramaic and later partially translated in order to include the book in the canon of the Hebrew Bible. But they offer no explanation of why the translation was not completed. Other scholars have proposed that Daniel may be a composite text compiled by several authors. To support this second theory, they point out the book's varied structure: the first six chapters are stories of Daniel's exploits written in the third person, but the last six chapters are first-person accounts of Daniel's dream visions and his explanations of their meanings.

Dating of Daniel The Book of Daniel has the distinction of being the earliest apocalyptic work in the Bible. Historical apocalypses such as Daniel (and the Book of Revelation in the New Testament) are concerned with times of great national or community crises. The authors observe history unfolding as if they were prophesying events from an earlier date. Their writing looks ahead to a new age when the world will be a better place.

Because the Book of Daniel describes events taking place at Nebuchadnezzar's court in Babylon, the text seems to date from the time of the Babylonian Exile in the sixth century B.C. However, evidence within the book itself indicates otherwise. For one thing, the text includes words of Greek and Persian origin, which may not have been known to the Jewish community at the time of the Exile. In addition, the author confuses known historical dates and appears to invent others, indicating, perhaps, that Daniel was written many years after the events portrayed. These and other bits of evidence have led many scholars to conclude that the Book of Daniel was compiled during another period of intense hardship for the Jews—the period of the Maccabean revolt. The importance of Daniel's example to the Jews of that period is made clear by the mention of his deeds in 1 Maccabees 2:60. At that time, about 167 B.C., Judea was ruled by the Seleucid (Syrian) king Antiochus IV, who attempted to destroy Judaism and who defiled the Temple by erecting an altar to the pagan god Zeus. Led by the Maccabean family, Jews revolted against the tyranny, but their battle continued for three years before Jerusalem was liberated,

Finding the Meaning of Daniel It is thought that the author of the Book of Daniel was a member of the Hassidim—pious Jews—who helped keep the faith during this difficult time. The Book of Daniel was part of that effort. The first six chapters encourage the struggling community by recalling events associated with the Babylonian Exile. In each of the episodes, Daniel or his friends overcome trials in a strange land. In each instance, they do so by living the Law and honoring God: they refuse rich foods and stick to the dietary laws of the Jews; Daniel seeks mercy in the Lord in order to interpret the king's dreams; and his friends refuse to worship the king's golden statue. Faith makes them strong and helps them to succeed. The stories in the first part of Daniel are thought to derive from earlier traditional tales, but their edifying message has meaning for all time.

In the second half of the book it is Daniel's own dream visions that require interpretation. As in other apocalyptic books, God's design for the future is hidden within complex symbolism and even Daniel cannot interpret it without the aid of angels. In Daniel's first vision, for instance, the despised King Antiochus IV, who gained his power by uprooting others, is symbolized as a little horn on a great beast. In Daniel 7:11 it is revealed that the little horn's arrogance will cause the beast (the Seleucid Empire) to be destroyed by fire. As difficult as the visions may be to interpret, they, like the first half of the Book of Daniel, deliver a message of hope and faith. ❖

The city of Babylon is depicted surrounded by serpents in the illustration below taken from a 10th-century copy of a commentary on the Book of Daniel by the Spanish monk Beatus of Liebana. Within the walls of Babylon the artist shows Shadrach, Meshach, and Abednego lying in sarcophagi in the furnace.

Choosing the 24 Books of the Hebrew Bible

THE SELECTING AND SEQUENCING OF THE BOOKS RECOGNIZED AS THE HEBREW BIBLE, OR OLD TESTAMENT, TOOK PLACE OVER SEVERAL CENTURIES.

No one knows how the books of the Hebrew Bible were chosen. The Bible itself says nothing about the considerations and concerns that led to selecting the canon, or authorized books. Scholars can only speculate about how the process might have taken place.

The word *canon* comes from the Greek *kanon*, which initially meant "reed" or "measuring rod" and subsequently took on the meaning of "rule" or "standard of excellence." It was first used by the early Christian Church Fathers to refer to a list of books that Christians considered sacred. By the late fourth century A.D., the word *canon* came to be applied to the books and order of the Hebrew Bible as well as Christian works.

There are 24 books in the Hebrew canon, which is divided into three parts: Torah (Pentateuch or Law), Prophets, and Writings. The Torah contains five books: Genesis, Exodus, Leviticus, Numbers, and Deuteronomy. The Prophets has eight books: Joshua, Judges, Samuel, and Kings (known as the Former Prophets); and Isaiah, Jeremiah, Ezekiel, and the Twelve (called the Latter Prophets). The Writings contains a total of 11 books: Psalms, Proverbs, Job, Song of Solomon, Ruth, Lamentations, Ecclesiastes, Esther, Daniel, Ezra-Nehemiah, and Chronicles.

Books cannot be added or taken away from the Hebrew canon. However, a seeming variation in the number of books did occur in the first century A.D. when the Jewish historian Josephus described the canon as containing 22 books. Apparently Josephus derived his number by joining Ruth and Judges and doing the same with Jeremiah and Lamentations.

The Hebrew Bible is recognized by Christians as the Old Testament. Nevertheless, the number of books in the Old Testament canon varies from that of the Hebrew Bible because the Christians split up the Twelve (the Minor Prophets), giving one book for each of them; they separate Ezra-Nehemiah into two books; and they divide Samuel, Kings, and Chronicles into two books

*T*orah scrolls covered with embroidered mantles are stored in the Ark of the Law. The carved wooden Ark above was made in Venice in the 18th century and moved to a synagogue in Jerusalem in 1952.

*S*croll cases, like the 19th-century example at left, are the traditional housing for hand-written Torah scrolls. Shown almost actual size in the foreground at left is a silver yad, or pointer. Since it is forbidden to touch the parchment during the reading of the Torah, readers use a yad to keep their place in the text.

each. The order of the books of the Old Testament in Christian Bibles also differs from that of the Hebrew Bible.

Many scholars believe that the canonization of the Hebrew Bible took place over a long period of time and that the three divisions of the Bible represent the stages of canonization. The entire canon was probably complete sometime in the first century A.D. A passage from 2 Esdras, supposedly written during the first or early second century A.D., mentions the 24 books. "Make public the twenty-four books that you wrote first, and let the worthy and the unworthy read them; but keep the seventy that were written last, in order to give them to the wise among your people [2 Esdras 14:45-46]." This passage is thought to distinguish between the books of the Hebrew canon and the apocryphal and pseudepigraphal (noncanonical) works.

Dating the Torah The five books of the Torah are believed to have been accepted as having spiritual authority during or just after the Babylonian Exile in the sixth century B.C., when the texts were probably given their final form. With its emphasis on Mosaic Law, the Torah created a legal yardstick for the people as they returned from exile to rebuild their lives once more in their own land.

The sequence of the five books of the Torah is invariable and appears to have been so since the books' completion. That has not been true of the Prophets and Writings. Early manuscripts of these books suggest that their order did not become fixed until much later. However, defining a set arrangement of books was not necessary initially because each book was written on an individual scroll that was selected for reading at the appropriate time.

Canonizing the Prophets Recognition of the Former and Latter Prophets as spokesmen for God began during the Babylonian Exile, at which time many of the books of the Prophets were compiled. This division of the Hebrew Bible is thought to have developed between the fifth century B.C. (the date of Malachai, the last of the books of the Prophets) and the second century B.C., perhaps, just before the Book of Daniel is judged to have been written. One basis for this claim is that since it is considered by some a prophetic work, the Book of Daniel would have been included in the second division if the canon of the Prophets had not already been closed.

Another indication that the canon of the Prophets was developed, if not yet closed, by the second century B.C. is found in the prologue that was added to the noncanonical Book of Ecclesiasticus about 130 B.C. In it the writer refers three times to the Torah, the Prophets, and "the other books" or "the rest of the books." As with the books of the Torah, those of the Prophets had probably long been accepted as divinely inspired by the time they were canonized.

This page from a Spanish Bible dated 1300 shows the prophet Zechariah's vision of two olive trees providing oil for a menorah. The olive trees are thought to symbolize Joshua and Zerubbabel; the seven lamps of the menorah are said to represent God's omnipresence.

Canonizing the Writings The division of the Hebrew Bible called the Writings may well have been the last to be canonized, but not all of its books were the last to be written. In fact the dates of the books in the Writings vary more widely than do those in the other divisions. Some of the material, including many of the psalms and proverbs and the poetry of Lamentations, is probably at least as old as some of the books of the Prophets. But the Writings also includes the last-written canonical books.

The fact that a book's age and tradition in the community were important to its inclusion in the canon appears not to have been lost on later authors. The author of the Book of Daniel, for instance, set his story three centuries earlier than the time it was actually written. Additionally, some of the tales in Daniel, as well as those in another relatively late work, the Book of Esther, derive from earlier lore that had been familiar to generations of people.

Some of the books that were written too late for acceptance in the Hebrew canon are included in the canons of the Roman Catholic, Greek, Armenian, Ethiopian, and Slavonic Bibles. In Protestant Bibles,

these books are either grouped together as the Apocrypha or they are left out entirely.

The rationale behind the selection of the books of the Writings is less clear than in the other divisions, and yet the selection is not random. Some scholars have pointed out that the books of the Writings collectively tell the faithful how to live good and religious lives, just as the books of the Prophets together stress the need to follow God's laws and the books of the Torah reveal the laws themselves. Sociopolitical factors and community needs seem to have played a strong role, if not the most important one, in determining canonicity. The canon of the Hebrew Bible was readily embraced by the people because it ratified what was already accepted as true.

However long the process of canonization went on and in however many stages, the selection and arrangement of the books in the Hebrew canon forms a unity. It is a history of a people, their developing faith, and their relationship to God that begins in Genesis and is recapitulated at the very end in Chronicles. Each of its three divisions narrates part of the history. Moreover, each represents the differing points of view of the people as they lived in Israel, Judah, Babylon, and Egypt over the course of some 1,500 years. Each division has its particular lessons to impart. However, one overriding lesson carries through from beginning to end: empires rise and fall but the one God of the Hebrews remains constant. ❖

*T*he 19th-century French Esther scroll above is inscribed on parchment. Its protective sandalwood cover is carved with scenes from the story of Esther.

What Was Left Out

THE COLLECTIONS OF RELIGIOUS WRITINGS NOW REFERRED TO AS THE APOCRYPHA AND THE PSEUDEPIGRAPHA WERE NOT INCLUDED IN THE CANON OF THE HEBREW BIBLE.

A number of religious works written between 300 B.C. and A.D. 200, although considered instructive and even inspired, were not included in the canon of the Hebrew Bible. These books have survived as parts of two general groups of works—the Apocrypha and the Pseudepigrapha.

The Apocrypha The books of the Apocrypha were written by Jews between 300 B.C. and A.D. 70, but the term *apocrypha* (Greek for "hidden") was applied to them only later by Christians. The books include histories, romantic stories, wisdom, prayers, and additions to Old Testament books. The themes of many of the works are concerned with the fate of Israel and the struggle against idolatry in an age when prophecy was believed to have ended. There is no standard list of books of the Apocrypha, but the number of works is generally set at 13 and includes Tobit, Judith, the Additions to the Book of Esther, the Wisdom of Solomon, Ecclesiasticus (Sirach), Baruch, the Letter of Jeremiah, the Prayer of Azariah and the Song of the Three Jews, Susanna, Bel and the Dragon, 1 and 2 Maccabees, and 1 Esdras (also called 3 Ezra or 3 Esdras).

Although considered extracanonical by the Jews, the Apocrypha was included in the Septuagint, the Greek translation of the Hebrew Bible. Roman Catholic, Greek, Slavonic, Armenian, and Ethiopian Bibles follow the Septuagint and add the Apocrypha to their Old Testament canons, though Catholic Bibles omit 1 Esdras. Protestant Bibles do not include any of these books but sometimes print them in an appendix.

The Pseudepigrapha The number of writings in the Pseudepigrapha is even larger. The works, written by Jews and Christians from about 200 B.C. to A.D. 200, were not included in the Septuagint and are not accepted as canoni-

One of the heroines of the Apocrypha, Judith, is depicted by Donatello in this 15th-century bronze sculpture. Judith helped the Jews defeat the Assyrians by cutting off the head of their leader, Holofernes.

The detail, above, from an Italian ivory comb made during the Renaissance, shows a scene from the apocryphal tale of Susanna and the Elders. In the tale, the hero Daniel proves the honesty of Susanna while exposing the deceit of the elders.

cal by any Western church. However, some Eastern churches include pseudepigraphical books in their canons, which is why the Pseudepigrapha has largely come down to us in such languages as Syriac, Ethiopic, Coptic, Georgian, Armenian, and Slavonic. The Bible of the Ethiopian Church, for instance, includes *Jubilees* and *1 Enoch*.

Many of the authors of the Pseudepigrapha attempted to mold their writings in the form of works from the bygone age of prophecy. To give their writings the appearance of added authority, authors often attributed their books to ancient worthies, including Moses, Elijah, Solomon, and Ezekiel. It is possible that this practice prompted the name *Pseudepigrapha*, or "false inscription," for the books.

Scholars disagree over exactly what constitutes the Pseudepigrapha, but 52 appears to be the accepted number of main documents. These include 19 apocalyptic works, 8 testaments, 13 legends and expansions of biblical stories, such as the *Martyrdom and Ascension of Isaiah* and the *Life of Adam and Eve*, 5 books of wisdom, and 7 books of prayers and psalms, including *Hellenistic Synagogal Prayers*. Some of the works, such as *The Testaments of the Twelve Patriarchs* and parts of *1 Enoch*, may have been expanded or rewritten by Christians.

Accepting and Rejecting New Beliefs From the books of the Apocrypha and Pseudepigrapha it can be illustrated that Judaism in the last centuries B.C. and early centuries A.D. was open to and influenced deeply by other cultures and that there was a growing diversity of beliefs within Judaism itself. The authors of the books were aware of the various beliefs and ideas of the time. They

Tobit, here pictured with his wife by Rembrandt, lost his sight because he buried an executed Jew. At the end of an adventurous tale involving the old man's son and the angel Raphael, God rewards Tobit with renewed sight and a pious daughter-in-law.

119

incorporated into their texts whatever they deemed to be compatible with their own traditions and rejected the rest. Two books of the Apocrypha, 1 and 2 Maccabees, record the battle that Judeans were willing to wage when foreign rulers tried to force them to adopt pagan beliefs. The differing versions of the story expressed in the two books suggest the political and theological purposes of the authors.

In 198 B.C. Judea came under the control of the Seleucid (Syrian) king Antiochus III, who, like the Greek-speaking Ptolemaic rulers before him, tried to Hellenize his conquered people. But there was a clash between the beliefs of the Jews, who would have nothing to do with idolatry, and the pagan beliefs of the Greek culture. The conflict reached a peak during the rule of Antiochus IV, who was determined to destroy the Jewish faith. He massacred 40,000 Jews, sold another 40,000 into slavery (2 Maccabees 5:14), compelled his subjects to take part in celebrations honoring the Greek god Dionysus (2 Maccabees 6:7), and defiled the Temple by dedicating it to the god Zeus (2 Maccabees 6:2).

Mattathias, the priest, is shown with his family and animals in this 19th-century German engraving by Schnorr von Carolsfeld. "At that time many who were seeking righteousness and justice went down to the wilderness to live there, they, their sons, their wives, and their livestock, because troubles pressed heavily upon them [1 Maccabees 2: 29-30]."

The Maccabean War A priest named Mattathias, father of five sons, refused to offer a pagan sacrifice when commanded to do so by an agent of the king and then proceeded to slay both the the agent and a Jew who did offer the sacrifice. Calling out, "Let everyone who is zealous for the law and supports the covenant come out with me [1 Maccabees 2: 27]!" Mattathias and his followers fled to the hills and launched a war against Antiochus. Although Mattathias soon died, the battle was continued by his son Judas, called Maccabeus, or "the hammer." Eventually the name would be applied to all the heroes of the rebellion.

In 164 B.C., after three years of fighting, Judas seized control of the Temple in Jerusalem, tore down the pagan altar, purified the sanctuary, and rededicated the Temple to God with "songs and harps and lutes and cymbals [1 Maccabees 4:54]." The dedication went on for eight days and has been celebrated by Jews every year since in the festival of Hanukkah.

Eventually, Judas' family, the Hasmoneans, gained control of Judea. Their dynasty ruled independently until 63 B.C. and then ruled under the protection of Rome until 37 B.C., when Herod took control.

The Writing of the Books The revolt is described in 1 Maccabees in a straightforward style. The book was originally written in Hebrew and has a pro-Hasmonean slant. It is considered an accurate historical account that is often corroborated by first-century Greek historians. Second Maccabees, which covers the same historical events as the first eight chapters of 1 Maccabees, was written in Greek. Its author shows

The Maccabee brothers confront Antiochus IV outside and inside city walls in this illustration from a 15th-century French manuscript of The Jewish War *by the Jewish historian Flavius Josephus. This late-first-century book includes another version of the story told in 1 and 2 Maccabees. The coin, below, dates from about 40 B.C. and bears an image of a menorah, a symbol of Hanukkah.*

no interest in trumpeting the goodness of the Hasmonean family, but rather his point is to emphasize the holiness of the Temple.

Between Old and New Testaments The Apocrypha and Pseudepigrapha are fascinating texts that mark the religious influences, transition of beliefs, and movements of groups of people between the Old and New Testaments. The stories and ideas that emerge from them remain integral for understanding the Judeo-Christian tradition. For example, 2 Maccabees presents several concepts—such as the resurrection of the body and the efficacy of offering prayers for the dead—that are not found in Hebrew Scriptures. These ideas would become important elements of Christianity. Similarly, symbols and terms associated with Jesus—the Son of Man, and the kingdom of God, for instance—are expressed in works in the Pseudepigrapha. ❖

Qumran and the Dead Sea Scrolls

THE MACCABEAN REVOLT SPURRED ONE JEWISH SECT TO SEPARATE FROM "THE MEN OF PERVERSITY . . . TO PREPARE THE WAY OF HIM."

In 1947, while searching for a lost goat along the barren cliffs near the Dead Sea, a young Bedouin accidentally discovered a treasure: the first of the manuscripts that came to be known as the Dead Sea Scrolls. But the cache found in Cave 1 (see map to right) would soon be eclipsed by the most spectacular finds of all, from Cave 4 (shown above), including the oldest surviving books of the Bible—dating from the third century B.C. Across a ravine from Cave 4 lie the ruins of the Qumran complex (above, right), excavated by archeologists beginning in 1951.

The Book of Joel issues a dire warning: "Alas for the day! For the day of the Lord is near, and as destruction from the Almighty it comes [Joel 1:15]." From their desert community at Qumran, about 14 miles east of Jerusalem near the Dead Sea, the members of a Jewish sect lived out their days awaiting the apocalypse. Confident that they were among God's elect, they readied themselves to inherit the new age. "All the children of righteousness are ruled by the Prince of Light and walk in the ways of light, but all the children of falsehood are ruled by the Angel of Darkness and walk in the ways of darkness," they wrote. These "Sons of Light" would ride on the final day with God's army to defeat Rome and the "Sons of Darkness."

The settlement at Qumran, founded in the mid-second century B.C., came to a violent end at the hands of those very sons of darkness:

the Romans extinguished the brotherhood in A.D. 68 during their drive to crush the Jewish revolt against Rome that had begun two years earlier. But the sect left behind a rich legacy, not for its own generation but for the distant future. In the period before Roman soldiers stormed the site, the inhabitants of the community gathered up their own precious library, placed it in clay jars, and transported the jars to nearby caves. Safely tucked away for centuries in their rocky shelters lay a veritable treasure trove of writings preserved on hundreds of leather and papyrus scrolls.

There the scrolls remained until, in 1947, a Bedouin shepherd boy chanced upon some of them. In the years to come parts of some 800 Dead Sea Scrolls would be brought to light, taken from dozens of caves and crevices dotting the cliffs around the Qumran site. A few of the manuscripts survived the centuries in good condition. Others had decayed and fragmented, creating an intricate jigsaw puzzle. To this day scholars are hard at work painstakingly assembling them.

The majority of the writings are in Hebrew. They include copies of almost all the books of the Old Testament, ranging in date from the third century B.C. to the first century A.D., plus commentaries on Scripture, and documents of instruction and on worship. Until their discovery, the earliest-known substantial Hebrew manuscripts of the Old Testament were texts transcribed by Jewish scholars in the ninth century A.D. The scrolls take us back nearly a thousand years in the history of the Bible, to a period predating the beginning of Christianity.

The Righteous Remnant The Qumran site has been identified with the Essenes, a Jewish sect descended from an ancient line of high priests. The word *Essenes* is most often translated as "pious ones" or "healers." In 152 B.C., after leading the Jews in a war of independence, Jonathan, brother of Judas Maccabeus, assumed the title of high priest in Jerusalem. This usurpation by a pretender prompted the Essenes to declare the priesthood illegitimate. They broke away from the Temple and severed all ties with their fellow Jews. They even rejected the Jewish calendar and marked the holy days by their own reckoning. Calling themselves the "righteous remnant" of Israel, the sect withdrew from society and established monastic-like brotherhoods—the first in Judaic history. This sect spread in towns throughout the country but concentrated in the region between Jericho and the Dead Sea. There, separated from the corrupt society of the time, and no longer under the authority of the Temple, the brothers answered instead to "the priests who keep the covenant."

One of the Dead Sea Scrolls records that the settlers of Qumran lived their first 20 years "like blind men groping their way at noon," until a priestly leader, the Teacher of Righteousness, rose among them. He was a man "to whom God made known all the mysteries of the

Continued on page 126

123

LAST DAYS OF QUMRAN

The Qumran settlers had survived natural disaster and hostile occupation only to rebuild, add new members, and carry on their sacred work. But A.D. 68 would mark their final year. As the Jewish revolt raged, Roman troops neared the desert outpost—ideal as a site for a military garrison with its tall tower and commanding view—and the settlers hastily evacuated. Their greatest treasure, the writings they had diligently copied onto scrolls, were deposited in jars and transported to nearby caves (some shown upper left). Soon thereafter, the Romans captured Qumran, bringing an end to the sect.

LOCATOR KEY

1. Caves	8. Council chamber
2. Pools	9. Scriptorium
3. Pottery workshops	10. Kitchen
4. Dyers' workshops	11. Tower
5. Main hall	12. Cistern
6. Pantry	13. Storerooms
7. Stable	14. Entrance
	15. Settling pool
	16. Aqueduct

words of his servants the prophets." Scholars have failed to identify the teacher; but whoever he was, his followers pinned their hopes for salvation on his visionary words. He instructed his people to interpret the lessons of the Bible; for encoded within Scripture were prophecies that shed light on current events and end times, concepts that members of the sect viewed as one and the same. The Bible, said the teacher, revealed that the wicked would soon be destroyed. In the aftermath, three figures would emerge to restore the Essenes to their rightful place in Jerusalem: a great prophet, a messiah descended from King David, and a second, priestly messiah, the "anointed of Aaron." Until that day, the Essenes must dedicate their lives to worship, study, and spiritual purification.

Life in the Wilderness Aside from the scrolls, the most complete account of Essene organization, initiation, and beliefs comes from the first-century Jewish historian Flavius Josephus. The Jewish philosopher Philo Judeaus of Alexandria and the Roman historian Pliny the Elder, also in the first century, give additional early descriptions of the sect. All these sources depict a life defined by hardship, self-deprivation, and a military-style discipline.

Qumran's elaborate network of conduits and cisterns was fed by river water channeled to the site along an aqueduct. The Essenes, who associated ritual cleanliness with spiritual purity, immersed themselves daily in ritual baths to ready their souls for the coming age.

A complex hierarchy of officials, headed by a council made up of 3 priests and 12 laymen, governed the community according to a strict application of biblical law. Members shunned wealth, dressed modestly, took a vow of celibacy, and deferred to their superiors. Like fellow Jews, they ceased all activity on the Sabbath. But they took the practice to greater extremes and resisted even natural bodily functions on the holy day.

The Essene initiation process lasted at least three years. The candidate for membership spent one year living apart from the settlement. Next he faced an examination, first by the leader then by the full assembly. If accepted, he became an apprentice of the sect and then worked his way up to full membership. Josephus reports that the oath of admission included the inductee's solemn promise "forever [to] hate the unjust and fight the battle of the just." Each new apprentice was issued a linen robe, a loincloth, and an ax, the last used primarily to survive in the wilderness but also to dispose of human waste in accordance with the rules of purity. After living for a year within the community, the apprentice relinquished his valuables and assumed some of the responsibilities of the sect. After the second year, he achieved full membership privileges and was permitted to join the community's table.

The highly regimented daily routine began after a short night's sleep. The Essenes arose in silence before sunrise and donned their robes. The first words they uttered were prayers offered in the direction of the rising sun, "as though entreating him to rise," wrote Josephus. From the sunrise prayer service they went to their chores, laboring until midday in the fields, flour mill, kitchen, stable, smelting furnaces, and pottery kiln. Some became experts on the healing powers of herbs and gemstones. Others, the community's scribes, sat bent over unfurled scrolls meticulously copying Scripture. In the late morning they immersed themselves in cold water, disdaining the oil generally used for cleansing, which they thought impure. Then they filed into the refectory to eat the first meal of the day. Afterward, they resumed work until time for the second meal. Evenings were devoted to worship and the study of Scripture.

Punishment for breaking the rules was severe. Transgressors were sometimes deprived of food, a precious commodity in the wilderness. The rations of any member who failed to give his belongings to the community could be reduced by one fourth, with the offender cut off from participation in the group for a year. Anyone who fell asleep during a meeting served one month's penance; if a man was caught laughing in a boisterous manner, a portion of his food was denied for 30 days. The punishment for indecent dress was meted out over six months. Those who spoke God's name aloud risked expulsion.

The Dead Sea Scrolls and the Bible "[F]or a third of the night all through the year," the Rule of the Community states, "the congregation shall stay awake together to read from the Book, to study Law, and to pray together." Testimony such as this, along with the massive Dead Sea Scroll library and the probable identification of a scriptorium and related artifacts at Qumran, amply demonstrate the central place that reading and studying Scripture held within the Qumran community. The Book, as interpreted through the sect's writings, guided not only the religious lives of the members but the most minute details of their daily existence.

Beside what they tell us about the Qumran sect itself, the scrolls offer tantalizing clues to the development of the Bible canon. In addition to the some 170 biblical manuscripts yielded by the caves, books from outside the canon were also found at Qumran. Two such are the *The Testaments of the Twelve Patriarchs*, alleged to be an account of the last words of the Patriarchs, and *Jubilees*, a detailed interpretation of the chronology of biblical history. In a number of instances the scroll writings depart from later convention; for example, the Book of Isaiah occurs in two different versions, and the arrangement of the Psalms is unusual and includes three previously unknown psalms. Still, much of the Scripture recorded in the Dead Sea Scrolls remains remarkably close to traditional Old Testament texts, an indication to some scholars that there was a trend toward standardization of the text during the first century A.D. ❖

WAS JOHN THE BAPTIST AN ESSENE?

Scholars have drawn striking parallels between the Essenes and the early Christians. Some have even gone so far as to suggest that Jesus may once have belonged to the sect. Though this assertion is highly dubious, a better argument can be made that John the Baptist was raised by Essenes.

The Gospel of Luke suggests that even as a child John lived in the Judean wilderness, site of the Qumran settlement. Like the Essenes, he forsook civilization for an ascetic life. Where Essene initiates were administered ritual cleansing similar to baptism, John baptized sinners in the nearby Jordan River. Yet, John's name is absent from the scrolls, and nowhere in the Bible is he described as an Essene, making it likely that if John had grown up in the order, he later left it.

Remains of I Samuel found in Cave 4 supply previously unknown details of the story of Saul. A fragment is shown below.

Scrolls were recovered in various states of condition, from the tens of thousands of fragments of more than 500 scrolls found in Cave 4, shown above, to a handful of nearly intact manuscripts, some of which were protected by clay jars (far right). Time and the elements spared most of the Temple Scroll (right), which outlines plans for building an ideal temple.

Recovering the Scrolls

The scrolls that were extracted from 11 caves near the Qumran site are among the most important archeological discoveries of all time. They provide a rich source for studying the varieties of Judaism at the beginning of the Christian Era and the diversity of biblical texts in circulation before the Scriptures became standardized. Sectarian documents such as the Rule of the Community, War Rule, Thanksgiving Hymns, and the Temple Scroll give us important insights into the lives and beliefs of community members.

The Dead Sea Scrolls have suffered the ravages of time. Most of them exist in a fragmentary state, with many pieces providing at most a few words of text. Rot has overtaken some manuscripts, making them legible only by infrared photography. The ink used in writing the Genesis Apocryphon has corroded the leather. Indeed, it is remarkable that the papyrus and leather scrolls endured the march of centuries at all.

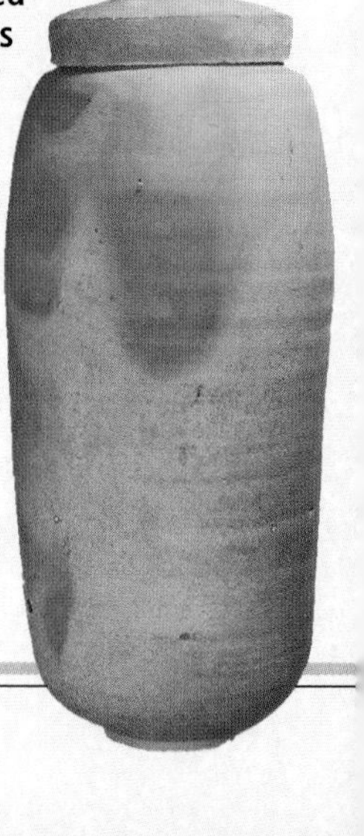

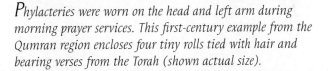

The Isaiah Scroll dates from c. 100 B.C. and is among the texts that survived their cave environment nearly intact. Prior to its discovery, the oldest extant version of a prophetic book written in Hebrew dated only from A.D. 895.

Phylacteries were worn on the head and left arm during morning prayer services. This first-century example from the Qumran region encloses four tiny rolls tied with hair and bearing verses from the Torah (shown actual size).

Restorers used scalpels to peel back adhered layers of the Temple Scroll that resisted unrolling and then reassembled the pieces.

The Shrine of the Book in Jerusalem displays the Temple Scroll and a facsimile of the nearly complete Isaiah Scroll found in one of the caves.

Words of a New Faith

Like the earlier tales of the Patriarchs, the stories of Jesus' ministry on earth were passed along by word of mouth for some time before they were written down. The earliest Christian writings were letters from Paul to newly founded churches. Then various gospels, acts, apocalyptic works, and other letters were written and circulated among Christian communities. It took more than 200 years, however, for Christians finally to decide which books would make up what we now know as the New Testament.

Street in Ephesus on which Paul may have walked

From the Roman Conquest of Judea to the Establishment of the Christian Canon

PART THREE TIMELINE (Many of the dates below are based on scholarly speculation and are approximate.)

| 4000 B.C. | 3000 B.C. | 2000 B.C. | 1000 B.C. | 65 B.C. A.D. 400 | A.D. 1000 | A.D. 2000 |

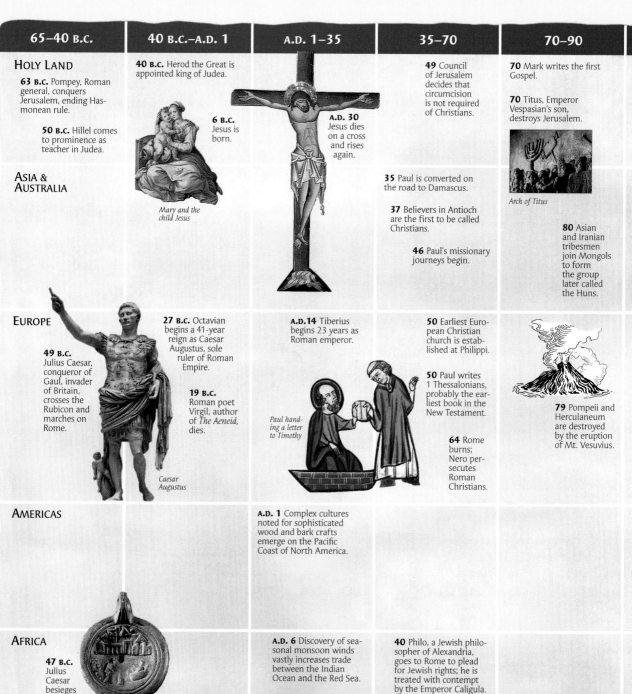

	65–40 B.C.	40 B.C.–A.D. 1	A.D. 1–35	35–70	70–90
HOLY LAND	**63 B.C.** Pompey, Roman general, conquers Jerusalem, ending Hasmonean rule. **50 B.C.** Hillel comes to prominence as teacher in Judea.	**40 B.C.** Herod the Great is appointed king of Judea. **6 B.C.** Jesus is born. *Mary and the child Jesus*	**A.D. 30** Jesus dies on a cross and rises again.	**49** Council of Jerusalem decides that circumcision is not required of Christians.	**70** Mark writes the first Gospel. **70** Titus, Emperor Vespasian's son, destroys Jerusalem.
ASIA & AUSTRALIA				**35** Paul is converted on the road to Damascus. **37** Believers in Antioch are the first to be called Christians. **46** Paul's missionary journeys begin.	*Arch of Titus* **80** Asian and Iranian tribesmen join Mongols to form the group later called the Huns.
EUROPE	**49 B.C.** Julius Caesar, conqueror of Gaul, invader of Britain, crosses the Rubicon and marches on Rome. *Caesar Augustus*	**27 B.C.** Octavian begins a 41-year reign as Caesar Augustus, sole ruler of Roman Empire. **19 B.C.** Roman poet Virgil, author of *The Aeneid*, dies.	**A.D. 14** Tiberius begins 23 years as Roman emperor. *Paul handing a letter to Timothy*	**50** Earliest European Christian church is established at Philippi. **50** Paul writes 1 Thessalonians, probably the earliest book in the New Testament. **64** Rome burns; Nero persecutes Roman Christians.	**79** Pompeii and Herculaneum are destroyed by the eruption of Mt. Vesuvius.
AMERICAS			**A.D. 1** Complex cultures noted for sophisticated wood and bark crafts emerge on the Pacific Coast of North America.		
AFRICA	**47 B.C.** Julius Caesar besieges Alexandria, and its great library is partially destroyed. *Pottery oil lamp with scene of the port of Alexandria*		**A.D. 6** Discovery of seasonal monsoon winds vastly increases trade between the Indian Ocean and the Red Sea.	**40** Philo, a Jewish philosopher of Alexandria, goes to Rome to plead for Jewish rights; he is treated with contempt by the Emperor Caligula.	

90–120	120–175	175–250	250–325	325–400

135 Bar Kokhba revolt against Hadrian's Rome fails, leading to an extensive dispersion of the Jews; Jerusalem is destroyed.

200 The Mishnah, the written collection of Jewish oral law, is compiled.

254 Origen, the great Christian writer and author of the *Hexapla*, a massive synopsis of extant editions of the Old Testament, dies.

354 Pagan temples are closed throughout the Roman Empire.

Coin from the time of the Bar Kokhba revolt

Roman temple

105 Paper is invented in China.

150 Buddhism comes to China by way of trade routes from India.

200 The *Mahabharata*, the epic containing the *Bhagavad-Gita*, the essence of Hindu Scripture, is completed.

271 Magnetic compass is used in China.

220 Chinese invent gunpowder.

303 Armenia becomes the first Christian state.

Chinese gilt bronze Buddha

Marcus Aurelius

120 Christians begin to use the codex, or book, in place of the scroll.

175 Emperor-philosopher Marcus Aurelius completes his *Meditations*.

250 Decius begins the first systematic, empire-wide persecution of Christians.

325 Council of Nicaea adopts a creed summarizing the core of Christian doctrine.

95 Revelation is written by John of Patmos.

303 Diocletian's persecution of Christians begins.

John of Patmos

An early codex of the Book of Psalms

177 Roman persecution of Christians intensifies; the fish becomes a Christian symbol.

313 The Edict of Milan decrees that Christianity will be tolerated throughout the empire.

The Arch of Constantine in Rome

330 Constantinople, the "New Rome," is founded at Byzantium.

100 In Guatemala, pre-classic Mayan civilization flourishes.

200 Hopewell people develop a trade network in what is now the eastern United States.

300 Monte Albán, a huge Zapotec Indian ceremonial center, flourishes in Oaxaca, Mexico.

200 Mochica (Moche) people build pyramids in southern Peru.

356 Anthony of Egypt, founder of Christian monasticism, dies.

Mochica portrait vessel

367 Athanasius establishes the New Testament canon in his Pascal letter.

The World of Jesus

THE BIRTHPLACE OF JESUS WAS JUDEA, THE JEWISH TERRITORY RULED BY ROME. DIVIDED BY RELIGIOUS FACTIONALISM, ITS PEOPLE WERE AWAITING THE ARRIVAL OF THE MESSIAH AND SALVATION.

Jesus lived on the eastern edge of the Roman Empire, a vast realm that stretched for 2,000 miles and encompassed most of the land around the Mediterranean Sea. There was peace inside this world, but it was the uneasy peace that comes when a conquered people must bow to a foreign master and its occupying forces. And nowhere was the Pax Romana, this peace, more unstable than in Judea, the land that God had promised the descendants of Abraham.

Romans Invited to Judea Nearly 80 years of independence under the Hasmoneans had ended for the Jews shortly after their queen, Salome Alexandra, died in 67 B.C. Alexandra had left the kingship to her eldest son, the high priest Hyrcanus, but his brother, Aristobulus, commander of the army, also coveted the throne. Both men appealed to the Roman commander Pompey, who sided with Hyrcanus. In the summer of 63 B.C., Hyrcanus defeated his brother in battle. But Roman intervention came at a high price: the Jews were forced to turn over their territorial possessions to the empire and submit to the authority of the Roman governor of Syria.

The Romans controlled Judea until 40 B.C., when Parthian invaders overran the region. Herod, a military leader of Idumean origin and the son of a governor of Judea, fled to Rome, where Mark Antony and Octavian (later Caesar Augustus) persuaded the Senate to appoint him king of the Jews in absentia. The Romans swiftly defeated the Parthians, and in 37 B.C. Herod won Judea back.

Over the 33 years of his reign, Herod the Great expanded the borders of his domain nearly as far as King David had almost 1,000 years earlier. Herod's ambitious building program dramatically altered the landscape. On the site of the Second Temple, he erected the largest and most magnificent place of worship the Jews had ever known—a 35-acre complex one-sixth the area of the city of Jerusalem and constructed of the finest cedar, marble, and gold. But many of the people of Judea hated Herod, a foreigner, whose claim to Jewish allegiance, through his Hasmonean wife, they thought tenuous. More distressing, Herod was a loyal friend of Rome and regularly aided Roman forces in their military campaigns.

As king of the Jews, Herod seized absolute control in Judea and killed off possible rivals among the descendants of the royal dynasty. He also executed Hasmonean supporters in the 70-member Jewish legislature-court known as the Sanhedrin and then appointed a new Sanhedrin but curtailed its jurisdiction. The Gospel of Matthew indicates that his bloody deeds culminated in the Slaughter of the Innocents, the infants in and around Bethlehem.

Herod's Legacy When Herod died in 4 B.C., Emperor Augustus divided the Jewish kingdom among Herod's three sons: Herod Archelaus, who was awarded the higher title of ethnarch, inherited the territory called Judea (including Jerusalem) and neighboring Samaria. His brothers, who were given the title of tetrarch, governed smaller states. Herod Antipas received Galilee, to the north, and Perea, along the east bank of the Jordan River. He set up his capital at Sepphoris, about three miles northwest of Nazareth, where he reigned throughout the lifetime of Jesus. Herod Philip, the third son, ruled Ituraea and Trachonitis, the Gentile territories northeast of Galilee.

Herod Archelaus was as ruthless as his father, but lacking Herod's political savvy, he lasted only 10 years in office. A delegation of Jews and Samaritans prevailed upon Augustus to depose him, and his land was turned over to Roman dominion under Quirinius, the governor of Syria. Quirinius immediately ordered the taking of a census to evaluate the

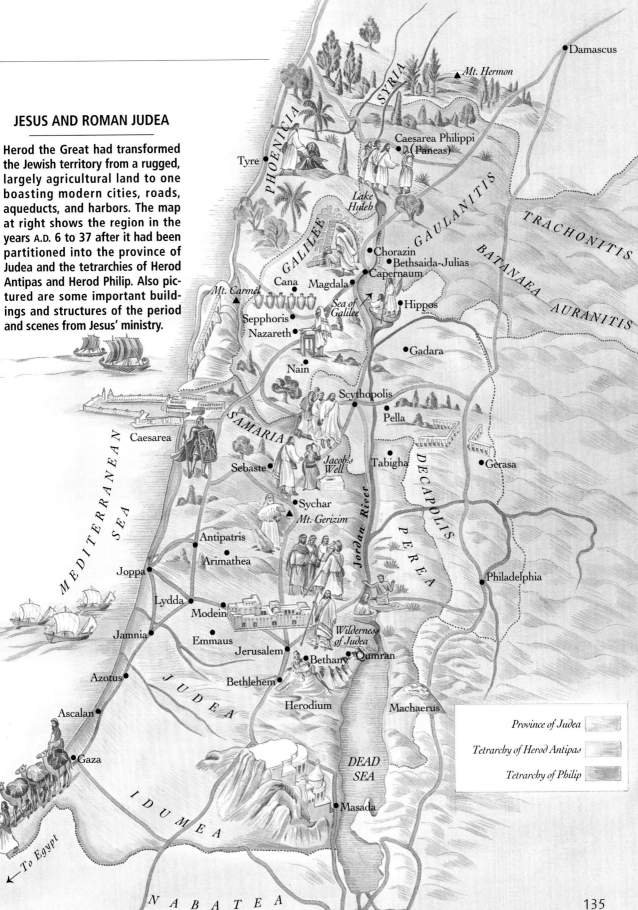

JESUS AND ROMAN JUDEA

Herod the Great had transformed the Jewish territory from a rugged, largely agricultural land to one boasting modern cities, roads, aqueducts, and harbors. The map at right shows the region in the years A.D. 6 to 37 after it had been partitioned into the province of Judea and the tetrarchies of Herod Antipas and Herod Philip. Also pictured are some important buildings and structures of the period and scenes from Jesus' ministry.

Damascus

Mt. Hermon

SYRIA

PHOENICIA

Tyre

Caesarea Philippi
(Paneas)

Lake
Huleh

GALILEE

GAULANITIS

TRACHONITIS

BATANAEA

Chorazin

Bethsaida-Julias

Capernaum

Cana

Magdala

Hippos

AURANITIS

Mt. Carmel

Sepphoris

Nazareth

Sea of
Galilee

Gadara

Nain

Scythopolis

SAMARIA

Pella

DECAPOLIS

Caesarea

Sebaste

Jacob's
Well

Tabigha

Gerasa

Sychar

Mt. Gerizim

Jordan River

PEREA

MEDITERRANEAN
SEA

Antipatris

Arimathea

Joppa

Philadelphia

Lydda

Modein

Emmaus

Wilderness
of Judea

Jamnia

Jerusalem

Qumran

Bethany

Azotus

Bethlehem

JUDEA

Ascalan

Herodium

Machaerus

Gaza

DEAD
SEA

IDUMEA

Masada

To Egypt

NABATEA

Province of Judea

Tetrarchy of Herod Antipas

Tetrarchy of Philip

135

This first-century B.C. relief shows the census-taking process in Rome, from enrollment through a sacrifice to Mars. Judeans' registration with the censor, for tax-collecting purposes, was a sore reminder of their conquered status. In deference to the Jewish law against graven images, however, most Judean governors stamped their coins with symbols instead of the portraits used on coins from imperial mints (an Antiochian example showing Augustus appears at top). A date-palm tree appears on the procurator Coponius' coin, the augur's staff on the Pontius Pilate coin, and a helmet on the Herod Archelaus coin.

area's tax potential. From then on, the Jews would pay their taxes directly to Rome. Many Jews bitterly opposed such taxation and rule as incompatible with their obedience to God's law.

From A.D. 6 to 41 Judea was ruled by a series of seven Roman governors appointed by the governor of Syria. Most of these military bureaucrats had little sympathy for or understanding of the culture or religion of the Jews. The most infamous of these was Pontius Pilate, who ruled A.D. 26 to 36 and ordered the crucifixion of Jesus. Pilate openly antagonized his Jewish subjects. In Jerusalem he mounted standards adorned with the image of the emperor and had coins minted bearing the symbols of Roman sovereignty. He also executed dissidents mercilessly. Rome finally discharged him after he ordered soldiers to massacre a group of Samaritans.

Competing Faiths and Factions The Romans encountered in the Jewish world a mix of traditions and philosophies. The nation had for centuries suffered foreign invasions and been buffeted by powerful cultural forces from outside. The most potent influence was that of Greek civilization, which swept through the region with the army of Alexander the Great and was supported for centuries by Hellenistic overlords in Egypt and Syria.

The Jews themselves were divided over subjects ranging from the legitimacy of the priesthood to the acceptance of certain books into the canon. One group, the Essenes, rejected the priesthood entirely. Samaritans formulated doctrines unique to themselves; for instance, they considered Mount Gerizim in Samaria the only proper place to worship God. Various cadres of religious zealots dedicated themselves to the task of overthrowing the Romans. The most dominant groups in Jesus' time, however, were the Sadducees and Pharisees.

The Sadducees were closely associated with the aristocratic clans that made up the priesthood in Jerusalem. Their prestige derived from their claim to exclusive supervision over the Temple. The Temple, God's sanctuary and the only lawful place for sacrificial offerings, was

a rallying point for Jews dispersed throughout the region, who made regular pilgrimages there on the holy days. The Sadducees ingratiated themselves with Rome and acquiesced when Herod and later the Roman governors ignored the traditional hereditary character of the high priestly office and appropriated the right to appoint or dismiss the high priest. In turn, Rome granted the Sadducees, who were leaders in the Sanhedrin, the power to rule locally.

The Pharisees adopted a more progressive outlook than the Sadducees. While the Sadducees did not accept the books of the Prophets and Writings, the Pharisees not only admitted these books but, in addition, believed in angels, demons, resurrection, and—like the Essenes and other groups—in the coming of the Messiah. The Pharisees devoted their lives to studying the Law and developed a growing body of unrecorded commentary on Scripture and rulings by Jewish sages. This oral law was intended to help Jews adapt the ancient Law of Moses to the circumstances of their own time. On several occasions mentioned in the Gospels, Jesus repudiates the dos and don'ts of the oral law.

The remains of a fourth-century synagogue in Capernaum, on the western shore of the Sea of Galilee, bespeak its former grandeur. Excavations on the site have also unearthed the foundations of an earlier synagogue, perhaps the one in which, according to the Gospels, Jesus taught and healed a possessed man.

The Diaspora Communities that, centuries earlier, had been scattered far from the Temple, had developed new ways to sustain their faith. These communities, known as the Diaspora, turned increasingly to Scripture and to interpretation of the Law. They also established synagogues—places of assembly—that functioned as centers for prayer, study, and the administering of local Jewish affairs. It was in the synagogues of Galilee that Jesus began his ministry, and to other synagogues, dotting the Mediterranean world from Antioch to Rome, that Paul later spread the message of the arrival of the Messiah and of his crucifixion and resurrection. ❖

137

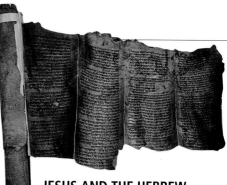

The Life and Ministry of Jesus

DURING HIS BRIEF MINISTRY AMONG POOR PEOPLE IN A POWERLESS LAND, JESUS BEGAN A MOVEMENT OF FAITH THAT MARKED A GREAT TURNING POINT IN HISTORY.

JESUS AND THE HEBREW SCRIPTURES

Jesus grew up using the Hebrew Scriptures. They formed the basic textbook for his education in the synagogue, and he quoted and alluded to them scores of times in his teaching. Jesus often gave his own thoughtful and controversial interpretation of important texts. He firmly believed in the authority of the Scriptures, saying that he had "come not to abolish [the Law or the prophets] but to fulfill [Matthew 5:17]." But Jesus was never afraid to challenge traditional understandings of the Scriptures. When asked what was the first commandment, he unhesitatingly quoted the command in Deuteronomy 6:4–5, to love God, and added the command in Leviticus 19:18, to love one's neighbor.

Jesus was born in the last years of the ruthless king Herod the Great, who died in 4 B.C. The Gospels of Matthew and Luke describe the events surrounding his birth and make it possible to estimate his birth date at about 6 B.C. Of the next 30 or so years until his public ministry began, few details are known. Jesus apparently grew up in a thriving Jewish family in the town of Nazareth among the green hills of Galilee. Like other boys he was likely educated in the town synagogue. He spoke the local Aramaic but learned to read the Hebrew of the Scriptures and probably to get by in Greek, the language of commerce. He learned a trade and worked for several years as a carpenter.

Beginning of His Ministry When Jesus was about 30 years old, he went out to the banks of the Jordan River. There his kinsman John the Baptist was preaching repentance to a large number of followers in preparation for the coming of another, who was so powerful, John claimed, that "I am not worthy to stoop down and untie the thong of his sandals. I have baptized you with water," John added, "but he will baptize you with the Holy Spirit [Mark 1:7–8]." John baptized Jesus, and as Jesus emerged from the water, he saw the heavens torn open and the Holy Spirit descending like a dove, and he heard a heavenly voice say: "You are my Son, the Beloved; with you I am well pleased [Mark 1:11]."

Following this revelation of Jesus' special relationship with God, the Spirit led Jesus into a desert area of Judea, where he fasted and prayed for 40 days. From the wilderness, Jesus returned to Galilee, the setting of much of his ministry, which lasted approximately three years. He moved from Nazareth to Capernaum, where, along the shores of the Sea of Galilee, he gathered his first disciples. It is

impossible to draw a precise itinerary of Jesus' subsequent movements since the order of events in the Gospels varies. John's account, in particular, differs in important respects from those of Matthew, Mark, and Luke, which are called the synoptic Gospels. For example, John begins Jesus' ministry with his miraculous sign of changing water to wine at a wedding in Cana of Galilee but concentrates most of Jesus' ministry in Judea rather than Galilee.

Radical Ministry From the start of his ministry Jesus went directly to the people. He made no attempt to create a pure community but attracted many followers who were considered sinners and outcasts. Indeed, the company Jesus kept was a revolutionary and, to some, highly objectionable, aspect of his ministry. He touched lepers, helped prostitutes, praised the faith of a mercenary centurion, called an anti-Roman Zealot as a disciple, and welcomed as a follower the wife of a courtier of Herod Antipas, ruler of Galilee. His ministry broke down walls in society. He blessed the poor, for as he said, "Yours is the kingdom of God [Luke 6:20]," but he also called a despised tax collector as a disciple. When he spoke to a woman at a well in the land of the Samaritans, between whom and the Jews there was historic animosity, she was astonished: "How is it that you, a Jew, ask a drink of me, a woman of Samaria [John 4:9]." The fact that Jesus had a circle of women disciples set him apart from any other Jewish teacher of the period.

Jesus proclaimed the message that God's kingdom was at hand. The miracles he performed—of healing, exorcism, and the control of nature—gave evidence of his role as God's agent for this momentous process. Jesus worked these miracles without fanfare: he once advised two men he had cured of blindness to "see that no one knows of this [Matthew 9:30]." But he also engaged in controversies with religious opponents that solidified opposition to his ministry. The Pharisees in particular thought that Jesus was dangerous because of his disregard for many traditional rites of purity, his rejection of the practice of fasting, and his repeated challenges to their understanding of Sabbath observance. The Gospel of Mark says that these issues led to a decision by some of them to try "to destroy him [Mark 3:6]."

Jesus' Galilean mission had many remarkable moments. Once after great throngs had followed him all day in open country listening to his teaching, he fed them—more than 5,000 the Gospels report—

*W*hile visiting the synagogue in his hometown of Nazareth, Jesus read from the scroll of Isaiah: "The Spirit of the Lord is upon me, because he has anointed me [Luke 4:18]." When he announced that the prophecy was being fulfilled, the townspeople were amazed at his words. The above book illustration is by the 19th-century French painter James J. Tissot.

*J*ohn the Baptist baptizes Jesus in a painting by the 16th-century Italian artist Paris Bordone.

using only a few loaves and fish. After this miracle he spent the evening alone in prayer high on a mountainside. A crucial moment came one day as he traveled near Caesarea Philippi with his disciples. "Who do you say that I am?" he asked them. At once, Peter confessed, "You are the Messiah [Mark 8:29]."

Six days later, Jesus took three of his disciples to a mountain in Galilee. There he appeared in a blaze of light, flanked by the prophets Moses and Elijah. The Transfiguration, which revealed the divine aspect of Jesus, marked a turning point in his ministry. Afterwards events moved rapidly toward their dramatic conclusion.

His Final Days On the Sunday before Passover in A.D. 30 Jesus was hailed with cries of "Hosanna to the son of David" as he rode into Jerusalem on a donkey. Jesus himself perhaps recalled the prophecy in Zechariah: "Lo, your king comes to you; triumphant and victorious is he, humble and riding on a donkey [Zechariah 9:9]." According to the Gospel of John, Jesus had been teaching in Jerusalem during the preceding months. Mark describes only a single week he spent in the city.

On Monday (in Matthew, Sunday) Jesus drove merchants from the Temple and upset the stalls of money changers and pigeon sellers, denouncing them for turning the house of God into "a den of robbers [Mark 11:17]." The next day he dealt adroitly with the Pharisees' attempt to paint him as either a traitor to his own people or an enemy of the Roman Empire: When asked if it was lawful to pay taxes to Caesar, he replied, "Give therefore to the emperor the things that are the emperor's, and to God the things that are God's [Matthew 22:21]." He silenced the Sadducees by arguing eloquently for life after death. Then he predicted the Temple's destruction and evoked the Last Judgment.

The following day Jesus dined in Bethany at the house of Simon the leper, where a woman anointed his head. The disciples protested that the expensive ointment should have been sold instead to benefit the poor, but Jesus reproved them, saying it would serve for his burial.

On Thursday evening, Jesus shared the Passover meal with his disciples in Jerusalem. As he blessed the bread and wine, he spoke mys-

The Gospel of John recounts the story of the woman taken in adultery, shown here in a 16th-century painting by Jan Sanders van Hemessen. When the Pharisees cited Mosaic Law pronouncing the woman's sin punishable by stoning, Jesus wrote on the ground and said, "Let anyone among you who is without sin be the first to throw a stone at her [John 8:7]."

teriously of the bread as his body and of the wine as his blood. The disciples later remembered and reenacted this event to symbolize their union with Jesus' life and death.

After the meal, Jesus and his disciples retreated to a garden on a hill just outside Jerusalem, where Jesus prayed three times for deliverance from his coming ordeal but submitted himself to God's will. Soon Judas arrived with a mob; Jesus was seized, and the disciples fled.

Mark tells us that in the early morning hours Jesus was interrogated by officials of the Sanhedrin. When asked if he were "the Messiah, the Son of the Blessed One [Mark 14:62]," his affirmative answer caused his accusers to cry that he deserved death. They remanded Jesus for trial to the Roman governor Pontius Pilate. Pilate, a notorious hater of the Jews and their leaders, handed Jesus over to Herod Antipas, who questioned him briefly, mocked him, and sent him back.

Pilate tried to use Jesus' former popularity for his own purposes. In accordance with Passover tradition, he gave the crowds a chance to free a prisoner—either Jesus or else Barabbas, a political rebel dangerous to Rome. The crowds, eager to spite Rome, cried "Release Barabbas for us [Luke 23:18]!" Foiled, Pilate mockingly condemned Jesus as a rebel "king of the Jews" and sentenced him to crucifixion.

Crucifixion and Resurrection Jesus' punishment was immediately carried out. By nine o'clock, he was scourged and nailed to a cross at Golgotha, place of the skull. Within hours he was dead, his last words according to Mark the cry of Psalm 22: "My God, my God, why have you forsaken me?" A secret follower, Joseph of Arimathea, removed Jesus from the cross. He prepared the body according to Jewish tradition, deposited it in a tomb, and sealed the opening with a stone.

The ministry that had begun in such hope appeared to have ended in desolation. But on Sunday morning, several of Jesus' female followers went to the tomb and found the stone rolled away. In John's account, Jesus appeared to Mary Magdalene, the first of a number of post-Resurrection appearances. One poignant encounter, also in John, has Jesus coming to the disciples after they had spent an unsuccessful night fishing. He filled their nets with a tremendous catch and commanded them to continue his ministry. In his final appearance, after telling his disciples they would be visited by the Holy Spirit, Jesus rose to heaven. While Jesus' bodily presence had ended, the Ascension confirmed his spiritual influence and ignited a lasting faith. ❖

For the followers of Jesus, the miracle of his resurrection fulfilled the messianic hope expressed in contemporary Jewish writing. This glazed terra-cotta relief, executed by the Renaissance sculptor Luca della Robbia for Santa Maria del Fiore, Florence, illustrates the passage in Matthew in which the Roman soldiers guarding the tomb become "like dead men [Matthew 28:4]" at the sight of the risen Christ.

Spreading the Good News

TEN DAYS AFTER JESUS' ASCENSION, THE APOSTLES AND OTHERS GATHERED IN JERUSALEM TO CELEBRATE
THE FEAST OF PENTECOST. SUDDENLY AND DRAMATICALLY THEY WERE FIRED BY THE HOLY SPIRIT AND
IMMEDIATELY WENT OUT TO PROCLAIM THE WORD OF THE COMING OF THE MESSIAH.

Thousands of Jews from the far reaches of the Mediterranean world thronged Jerusalem during Pentecost, the Feast of Weeks marking the end of the grain harvest. The Acts of the Apostles tells us a group of those celebrants numbering 120 —among them the Apostles, Mary the mother of Jesus, and some of Jesus' other disciples— assembled in a house to await the arrival of the Holy Spirit as heralded by the resurrected Jesus. Suddenly the room reverberated with the sound of a violent wind. What seemed to be flames appeared and hovered above the disciples' heads. The Holy Spirit filled the company, who then began speaking in other tongues.

Upon hearing the noise, a crowd of Jews, hailing from Mesopotamia, Egypt, Libya, Crete, Rome, and other places, gathered. Each was amazed to hear Galileans speaking in the hearer's own language. Then from the group of Apostles, Peter stepped before the crowd to proclaim Jesus the Messiah, the one whom God had raised up, as foretold by the prophets, to deliver mankind. Peter called upon his listeners to repent, and some 3,000 were baptized that day in the name of Jesus.

Thus in the Christian tradition, Pentecost came to signify the birth of the church and the beginning of the Christian mission. The first Christians, who called their movement the Way, considered them-

*M*ary and the Holy Spirit, represented
by a dove, are the central figures in
a miniature Pentecost scene in the style of
the 15th-century artist Simon Marmion.

selves not part of a new religion but devout Jews. They followed the Law, observed the Sabbath, and "spent much time together in the temple [Acts 2:46]." They formed a distinct community, however, based on their faith in Jesus as the Messiah and their belief that the Holy Spirit, the Spirit of prophecy, was among them.

The 12 Apostles (Judas Iscariot had been replaced by Matthias) led the church in Jerusalem. At first Peter was most prominent among them, but after persecution forced him to leave Jerusalem, James the brother of Jesus emerged as leader. The Acts of the Apostles describes the first community of believers in ideal terms. Many of them sold their property and divided the proceeds so that "there was not a needy person among them [Acts 4:34]." They shared "with glad and generous hearts, praising God and having the goodwill of all the people [Acts 2:46–47]."

During the first 20 years of the new faith, no writings of any kind emerged. Jesus left no permanent writing, and his followers handed down his teachings and their proclamation about him entirely by word of mouth. The first writings that are preserved are letters from the Apostle Paul beginning about A.D. 50. At about the same time, an unknown Christian evidently compiled an anthology of Jesus' parables, prophetic and wisdom teachings, and exhortations. This collection, sometimes called Q (from the German word *Quelle* meaning "source"), is now lost but was used by both Matthew and Luke in writing their Gospels.

The First Christian Martyr Jerusalem was a cosmopolitan city with large communities of immigrant Jews who had grown up in Greek-speaking cities across the Roman Empire. From the start, the new faith attracted many of these Jews, known as Hellenists because of their language, as well as Aramaic-speaking Jews, who are sometimes called Hebrews in the Acts of the Apostles. The cultural differences between these groups evidently led to the first friction in the church, as some Hellenists complained that their widows did not receive the same daily distribution of food as the Hebrew widows. The Apostles resolved the dispute by appointing seven prominent Hellenists—including Stephen and Philip—to take care of it.

Soon sparks flared around Stephen as he debated against Hellenist Jews who rejected Jesus. In the Greek-speaking synagogues of Jerusalem, he began to argue that the work of Jesus as Messiah had made the Temple and its sacrifices obsolete. Many of the Hellenists were intensely devoted to the Temple and considered Stephen's arguments sheer blasphemy. They brought him before a council on charges of teaching that Jesus would destroy the Temple and change the Law. Rather than defend himself, Stephen attacked his accusers, using the Law and the words of the prophets against them. He quoted Jeremiah to show that the leaders were resisting God and had betrayed and murdered God's "Righteous One [Acts 7:52]." The council turned into a mob and stoned Stephen.

A wave of persecution broke out, especially against the Hellenist believers, scattering them northward to Samaria, Phoenicia, Syria, Cyprus, and on to Antioch. Everywhere they went the believers shared their faith in Jesus as Messiah with their fellow Jews, until in Antioch they began to tell Gentiles also about Jesus. ❖

THE MINISTRY OF PHILIP

Philip the evangelist fled Jerusalem after the death of Stephen and took the mission to Samaria. Summoned by an angel, he traveled the road between Jerusalem and Gaza, where he met "an Ethiopian eunuch, a court official of the Candace, queen of the Ethiopians [Acts 8:27]." The man—who was a convert to the Jewish faith in God and who had traveled hundreds of miles to worship in the Temple—sat in his chariot reading Isaiah. He asked Philip to interpret the prophecy and then baptize him. Thus the Ethiopian became one of the first Gentiles to be converted.

The 16th-century painter Michiel Coxie showed how Philip met, converted, and baptized the Ethiopian eunuch in a work now housed in St. Bavo Cathedral, Ghent.

Apostle to the Gentile World

THE OLDEST WRITINGS IN THE NEW TESTAMENT ARE THE LETTERS OF A PHARISEE WHO, ONCE CONVERTED, TRAVELED 10,000 MILES TO TELL THE GOOD NEWS TO JEWS AND GENTILES ALIKE.

One of those who participated in the stoning of Stephen was Saul, a Greek-speaking Jew raised in the commercial center of Tarsus in Cilicia (in what is now Turkey). The son of devout Jews, Paul (to use his Roman name) had studied in Jerusalem with Gamaliel, the most respected Pharisee of his day. Gamaliel treated followers of the Way with tolerance; his pupil became their ardent foe. Paul himself says he "was violently persecuting the church of God [Galatians 1:13]."

A Transforming Vision Paul's campaign of destruction ended abruptly about A.D. 35. Luke tells us that while Paul traveled to Damascus to round up Christians for trial, a blinding light struck and felled him. "I am Jesus, whom you are persecuting," a voice rang out. God had chosen Paul, the voice revealed, as messenger to the Gentiles, "to open their eyes so that they may turn from darkness to light [Acts 26:15–18]." As an enemy of the church, Paul was an unlikely missionary, but he had grown up in a Hellenized city, knew Greek, and enjoyed Roman citizenship. Through the forceful articulation of his message he penetrated the hostile environment of pagan cities and established permanent communities of Christians.

For a decade or so after his conversion, Paul worked in the eastern Mediterranean region. He preached in Damascus, but after raising the ire of Jews who saw him as a traitor, he had to escape the city by being lowered over the wall in a basket. He also spent more than two years preaching in the Arabian kingdom of the Nabataeans. From the time he began to preach, Paul welcomed Gentiles as believers, certain that Jesus had called him to bring Gentiles to faith in God without their having to convert first to Judaism. This practice was highly controversial among the Jewish Christians in Jerusalem, where Peter's baptism of the Gentile Cornelius provoked a serious dispute.

Though Paul had waited three years after his conversion to return to Jerusalem, he found himself greeted by intense suspicion. Only with the help of Barnabas, a trusted leader, was he accepted into the community. Paul spent two weeks with Peter and James, who was becoming the most prominent leader of the Jerusalem church. Soon, ironically, Paul became engaged in disputes with Hellenist Jews, and

The Apostle Paul (shown in a 12th-century panel painting from Spain) carried out three successful missionary journeys in the heart of the Roman Empire—prevailing against unruly seas, bandit-ridden roads, and opponents to his message—before he was taken to Rome for trial.

BLACK SEA

BITHYNIA and PONTUS

MACEDONIA
THRACIA
Philippi
Thessalonica
Neapolis
Berea
SAMOTHRACE
Apollonia
Bosporus
GALATIA
CAPPADOCIA
Mt. Olympus
AEGEAN SEA
Troas
Assos
MYSIA
Pergamum
Thyatira
ASIA
PHRYGIA
Cilician Gates
Mitylene
Sardis
Smyrna
Antioch
PISIDIA
Iconium
CILICIA
ACHAIA
CHIOS
Philadelphia
Lystra
Issus
Delphi
Ephesus
Colossae
Derbe
Tarsus
Athens
Miletus
Laodicea
LYCAONIA
Corinth
SAMOS
PAMPHYLIA
Perga
Taurus Mountains
Antioch
Cenchreae
Attalia
Seleucia Pieria
Cnidus
LYCIA
SYRIA
Myra
Rhodes
Patara
RHODES
CYPRUS
Salamis
CRETE
Cape Salmone
Paphos
Damascus
Phoenix
Sidon
Fair Havens
Tyre
CAUDA
Ptolemais
Caesarea
MEDITERRANEAN SEA
Jordan River
Jerusalem
Dead Sea
CYRENAICA
JUDEA
Alexandria
AEGYPTUS
Petra

PAUL'S JOURNEYS

First Journey c. A.D. 46–48

Second Journey c. A.D. 49–winter 51–52

Third Journey c. A.D. 53–57

Voyage to Rome c. A.D. 59–62

A broken line indicates the presumed route taken by Paul when his exact course is unknown.

threats to his life forced him to leave Jerusalem for his hometown of Tarsus. He continued to preach in Cilicia until Barnabas, who had been sent from Jerusalem to Antioch in Syria, asked him to join in leading the work there. Their mission in that city evidently alerted the authorities to the fact that the believers were not simply a sect of Judaism, and they began to call them Christians.

Paul's Travels A new stage of Paul's life began when the Holy Spirit, as Acts indicates, summoned Barnabas and Paul. The Antioch church, which by then had numerous leaders, sent them out to preach in areas where their message had not yet been heard. They set sail on their first missionary journey for Barnabas' native island of Cyprus and then crossed to the southern shore of Asia Minor and traveled inland through the regions of Pamphylia, Pisidia, and Lycaonia.

In every place, they went first to the synagogue, where people knew the Scriptures and understood the meaning of God's promise to his people. Generally, it seems, when Paul and Barnabas claimed that Jesus was the Messiah, only a few of the Jews believed the message— no one expected the Messiah to be crucified. Often the most receptive hearers were Gentiles who were attracted to Judaism's teachings (and so were often called God-fearers) but who had not become full proselytes. Drawing converts from those who did believe, Paul and Barnabas established small communities of believers in several cities.

However, the reaction to the message was often explosive. The missionaries were driven out of Antioch in Pisidia and threatened with stoning in Iconium. Paul was actually stoned in Lystra and barely survived. He later looked back on these times: "Five times I have received from the Jews the forty lashes minus one. Three times I was beaten with rods. Once I received a stoning [2 Corinthians 11:24–25]."

Council of Jerusalem In A.D. 49 Paul, Barnabas, and other representatives of the Antioch church went to Jerusalem to meet with Peter, James, and other church leaders. Their purpose was to settle a burning issue: could Gentiles be accepted as believers without converting to Judaism and keeping the Law of Moses, notably the covenant of circumcision? Peter, alluding to his conversion of the Gentile Cornelius, sided with Paul, as did James. The council produced a letter affirming acceptance of Gentile believers and thus averted a schism.

Soon after the council disbanded Barnabas returned to Cyprus, and Paul launched his second mission with a new companion, Silas. They revisited the churches Paul had planted on his first trip and pushed onward to the western tip of Asia Minor and over to Europe. Paul traveled through Macedonia and Greece, establishing churches in Philippi, Thessalonica, Beroea, and Corinth. He spent a year and a half in Corinth before traveling to Ephesus, Jerusalem, and Antioch.

On his third mission, Paul preached in central Asia Minor, spent three years in Ephesus, revisited Macedonia and Greece, and returned to Syria. Proceeding to Jerusalem, he was arrested on the false charge of profaning the Temple and was ultimately taken to Rome for trial.

Paul's Letters As the founder of numerous churches, Paul fulfilled his responsibility to guide these communities by writing letters that substituted for his presence among the converts. In these letters, he often responded to questions, showing Christians how the message of Jesus applied to their daily lives. He guided congregants' beliefs and gave them courage in the face of strong challenges coming both from inside and outside Christianity.

Paul generally dictated his letters to a scribe: the only one known is Tertius, who added a personal greeting to Paul's Letter to the

Jesus, seated upon his heavenly throne, hands the Law over to Peter with Paul in attendance. This relief is one of 10 Old Testament and Christian scenes carved on the fourth-century sarcophagus of a Roman prefect and Christian convert named Junius Bassus.

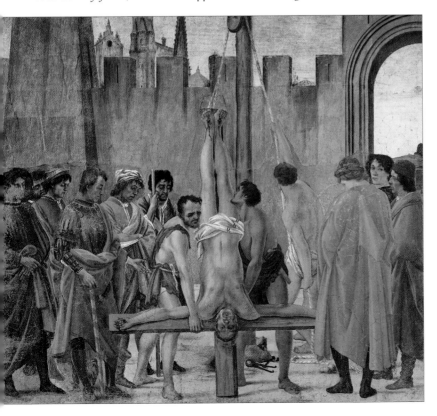

Romans, but Timothy may also have served as a scribe. Messengers hand-delivered the letters, and if knowledgeable on the topic, he or she—Romans 16:1–2 implies a woman named Phoebe was a messenger—read the letter to the congregation, interpreted it, and helped resolve any disputes that arose.

Of the 14 letters in the New Testament traditionally ascribed to Paul, 7 are firmly attributed to him by even the most skeptical scholars: Romans, 1 Thessalonians, 1 and 2 Corinthians, Galatians, Philippians, and Philemon. Scholars continue to debate the authenticity of 6 other letters: 2 Thessalonians and Colossians are widely accepted as Paul's own writing; Ephesians and the Pastoral letters (1 and 2 Timothy and Titus) are more often questioned. Hebrews is almost universally agreed to be from another writer. ❖

According to tradition, Peter asked to be crucified upside down, as shown in a 15th-century fresco, so as not to appear to be imitating Christ.

MARTYRDOM OF THE APOSTLES

Since the Bible gives no information about the fates of most of the Apostles, tradition over the centuries supplied stories and legends to fill in the gaps. Tradition assigns a martyr's death to almost all the Apostles, though there is clear evidence in only a few cases. The New Testament records the martyrdom of only one Apostle, James the son of Zebedee, who according to Acts was beheaded by command of Herod Agrippa I.

Although 2 Timothy and 2 Peter point to the deaths of Paul and Peter respectively, no details are given. A second-century tradition describes their martyrdom in Rome about the time of the Neronean persecution. According to other legends, Matthew's martyrdom took place variously in Ethiopia, Persia, or Pontus; Thomas died in India; Simon the Zealot and Jude were martyred in Persia; Bartholomew was flayed alive in Armenia; and Andrew was crucified in Greece on an X-shaped cross.

Rarely can modern evidence aid in analyzing these traditions. Excavations on Vatican Hill in Rome have shown that the spot has been revered in connection with Peter since the second century, but claims that Peter's bones were found there are largely discounted.

147

Letter Writing in the First Century

THE POWER OF THE EPISTLES, ESPECIALLY THOSE OF PAUL, LAY PARTLY IN THEIR ADHERENCE TO A STRUCTURE RECOGNIZED BY EDUCATED PEOPLE THROUGHOUT THE GREEK-SPEAKING WORLD.

In their work, scribes used pottery inkwells and occasionally bronze pens like the ones above from first-century Rome. During their travels, Paul and his scribes might have used a portable pen case with built-in inkwell and hand-cut reed pens, like the ones below from Roman Egypt. Ink was made from black soot mixed with gum and water.

By his own admission, Paul was not particularly impressive or persuasive in person. Part of his success as a founder of churches lay in his ability to use well-crafted letters to communicate his teachings to the widely scattered communities he founded and to deal with their problems. Like all educated people of the time, Paul made use of the formal structure for letter writing that had been well established in the Hellenistic world for many years. Not unlike the rules for presenting an argument known to any good writer today, Greek convention divided a letter into five segments: the opening (the name of the writer and greetings), the exordium (thanksgiving, intercession, and praise), the proof (an appeal for action), the peroration (a reiteration and expansion of the appeal), and the conclusion (more greetings and a closing).

Although Paul followed this form in writing his letters, he transformed it into his own distinctive tool for communicating the Christian faith. For example, the standard greeting in a Greek letter was simply *Chairein* ("Greetings"), but Paul expanded it into a distinctly Christian message: "Grace to you and peace from God our Father and the Lord Jesus Christ." Other ways in which Paul created his own revised form of the Greek structure can most easily be seen in the Letter to Philemon reproduced on the opposite page.

Paul generally dictated his letters to a scribe; when he did write in his own hand, he often called attention to that fact in order to add a personal immediacy to his argument, as in Philemon, verse 19. The scroll would then be sent by messenger or with any friend who would be traveling close by its destination (in Philemon, the runaway slave who is the subject of the message was also the messenger). In this way, Paul was able to spread his interpretation of the gospel farther and more frequently than by his own extensive travels. The letters conveyed his authority as powerfully as his own presence, if not more so, and his letter style was so effective that it became the standard for written theological arguments for many years to come. ❖

To withstand the hardships of the road, letters written on papyrus scrolls (opposite) were tightly rolled, folded, bound with twine, and sealed with wax.

THE LETTER OF PAUL TO PHILEMON

Although it is Paul's briefest letter and concerns only a single, personal request on behalf of a runaway slave, the Letter to Philemon is one of the purest examples of the Hellenistic letter-writing format as adapted by Paul to fit his own rhetorical style.

[Opening:] ¹Paul, a prisoner of Christ Jesus, and Timothy our brother,

To Philemon our dear friend and co-worker, ²to Apphia our sister, to Archippus our fellow soldier, and to the church in your house:

³Grace to you and peace from God our Father and the Lord Jesus Christ.

[Exordium (thanksgiving, intercession, and praise):] ⁴When I remember you in my prayers, I always thank my God ⁵because I hear of your love for all the saints and your faith toward the Lord Jesus. ⁶I pray that the sharing of your faith may become effective when you perceive all the good that we may do for Christ. ⁷I have indeed received much joy and encouragement from your love, because the hearts of the saints have been refreshed through you, my brother.

[Proof (the appeal on behalf of Onesimus):] ⁸For this reason, though I am bold enough in Christ to command you to do your duty, ⁹yet I would rather appeal to you on the basis of love—and I, Paul, do this as an old man, and now also as a prisoner of Christ Jesus. ¹⁰I am appealing to you for my child, Onesimus, whose father I have become during my imprisonment. ¹¹Formerly he was useless to you, but now he is indeed useful both to you and to me. ¹²I am sending him, that is, my own heart, back to you. ¹³I wanted to keep him with me, so that he might be of service to me in your place during my imprisonment for the gospel; ¹⁴but I preferred to do nothing without your consent, in order that your good deed might be voluntary and not something forced. ¹⁵Perhaps this is the reason he was separated from you for a while, so that you might have him back forever, ¹⁶no longer as a slave but more than a slave, a beloved brother—especially to me but how much more to you, both in the flesh and in the Lord.

[Peroration (the reiteration and expansion of the appeal):] ¹⁷So if you consider me your partner, welcome him as you would welcome me. ¹⁸If he has wronged you in any way, or owes you anything, charge that to my account. ¹⁹I, Paul, am writing this with my own hand: I will repay it. I say nothing about your owing me even your own self. ²⁰Yes, brother, let me have this benefit from you in the Lord! Refresh my heart in Christ. ²¹Confident of your obedience, I am writing to you, knowing that you will do even more than I say.

²²One thing more—prepare a guest room for me, for I am hoping through your prayers to be restored to you.

[Conclusion:] ²³Epaphras, my fellow prisoner in Christ Jesus, sends greetings to you, ²⁴and so do Mark, Aristarchus, Demas, and Luke, my fellow workers.

²⁵The grace of the Lord Jesus Christ be with your spirit.

Opening: (Verse 1) Paul introduces himself; the choice of "prisoner" rather than "Apostle in Christ" refers to the fact that he is currently under arrest but still claims Christ as his master. Paul often named others as co-senders of a letter; here it is Timothy, who shares his imprisonment. The implication is not that Timothy has contributed to the letter but only that he shares in the views expressed.

(Verses 2–3) Although the letter is addressed solely to Philemon, Paul extends his greeting to Philemon's family and to his congregation, implying that they will have an interest in Philemon's response.

Exordium: (Verses 4–7) Paul thanks God for Philemon's faith and prays that it will deepen, leading him to grant the appeal he is about to make.

Proof: (Verses 8–16) The slave Onesimus ran away from Philemon and met Paul, who converted him to Christ. Paul is sending the slave back with this letter, asking Philemon to forgive the slave, charge to Paul any expenses caused by the slave's absence, and, by implication, set Onesimus free. Paul does not command obedience but rather recommends a voluntary act of Christian charity.

Peroration: (Verses 17–21) Paul repeats his request, stressing once again that Philemon's treatment of Onesimus as an equal will increase the value of both men in the eyes of the Lord.

(Verse 19) Philemon is indebted to Paul for his salvation, a point Paul presses by pretending to dismiss it.

(Verse 22) By inviting himself to stay at Philemon's house, Paul does him an honor. He also gets an opportunity to observe how Onesimus is being treated.

Conclusion: (Verses 23–24) By conveying the best wishes of these colleagues, Paul implies their support for his appeal.

(Verse 25) Paul closes with a blessing.

Thessalonians and Galatians

PAUL WROTE WHAT ARE LIKELY THE OLDEST NEW TESTAMENT BOOKS: 1 THESSALONIANS
AND GALATIANS. TOGETHER THEY PROVIDE A VIVID PICTURE OF THE EMERGING GENTILE CHURCH.

The Book of Acts tells us about an incident that changed the future course of Christianity. Having gone over a thousand miles into his second missionary journey and about to head back toward home, Paul stopped over in the port city of Troas on the western edge of Asia Minor. One night he had a vision in which a man pleaded with him to cross the Aegean Sea to Macedonia. Interpreting the dream as a sign from God that he should "proclaim the good news to them [Acts 16:10]," Paul set sail immediately.

Europe The Apostle was in Philippi only a short time when residents charged him with disturbing the peace and he was forced to leave. He proceeded on to Thessalonica, capital of and largest city in the Roman province of Macedonia. There he preached in the synagogue and attracted a number of converts. But once the full implications of his message became apparent, riots broke out. A mob rushed the house where Paul and his co-workers were staying, and after failing to find the missionaries, they dragged Paul's host before the city officials. This man, they said, was abetting traitors who claimed Jesus as their king, a direct affront to Caesar. Paul left town. However, he had already succeeded in converting numerous "God-fearing" Gentiles and pagans and some Jews as well.

Paul traveled next to Athens and then to Corinth, where he remained for a year and a half. While there he received reports about the fledgling assembly of Christians he had left behind in Thessalonica. It seems they were grappling with perplexing questions about their new faith and needed his counsel. Paul's solution was innovative: he educated and nurtured the congregation through letters. Thus he was able to further his missionary work in Thessalonica without being there in person.

The First Letter Along with his companions Timothy and Silas, Paul wrote what many scholars believe to be his first letter, to the Thessalonians, about A.D. 50. The message seems meant to boost the morale of church members. It begins with praise for the community's "work of faith and labor of love and steadfastness of hope in our Lord Jesus Christ [1 Thessalonians 1:3]." Paul then discusses the community's anxiety over end times. Like other Christians, the Thessalonians

In the Letter to the Galatians, Paul describes his personal calling from God at the time of his conversion, shown above in a painting by the 18th-century artist Benjamin West.

eagerly awaited the advent of the Parousia: the Second Coming of Jesus and the Last Judgment. But they feared for their own salvation and especially for that of their deceased brethren. In the letter Paul states his high hope that the Thessalonians will be judged "blameless" by God and assures them the dead will obtain their salvation through Jesus, "who died for us, so that whether we are awake or asleep we may live with him [1 Thessalonians 5:10]."

A second letter to the community—sometimes attributed not to Paul but to one of his companions or to another, unknown author—

reiterates many of these same points, but the writer tries to correct his audience's impression that the "day of the Lord" has already arrived: "Let no one deceive you in any way; for that day will not come unless the rebellion comes first [2 Thessalonians 2:2–3]."

An Urgent Letter On his second journey Paul had established churches among the Galatian people in the heart of Asia Minor. But in the mid-50's, the Galatians experienced a crisis that threatened to undermine Paul's work in the region. The Apostle had told the Galatians that they need only have faith in Jesus to become Christians. Other missionaries contradicted Paul's teaching, however, by insisting that these Gentile converts obey Mosaic Law. It was an issue that had already been debated and decided in Paul's favor at the Council of Jerusalem in A.D. 49, described by Paul in Galatians 2:1–10.

Paul's Letter to the Galatians is an eloquent, often vehement, defense of his spiritual authority and the founding principles of his mission. He swiftly penetrates to the heart of the matter, dispensing with the customary opening expression of gratitude in favor of a stern rebuke: "I am astonished that you are so quickly deserting the one who called you in the grace of Christ [Galatians 1:6]." He next offers a brief account of his life, reminding the reader that God had chosen him to take the word to the Gentiles. He recounts his struggles to defend the principle that people stand innocent before God not by obedience to a law but "through faith in Jesus Christ [Galatians 2:16]." He uses Abraham as an example of one whose faith God counted "as righteousness [Galatians 3:6]." The Law of Moses, he argued, was intended to serve in the interim until the Messiah arrived. Believers are "called to freedom [Galatians 5:13]," he asserts, while the Spirit of God works directly in their hearts to transform their lives. ❖

The success of Paul's letter-writing ministry depended heavily upon the soundness of the Roman highways and the many smaller roads that cut through the empire. Stretches along a number of these roads, such as the one connecting Damascus and Aleppo, Syria (shown above), survive to this day— a testament to the highly skilled workmanship of Roman engineers.

Corinthians and Philippians

PAUL'S LETTERS TO THE CORINTHIANS AND THE PHILIPPIANS SHOW HOW THE APOSTLE'S RELATIONSHIP WITH THE CHURCHES IN THESE COMMUNITIES EVOLVED OVER TIME.

Paul toured the Mediterranean at a frenetic pace, rarely tarrying in a town more than a few weeks. But his stay in Corinth was different. Located near a narrow isthmus between the Aegean Sea and the Adriatic, Corinth was "master of two harbors," in the words of the first-century geographer Strabo. It was an ideal place for Paul to encounter travelers, who might take word of his teachings back to their native lands. He arrived in Corinth in the mid-50's and set up residency there for about a year and a half before he returned to Palestine.

Turmoil in the Corinthian Church Paul evidently wrote at least four letters to the Christian community at Corinth. The first is lost; it is known only by a reference in 1 Corinthians 5:9 and seems to have been a warning to church members not to associate with sexually immoral people. Paul dispatched the second letter (1 Corinthians) after representatives of the church wrote him to ask about Christian life and sent news of growing factionalism among their leaders. In the letter Paul called for unity: "Now I appeal to you, brothers and sisters, by the name of our Lord Jesus Christ, that all of you be in agreement [1 Corinthians 1:10]." The letter goes on to address the Corinthians' concerns about social issues such as marriage, life among the pagans, and propriety in worship. In an especially eloquent passage (Chapter 13) Paul

Paul hands a letter to Timothy in a 13th-century biblical commentary. Above, a codex page dated about A.D. 200 records 2 Corinthians 13:5–13.

When Paul reached the agora of Corinth, at the end of the Via Lechaeum leading from the city's port, he encountered a market, public bath, shops, the synagogue, and a temple of the sixth century B.C. dedicated to Apollo (shown above with the acropolis citadel behind).

TIMOTHY AND TITUS

Timothy, Paul's "beloved and faithful child in the Lord [1 Corinthians 4:17]," and Titus, his "partner and co-worker [2 Corinthians 8:23]," were the Apostle's most valued associates and his personal emissaries in the Greek-speaking world. Timothy accompanied Paul to Thessalonica and later took responsibility for the ministry there. He also helped the Apostle in dealing with the unruly Corinthians; but when relations with the church in Corinth deteriorated, Paul sent Titus to intervene on his behalf.

Paul's name has been attached to three letters—1 and 2 Timothy and Titus—called Pastoral epistles because they concern matters of church order. But the tone and style of the letters sound curiously unlike Paul's writing. Often basic terms, such as "faith," are used in a sense different from the other letters. Because of such variations many scholars have questioned Paul's authorship and have suggested that the Pastoral epistles were written by a second- or third-generation follower of the Apostle who was calling on Paul's authority to treat problems of his own day.

wrote that the greatest virtue is love, and that one who has no love has nothing. In answer to questions on resurrection, he replied, "As all die in Adam, so all will be made alive in Christ [1 Corinthians 15:22]."

Subsequently, Paul made a "painful visit [2 Corinthians 2:1]" to Corinth during which he was confronted by Christians from outside the community who had turned his own church against him. Some scholars maintain that Paul's next letter, which was written "with many tears [2 Corinthians 2:4]," is attached to 2 Corinthians as chapters 10–13. With the aid of Titus, Paul soon patched things up with the Corinthians, for he expresses great fondness for them in what some scholars consider to be a fourth distinct letter, 2 Corinthians 1–9: "I rejoice because I have complete confidence in you [2 Corinthians 7:16]."

Brothers and Sisters Paul founded his first European church in Philippi, an important stop on a major east–west road that cut through the Roman Empire. His first convert there was Lydia, a dealer in expensive purple cloth and a "God-fearing" Gentile, someone attracted to Judaism. At Lydia's invitation Paul stayed at her home; and after he had left, a congregation apparently met there regularly.

Like 2 Corinthians, the Letter to the Philippians may also be a composite. Paul wrote most of it while awaiting trial in prison, probably in Ephesus. In it, he urges the Philippians to meet their opponents with courage, reminding them of the good that has come of his own unfortunate circumstances: "I want you to know, beloved, that what has happened to me has actually helped to spread the gospel, so that it has become known throughout the whole imperial guard and to everyone else that my imprisonment is for Christ [Philippians 1:12–13]." The tenor of the letter changes abruptly in passages 3:2 to 3:3 as Paul condemns the proponents of circumcision. Then his tone softens. He urges joy and contentment and offers the Philippians his gratitude for the generous gifts they have sent him in jail. ❖

Romans, Colossians, Ephesians

A MASTERFULLY CRAFTED SUMMARY OF MANY CHRISTIAN BELIEFS, ROMANS IS PAUL'S MOST INFLUENTIAL LETTER. COLOSSIANS AND EPHESIANS GLORIFY CHRIST'S COSMIC POWER OVER SUPERNATURAL FORCES.

Just over a decade into his public ministry (probably in the mid-50's), Paul had completed his third missionary journey and was wintering in Corinth. He felt that his job was done along the Aegean and in the interior of Asia Minor, and he set his sights on Spain, where no Christian communities yet existed. But before setting out for Spain, Paul planned to deliver to Jerusalem the gifts he had collected among his Gentile churches for the impoverished Jewish Christians. He hoped to reconcile the Jewish and Gentile Christians, who argued over how Jewish traditions fit into the Christian faith. But tensions were high, and Paul knew he would find enemies in Jerusalem and that the Sanhedrin might arrest him.

Paul's Legacy to the Church Before leaving for Jerusalem, Paul wrote a letter to the church in Rome, introducing himself and requesting hospitality. "I desire," he wrote, "as I have for many years, to come to you when I go to Spain [Romans 15:23]." But the letter is more than a letter of introduction, it is an extended expression of Paul's faith and passionate trust in Jesus. Although it does not present a systematic theology, it does summarize many of the issues touching Jewish and Gentile Christians and Mosaic Law that had been important for Paul's work, and it gives the Apostle's views on many aspects of God's plan of salvation, including sin, grace, faith, justification, and redemption.

In Jerusalem Paul was welcomed by James and the elders, but he was soon arrested in the Temple and sent to Caesarea, where he was held as a Roman prisoner for two years. Upon his request for a hearing before the emperor, he was then sent to Rome, surviving a shipwreck on the way. When he arrived in Rome in A.D. 60, he finally met the Christians of that city, but as a prisoner. He remained under house

Paul lived under house arrest in Rome for about two years. In this painting, attributed to Rembrandt, the imprisoned Apostle is hard at work on a letter. The sword, seen here in the shadows, prefigures the Apostle's martyrdom; it is seen in nearly all depictions of Paul.

arrest; nevertheless, he was able to carry out his work with the help of John Mark, Luke, and others.

Last Letters When the imprisoned Paul heard that a speculative philosophy that combined elements of Judaism and asceticism was making inroads into the church at Colossae, he wrote to the Colossians exhorting them to believe solely in the supreme power of Jesus Christ, "the firstborn of all creation [Colossians 1:15]." He also wrote a letter to the Colossian Philemon, urging him to free his slave Onesimus as an act of love.

The Letter to the Ephesians seems to comment on and expand what is said in Colossians, and so many scholars believe that it was written shortly after. It may also have been a circular letter, sent to a number of churches. The oldest manuscripts do not identify any one church as recipient, nor are there any personal greetings at the end. The writer speaks of Christ's cosmic power over supernatural forces, and the new unity of Jewish and Gentile believers. He urges his readers to refrain from lying, stealing, and other immoral acts, and "do not let the sun go down on your anger [Ephesians 4:26]." Instead, "be kind to one another, tenderhearted, forgiving one another, as God in Christ has forgiven you [Ephesians 4:32]."

For some 1,700 years no one questioned that Paul wrote Colossians and Ephesians. But some modern scholars question their authorship, especially that of Ephesians, observing that each letter varies considerably from the writing style and vocabulary common in Paul's authenticated letters. They believe that one or more of Paul's close associates, such as Timothy, wrote the letters after Paul died, applying Paul's theology to new threats facing believers. These disciples would have signed Paul's name as part of a widespread practice among Greek and Jewish writers that honored their master and drew on his authority. Scholars who hold that Paul wrote both letters say the changes in theology show Paul was capable of growing and adapting. The wordy prose, they say, is a result of Paul's drawing from early church hymns and prayers—prevalent in both letters.

According to some scholars, Paul was tried and executed in A.D. 62. Others say he was released and returned to the Aegean area before being arrested again and executed in Rome in the mid-60's. ❖

At the great Greek amphitheater of Ephesus, silversmiths initiated a riot against Paul because he preached against the worship of Artemis and so threatened their livelihood—the selling of likenesses of the fertility goddess. However, Christians in Ephesus remained faithful to Paul, and later the Letter to the Ephesians was addressed to them.

Who Wrote the "Other" Epistles?

THOUGH THEY DIFFER IN ORIGIN AND PURPOSE, THE
NON-PAULINE EPISTLES ARE UNITED IN THE EFFORT TO AID,
INSPIRE, AND UPLIFT THE EARLY CHRISTIAN COMMUNITIES.

Peter, inspired by an angel, dictates a letter to his close associate Mark in this 11th-century ivory from southern Italy. Though Peter may well have written letters to Christian communities, many scholars believe it unlikely that the epistles coming down to us in Peter's name were written by him.

Paul was not the only early church leader to write letters of guidance to Christian communities. The New Testament includes a number of epistles written by others: Hebrews, James, 1 and 2 Peter, Jude, and 1, 2, and 3 John. (For an account of the Johannine epistles, see pages 174–177.) An epistle is a sermon or essay-like communication that adopts some of the conventions of the letter but is addressed to a large audience. The "other" epistles date from Paul's time to the early second century.

Hebrews and James The longest of the non-Pauline epistles is Hebrews, a detailed argument for the Christian message that exalts Jesus as the "great high priest [Hebrews 4:14]" who offers himself as a sacrifice for his people. Like the high priests on the Day of Atonement, Jesus enters the holy of holies of the heavenly temple to atone for his people's sins. According to Western tradition, the anonymous work was written by Paul himself. Yet nowhere does the text mention Paul or claim his authority. In addition, the style of writing and argument in Hebrews is so different from the style of Paul's letters that even in ancient times many scholars recognized that it did not come from Paul. Through the centuries, various New Testament figures—including Barnabas, Apollos, Silas, and Priscilla—have been proposed as authors, but the evidence reveals only that the author was a Greek-speaking Christian writing between A.D. 60 and 90 who was well acquainted with the Greek Septuagint translation of the Hebrew Bible. Even the title "To the Hebrews" is probably a conjecture, since other New Testament writings show that Gentile as well as Jewish Christians were concerned with the problems addressed by the work.

The Letter of James, which provides numerous practical lessons on the principles of the Christian life, has also sparked questions of authorship. The writer calls himself simply "James, a servant of God and of the Lord Jesus Christ [James 1:1]," but in the fourth century he was equated with James of Jerusalem. Scholars are divided on the accuracy of this attribution and date the epistle anywhere from the middle of the first century to the early second. Lacking a reference to a particular community, the letter is termed a "catholic," or general, epistle, and its address to the "twelve tribes in the Dispersions" suggests that it was directed either to Jewish Christians or to the church at large ("the new Israel").

Jude and Peter The author of the Letter of Jude describes himself as "a servant of Jesus Christ and brother of James [Jude 1]," leading to a traditional identification with the Judas who, with James, is called a brother of Jesus in Matthew 13:54 and Mark 6:3. But the letter apparently attacks a school of thought that claimed freedom from moral constraints against sexual libertinism. Because such a school arose after the time of the Apostles, many scholars date the letter to the end of the first century, too late to have been written by this Judas. Some venture it was written by an unknown Jude, held in high esteem in his time but lost to history.

The First Letter of Peter was written to sustain and inspire Christian communities facing persecution in Asia Minor. If the letter was indeed written by the Apostle Peter, as many scholars believe, these persecutions were probably unofficial localized outbreaks during the early 60's, when Christians came more and more to be viewed as an alien cult that rejected the life of pagan society. Other scholars believe that the "fiery ordeal [1 Peter 4:12]" of the letter refers to persecutions near the end of the first century, some 30 years after the Apostle's death. They hold that the letter was written in Peter's name by one of his followers.

The Second Letter of Peter takes the form of a last testament. The author identifies himself as Peter, even claiming to have witnessed Jesus' Transfiguration; yet, from its earliest mention outside the Bible, the authenticity of the letter has been in doubt. The letter is very different in style from 1 Peter, and in its central section, it seems to be closely dependent on Jude in content and wording. Parallels between Jude 4–13, 16–18 and 2 Peter 2:1–17, 3:1–3 are striking. Consequently, many scholars attribute 2 Peter to a Christian writing in the second century, in which case it was probably the last New Testament book to be written. ❖

The Letter to the Hebrews evokes events in the Old Testament such as the sacrifice of Isaac (shown in a French miniature from about 1350) to support its argument that "faith is the assurance of things hoped for, the conviction of things not seen [Hebrews 11:1]:"

Telling the Story of Jesus

IT WAS NOT ONLY THE STORY OF JESUS THAT LIVED IN THE MEMORIES OF EARLY CHRISTIANS BUT ALSO THE MANY PROVERBS, PARABLES, AND OTHER FORMS OF TEACHING HE PASSED ON TO HIS DISCIPLES.

"Each tree is known by its own fruit. Figs are not gathered from thorns, nor are grapes picked from a bramble bush."

(Luke 6:44)

It is hard to imagine Christianity without the Gospels that bear witness to Jesus; but for a hundred years after Jesus' crucifixion—and decades after the last of the four Gospels was written—most Christians knew of his teachings and deeds primarily by word of mouth. Jesus himself wrote nothing, and his circle of Apostles and perhaps hundreds of devoted disciples passed on his teachings orally. Hence newcomers to the faith were taught the sayings of Jesus and learned about episodes in his life through the oral tradition.

Remembering Jesus Acts 20:35 gives an example of how the memories of Jesus were handed down. As Paul bids farewell to some Christians from Ephesus, he exhorts them to support the weak among them, "remembering the words of the Lord Jesus, for he himself said, 'It is more blessed to give than to receive.'" This short proverb is quoted without any indication when, where, or to whom Jesus said it. As it happens, the saying, like many others known in those early years, was never included in any of the Gospels.

Only some 20 to 30 years after Jesus' death did Christians begin to write down brief collections of his teachings. The best-known is a lost collection called the sayings source, sometimes designated by the letter *Q* for *Quelle*, the German word for "source." The first of the four Gospels, Mark, was evidently written about 40 years after Jesus' death, when his early followers were aged or had died. Some time elapsed, however, before the Gospels were widely distributed and accepted, and as a result Christian writers in the first quarter of the second century still quoted Jesus' teachings primarily as they had learned them through the oral tradition.

The Gospels—especially those of Matthew, Mark, and Luke—reflect person-to-person retellings of Jesus' life. The accounts consist of segments, ranging in length from a sentence to a few paragraphs; they focus on what was important to instruct and sustain Christian communities. Very little of a personal nature about Jesus was kept; aside

The detail of a fruit tree, above left, is from a 15th-century tapestry.

from stories of his birth, only a single incident from the first 30 years of his life is recorded. None of the Gospels describes Jesus' appearance, voice, clothing, schooling, or a thousand other things a modern biographer would like to know about a man who changed history. Nevertheless, the character and conduct of this singular teacher come through.

Proverbs and Pronouncement Stories Jesus often cast his words in the form of proverbs. His disciples remembered, for example, how he urged them, "So do not worry about tomorrow, for tomorrow will bring worries of its own. Today's trouble is enough for today [Matthew 6:34]." He warned them further, "Do not give what is holy to dogs; and do not throw your pearls before swine, or they will trample them under foot and turn and maul you [Matthew 7:6]."

Wisdom teachers typically instructed followers that if they led lives of piety they would gain honor and wealth. But Jesus spoke of wealth as a threat: "One's life does not consist in the abundance of possessions [Luke 12:15]." He cautioned, "It is easier for a camel to go through the eye of a needle than for someone who is rich to enter the kingdom of God [Mark 10:25]." And he condemned those who, in the pursuit of honor, "like to walk around in long robes, and to be greeted with respect in the marketplaces [Mark 12:38]."

In an attempt to retain the force of Jesus' words as well as to make them clear and memorable, Christian teachers often described his teachings within their original settings. Brief narrative vignettes centering on a saying of Jesus, sometimes called pronouncement stories, are common in the Gospels. An example is found in the account of a controversy that arose after Jesus sat down for a meal with "tax collectors and sinners." The heart of the story is Jesus' reply to his critics: "Those who are well have no need of a physician, but those who are sick; I have come to call not the righteous, but sinners [Mark 2:15–17]."

*W*hen Jesus spoke in the Temple in Jerusalem— an event depicted in a 12th-century ceiling painting from St. Martin's at Zillis in Switzerland—"the whole crowd was spellbound by his teaching [Mark 11:18]."

Jesus told the parable of the Good Samaritan, who, by tending the wounds of a beaten man, acted more mercifully than a priest and a Levite (Luke 10:29–37). This letter was illuminated by Liberale da Verona for a 15th-century hymnal.

Until the Gospels became the authoritative record of Jesus' teachings, the Apostles, preachers, and ordinary believers kept the memory of his ministry alive with scores of such dramatic vignettes, prophetic proclamations, and wisdom sayings.

The Parables Jesus also used parables and other indirect means to convey his teachings. For example, instead of instructing his listeners to examine their own faults before finding fault in others, he asked them, "Why do you see the speck in your neighbor's eye, but do not notice the log in your own eye [Luke 6:41]?" Rather than extol the virtues of avoiding violence, he pricked his hearers' consciences, saying, "If anyone strikes you on the right cheek, turn the other also [Matthew 5:39]." When asked why his disciples did not fast he answered in simple parables. First he rejected fasting by asking, "The wedding guests cannot fast while the bridegroom is with them, can they [Mark 2:19]?" He then painted images—putting a patch on an old garment and pouring new wine into old wineskins—to communicate the freshness of his own work.

The Greek word *parabole*, used in reference to the Gospels, can mean anything from an image sketched in a few words to an extended story. At the core of each parable is an analogy: something unknown is illuminated by comparison with something familiar. On one level the parables are vivid stories that anyone might enjoy and then forget. But for those who, as Jesus said, had "ears to hear [Mark 4:9]," the parables were doorways to perceiving the reality of God's kingdom.

Extended parables occur in the Hebrew Bible as well, and in at least one instance Jesus used an Old Testament parable—the "Song of the Vineyard" in Isaiah 5:1–2—as the model for his own (the parable of the evil tenants in the vineyard in Mark 12:1–12). Jesus' longer narrative parables frequently involve a reversal of ordinary values or sta-

tus, a twist that caught the imagination and, as one modern scholar has said, would "tease it into active thought." The disciples related, for example, how Jesus revealed the grace of God through the story of a father who forgets his dignity to run to his returning prodigal son and then urges his resentful older son to share in his joy (Luke 15:11–32).

Certain ideas and themes recur in the parables. The kingdom of God, for example, is compared to a treasure found hidden in a field; it is a merchant intent on acquiring the best pearl (Matthew 13:44–45). The advent of the kingdom is like a sower scattering seed. Much of the seed falls on fallow soil, but the seed that takes root produces a great bounty (Mark 4:3–8). Jesus' story of a banquet showed the inclusiveness of God's kingdom: Many of the invited guests made excuses not to come, but the host sent his slave into the city to "bring in the poor, the crippled, the blind, and the lame [Luke 14:21]."

While Jesus was not alone in using images to teach, no other ancient body of instruction is so weighted toward parable. Some 40 of Jesus' parables survive in the Gospels of Matthew, Mark, and Luke and the noncanonical *Gospel of Thomas*. As the parables were retold, their original context was often forgotten; perhaps the parables that have come down to us are only outlines or summaries of longer stories that have been reduced to their essence.

Jesus' Deeds Jesus did so many things, says the Gospel of John, that "if every one of them were written down . . . the world itself could not contain the books that would be written [John 21:25]." During the

---

A 12th-century Italian enameled plaque depicts the parable of the evil tenants of the vineyard as it is related in the Gospels of Matthew, Mark, and Luke and the noncanonical Gospel of Thomas.

THE GOSPEL OF THOMAS

The *Gospel of Thomas* (title page shown above), a collection of 114 sayings attributed to Jesus, is one of a group of books unearthed at Nag Hammadi, Egypt, in 1945. The text identifies the author as Didymus Judas Thomas, a man later revered by some in the Syriac church as Jesus' twin brother. Most scholars believe this gospel may have originated in the first century A.D. It was recorded in Greek about A.D. 140 and was translated into Coptic by the fourth century.

The aphorisms, proverbs, and parables in the *Gospel of Thomas* urge readers to gain the wisdom needed to avert death and reunite with "the living Jesus." The gospel does not describe Jesus' death or resurrection, nor is it concerned with the coming of the kingdom of God. Though many of its features point to a development independent of Matthew, Mark, and Luke, 68 of its sayings find more or less close parallels in them.

With the words, "Lazarus, come out [John 11:43]!" Jesus raised the dead man from his tomb (shown in a 14th-century fresco by Giotto). Jesus' miraculous powers contrasted sharply with contemporary magic practices that used objects such as incantation bowls to ward off evil. (Aramaic incantation bowls of the 5th to 6th centuries are shown below.)

first century, Jesus' deeds were recounted side by side with his words. But
unlike the traditions of his teachings,
which were taken directly from his words
and forms of speech, the narratives of Jesus'
deeds originated with the disciples. As time passed
and these accounts were honed by teaching, they fell into patterns.
The tradition of the Last Supper, for example, takes much
the same form in Paul's First Letter to the Corinthians as it does in
the Gospel of Mark, written about 20 years later.

The narratives are almost always brief with a minimum of rhetorical expansion or dramatic flair. They emphasize the simple power of
Jesus, which needed no extravagant display.

Certain types of stories, such as the miracles, conform to an
underlying pattern. A healing narrative might begin, for example, with
Jesus encountering the afflicted person. A description of the disease
follows, sometimes stressing its duration (Luke 13:11), earlier failed
attempts to heal the condition (Mark 5:26), or else an observer's skepticism toward Jesus' powers (Mark 9:22–23). Next comes the healing
itself, usually effected by Jesus' touch or word (Matthew 8:3, 13, 15).
Occasionally, accounts of other wondrous events are related, as, for
example, when a woman touched Jesus' garment and was healed
(Mark 5:28-29) or when Jesus cured a man of blindness by applying
mud to his eyes (John 9:6). The story then offers tangible proof of

An account of Jesus washing the disciples' feet is illustrated in a 16th-century woodcut by Albrecht Dürer.

Jesus' success: a paralyzed man walking (Mark 2:12) or a dead child awakening as if from sleep (Mark 5:42). Lastly there is a description of the awed response of witnesses to the astounding recovery (Mark 2:12) and often Jesus' instruction to the witnesses or to the healed person or persons that they keep silent about it (Mark 5:43).

Passion and Birth Narratives The narrative of Jesus' trial, crucifixion, and resurrection was probably the earliest extensive portion of the Gospel story to take shape. It survives in several apparently independent versions that may have originated in different regions. The same version is found in the Gospels of Mark and Matthew; another is given in the Gospel of Luke; a third, in the Gospel of John; and a fourth, in the fragmentary noncanonical work called the *Gospel of Peter*. All share the same basic story but include distinctive elements and a characteristic emphasis. Mark and Matthew describe Jesus' trial taking place at night before the Sanhedrin and have him cry, "My God, my God, why have you forsaken me?" The version in Luke includes Jesus' trial before Herod Antipas, his conversation with the repentant thief, and incidents omitted by the other Gospel writers. John treats of Jesus' extended trial before Pilate and gives a different date for the crucifixion—the day before Passover instead of Passover itself.

Probably the last of the traditions to come into final form were the birth narratives, which are found only in the Gospels of Matthew and Luke. Here, as with the Passion, two distinct traditions developed in different regions. The accounts share basic elements but diverge in the details. Both authors employ literary devices found in the Hebrew Scriptures (for example, genealogies, dream narratives, hymns, and appearances of angels).

Thus close examination of the Gospels reveals something of the narrative development that preceded their writing. Their shape was molded by the dedicated labor of Christian followers and teachers, passing along their loving memories of Jesus. ❖

Jesus stilled the tempest that arose on the Sea of Galilee "and there was a dead calm [Matthew 8:26]." The miracle is shown in a stained-glass window of the 16th century.

Language of the New Testament

THE CHRISTIAN SCRIPTURES WERE WRITTEN IN GREEK, A LANGUAGE COMMON TO PAGANS, JEWS, AND THE FOLLOWERS OF JESUS.

A picture painted in the 17th century by José Ribera shows Peter and Paul engaged in an animated discussion of a passage of Scripture written in Greek on the unfurled scroll before them.

There were four languages current in Palestine during the centuries when the books of the New Testament were written. Hebrew survived as the language of Jewish worship and scholarship, but the everyday language was Aramaic, which was probably spoken by Jesus. Latin came with the Romans in the first century B.C. and was used in imperial proclamations and inscriptions. And Greek—promoted by the Romans as the common tongue of their farflung empire—was the primary language of commerce, literature, and government in the eastern part of the Roman Empire.

The *koine,* or common, Greek of this period was a hybrid of regional dialects dating from the time of Alexander the Great. When, in the first century A.D., the Jews were dispersed to regions outside their native Palestine, they adopted the Greek tongue in order to communicate in their new surroundings. Some Diaspora Jews abandoned Hebrew and Aramaic altogether.

Christian Scriptures The books of the New Testament were written entirely in Greek between the years A.D. 50 and 100. The quality of Greek varies widely, from the elevated *koine* of the Letter to the Hebrews to the almost colloquial language of the Book of Revelation.

There are several reasons why Greek became the language of the Christian Scriptures. One is that Christians followed convention by writing in the language of their literary contemporaries. Another is that the Hebrew Bible inherited by the early Christians and used in the emergent church was the translation into Greek known as the Septuagint. When Christians quoted from the Old Testament, they invariably took their wording from the Septuagint.

Christian writers also wrote in Greek in the hope of reaching a wide audience, both in Palestine and among the communities of Greek-speaking Jews and Gentiles that were scattered throughout the

Letter	Name	Letter	Name
Α α	alpha	Ν ν	nu
Β β	beta	Ξ ξ	xi
Γ γ	gamma	Ο ο	omicron
Δ δ	delta	Π π	pi
Ε ε	epsilon	Ρ ρ	rho
Ζ ζ	zeta	Σ σ, ς	sigma
Η η	eta	Τ τ	tau
Θ θ	theta	Υ υ	upsilon
Ι ι	iota	Φ φ	phi
Κ κ	kappa	Χ χ	chi
Λ λ	lambda	Ψ ψ	psi
Μ μ	mu	Ω ω	omega

Greek Word	Transliteration	Translation
ʼΑΠΟΣΤΟΛΟΣ	apostolos	Apostle
ʼΕΠΙΣΚΟΠΟΣ	episcopos	bishop
ΘΕΟΣ	theos	God
ʼΙΗΣΟΥΣ	Iesous	Jesus
ΜΥΣΤΗΡΙΟΝ	mysterion	mystery
ΡΑΒΒΙ	rabbi	master
ΧΡΙΣΤΟΣ	christos	Messiah

The chart to the left shows, at top, the Greek letters and their names. Below the alphabet is a sampling of Greek words used in the Bible. Although both majuscule and minuscule characters are shown in the chart, early manuscripts used mainly majuscule letters as shown in the sample words given below.

Pilate's trilingual inscription, "Jesus of Nazareth, the King of the Jews," appears on the cross above Jesus' head in this detail from a 1620 painting by Peter Paul Rubens.

empire. Paul, for instance, wrote all his letters in Greek, whether to churches in Macedonia, Asia Minor, or Rome.

The books of the New Testament also contain ample evidence of the multilingual culture of their readers. It shows up in the Aramaic, Hebrew, and even Latin phrases, uses, constructions, and occasional words found in the texts. The most striking example occurs in the Gospel of John account of Jesus' crucifixion: Pontius Pilate ordered the making of a sign to be inscribed and hung on the cross, which read, "Jesus of Nazareth, the King of the Jews"—written "in Hebrew, in Latin, and in Greek [John 19:19-21]." ❖

The Gospel of Mark

PORTIONS OF THE STORY OF JESUS HAD BEEN RECITED ALOUD THOUSANDS OF TIMES, BUT UNTIL MARK NO ONE HAD CREATED A SINGLE NARRATIVE OF JESUS' LIFE AND MESSAGE.

Mark contemplates his Gospel in a ninth-century French illumination. The evangelist's symbol, above right, is a detail from the ceiling of San Francesco Cathedral, Montefalco, Italy. Since the second century a symbol deriving from one of the "four living creatures" of Ezekiel 1:10 has been paired with each of the evangelists, according to a passage near the start of his Gospel. Mark's lion corresponds to the roar of the "voice of one crying out in the wilderness [Mark 1:3]."

One of the pivotal events in the history of Christianity occurred when a Christian put pen to papyrus and wrote in Greek, "The beginning of the good news of Jesus Christ, the Son of God [Mark 1:1]." The name of this Christian who wrote the Gospel According to Mark is uncertain. The second-century bishop Papias identified him as John Mark, a young associate of the Apostle Peter. According to Papias, John Mark had served as Peter's interpreter in Rome and based his Gospel on Peter's preaching. Another early Christian writer claimed that the Gospel was written in Alexandria, Egypt. The Gospel itself gives no indication of either author or place of composition. But the Gospel writer's explanation of Jewish practices, his use of translated Aramaic words, and his unfamiliarity with Palestinian geography all point to someone not native to Palestine writing for a Gentile audience. The Gospel of Mark was most likely written about A.D. 70, the year the Romans destroyed the Temple.

Whoever Mark was, the importance of his Gospel can hardly be exaggerated. In it he united the traditions of Jesus as wise teacher and miracle worker and linked them to an account of his crucifixion.

Confessions of Faith The Gospel of Mark relates the drama of how Jesus' listeners come to recognize him as Christ, the Messiah. The Gospel's opening confession of "Jesus Christ, the Son of God" is affirmed by God at Jesus' baptism—"You are my Son, the Beloved [Mark 1:11]"—and by a man possessed by a demon—"I know who you are, the Holy One of God [Mark 1:24]." The identity of Jesus as Messiah becomes apparent as he calls the disciples, teaches, heals, and performs other miraculous deeds. But Jesus, unlike the anticipated Messiah, is on the road to rejection and death, not glory.

Mark explores the difficulty of faith in this doomed Messiah—one who came "to give his life as a ransom for many [Mark 10:45]"—chiefly through the disciples. For, though they were close to Jesus' ministry, the disciples often failed to grasp its meaning. They did not understand the parables, and Jesus' deeds often provoked their fear rather than faith. Only near the end of Jesus' Galilean ministry does Peter confess, "You are the Messiah [Mark 8:29]." Mark reveals, however, that Peter's definition of *Messiah* allowed no room for the suffering and violent death that were to befall Jesus.

For Mark, like Paul who wrote before him, the cross lies at the heart of the Christian message. By the third chapter of his Gospel, Mark describes the beginnings of a plot to kill Jesus, and Jesus predicts his own death three times. Fully a third of the Gospel is devoted to the last week of Jesus' life as Mark carries the reader through Jesus' triumph and reversal. The reader overhears Jesus pray to God in Gethsemane to "remove this cup from me [Mark 14:36]" and witnesses Jesus' submission to God's will. Then, out of the utter desolation of Jesus' crucifixion, emerges a realization of his identity: The centurion who carried out the execution cries, "Truly this man was God's Son [Mark 15:39]!"

The agony suffered by Jesus as he carried the cross to Calvary is made palpable in this 16th-century painting by El Greco.

Different Endings In the earliest extant Bible codices on parchment, dating from the fourth century, Mark's Gospel ends with the women who visited Jesus' tomb saying "nothing to anyone, for they were afraid [Mark 16:8]." This abrupt and negative ending, which reflects the version of the Gospel inherited by the early church, has troubled readers since that time. A second-century Christian writer drew on the other Gospels and the Acts of the Apostles to compose a new, longer ending. Another writer composed a two-sentence ending that has survived in only half a dozen Greek manuscripts. The longer appendix gradually gained popularity, and from the fifth century on most copies of Mark's Gospel included it, some with a few further additions.

Scholars are divided over whether the abrupt ending was intended or is the result of a mishap. Did Mark collapse and die in mid-sentence? Was his scroll torn en route to the copyist? Any lost ending was apparently lost by the time Matthew and Luke read Mark, as their wording coincides with Mark and each other up to that passage but then diverges. Most scholars accept 16:8 as the original ending, arguing that Mark is again showing the difficulty of comprehending God's intervention in the world. ❖

The Gospel of Matthew

THE GOSPEL OF MATTHEW RELIES ON MARK'S NARRATIVE BUT DRAMATICALLY INTERWEAVES NEW MATERIAL THROUGH A SERIES OF FIVE LENGTHY SPEECHES BY JESUS.

Matthew's symbol is a winged human being because his Gospel begins with a genealogy of Jesus, "the son of David, the son of Abraham [Matthew 1:1]." The symbol is shown here in a ceiling painting from San Francesco Cathedral, Montefalco, Italy.

By the 14th century, when Theodoric of the Bohemian school painted his portrait of Matthew, shown at right, the convention was to represent the Apostle as bearded and pensive.

After Christians began to copy down Mark's Gospel and disseminate it among the scattered churches, other disciples were inspired to write the accounts of Jesus that had been lovingly handed on from the first generation of believers by word of mouth. Two of the great works that were inspired by Mark's Gospel have survived—the Gospels of Matthew and Luke.

Many scholars believe that the Gospel According to Matthew was written in or near Antioch, Syria, about A.D. 85. The Gospel itself says nothing about its author, who is generally considered to be an unknown Hebrew Christian or Gentile believer. The tradition that the Apostle Matthew wrote this Gospel originates with the second-century bishop Papias, who claimed that Matthew compiled "the oracles [of Jesus] in the Hebrew language." But Papias' statement is puzzling. The word *oracles* implies not a Gospel but sayings, and our Gospel of Matthew was written not in Hebrew but in the Greek language and it was based on Greek sources. Some have speculated that Papias was referring to a collection of sayings that predates our Gospels.

Mark's Example The author of Matthew took much of his material from the Gospel of Mark, but he also drew from oral traditions about Jesus; from the sayings source, or *Q*, which had been in circulation for 30 years or more; and perhaps from other written documents. Matthew's writer used the narrative in Mark as a framework for his own story, then revised the wording and expanded and rearranged events from the other sources to bring his own message into focus.

The writer added the teaching traditions not found in Mark's Gospel in the form of a series of discourses. Each of these five discourses concludes with a phrase such as "when Jesus had finished saying these things [Matthew 7:28]," marking the transition back to narrative. Thus Matthew's account of Jesus' ministry moves in a stately cadence, alternating speech and action, word and deed, teaching and narrative.

According to Matthew The Gospel of Matthew opens with a birth narrative, distinctive to Matthew, that introduces Jesus as "'Emmanuel,' which means, 'God is with us' [Matthew 1:23]." Jesus' ministry begins, as in Mark, with Jesus' baptism and temptation, his calling of the disciples, and stories of his preaching and healing. This material serves to introduce the first great discourse in Matthew, the Sermon on the Mount, which sets forth the heart of Jesus' message—calling people to seek "first the kingdom of God and his righteousness [Matthew 6:33]." Nine miracle stories follow, taken from various places in Mark and linked together in three groups of three. The miracles highlight the power of Jesus' words and deeds and reinforce the theme of discipleship, which is the subject of the second of the five added discourses.

A series of controversies and false accusations comes next, ending with the third discourse, which is on the parables. The narrative that follows focuses on Jesus' identity as revealed through his power to feed and heal and his role as the suffering Messiah and Son of God. The fourth discourse is on reconciliation. In Jerusalem, Jesus' confrontations with Temple authorities lead to warnings against hypocrisy (not found in Mark). Then comes the Markan material on the end times, followed by Matthew's extended discourse on the subject.

In the climactic account of Jesus' final hours, Matthew follows Mark closely but with changes in detail. He transforms Mark's ending by including memories of Jesus' resurrection appearances and his command to the disciples to take his message to all nations. The Gospel concludes with Jesus' promise, "Remember, I am with you always, to the end of the age [Matthew 28:20]."

Matthew's Gospel proved to be powerful indeed. It was placed first in the New Testament canon, and in later centuries Matthew's was the Gospel most often quoted by Christian writers. ❖

The Gospel of Matthew gives the only New Testament account of the flight into Egypt, an event said to fulfill God's word that "out of Egypt I called my son [Hosea 11:1]." The subject, shown here in a painting by the 15th-century Italian Cosimo Tura, proved popular in art.

169

The Gospel of Luke and Acts

IN HIS TWO-PART GOSPEL, LUKE PORTRAYS GOD AS OFFERING SALVATION TO ALL PEOPLE, WHETHER JEW OR GENTILE, MAN OR WOMAN, RICH OR POOR, PRIVILEGED OR OUTCAST.

A winged ox is used to represent Luke because his Gospel begins with a sacrifice by the priest Zechariah. The emblem at right is from the ceiling of San Francesco Cathedral, Montefalco, Italy. The image of Luke shown below is a detail from a 13th-century Armenian Gospel.

In the Gospels of Mark and Matthew the narratives are limited to Jesus' life. The writings of Luke, however, combine the story of Jesus with that of the early Christians. Although the New Testament splits Luke's work into the Gospel According to Luke and the Acts of the Apostles, common themes unite the two volumes into a single narrative. The great, overarching theme of Luke-Acts is how the ever faithful God brought his people from the traditional ways of Israel's piety to the new universal faith that was spreading rapidly among the Gentiles. Luke begins his Gospel narrative at the very heartbeat of Israel's faith—inside the Temple sanctuary, where the priest Zechariah is offering incense to the Lord. Through two volumes Luke lets his readers see how God's intervention and miraculous power moved the course of events step by step from Jerusalem, the Jewish capital, to Rome, the center of Gentile power, and to Paul's statement at the end of Acts, "This salvation of God has been sent to the Gentiles; they will listen [Acts 28:28]."

Authorship and Sources As with the other Gospels, Luke-Acts names no author, but in the second century it was attributed to Luke, whom Paul called "the beloved physician [Colossians 4:14]." Although unprovable, the attribution is generally accepted.

Luke does not say where he was doing his writing, but he was probably among Gentile Christians in one of the churches mentioned in Acts. Although he writes with a broad view to the whole church, he shows no specific knowledge of Christians in North Africa, Egypt, or eastern Syria, among other places. Scholars are divided on the date of the writing of Luke-Acts, hypothesizing anywhere from after A.D. 70 to about A.D. 90.

In the prologue to his Gospel, Luke portrays himself as one of many who have "set down an orderly account of the events that have been fulfilled among us [Luke 1:1]." Among the other accounts were evidently Mark's Gospel and the sayings source, or Q, both of which Matthew also used, but about half of Luke's Gospel is unique to Luke and apparently based on other sources. No sources for Acts are known, but in three passages (Acts: 16:10–17; 20:5–21:18; and 27:1–28:16) the narrative inexplicably switches from third person to first. In these "we-passages"—all of which describe sea voyages—the author is apparently either writing from personal experience or using a source that was written as a first-person narrative.

Gospel of Luke Like Matthew, Luke chose to use the Gospel of Mark as the basic outline of his own Gospel and to add material to it. Again as in Matthew, Luke began his Gospel with a narrative of Jesus' birth and ended it with one of Jesus' resurrection appearances (both quite different from Matthew's). Between these brackets of birth and resurrection, however, Matthew and Luke followed different practices in expanding Mark's narrative. Matthew brought most of his added material together in five thematic discourses by Jesus, but Luke put his extra material in two large sections, each of which interweaves episodes of teaching and action in a continual flow. The first and shorter section (Luke 6:17–8:3) shows Jesus teaching and healing during his Galilean ministry. It includes Jesus' Sermon on the Plain, which corresponds to the Sermon on the Mount in Matthew, although it is much shorter.

The second, more extensive section begins where Jesus' Galilean ministry ends: "When the days drew near for him to be taken up, he set his face to go to Jerusalem [Luke 9:51]." Whereas Mark covers the journey south to Judea in a single verse (Mark 10:1), Luke expands it into nine chapters filled with wide-ranging controversies, teachings, and healings. Many of Jesus' best-known parables, including the Good Samaritan (Luke 10:29–37) and the Prodigal Son (Luke 15:11–32), are included here— and nowhere else. Little is said about Jesus' actual itinerary, but all the events that occur from Luke 9:51 to 19:44 are seen through the lens of Jesus' impending confrontation with death in Jerusalem. Through detailed episodes of action and instruction, Luke describes Jesus' ministry as moving in a purposeful direction from the provincial village of Nazareth to the holy and rebellious city of Jerusalem. There Jesus in his crucifixion and resurrection fulfills his role of prophet and Messiah and commands his disciples to wait "in the city" until they receive "power from on high [Luke 24:49]." Luke's second volume, the Acts of the Apostles, reverses that direction as the disciples journey from Jerusalem into "Judea and Samaria, and to the ends of the earth [Acts 1:8]" represented by the city of Rome.

This miniature from a 13th-century psalter combines the various versions of a Gospel story: Mark and Matthew tell of a woman anointing Jesus' head, while Luke has "a sinner" anointing his feet; according to John, it is Mary, sister of Lazarus and Martha, who pours precious oil over Jesus' feet.

Jesus is described as ascending to heaven at the end of the Gospel of Luke and again at the start of Acts, thus linking the books together; none of the other Gospels describe the event. The depiction of the Ascension at right is by the 15th-century Italian painter Andrea Mantegna.

Acts of the Apostles Although Acts focuses on a few major figures—Peter in much of the first half and Paul in the second, with segments about Stephen, Philip, and Barnabas—in many ways God, or the Holy Spirit, is the most important figure. At each major step in the story, explicit divine intervention pushes the human characters toward the goal God has in mind. For example, the Holy Spirit empowers Peter to preach to a multinational crowd in Jerusalem at Pentecost, inspires Stephen's confrontation with the authorities that leads to his martyrdom, and leads Paul on his missionary journeys to the Gentiles. In fact, the Holy Spirit is such a major force some have quipped that the work could be called the Acts of the Holy Spirit.

Luke makes no attempt to tell the whole story of the early church or to recount the lives of its heroes. Often he presents his material in the context of a speech given at a key point in the history, rather than writing a detailed narrative. Though Luke may have had source material for some of these speeches, most of them were probably his own summaries of what was at stake at that particular point in history. This method for interpreting events was common in ancient histories.

Even when Luke focuses on the heroes of faith, such as Peter and Paul, his interest is not biographical, and he feels no need to tell the reader the entire course of their lives or even how they died as martyrs. Though Luke admires Peter and Paul, his primary concern is the work of God. Stretching from the moment God sends his messenger Gabriel to Zechariah in Luke 1 until he brings his messenger Paul safe to Rome in Acts 28, Luke wanted his readers to understand the grand scope of "the events that have been fulfilled among us [Luke 1:1]." ❖

As told in Acts, early Christians were expected to share their wealth, but one couple, Ananias and Sapphira, withheld some profits from the sale of a piece of property. When Peter confronted Ananias with his lie, the man fell dead. In this detail from a fourth-century ivory, while Ananias is being carried out for burial, Peter questions Sapphira about the sale price; she also lies.

THE USE OF MARK'S GOSPEL IN MATTHEW AND LUKE

The authors of the Gospels According to Matthew and Luke used Mark's Gospel as a starting point and expanded it to build their own Gospels, sometimes rearranging events in the process. This chart shows, through color, the material that is found in Mark and the material that was added to the other two Gospels.

COLOR KEY

Found in Mark

Added in Matthew

Added in Luke

MARK

1 Baptism of Jesus; temptation; beginning of ministry; calling disciples

2 Healing and controversy

3 Calling the Twelve

4 Parables; stilling the storm

5 Exorcism; raising the dead

6 Mission of the Twelve

7 Trip to Phoenicia

8 Peter calling Jesus the Messiah

9 The Transfiguration

10 Trip to Judea; teaching

11 Entrance to Jerusalem

12 Teaching in the Temple

13 Prophecies of the end

14 Last Supper; arrest; trial before priests and scribes

15 Pilate; the Crucifixion

16 Empty tomb

MATTHEW

1 Birth of Jesus

2 Visit of Magi; flight to Egypt

3 Baptism of Jesus

4 Temptation; beginning of ministry; calling disciples

5
6 } Discourse 1: Sermon on the Mount
7

8 Healing; discipleship; storm; exorcism

9 Healing; authority of Jesus

10 Calling the Twelve Discourse 2: discipleship

11 John the Baptist and Jesus

12 Controversies; accusations

13 Discourse 3: parables

14 Death of John the Baptist; Jesus' miracles

15 Trip to Phoenicia

16 Peter calling Jesus the Messiah

17 The Transfiguration

18 Discourse 4: forgiveness

19 Trip to Judea; on wealth

20 On greatness, service

21 Entrance to Jerusalem

22 Teaching in the Temple

23 Warnings against hypocrisy

24 Prophecies of the end

25 Discourse 5: the end times

26 Last Supper; arrest; trial before priests and scribes

27 Pilate; the Crucifixion

28 Resurrection appearances

LUKE

1 Birth of John the Baptist

2 Birth, childhood of Jesus

3 Baptism of Jesus

4 Temptation; beginning of ministry; Nazareth sermon

5 Calling disciples; healing

6 On observing the Sabbath; calling the Twelve; Sermon on the Plain

7 Healing and teaching

8 Parables; storm; exorcism

9 Peter calling Jesus the Messiah; the Transfiguration; start of journey to Jerusalem

10 The Seventy; parable of the Good Samaritan

11 On prayer, Beelzebub, etc.

12 On wealth and greed

13 Kingdom of God; lament for Jerusalem

14 On humility, discipleship

15 Parables of lost and found, including the Prodigal Son

16 On faithfulness

17 On forgiveness, faith, the coming kingdom

18 Parables on prayer; teaching; healing

19 Entrance to Jerusalem

20 Teaching in the Temple

21 Prophecies of the end

22 Last Supper; arrest; trial before priests and scribes

23 Pilate; the Crucifixion

24 Resurrection appearances

The Gospel and Letters of John

ITS POETIC LANGUAGE AND ITS THEME OF LOVE MAKE JOHN'S GOSPEL ONE OF THE MOST POWERFUL AND MYSTERIOUS OF ALL CHRISTIAN WRITINGS. THE LETTERS SHARE THE GOSPEL'S LANGUAGE AND THEME.

John's eagle (shown in a detail of the ceiling of San Francesco Cathedral in Montefalco, Italy) symbolizes his location of the "Word" in the heavenly sphere, where eagles soar.

The most cherished verse perhaps in the entire New Testament is from the Gospel According to John: "For God so loved the world that he gave his only Son so that everyone who believes in him may not perish but may have eternal life [John 3:16]." In this passage lies the essence of the Gospel—the power of God's love, Jesus as the Son of God, and the salvation of humanity through belief in Jesus.

John's Gospel is the most distinctive of the four, representing an independent account of early Christian memories. But scholars cannot agree on who wrote it. In the second century, a tradition arose that the Gospel, along with the Book of Revelation and three letters, were all written by the Apostle John, the son of Zebedee, who is further identified with the "disciple whom Jesus loved [John 21:7]." The Gospel itself never names the author, stating only that its account is based on direct experience and eyewitness testimony. Two of the letters attributed to John call their author simply "the elder" (2 John 1; 3 John 1).

Few scholars today are convinced that the Apostle John wrote any of the works attributed to him. Some maintain, however,

The Gospel writer is shown seated on a throne within a monumental architectural setting in this detail from the early ninth-century Soissons Gospels, one of the most important books produced by the Court school of Charlemagne.

that there is scant internal evidence that John did not write at least the Gospel and that longstanding tradition should carry more weight in assigning its authorship to him.

There is not much more agreement concerning the Gospel writer's intended audience, but a widely accepted hypothesis states that he directed it to a group or several groups of Hebrew Christians in order to support them in conflicts with Jewish kinsmen over their belief in Jesus as the Messiah. The Gospel is generally dated about A.D. 90 to 95.

The "Spiritual Gospel"

All four of the Gospels tell how John the Baptist prepared the way for Jesus and describe Jesus' ministry and resurrection. But beyond these benchmarks in Jesus' life, the Gospel of John shares little else with the other three Gospels, called the Synoptic Gospels because they are closely related to one another.

As the author of the fourth Gospel himself notes twice, his narrative omits many of the deeds performed by Jesus. Among the events chronicled by the other evangelists that go unrecorded in John are Jesus' baptism and temptation, his teaching in parables and casting out demons, his transfiguration, the agony in the garden, and the trial before the Sanhedrin.

In contrast, the Gospel of John enriches our knowledge of the traditions about Jesus with stories left out of the Synoptic Gospels. John is the only canonical Gospel source for the raising of Lazarus, the meeting with the Samaritan woman, the washing of the disciples' feet, the doubting Thomas incident, and numerous other events. Only a single miracle story—the multiplication of the loaves and fishes—is common to all four Gospels (Matthew 14:13–21; Mark 6:32–44; Luke 9:10–17; John 6:1–15).

The Gospel of John gives a unique account of where and when Jesus taught. In the Synoptics, Jesus' ministry takes place almost entirely in Galilee and over the course of a single year—one Passover season. In John, the ministry is acted out over a larger geographic area, taking in Judea and Jerusalem with only brief stays in Galilee. The Gospel extends the ministry to three years marked by three Passover feasts and "a festival of the Jews [John 5:1]," usually interpreted as a fourth Passover.

The Gospel also departs from the Synoptics by describing two opposing realms. The realm of God (representing light, spirit, eternal life, truth, "above") stands against the realm of Satan (that of darkness, flesh, death, falsehood, "below"). Salvation graces those who, as Jesus urged, "believe in the light, so that you may become children of light [John 12:36]." And light, in the person of Jesus, reaches its greatest brilliance in John when Jesus is "glorified," paradoxically with his

The opening line to John's prologue ("In the beginning was the Word") inspired illuminators of the Gospel to create a highly decorated initial page. This example is from the 10th-century Codex Aureus.

WAS THERE A SIGNS SOURCE?

Many scholars believe that the author of the Gospel of John made use of a signs source in composing his first 12 chapters. This source is a hypothetical document that is thought to have listed miracles performed by Jesus. (The illustration to the right, from Queen Mary's Psalter of the 14th century, depicts the setting of the first sign, the marriage at Cana.)

Though no actual signs source survives, several features in the Gospel of John have caused scholars to argue for its existence. For example, the first two signs in John (John 2:11, 4:54) are explicitly numbered first and second, even though the text implies that Jesus worked a variety of other signs between them (John 2:23, 3:2). This suggests that the two numbered signs are part of a series whose numbering is only partially incorporated into the Gospel. Scholars have also noted that abrupt shifts characterize the first half of the Gospel, and that these *aporias* occur wherever the writer appropriated a miracle from the signs source. Thus the *aporias* mark the seams between the writer's own narrative and the words of the signs source.

But whether the signs derive from a source or from the author himself, they remain one of the distinctive elements of the Gospel's presentation of Jesus' ministry.

crucifixion. To a crowd of listeners in Jerusalem Jesus had promised, "And I, when I am lifted up from the earth, will draw all people to myself [John 12:32]." Thus as he faced death, Jesus prayed, "Glorify your Son so that the Son may glorify you [John 17:1]."

Signs and Pronouncements The Gospel of John begins where the others end—with a recognition of Jesus' identity. In the first chapter, Jesus is called "the Word," "God the only Son," and "the Son of Man," and various people confess him as "Messiah," "Son of God," "the Lamb of God who takes away the sin of the world," and "the King of Israel."

The meaning of these titles is explored primarily through Jesus' miracles, or "signs," for these pointed beyond themselves to Jesus' identity and "revealed his glory [John 2:11]." Chapters 1 to 11 of the Gospel are structured around seven such signs: Jesus changing water to wine in Cana, healing the royal official's son, healing a paralyzed man, feeding the 5,000, walking on the Sea of Galilee, curing a blind man, and raising Lazarus from the dead. These signs frequently serve to spark a series of incidents, as when the healing of a blind man in John 9 leads to the man being driven out of the community as a defender of Jesus. The formerly blind man experiences a genuine sign as he sees that Jesus was truly from God, while the religious leaders remain blind to that truth.

The Gospel's narrative is distinctive in stressing the potential of Jesus' encounters for revealing his identity and mission. Often, when Jesus converses with someone, he utters words that are mysterious or easily misinterpreted. His listeners, left puzzling over his meaning, are forced to seek a deeper understanding. At the wedding in Cana, for example, Jesus' mother tells him, "They have no wine," and he responds cryptically, "Woman, what concern is that to you and to me? My hour has not yet come [John 2:3-4]." He explains neither why he refers to his mother in this impersonal manner nor what he means by "my hour," but his words suggest that his life follows a divine plan.

Jesus' identity as the Messiah is revealed most strikingly through the "I am" pronouncements. Numerous extended discourses, taking up more than a third of the Gospel, begin with Jesus saying, "I am . . . ." The words recall God's command to Moses to tell the Israelites: "I am has sent me to you [Exodus 3:14]."

The phrase first appears when the Samaritan woman says, "I know that Messiah is coming," and Jesus answers, "I am he, the one who is speaking to you [John 4:25-26]." In the next 11 chapters seven proclamations of Jesus' divine identity follow, rich in their symbolic language: "I am," Jesus states, "the bread of life [6:35]"; "the light of the world [8:12]"; "the gate for the sheep [10:7]"; "the good shepherd [10:11]"; "the resurrection, and the life [11:25]"; "the way, and the truth, and the life [14:6]"; and "the true vine [15:1]." The statements and supporting discourses powerfully express the notion that salvation is possible uniquely through Jesus. When asked by the Apostle Thomas, "How can we know the way?" Jesus answered, "No one comes to the Father except through me [John 14:5-6]."

The Letters of John

The First, Second, and Third Letters of John reflect the struggles of a Christian community cut off from their Jewish heritage and engaged in theological struggles over the nature of Jesus. The first letter uses the same dualistic language as the Gospel, but the writer applies the negative side of these opposing forces to a group of Christians he terms "antichrists [1 John 2:18]." The group had broken fellowship with other believers by denying Jesus' physical nature and considering him so divine as to be pure spirit. The second letter continues along the same themes, and the third addresses the particular situation of a church that has come under the control of one Diotrephes, an opponent of John's teaching.

The letters provide insight into early understandings of the Gospel of John and illuminate its message concerning the nature of Jesus. The issue of Jesus' nature would dominate theological debate up to 451, when the dictum of the Council of Chalcedon stated that Jesus' divine and human natures were at once distinct and inseparable. ❖

The historical authenticity of Joseph Caiaphas—the Temple high priest who, referring to Jesus, said, "it was better to have one person die for the people [John 18:14]"—was reconfirmed in 1990 with the discovery of the Caiaphas family tomb and an ossuary bearing the high priest's name in Aramaic.

Present at the Apocalypse

CHARACTERIZED BY DRAMATIC VISIONS, COSMIC UPHEAVALS, AND STRANGE SYMBOLISM, APOCALYPTIC WRITINGS REVEAL THE WICKEDNESS OF THE DAY AND A RADICALLY ALTERED FUTURE.

The opening verse of The Revelation to John, also known as the Apocalypse, reads: "The revelation of Jesus Christ, which God gave him to show his servants what must soon take place; he made it known by sending his angel to his servant John [Revelation 1:1]." In the original Greek the word for "revelation" is *apocalypsis*, which also connotes "an unveiling." Because of the cataclysmic events foretold in Revelation, the word *apocalypse* has come to mean a world-shattering catastrophe.

John's book was part of a tradition of apocalyptic literature whose antecedents reach back to the Babylonian Exile, when Israelites were exposed to Persian ideas. This largely noncanonical literature flourished from about 200 B.C. to A.D. 200, a period when Jews and later Christians were frequently subject to attack and persecution. Though parts of the Books of Isaiah and Ezekiel resemble apocalyptic writings, the only true example of the genre in the Hebrew Bible is the visionary section of the Book of Daniel, probably written about 165 B.C. during the Seleucid oppression of the Jews.

In most examples of the genre, the writer assumes the identity of a biblical hero or prophet,

Revelation, like the Book of Daniel, prophesies the course of history. One of 90 tapestries executed in the 14th century for Louis, duke of Anjou, depicts the fall of Babylon (symbol of Rome) as told in Revelation 17:1–18:24.

such as Ezekiel, Baruch, Elijah, Moses, or even Adam. Through the voices of these earlier figures the events of the day are foretold and interpreted to show that history unfolds in accord with a divine plan. This outlook may have given comfort to readers, who could take heart in the belief that God's purpose would soon be achieved and a glorious new age ushered in.

Apocalyptic Times An important example of Jewish apocalyptic writing is *1 Enoch* of the Pseudepigrapha, a body of writings not included in the Bible or the Apocrypha. Probably composed between the early second century B.C. and the first century A.D., *1 Enoch*, like other apocalypses, can be called a prophetic fiction: it claims to reveal the moral teachings of an ancient biblical figure—Enoch, a descendant of Adam and the father of Methuselah. The book is a lengthy compendium of visions, symbolic similitudes, and wise counsel in which Enoch, in the company of an angel, makes a series of journeys to heaven and looks into the future.

Another noncanonical apocalyptic book, *2 Esdras* (also known as *4 Ezra* or *4 Esdras*), is told through the person of the lawgiver Ezra. It is a composite of Jewish and Christian writings. The Jewish core of the book was probably written in the bleak period following the Roman destruction of the Temple in A.D. 70. Like *1 Enoch*, the visions of *2 Esdras* assured readers that current injustices would be corrected and righteousness rewarded with the arrival of the second age.

A 15th-century French miniature by Jean Fouquet identifies John of Patmos with John the evangelist and shows him with his symbol, the eagle.

The Revelation to John clearly belongs to the tradition of apocalyptic literature, but it also stands apart. The writer speaks not as an ancient authority, as in other apocalyptic works, but in his own voice as a Christian teacher. Though the book has been attributed to John the Apostle, the text identifies the author as simply: "I, John, your brother who share with you in Jesus the persecution and the kingdom." John "was on the island called Patmos because of the word of God and the testimony of Jesus [Revelation 1:9]."

The author of Revelation was probably the person this prologue describes, a Christian named John whose preaching

*J*ohn addresses The Revelation to seven Asian churches that are suffering persecution. Chapters 2 and 3 include a letter to each of the churches (shown on the main map and located on the inset).

ended with his exile to Patmos, a small, rocky island in the Aegean Sea. The most likely date of composition is A.D. 90 to 95, toward the end of Domitian's reign when the Roman emperor harshly persecuted Christians. John's purpose in setting down his visions was to encourage the Christian churches of Asia to resist the allure of pagan culture, reject false teachings, and remain faithful under persecution.

Mysterious Symbols and Numbers John filled his visions with biblical language and allusions to Old Testament prophecies. For example, the four creatures surrounding God's throne are analogous to the creatures of Ezekiel's vision. Their song—"Holy, holy, holy"—recalls the song of the seraphim in the Book of Isaiah. The visions are also structured around significant numbers, especially the number seven, a symbol of perfection or totality.

At the beginning of John's quest the heavenly Christ dictates seven letters to seven angels of the seven churches of Asia: Ephesus, Smyrna, Pergamum, Thyatira, Sardis, Philadelphia, and Laodicea. By making the number of churches seven, John suggests that the letters also address the universal church. A spirit leads John into heaven, where he experiences marvelous visions that are patterned on numbers with varied positive and negative meanings.

The four horsemen of the Apocalypse—the first carried a bow; the second brandished a great sword; the third held a pair of scales; and the fourth, whose name was Death –are portrayed in an altarpiece of about 1400 from the workshop of Master Bertram of Germany.

In heaven John beholds God in his glory, holding a scroll with seven seals. None among the heavenly court is found worthy to open the seals except Christ. As each seal is broken, it brings a new vision. The four horsemen of the Apocalypse appear, symbols of conquest, war, famine, and death. The martyrs cry out to God for vengeance, destruction befalls the earth, and the triumph of God's people is revealed: The 12 tribes of Israel appear followed by a multitude of the saved, who "have washed their robes and made them white in the blood of the Lamb [Revelation 7:14]."

Silence falls as the seventh seal is opened, and then other visions follow. Trumpets sound—heralding destruction, persecution, martyrdom, and God's judgment on the evils of humanity—and the seventh trumpet proclaims the kingdom of God and Christ. This cycle of persecution, judgment, and triumph replays continuously throughout the book, each time viewed through the kaleidoscope of a different vision of John.

As the visions progress, they become more emphatic in condemning Rome, the enemy of all that is good. In chapter 13 the Roman Empire takes the shape of two hideous monsters born of Satan: a

The labels visible within the illustration include: CERUBIN, SERAFIN, SONI, ORES, TRO, NVS, SOL, hicsolobscurabitur etluna insanquine uersaest, hicuribou neodicebunt montibus cadozesupnos, ercollibus coo nite nos

When the sixth seal was opened,
"there came a great earthquake;
the sun became black as sackcloth,
the full moon became like blood
[Revelation 6:12]." These horrific
events are evoked in a 10th-century
copy of the Commentary on the
Apocalypse *by Beatus of Liébana.*

APOCALYPSE OF PETER

The *Apocalypse of Peter* is perhaps the most important noncanonical example of Christian apocalyptic literature. It is believed to date from sometime shortly after A.D. 132, the year Simon Bar Kokhba led a revolt against Rome in Judea. The unknown author of the apocalypse was probably a Christian living in Judea who perceived Bar Kokhba's mission as a threat.

Modern scholars have long been aware of the *Apocalypse of Peter* from references to it in Christian writings; but the first actual text came to light only in 1887, when a fragment written in Greek was found in Akhmim, Egypt. A complete Ethiopic version was uncovered in 1910.

In this apocalypse, Jesus reveals heaven and hell to Peter and the other disciples. The book's graphic description of the torments of hell, set against the joys of heaven, influenced many later writings, including Dante's masterpiece, *The Divine Comedy*. The *Apocalypse of Peter* was considered canonical by Clement, and as late as the fifth century A.D. it continued to be read in some Christian churches.

seven-headed beast from the sea, symbolizing the empire, and a beast from the earth, who compels men to worship the sea monster. The second beast is equated with the number 666, probably a play on the ancient numerical value of Emperor Nero's name.

In other visions Rome appears as a gaudy "whore" drunk with human blood and as the fallen city of Babylon, the haunt of foul spirits and beasts. A lengthy triumphal dirge in several parts celebrates the fall of Rome. The power behind the Roman beast—"the great dragon . . . who is called the Devil and Satan [Revelation 12:9]"—is at last overthrown when Christ emerges as "King of kings and Lord of lords [Revelation 19:16]." The Devil is destroyed and condemned to everlasting torment in a lake of fire and sulfur.

In contrast to Rome, characterized as a "whore" city lying in ruins amid a destroyed earth, are the victorious faithful and a new heaven and earth with "the new Jerusalem, coming down out of heaven from God, prepared as a bride adorned for her husband [Revelation 21:2]." God dwells with his people. All evil is past, and tenderness, beauty, and joy suffuse a paradise restored. ❖

Josephus

THE WRITINGS OF A JEWISH HISTORIAN PROVIDE VITAL ACCOUNTS OF EVENTS IN JUDEA BETWEEN THE TESTAMENTS AND OF JESUS AND HIS CONTEMPORARIES.

The first-century Jewish historian Joseph ben Mattathias, known by his Roman name, Flavius Josephus, recorded the sweeping story of the Jewish people, beginning with the biblical account of the Creation up to events in his own lifetime. Josephus provides our most extensive source for the history of the Jews in the first centuries B.C. and A.D., but like many Jewish works of this period, Josephus' writings were preserved because Christian scribes found in them matters of interest for Christian apologetics.

Life of a Survivor Josephus was born in A.D. 37 to an affluently priestly Jerusalem family. In his autobiography he described himself as a precocious youngster, boasting that, when he was only 14, Jewish teachers consulted him for advice on rabbinical law. Two years later he studied the teachings of several Jewish groups and then joined the Pharisees. But the formative experience of his life occurred when, at 27 years old, he was sent to Rome to win the release of Jewish priests who were imprisoned there. Even at this young age, Josephus displayed a gift for diplomacy. He obtained the priests' freedom by appealing to the Emperor Nero's consort, who sympathized with their plight.

Josephus returned to his homeland, where he found that resentment against the Romans was growing. He considered rebellion against Rome impossible and attempted at first to silence the rumblings. When a full-fledged revolt broke out, Jewish leaders turned to Josephus. They appointed him commander of the forces in Galilee, the obvious first target for the Roman legions under General Vespasian, who was attacking from the north. Galilee was deeply divided about the revolt, and most cities and villages offered the Romans no resistance. Josephus held out with his forces in Jotapata through a 47-day siege. In the end Josephus joined his surviving soldiers in a suicide pact; but he survived the experience, possibly by rigging it in his favor. After surrendering to Vespasian, Josephus prophesied that the general would soon be named emperor. When the prophecy came true shortly thereafter, Vespasian's son Titus took over the Roman forces, and

Roman soldiers march in triumph carrying plunder taken from the Temple after Jerusalem's fall in A.D. 70. This relief from the Arch of Titus in Rome (shown in a reconstruction) seems to have drawn inspiration from Josephus' eyewitness account of the triumphal procession: "Most of the spoils . . . were heaped indiscriminately, but more prominent than all the rest were those captured in the Temple at Jerusalem — a golden table . . . and a lampstand similarly made of gold. . . . The central shaft was fixed to a base, and from it extended slender branches placed like the prongs of a trident, and with the end of each one forged into a lamp: these numbered seven, signifying the honor paid to that number by the Jews." (The Jewish War)

Josephus, then part of their entourage, became Titus' indispensable aide. By A.D. 70, when the Romans attacked Jerusalem, the rebel forces in the city were divided into radical factions that had been engaged in a year-long reign of terror. Josephus stood before the Jerusalem defenders alongside 80,000 Roman troops and urged the Jews to surrender. "You are not fighting the Romans but God," he said. "God has deserted the sanctuary and now stands on the side of your enemies." After Jerusalem fell, Josephus traveled to Rome with the conquerors, never to see Judea again.

*A**n** engraving from the first American edition of the works of Josephus (published 1792) pictures the writer in the company of Moses.*

A Jewish Historian in Rome In recognition of his service to the empire, Josephus was granted Roman citizenship, awarded an imperial pension, and given his own apartment inside the palace. Thus generously provided for, he was free to pursue his scholarly interests. He produced two histories over the next 20 years, *The Jewish War* and *Jewish Antiquities*, the latter of which presented the entire history of the Jews. In these works the writer celebrated his Jewish heritage while presenting events in a way that was attractive to the Romans. For example, he attributes the origin of the Jewish revolt to fanatical groups reacting to the policies of some corrupt Roman officials who had been condemned by the emperor.

That so many of Josephus' writings have survived is owed above all to passing references in them to three important Christian figures: Jesus, his brother James, and John the Baptist. The early Church Fathers, notably Jerome, seized on Josephus' histories as independent corroboration of the messiahship of Jesus, and the works were transcribed and passed on. But questions have arisen as to the authenticity of the text on Jesus. Some of the language sounds out of character. Would Josephus really have called Jesus the Messiah? Is it likely that he would have spoken of Jesus' resurrection? Most scholars have concluded that third-century Christians, embroiled in a debate over Jesus' nature, probably embellished Josephus' depiction. Their transcriptions of Josephus became in part professions of their own deep faith in Jesus. ❖

Testimony on Jesus

Josephus and the Roman writers Tacitus and Suetonius (both writing in the early second century) are among the first nonbiblical witnesses to Jesus. Here is what they said:

Josephus:

"About this time there lived Jesus, a wise man, if indeed one ought to call him a man. For he was one who wrought surprising feats and was a teacher of such people as accept the truth gladly. He won over many Jews and many of the Greeks. He was the Messiah. When Pilate, upon hearing him accused by men of the highest standing amongst us, had condemned him to be crucified, those who had in the first place come to love him did not give up their affection for him. On the third day he appeared to them restored to life."

Tacitus:

"[The name Christian*] comes from Christ, who in the reign of Tiberius was condemned to death by Pontius Pilate."*

Suetonius:

"[Claudius] drove out of Rome the Jews, who were perpetually stirring up trouble at the instigation of Chrestus."

Shaping the Mishnah

WITH THE DESTRUCTION OF THE TEMPLE IN JERUSALEM, THE CODIFICATION AND EDITING OF THE ORAL LAW BECAME A NECESSITY.

Rabbi Akiba (about A.D. 50–135) was the most prominent Hebrew scholar of his day. Echoing Deuteronomy 30:20 on faithfulness to God, he wrote that study of the Torah is "life to you and length of days." He is depicted here in a 14th-century Passover Haggadah.

Angered by a succession of corrupt and oppressive Roman rulers and spurred by a rising tide of nationalism, the Jews of Judea rose up in rebellion in A.D 66. But they were no match for Rome's legions. One by one, Jewish strongholds were crushed and tens of thousands of Jews died or were enslaved. Jerusalem itself was captured in A.D. 70, and four years later the Romans took the last rebel bastion, the mountain fortress of Masada on the western shore of the Dead Sea.

The fall of Jerusalem marked a turning point in Jewish history. The Temple, the focal point of Jewish worship and the priesthood, lay in ruins, and an entire people was barred from returning to their holy city. The survival of Judaism no longer depended on the Temple or priests but on the rabbinical scholars whose teachings would keep the traditions alive.

Studying the Jewish Laws After Jerusalem fell, Emperor Vespasian permitted the rabbi Johanan ben Zakkai to set up a Jewish academy at Jamnia, a town west of Jerusalem near the coast. Johanan also established a religious court, the Bet Din, to rule, as the Sanhedrin once had, on Jewish spiritual and secular matters.

In Jamnia, the rabbi and his followers studied the written Torah and the oral law, both of which were believed to have been revealed to Moses at Sinai. Following in Johanan's footsteps were other outstanding scholars: Gamaliel II, an authority recognized by the Jewish community and Rome; Akiba, whose pupils and successors wrote the largest body of teachings; and Meir, the author of witty parables and fables who worked to complete the codification of the oral law.

The most celebrated of the rabbinical scholars—a man who, like Moses, was said to combine "Torah and political greatness in one person"—was Judah ha-Nasi. Judah was a descendant of the eminent rabbi Hillel and a learned teacher in his own right. Under his supervision, the long labors of the rabbis were finally brought to fruition.

THE TALMUD

In the 300 years following the completion of the Mishnah, rabbis in Galilee and Babylonia continued to expound on its precepts. These discussions, known as the Gemara, also include digressions on legal and nonlegal subjects, including stories about rabbis, stories by rabbis about characters and events in the Bible, medical treatments, and science. The Gemara was eventually combined with the texts of the Mishnah to form the Talmud.

There are two versions of the Talmud. The Jerusalem, or Palestinian, Talmud was completed about A.D. 450 and is the shorter and less developed of the two. The Babylonian Talmud, completed about A.D. 550, is the more logical, detailed, and widely accepted version. Study of the Law became the highest pursuit for a Jew, and Talmudic study remains central to Orthodox Jewish religious life.

Writing Down the Oral Law About A.D. 200, Rabbi Judah completed the enormous task of compiling and editing the Mishnah. Written in Hebrew, the Mishnah is the record of centuries of interpretation of the Torah, from the earliest oral judgments up to the written decisions of nearly 150 *Tannaim*, or teachers, active between about 70 B.C. and Judah's time. The laws instruct Jews on everything from proper celebration of the Sabbath to drawing up a contract to making donations to the poor. They also confirmed the permanence and sanctity of Israel under Roman occupation.

Judah and his assistants organized the Mishnah in six sections divided into 63 tractates (treatises) and 531 chapters. The first section, "Agriculture," contains laws on land use and produce. "Appointed Times" sets out the Hebrew calendar and the rules governing related observances. "Women" discusses laws on marriage, the role of women, and the family. "Damages" explains civil and criminal laws, "Holy Things" concerns Temple worship, and "Purities" lists the regulations pertaining to cultic cleanliness.

Serving both to complement and supplement the Torah, the Mishnah prescribed the application of the Law in day-to-day living. The regulations were seen as inviolable—each one should be followed to the letter. As the Mishnah itself cautioned, "Be equally conscientious in small as in great precepts, for you know not their individual rewards." The Mishnah laid the foundation for the rabbinic thought contained in the Talmud. ❖

Invention of the Book

THE BOOK AS WE KNOW IT TODAY HAD ITS ANTECEDENTS IN THE ROMAN CODEX, A PRACTICAL FORMAT THAT HELD SPECIAL APPEAL FOR THE EARLY CHRISTIANS.

Christians were among the earliest of ancient peoples to discard the 3,000-year-old tradition of recording literature on scrolls and adopt instead the codex, or leaf-book, format.

The link between Christianity and the codex is compelling: Every surviving New Testament manuscript or fragment, including some examples of the early second century, and most noncanonical Christian writings as well, comes from codices. By comparison, only about 14 of some 870 surviving non-Christian texts dating from the second century A.D are from codices.

The evangelist Mark is shown with inkpots and pens, copying from a scroll into a codex in a 16th-century illuminated manuscript from Moscow.

Birth of the Codex Long before the arrival of the codex, there was the notebook: two or more wooden tablets—called *caudex* from the Latin word for "log of wood"—pierced and strung together with ties something in the manner of today's three-ring binder. The tablet was hollowed out and filled with pigmented wax, and the writer inscribed the hardened surface with a metal stylus.

Corrections were made with the blunt end of the stylus, and by that method entire texts could be erased and the tablet reused. Since at least the second century B.C. Romans recorded every kind of thing—from poems to law codes and official documents—in notebooks.

Sometime over the next century thinner, more pliable parchment made

The oldest-surviving New Testament text is John 18:31–33, written in Greek on this second-century fragment from a papyrus codex.

A seven-leaved Roman wax tablet of the third century retains its Greek "shorthand" inscription—written with a metal stylus such as the one pictured—and the leather ties used to string the tablets together.

From an early date Christian scribes used enlarged initial letters to start new sections of Scripture, as shown in the exquisite mid-fourth-century Codex Vaticanus, one of the earliest entire Bibles extant.

from treated animal skins began to be substituted for the notebook's bulky wooden leaves. Several sheets of parchment were assembled and folded in half to create small notebooks called *membranae.*

Reed pens, some with metal tips, were used to write in parchment notebooks. The ink was usually a compound of iron sulfate and vegetable matter, to which a gum was sometimes added. This metallic ink adhered to animal skins better than the carbon-based inks employed for papyrus scrolls.

The move from the *membrana* notebook to the codex—made of several such gatherings of parchment stitched together—happened over time. But codices existed by at least A.D. 98, when the Roman poet Martial completed his *Epigrams.* In these verses Martial seems to say that bookshops were carrying codex editions of works by Homer, Virgil, Cicero, Livy, and Ovid. Under the heading "Homer in Parchment Handybooks," he notes: "The *Iliad* and the tale of Ulysses . . . lie stored in many-folded skins." Not long after Martial's writing, the papyrus codex was introduced, and the earliest surviving fragments of Christian codices are made of this material.

Christians and the Codex Scholars have tried to explain the apparent Christian preference for the codex in many ways. Some have suggested that Christians used the codex as a way of distinguishing their teachings from other, non-Christian writings on scrolls. Another theory holds that Mark the evangelist recorded his Gospel in a notebook and thus began the codex tradition.

But the early adoption of the codex by Christians is perhaps best accounted for by entirely pragmatic considerations. One advantage of the book format over the scroll was the book's compactness; for example, while the Gospel of Luke alone would have taken up about 31 feet of scroll, approaching that medium's practical maximum length, all four Gospels could be accommodated in a single codex. Codices were also highly portable— a special convenience for the peregrinations of the missionary life.

Handling a scroll could be awkward: a person unrolled one end while winding up the other. With a codex, the reader could flip to a marked passage and rest the book open on that page, and two books might be used side by side for liturgical readings. The ability to find a reference quickly was also an advantage in theological disputes.

But the codex had drawbacks as well. If the scribe writing on a scroll discovered that his text was running long, he simply attached fresh sheets of parchment to it. But the codex, by its design, required the scribe to determine in advance the number of sheets he would need. If he underestimated, he generally had to add an entire parchment sheet to the gathering of pages, and because of the way he had to fold the sheet and add it to the others, he would add blank pages at the beginning, where they were not wanted, as well as at the end of the gathering.

The sixth-century Rossano Gospels, a deluxe codex written in silver ink on purple-stained vellum, is the first known New Testament manuscript to contain miniatures. This page depicts Jesus standing before Pilate as an angry mob shouts, "Away with this fellow! Release Barabbas for us [Luke 23:18]."

A Special Commission In A.D. 301 the demand for parchment books was so great that Emperor Diocletian put a ceiling on the fees paid to scribes writing in books. Thirty-one years later, Emperor Constantine ordered 50 Bibles produced for the churches he was erecting in Constantinople. The books were "to be written on fine parchment, in legible manner, and in a convenient portable form, by professional scribes thoroughly accomplished in their art." Two magnificent Bibles have survived from the fourth century, the Codex Sinaiticus and the Codex Vaticanus—though these are probably not among the 50 that Constantine commissioned. The shift in the Western world from scroll to codex was virtually complete by the fifth century A.D. ❖

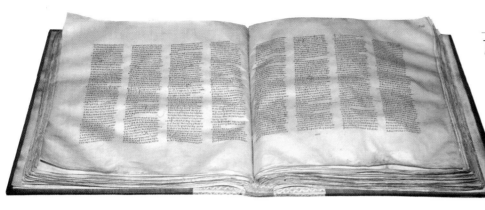

The arrangement of the text in the Codex Sinaiticus—in four narrow columns of 48 lines to the page—differs from the one or two columns per page common to most early codices.

A FOURTH-CENTURY CODEX

Perhaps the best way to understand how an early book was constructed is to take a look at a specific surviving example. The Codex Sinaiticus was rescued from oblivion in 1844 by a German biblical scholar named Constantin von Tischendorf. During a visit to the monastery of St. Catherine at Mount Sinai, something caught Tischendorf's eye: a pile of manuscript leaves lying in a wastebasket and about to be burned as fuel. They turned out to be portions of a fourth-century Bible codex, one of the oldest books ever recovered. After numerous return trips to St. Catherine's and with the help of intermediaries, Tischendorf obtained almost the entire book, which had originally contained at least 1,460 pages.

The Codex Sinaiticus contains portions of the Greek Septuagint translation of the Old Testament, all 27 books of the New Testament, plus the noncanonical *Epistle of Barnabas* and some of the *Shepherd of Hermas*. Its parchment pages, made from the skins of sheep and goats, currently measure 15 by 13½ inches.

Groups of four parchment sheets were layered so that the hair sides of adjacent sheets—and therefore their opposite skin sides—faced each other (see fig. 1). This arrangement of sheets was adopted for most parchment codices to give their facing pages a uniform appearance, since the hair and skin sides of parchment accept ink differently. The four sheets of parchment were then folded to create a gathering of 16 pages (see fig. 2). Gatherings were sent to scribes for copying and then collated and sewn together at the fold to form the final book.

The text in the Codex Sinaiticus is written in a remarkably uniform uncial script, a style of handwriting common for Christian literature up to the 9th century. Scholars have identified three scribal hands, distinguishable one from the other, in part, by their varying degree of spelling proficiency. Between the 4th and 12th centuries as many as nine "correctors" meticulously pored over the manuscript, fixing spelling errors and filling in careless omissions of text.

Fig. 1

Fig. 2

The restored portions of the Codex Sinaiticus show evidence that, on at least two separate occasions, different bindings were sewn to the gatherings of parchment with hemp thread and then further attached with glue.

Apostolic Fathers

SIGNS THAT MUCH NEW TESTAMENT LITERATURE HAD BEEN ACCEPTED
AS AUTHORITATIVE AS EARLY AS THE FIRST AND SECOND CENTURIES
APPEAR IN THE WRITINGS OF THE APOSTOLIC FATHERS.

Clement, bishop of Rome, is depicted celebrating mass in this detail from an 11th-century fresco in the basilica named after him in Rome. His influential letter known as I Clement was read along with Scripture at the church in Corinth as late as A.D. 170.

By the end of the first century, nearly all the works that would be included in the New Testament had been written. These and other Christian writings, including other gospels and letters, were circulated among the churches and read to growing congregations.

There was no official creed or universally accepted liturgy in the early church. Church leaders consequently looked to the writings in circulation for guidelines to what the church stood for and what its tasks should be. However, not all of the writings were considered divinely inspired or of equal value. As a result, writings based on the accounts of people who had known Jesus and had witnessed the events of his life firsthand took on a special role and were more likely to be considered authoritative documents of the Christian faith. By the early second century, Christians recognized that the tenets of the church must be defined and solidified if the church was to grow, and the need to determine which Christian texts were authentic (and which false) grew ever more apparent. Nonetheless, it would be a very long time before agreement was reached.

Notes of the Apostolic Fathers The best indication of which writings were accepted by the church in the late first and the second century comes from the writings of early church leaders—Ignatius, Clement of Rome, Polycarp, Hermas, and others, who are known as the Apostolic Fathers. In their influential epistles and treatises the Apostolic Fathers discussed points of Christian belief, often quoting liberally from the writings that they believed to be authoritative. Some of the writings of the Apostolic Fathers were read in churches along with passages from the Old Testament. For a time, these writings were themselves considered for inclusion in the New Testament canon.

Ignatius, the bishop of Antioch, wrote seven letters to various churches and to Polycarp, the bishop of Smyrna, about 107 on topics ranging from the importance of obeying church officials to combatting heresy. He was deeply influenced by Paul and in his writings borrowed freely from Paul, sometimes lifting entire sections verbatim.

In a letter known as 1 Clement, written to Christians in Corinth about A.D. 95, Clement, the bishop of Rome, pleaded for unity in the church in a time of strife. "Love admits no schism, love makes no sedition, love does all things in concord," he wrote. Clement's lengthy letter made clear his knowledge of the Gospels according to Matthew, Mark, and Luke, Acts of the Apostles, and the Epistles Romans, 1 Corinthians, Galatians, Ephesians, Philippians, 1 Timothy, Titus, Hebrews, and 1 Peter.

Like Ignatius and Clement, Polycarp quoted Paul and referred to him in his letters. In his epistle to the Christians of Philippi, written early in the second century, Polycarp asked the Philippians to read Paul's letters and "become edified in the faith which has been given to you." There are also portions from Matthew and Luke, and the letters of John and Peter in Polycarp's writings.

The Shepherd of Hermas

In an apocalyptic work called the *Shepherd* written about 140, a Christian prophet in Rome known as Hermas suggests his familiarity with the Book of Revelation when he uses the parallel imagery of the church as a woman and of the church's enemy as a beast. He also appears to have knowledge of the Gospels of Matthew, Mark, and John, and Paul's Letter to the Ephesians.

When taken all together, the evidence from these writers is compelling proof that much of the New Testament as we know it today was singled out as authentic by the beginning of the second century. However, it would be another two centuries before a canon of New Testament Scriptures was generally agreed upon. ❖

COLLECTED WORKS

In the 1930's a collection of 11 papyrus codices, or books, written in Greek was uncovered in Asia Minor. The find included the largest selection of early copies of New Testament writings that had ever come to light. Since then the collection—named the Chester Beatty Papyri after the man who purchased them—has furnished scholars with important information about the acceptance and use of the writings in the early church.

Prior to the discovery, for instance, scholars believed that the Gospels were circulated separately until sometime in the fourth century. But Papyrus I of the codices, which dates from the first half of the third century, contains the Gospels bound in the order of Matthew, John, Luke, Mark, and Acts.

Papyrus II, part of which is shown above, includes a nearly complete collection of the letters attributed to Paul. In it, Hebrews appears immediately after Romans, indicating that its authorship by Paul was not then disputed. Missing, however, are the Epistles to Timothy and Titus, which suggests that they may not have been accepted as Pauline or were simply unknown to the scribe.

The martyrdom of Ignatius, bishop of Antioch, is shown in this 10th-century illustration. Ignatius' seven letters were written while he traveled as a prisoner from Antioch to Rome, where he was put to death.

Role of the Bible in Early Christian Worship

OLD TESTAMENT READINGS WERE PART OF CHRISTIAN WORSHIP FROM THE START. CHRISTIAN WRITINGS WERE ALSO INSTRUMENTAL IN WORSHIP LONG BEFORE A NEW TESTAMENT CANON HAD BEEN FORMED.

There is very little record of how Christian worship was conducted in the earliest years of Christianity. From the end of the first century on, however, there are letters and documents from church leaders that give some details. Scholars believe that the earliest Christians, most of whom were formerly Jews, based their worship services on those of the the Jewish synagogue. In synagogues, reading and interpreting Scripture were central to worship. Selections from the Torah and the Prophets were read and psalms were probably sung at weekly services. The readings, arranged as a lectionary in a specific order, took three years to complete and were then begun again.

Readings The readings at services of Christian worship were not highly structured initially, although they became so. One of the earliest detailed descriptions of worship practices comes from Justin Martyr, who wrote from Rome about 155: "The memoirs of the apostles or the writings of the prophets are read as long as time permits." He went on to add that each reading was followed by a sermon that explained the

reading's message and its importance in daily life. Then all Christians who had been baptized celebrated the Lord's Supper by sharing a meal of bread and wine. This ritual became known as the Eucharist, from the Greek word for "thanksgiving." Initially it referred to the prayers said before Communion, but it eventually became the name for the communal meal itself.

In Remembrance The words Jesus had spoken at the Last Supper were recited during the Eucharist by the middle of the first century. The Apostle Paul repeats the words in a letter, describing how to conduct Communion. "[He] took a loaf of bread, and when he had given thanks, he broke it and said, 'This is my body that is for you. Do this in remembrance of me' [1 Corinthians 11: 24]." Originally the communal meal was extensive (lasting as long as several hours), but by the early second century, it had become much shorter. Although Communion services varied somewhat among congregations, they were all occasions of joy.

Just as in Jewish tradition, Christians assigned specific days of the week for fasting and for the

The third-century Christian, above, from the catacombs in Rome, holds his arms in the gesture of an orant, or praying figure. The name comes from orare, *a Latin word meaning "to pray."*

A relief from a third-century Roman sarcophagus, left, depicts the sharing of bread and wine. Objects used in worship had symbolic meaning. The light of lamps, such as the fourth-century example below, symbolized the splendor of God.

CHRISTIAN INSTRUCTION

Sometime in the last decades of the first century—although no exact date is known—a treatise was written to instruct Christians on how to worship. It is known as the *Didache,* or *The Teaching of the Lord Through the Twelve Apostles to the Gentiles.*

Variations in surviving *Didache* manuscripts show that Christian worship evolved over centuries and that it grew out of Jewish precedents. Like Jews, Christians are instructed to pray three times a day, according to the treatise, but, unlike Jews, Christians are told to make use of the Lord's Prayer.

In 16 chapters the *Didache* offers advice about fasting, prayer, celebration of the Eucharist, baptism, and the Sunday worship. It instructs on Christian behavior, at times quoting from Jesus: "If someone strikes you on the right cheek, turn to him the other too." And it sometimes reads like the gentle nudging of a spiritual leader. "If you can bear the Lord's full yoke, you will be perfect," it says, "but if you cannot, then do what you can."

Sabbath. Wednesday and Friday were chosen as the Christian days for fasting and penance because they corresponded with the days of Jesus' betrayal and burial. Sunday, which became the day of worship, was associated with the Resurrection and was consequently a day of celebration. Services of worship originally were held in homes.

Hymns and Prayers Scripture and other Christian writings were important sources for hymns and prayers. Hymn singing and the recitation of prayers followed the readings and the sermon. Among the universal prayers in the early church was the Lord's Prayer, taken from Matthew 6: 9-13. Conversely, an example of a liturgical prayer being quoted in Scripture is found in Philippians 2: 6-11. Early Christians continued the Jewish custom of reciting morning and evening prayers. In the *Apostolic Tradition*, Hippolytus, an early third-century leader of the Roman church, outlined the times for prayer as being in the morning, at the third, sixth, and ninth hours, and at night. The structure of daily prayer later developed as the Divine Office.

By the third century, Christians were pairing Scripture with particular dates in the church year. For example, during Easter week, people read from Job and Jonah because the two stories were considered Old Testament parallels to the suffering of Jesus. While Christians continued to revere the Old Testament because of its prophecies of a messiah, the Gospels also emerged as cherished writings because they told the story of God's fulfillment of the prophecies. "At the conclusion of all the Scriptures," said a third-century writer in the *Canons of Addai*, "let the Gospel be read, as the seal of all the scriptures; and let the people listen to it standing upon their feet, because it is the glad tidings of the salvation of all humankind." ❖

Christian Popular Literature

AMONG THE WRITINGS LEFT OUT OF THE NEW TESTAMENT WERE
MANY PIOUS ACCOUNTS, SOME OF DOUBTFUL VERACITY.

*Stories of Thecla and her triumphs
over persecution had wide appeal.
Perhaps a fictional character created
in the 1st century, Thecla was still
widely regarded as a saint in the
Middle Ages. Her portrait, above, is
part of a 12th-century fresco in a
church on Cyprus. Scenes from the*
Acts of Paul and Thecla *were carved
in the 12th to 14th-century cathedral
in Tarragona, Spain.*

As Christian writings and oral accounts circulated within the
early church, inspired listeners wanted to learn more
about the early years of Jesus and the lives of his disciples. In the second and third centuries A.D. a great
amount of material was developed in response to those interests.
These writings took the form of new gospels, apocalypses, acts, and
epistles, including one letter purported to be from Jesus himself.

By the end of the second century, church leaders had already
begun to label many of these stories apocryphal as they began to separate apostolic writings from more recent works. But the stories did
not necessarily disappear. Many of them were immensely popular and
were written down, translated, and passed along. These stories are of
great interest to scholars today because they provide a firsthand
record of the climate that fostered the young church, the piety of early
Christians, and the diversity of their beliefs.

Works About Jesus Some of the works may have been considered
for canonicity because they include Jesus' words or events from his life
that are not recorded elsewhere. Other stories were deemed doubtful
because they strayed from apostolic versions of events. Still others
seem to have been created purely to satisfy listeners' curiosity and to

give them a good story. The *Infancy Gospel of Thomas,* for example, purports to reveal miracles that Jesus performed as a child. It portrays Jesus as a vindictive boy who used supernatural powers to satisfy his childish whims. When he grew older and accompanied Joseph on carpentry jobs, the *Infancy Gospel* claims, Jesus used his powers to resize miscut beams. A writer identified simply as "Thomas, an Israelite" probably created this gospel in the second century. It was translated into at least 13 languages.

The *Epistle of Christ to Abgar,* which can be dated only from the early fourth century, takes a more pensive tone and is less concerned with narrative. It consists of a letter to Jesus from Abgar, a ruler of Edessa, requesting a cure, and Jesus' reply, assuring Abgar that though he himself cannot come he will send a disciple to cure him.

Tales of Mary and of Thecla   The *Protoevangelium* [First Gospel] *of James* describes the birth of the Virgin, her training in the Temple, and her marriage to Joseph. It appears to have been written to protect Mary's reputation against charges that Jesus was illegitimate. The author identifies himself as James, a stepbrother of Jesus, but errors regarding geography and customs in Palestine suggest it may have been written in Syria, where other stories about Mary were produced.

The *Acts of Paul and Thecla* tells of an 18-year-old woman who, on hearing the Apostle Paul's praise of chastity, rejected her fiancé in order to follow Paul. Many attempts to stop Thecla ensued. She escaped being burned at the stake when a cloudburst drenched the pyre. She was put in an arena with wild animals but was saved by a lioness. The authorities let Thecla go. She baptized herself and lived a monastic life, becoming famous for curing the sick and teaching others. According to one account, about the year 200, a church elder confessed that he had made up the tale out of devotion to the Apostle Paul. The man was forced to resign from his position apparently because his story clashed with Paul's teachings about marriage and women leaders in the church.

According to popular stories, Anne and her husband, Joachim, were an elderly couple when they learned that they would have a child, Mary. Giotto's "Birth of the Virgin" is from a series of frescoes depicting Mary's childhood in the 14th-century Scrovegni Chapel in Padua, Italy.

Early believers loved such tales, which entertained and offered moral teaching. Although the stories were not recognized as Scripture, they have been retold in Christian art and literature ever since. ❖

Map labels:

HIBERNIA

BRITANNIA
London

ATLANTIC OCEAN

GERMANIC TERRITORIES

Cologne
Rhine River
Trier

Seine R.
Paris

GAUL

Lyons

Loire R.

ALPS MOUNTAINS

Po River
Parentium

Danube River

DACIA

ILLYRICUM

THRACIA
Anchialus

BLACK

Astorga
PYRENEES MOUNTAINS
Ebro River

HISPANIA

Tagus River
Saragossa

Mérida

Córdoba
Seville
Cartagena
Elvira

BALEARIC ISLANDS

Marseilles

CORSICA

SARDINIA

ITALIA

Salonae

Rome

Puteoli

MACEDONIA
Philippi
Byzantium
Thessalonica
Nicaea
Nicomedia

BITHYNIA
GALATIA

GREECE
Nicopolis
Corinth
Pergamum
Athens
Smyrna

ASIA MINOR

Ephesus

SICILY
Syracuse

MALTA

MAURETANIA
ATLAS MOUNTAINS

Cirta Carthage
AFRICA

RHODES

CRETE

MEDITERRANEAN SEA

Cyrene

Alexandria

CYRENAICA

EGYPT

The Early Spread of Christianity

CONSTANTINE PROCLAIMED THE TOLERATION OF RELIGION, ENDING THE PERSECUTIONS THAT ACCOMPANIED THE CHURCH'S EARLY GROWTH AND DETERMINING THE COURSE OF CHRISTIANITY.

By the year A.D. 325, Christianity, which began as a minor sect of Judaism, claimed churches across the Roman Empire and had become the avowed faith of Emperor Constantine himself. Several factors help explain the rapid growth of the church. The first Roman emperor, Augustus, established a widespread and enduring peace. Greek was the common language. New roads and improvements to old ones made travel and commerce easier and safer. Under the pragmatic rule of the Roman emperors,

In the early years of the second century, as Rome made provinces of Dacia, Arabia, and Mesopotamia, extending the empire to its greatest reach, the young church was making its own quiet conquests. Christianity continued to grow, and by A.D. 325, when Constantine (shown above) convened the first ecumenical council in Nicaea, churches were scattered throughout the empire.

Jews, and therefore Christians, were permitted to worship a single god rather than the pantheon of Roman deities. The early empire's climate of order, security, and tolerance enabled the first missionaries to carry out their work with little fear of interference from Rome.

Martyrs and Victors When Christian missionaries arrived in a community, they went first to the local synagogue. The New Testament provides insights into the church in Antioch and those founded by Paul. But it has little to say on other early Christian communities in Phoenicia, Syria, and Asia Minor, at Pella in the Decapolis, at Dura-Europos and Edessa in Mesopotamia, and in the North African cities of Alexandria and Carthage. Even the beginnings of the church in Rome are obscure, though by the time Paul wrote his Letter to the Romans in the mid-first century A.D. the church was well established.

By A.D. 64 Rome's Christian population had grown large enough, and hostility toward it fervent enough, for Emperor Nero to incite a vicious massacre when he accused the community of setting a devastating fire in the city. Nero used the persecution of Christians to boost his declining favor, but his successors discontinued his policies, and the church began to thrive once more. Then about A.D. 95, Emperor Domitian ordered a crackdown on all Roman subjects who refused to recognize the state religion and the cult of the emperor. Christian proselytizing had come to be viewed as a threat to the social order.

Many Christians fell victim to the sporadic repressions of the next decades, among them Ignatius, bishop of Antioch, and Polycarp, bishop of Smyrna. Still, the church continued to grow, and Christians took heart in the belief that they would be rewarded for their martyrdom with eternal salvation. The Roman persecutions peaked in 303, when Diocletian made the most violent attempt to rid the empire of Christianity. He ordered the imprisonment of the clergy and called for churches to be razed and copies of the Scriptures burned.

The Patronage of Constantine Diocletian's division of the empire into East and West left his successors to vie for dominance. After Constantinius I, the chief ruler in the West, died, his son, Constantine, took command of the army and invaded Italy in an effort to claim his rightful title. As Constantine prepared to face his foe, Maxentius, at the Milvian Bridge, he saw a vision of a flaming cross emblazoned against the sky. Constantine's victory in battle that day convinced him that the cross symbolized the truth and power of Christianity.

Though not yet a full convert to Christianity, Constantine became a generous patron of the church. In the year 313 he and the ruler of the Eastern Empire reached an agreement later called the Edict of Milan, pronouncing freedom of worship for all religions. He declared Sunday a day of rest, restored the churches, and gave them permission to acquire property. And he exempted Christians from participating in pagan sacrifices. On his deathbed Constantine accepted the rite of baptism, making Christianity in effect the religion of the empire. ❖

Extent of Roman Empire
in A.D. 117

Church in A.D. 100

Church in A.D. 200

Church in A.D. 325

Catacomb paintings often portrayed Adam and Eve, as does this fresco from Sts. Peter and Marcellinus catacomb.

The raising of Lazarus (detail from the catacomb of the Giordani) was a subject befitting Christian funerary art.

The second- to fifth-century catacombs, underground burial chambers that lay outside Rome, are major sources of early Christian art. The Via Latina galleries, at left, feature both pagan figures and biblical scenes, including the crossing of the Red Sea, the three Hebrews in the fiery furnace, and the multiplication of the loaves and fishes.

The Jonah story—a subject that dominates early Christian art—was thought to symbolize divine deliverance. It is depicted here in a fourth-century mosaic.

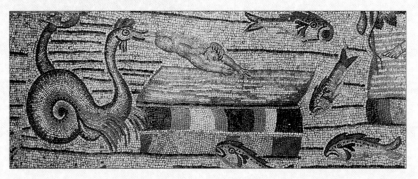

The image of the Good Shepherd, a symbol of Jesus in John 10:11-16, is shown here in a fifth-century mosaic from Ravenna, Italy.

Among the earliest representations of the passion is this fifth-century ivory relief of Pilate washing his hands, Jesus carrying the cross, and Peter's denial of Jesus.

Early Christian Art

Whereas Jewish law forbade the use of human or animal figures in art, Christianity—a movement that recognized an incarnate God—produced an art that reflected the visible world. Over the course of the first five centuries, Christians in the West developed a repertoire of images that gave vigorous expression to their faith.

The earliest Christian art was largely symbolic or schematic. Pagan symbols and images were endowed with Christian meanings and used to adorn sarcophagi and catacomb walls; among them, the anchor (hope), the dove (soul), and the peacock (immortality). Christians pictured Old Testament stories—such as Noah's ark, Jonah and the whale, and Daniel in the lions' den—to suggest New Testament salvation themes. Jesus was portrayed in the guise of the Good Shepherd or the Greek hero Orpheus, and later as a beardless youth being baptized by John, raising Lazarus, and performing other miracles. Jesus' passion and resurrection were not depicted until the fifth century.

When Rome officially recognized Christianity in A.D. 313, Christian art emerged from clandestine settings to be displayed openly. As churches were built, they acquired the rich mosaic decorations that announced the glories of Byzantium.

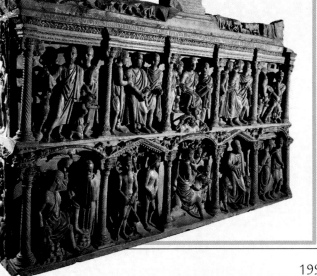

The elaborate carvings of the Junius Bassus sarcophagus, dating from A.D. 359, portray Jesus as ruler of the universe surrounded by Old and New Testament events.

The Gnostic Challenge

THE SPREAD OF GNOSTICISM AMONG CHRISTIANS IN THE SECOND
AND THIRD CENTURIES PROMPTED THE CHURCH TO SOLIDIFY ITS
TENETS AND ITS CANON.

While the church was seeking to define the Christian faith in its early years, other groups were also concerned with defining humanity's relationship to God. Followers of gnosticism (from the Greek word *gnosis*, meaning "knowledge") presented a considerable challenge to church leaders because many gnostic ideas appealed to Christians but countered concepts that other Christians considered basic to their faith.

Gnosticism was not a unified religion but encompassed a variety of sects that were organized around the teachings of individual leaders. The leaders devised their views by drawing on many sources: Judaism and Christianity, the religions of ancient Egypt and Asia Minor, and the ideas of poets and philosophers. There were Jewish gnostic sects and others that are called Christian because Jesus played a part in their beliefs, as did the writings that would become the New Testament. Gnostics, however, interpreted Jesus' role and the writings differently from mainstream Christians. Many gnostic groups thought that Christians were wrong to interpret the texts literally. According to them, the Gospels and other writings had hidden meanings that could be interpreted only by the enlightened. Gnostic groups also considered additional writings—including some by their own leaders—to be of equal importance. Church leaders viewed their ideas as heresy.

A Dualistic World Many gnostic groups, including those led by one of the most important second-century gnostic leaders, Valentinus in Rome, believed that there were two worlds and two gods. The mundane world, in Valentinus' view, was a world of darkness created by an inferior god—the God of the Old Testament. Valentinian gnostics rejected the Old Testament. They also rejected all material aspects of this world—including the human body—as burdens that humanity was forced to endure.

The other world, accordingly, was a spiritual world of light and knowledge ruled by a Supreme Being. Salvation was possible only through knowledge of this divine world and the Supreme Being's mysteries, but salvation was available only to some. Some gnostics believed that there were three classes of people in the mundane

Mary Magdalene played a part in gnostic writings such as the Gospel of Mary. *Jesus' closeness with Mary suggested he shared special knowledge with her. Above is a detail from a 13th-century painting by the Magdalene Master.*

world. On the highest level were those few who were born with *gnosis* and could reveal knowledge and truth to others. Jesus was seen as the great revealer of divine truth. On the next level were people who desired knowledge and were capable of achieving salvation through tutelage—this idea appealed to many Christians. At the third level, however, were the vast majority of people, who were incapable of enlightenment and who would forever be enslaved by the material world. Church leaders could not accept the gnostic rejection of God and creation. Nor could they accept the gnostics' exclusionist view of salvation, since the church taught that all people could be saved.

No Incarnation Other ideas that went against orthodoxy were recorded in the *Gospel of Truth*, which many scholars believe was written by Valentinus. Jesus, in the gnostic view, was not the son of the "inferior" God, nor did he become man, suffer human pain, or die on the cross. Resurrection, gnostics taught, was a spiritual linking of the soul with the savior and had nothing to do with a human body.

The gnostic rejection of the incarnation of Jesus and the resurrection of the body, among other beliefs, forced church leaders to make the definition of Christianity clear. The basic tenets of the faith were declared explicitly in the Apostles' Creed, which was drawn up in Rome about A.D. 150. Gnostic beliefs also provoked Iranaeus, the bishop of Lyons, to write *Against the Heresies*, the first important essay on Christian theology, about 185. As part of church doctrine, bishops were declared direct descendants of the Apostles and thus their role and authority were greatly strengthened. Church leaders also helped to begin the long process of debating the authority of Christian writings and formulating what would become the New Testament canon. ❖

This carved gemstone, dating from the third century, is believed to depict a female gnostic deity flanked by the twins Castor and Pollux.

A GNOSTIC FIND

For many centuries, anyone interested in studying gnostic thought had to rely mainly on the reports of early Christians who fought it. But in 1945 two Egyptian brothers uncovered the most important collection of gnostic literature known.

The men were digging in a cave near the town of Nag Hammadi when they unearthed a jar containing 12 papyrus codices (above). The manuscripts, copied from Greek into Coptic in the fourth century, include 52 essays, 40 of which were previously unavailable to scholars. The collection is actually a library that represents a wide variety of gnostic thought. The *Gospel of Thomas* is a collection of Jesus' sayings. Some of the writings rework elements of the Old Testament. In the *Testimony of Truth,* the story of Adam and Eve is told with the Creator as a jealous villain. Other essays, such as the *Apocalypse of Peter,* show a bias against the church. "They will cleave to the name of a dead man, thinking that they will become pure." And some, such as the *Discourse on Eighth and Ninth,* refer to Egyptian lore and have nothing to do with Judeo-Christian writings.

The manuscripts were probably buried at the site for safe keeping by followers. It is interesting that the same Nag Hammadi site saw the origins of Christian monasticism in the third century.

ΗΑΝΑCΤΑCΙC

IC   ΧΙ

The above 14th-century fresco, on the ceiling of a church in Istanbul, shows Jesus helping Adam and Eve from hell to join the company of saints. Marcion repudiated the Old Testament. In order to justify Jesus' preaching to the souls in hell, Marcion is said to have claimed that by Jesus' death on the cross he paid the God of the Old Testament a price for the souls he was to save.

Debating the New Testament Canon

IT WAS THE SECOND CENTURY BEFORE THE CHURCH DECIDED IT SHOULD HAVE A CHRISTIAN CANON. DECIDING WHAT WRITINGS BELONGED IN THE CANON TOOK AN EVEN LONGER TIME.

When early Christians spoke of Scriptures they meant the texts of the Hebrew Bible. These were the writings that Jesus said he came "not to abolish [Matthew 5: 17]." Even after the evangelists had completed their Gospels, Christians did not immediately regard them as equivalent to the earlier writings. The Apostle Paul used the authority of the Hebrew Bible to measure the truth of certain Christian claims. When he used the phrase "in accordance with the Scriptures (1 Corinthians 15: 3)," he declared that all of his assertions about the new faith were consistent with the prophecies contained in the Old Testament.

As the evangelists began to write down accounts of Jesus' life and teachings, they often referred to the ancient authoritative model. Yet, the reverence for Hebrew Scripture also inhibited Christians from producing their own documents and claiming comparable authority for them. Even so, by the end of the first century, when most of the Gospels had appeared in their present form and apostolic letters—particularly Paul's—were being collected, copied, circulated, and read in churches, a new, unofficial canon had begun to take shape.

Resistance to a Canon In part, resistance to a new Scripture stemmed from a belief in the authority of oral tradition: a living memory handed on verbally from one generation to the next. None of the evangelists recounted an occasion when Jesus wrote anything down or commanded his Apostles to record his words for posterity. Instead, Jesus commanded that the Apostles go out to teach, preach, heal, and baptize. But as the early church grew, written accounts took on greater value. The greater the number of years that separated some oral records from their original sources, the less reliable they became, but writing provided a certain permanence.

The first known instance in which apostolic writings were accorded scriptural stature occurred in the second century, when the gnostic teacher Basilides appealed to the Gospels of Matthew, Luke, and John, as well as to certain Pauline epistles, as "proof-texts" for his arguments. About that same time, church leaders began to cite the Gospels and epistles alongside Hebrew Scriptures when trying to settle internal disputes. The first known reference to Gospel reading in churches also comes from the second century. The writer Justin Martyr wrote that during worship services that he observed in Rome, either the "memoirs of the Apostles" or the "writings of the prophets" were read to the assembly.

The transition from oral tradition to written authority persisted into the second century. Papias, a bishop in Hierapolis, in Asia Minor, writing in the early decades of the second century, asserted his preference for the "living voice of the elders" who had been taught by the Apostles themselves.

The papyrus fragment below is all that remains of Tatian's Diatessaron, *composed in the second century. Tatian attempted to eliminate repetitions and inconsistencies in the four Gospels by "harmonizing" them into one story.*

Tatian's Harmonized Gospels Because the Gospels had arisen in different communities (and each told the story of Jesus in a slightly different way), communities hearing the various versions could not help but note discrepancies among them. Attempts were made to combine the four Gospels into one. In one such attempt, Tatian, a Syrian rhetorician and teacher, assumed the role of Gospel harmonizer. His *Diatessaron* ("harmony of four") was completed about 170 and remained the authorized text in many Syrian churches into the fifth century. Tatian obviously felt no inhibitions about blending Matthew, Mark, Luke, and John, along with some oral traditions, and his presumption demonstrates the absence of an inviolate sanctity concerning these documents.

Marcion's Rejection of the Hebrew Bible Ultimately, the church began to specify its authoritative sources, in part as a reaction to the views of a man named Marcion. Born and reared a Christian in the small Black Sea port of Sinope, Marcion probably arrived in Rome sometime in the late 130's and began to reconstruct the Christian message to conform to his own gnosticizing views. Most significantly he broke from tradition by repudiating the Hebrew Scriptures, claiming that they were inspired by an inferior, even wicked God. For Marcion, the Old Testament was entirely overridden and made irrelevant by the spiritual teaching of Jesus. Eventually Marcion founded his own church and developed a canon of texts.

Because of his gnostic denial of Jesus' humanity, Marcion's canon included only an edited version of Luke and excised from Paul's letters any mention of Jesus' incarnation or suffering. Marcion's absolute rejection of Hebrew tradition assured his retention of texts such as Galatians that supported his claim that Christianity superseded Judaism. Marcion's views were widely popular and his canon prompted the church to examine its need to establish a canon of its own.

The Montanist View A few decades after Marcion compiled his canon, Christians led by a certain Montanus claimed that they had received a revelation directly from God during a trancelike state of ecstasy. The Montanists insisted that the Christian canon could not be closed inasmuch as the age of revelation continued. Although the church did not deny the possibility of ongoing revelation, it declared that true prophets would be authorized by the community and that the only writings that would be considered scriptural were those linked to the Apostles themselves, a criterion that completed the transition from oral tradition to written document. Thus, while Marcion's activities demonstrated the need for an authorized, but open, canon, Montanus' followers provoked the closure of that canon, and criteria for determining what belonged in the canon began to emerge.

Determining Canonicity Only in the last decades of the second century did the church begin to speak officially of a Gospel or epistle as Scripture. To be considered authoritative, a book required apostolic authorship. Additionally, texts that had long been accepted by a significant number of communities were seen as having demonstrated sanctity. Irenaeus, the bishop of Lyons, was one of the first to speak of an Old Testament and a New Testament. He declared that the four Gospels in particular had been given by God to all Christians, each equally and fully the divine word. "It is not possible that the Gospels can be either more or fewer in number than they are," he explained.

A Christian figure with his hands raised in prayer appears on this funerary mosaic from Tunisia. In the second century, the city of Carthage, in what is now Tunisia, was the home of the writer Tertullian, whose ideas on forming a Christian canon were influential.

"For since there are four zones of the world in which we live, and four principal winds . . . it is fitting that the church should have four pillars." Four was also the perfect number because, in Irenaeus' view, the Gospels were symbolized in the four cherubim of Ezekiel 1: 5-10 and Revelation 4: 7. Each face (lion, ox, man, eagle) represented both an aspect of Jesus' work and a characteristic of a particular Gospel. Irenaeus linked the symbols with the evangelists.

Irenaeus' New Testament consisted of the four Gospels, Acts, 13 epistles presumed to be Paul's, 1 Peter, 1 and 2 John, Revelation, and the *Shepherd of Hermas*. Irenaeus' choices were supported by Tertullian, a theologian and writer in Carthage. Tertullian had earlier supported the Montanist point of view but came to believe, as Irenaeus did, that the canon should be closed and limited to apostolic texts.

Thus, by the end of the second century, Christians possessed a collection of books that closely approximated the canon used today. Yet, it was the late third century before the New Testament canon was

Christian imagery, including the Good Shepherd and a praying figure, appear on this third-century sarcophagus from France, where Irenaeus was bishop.

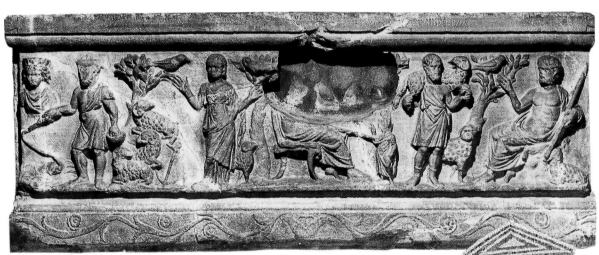

finally established. At one time scholars believed they had found a canon list dated by some authorities to the late second or early third century. This Syrian or Palestinian fragment, known as the Muratorian Canon, has been more recently dated in the fourth century. Whatever its date, the Muratorian fragment, with its rejection of some books (Hebrews and 1 and 2 Peter, for example) and its inclusion of others (the *Wisdom of Solomon* and the *Apocalypse of Peter*) demonstrates the fluidity of the canon and the struggle to find a compromise between the narrow Marcionite canon and the open-ended or deliberately obscure canons of the Montanists and gnostics. ❖

The four Gospels are shown stored in this cabinet, a detail from a mosaic dating from about 450 at Ravenna, Italy.

Revising the Septuagint

TO BRING THE GREEK BIBLICAL TEXT MORE IN LINE WITH THE CURRENT HEBREW TEXT, JEWISH SCRIBES MADE THREE NEW GREEK TRANSLATIONS.

By the first century A.D., the Christian communities within the Roman Empire, whose common language was Greek, had adopted the Greek translation of the Hebrew Bible, known as the Septuagint, as their own sacred Scriptures. Ironically, the Greek translation served Christians in their theological disputes with Jews.

For their part, Greek-speaking Jews needed a Greek translation that would not only faithfully represent the Hebrew Bible for their own religious needs but would also provide a basis for discussions with Christians. Since the Hebrew text had to some extent changed over the years during which the Septuagint translations were being made, the Jewish community felt the need to revise the Septuagint to adapt it to the most authoritative Hebrew text of their time.

New Greek Translations One of the earliest attempts at a complete, revised Greek translation was made about A.D. 130 by Aquila, a native of Pontus, Asia Minor. Aquila was a student of the famous rabbi Akiba,

Christians understood the Old Testament, known to them through the Septuagint, in light of the New Testament. The stories of Noah's deliverance from the Flood (shown above in a third-century catacomb painting) and Moses striking the rock (shown below in a fourth-century ivory relief) were thought to anticipate Christian baptism.

from whom he acquired the belief that every letter and word in the Bible is meaningful. So determined was Aquila to reproduce faithfully the precise meaning, word choice and order, grammar, and even the sound of the Hebrew text that he employed or invented fixed Greek equivalents for Hebrew terms.

Aquila's devotion to the principle of literalism frequently caused the meaning of the text to suffer, and his version often sounds distinctly un-Greek. Nevertheless, it was this bold literalism that recommended Aquila's work to Greek-speaking Jews. Aquila's translation replaced the Septuagint in many synagogues, including the Jewish community of Alexandria, Egypt, birthplace of the Septuagint.

At the end of the second century a second Greek revision was completed by Theodotion of Ephesus, a Diaspora Jew who may have been a Christian before returning to his original faith. Rather than produce a new Greek version, Theodotion revised an existing one to bring it nearer to the standard Hebrew text. A noteworthy feature of the translation is its transliteration of obscure words into Greek. Much of the translation has been lost; the Daniel text, however, was preserved because it supplanted the Septuagint version of that book.

Recent research has shown that documents predating Theodotion by a century appear to cite the translation. As a result, some scholars theorize that Theodotion did not work from the Septuagint translation but rather from an earlier Greek text that has survived in only a few early Christian quotations.

Symmachus' Elegant Translation A still more readable Greek translation dates from the end of the second century A.D. or the beginning of the third century. It was the work of Symmachus, a Samaritan who was either a convert to Judaism or a member of the Ebionite Jewish-Christian sect. Symmachus' translation exhibits a knowledge of classical literature and a familiarity with rabbinical interpretations of Scripture.

Symmachus was concerned less with a literal representation of the Hebrew than with giving his version felicitous expression in Greek. For instance, when he encountered an obscure Hebrew term, he typically avoided the awkward transliterations favored by his predecessors, opting instead for his best guess at a correct translation. Symmachus' elegant prose style has prompted one scholar to remark that his translation "reads like a direct challenge to Aquila's monstrosities," although such an effect seems to have been incidental.

Symmachus' Greek translation was admired by prominent Christian scholars and translators. In preparing his Latin translation of the Old Testament, Jerome drew on Symmachus more than on the other two second-century translations by Aquila and Theodotion. Perhaps Jerome found in Symmachus' version the embodiment of his own definition of the translator's task: to be true to the idiomatic essence of the original rather than to the literal meaning. ❖

THE TARGUMS

By the fifth century B.C., most Jews spoke Aramaic rather than Hebrew. Over the next centuries Aramaic translations and paraphrases of the Hebrew Scriptures, known as Targums, began to be read aloud in the synagogue.

The official Targum of the Pentateuch was written in the second or third century A.D by Onkelos, a figure tentatively identified with Aquila. (The colophon page from a 15th-century edition of Onkelos' Pentateuch appears above.) The official Aramaic translation of the Prophets, the Targum of Jonathan, was written between the second century B.C. and the seventh century A.D. Targums were eventually produced for every book of Writings except for Ezra–Nehemiah and Daniel, both of which contain large portions in Aramaic.

Origen and the Sixfold Bible

THE HEXAPLA, THE FIRST TEXTUAL STUDY OF THE OLD TESTAMENT, WAS AN UNPARALLELED ACHIEVEMENT.

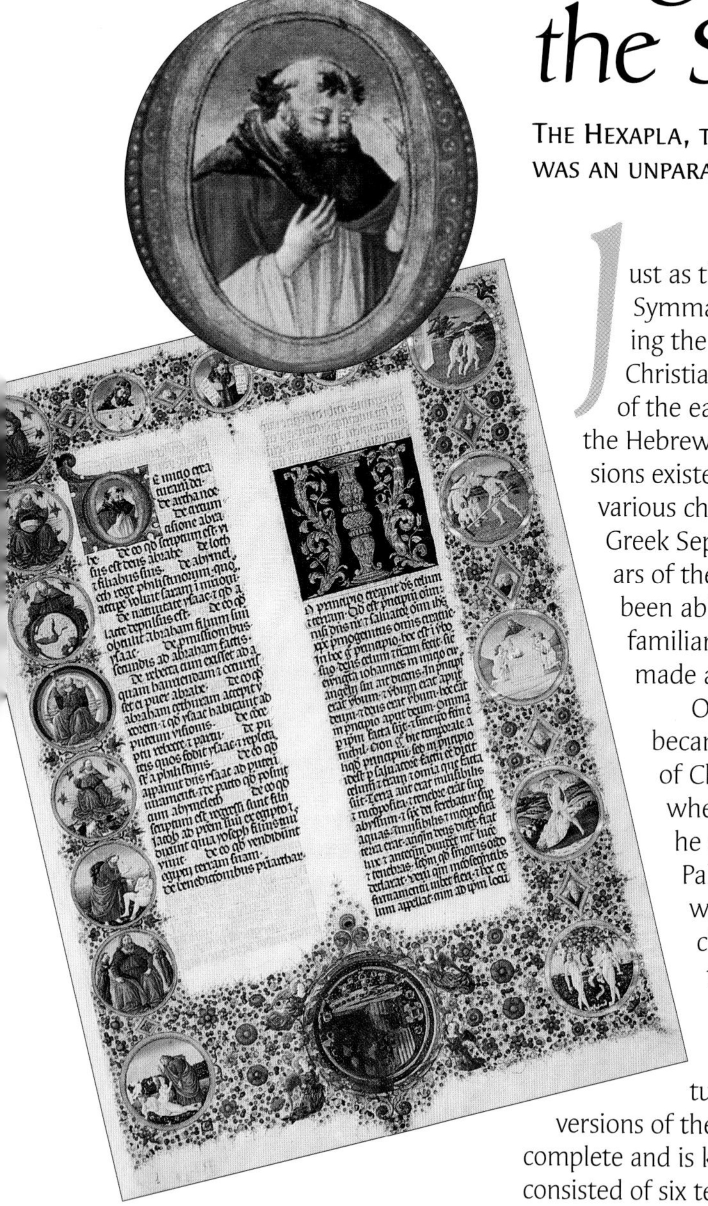

Just as the Jewish biblical scholars Aquila, Theodotion, and Symmachus applied themselves to reviewing and retranslating the Septuagint in the second century A.D., there were Christian scholars who did the same a century later. Most of the early church accepted the Septuagint as their version of the Hebrew Scriptures, or Old Testament. However, other versions existed and there were variations in the texts used by the various churches. There were also differences between the Greek Septuagint and Hebrew Scriptures. Most Christian scholars of the period did not read Hebrew and would not have been able to draw comparisons. But one scholar, Origen, who familiarized himself with Hebrew for this express purpose, made a lasting contribution to the study of Scripture.

Origen was born into a Christian family about 185 and became one of the greatest early teachers—and scholars—of Christianity. He began his life's work in Alexandria, where he is thought to have studied with Clement, and he continued his work in Caesarea, the Roman capital of Palestine, where he settled and was ordained. His many writings included biblical commentaries, textual criticism of the Old Testament, and *On First Principles*, a treatise on Christian theology.

The Hexapla Perhaps about 230 Origen embarked on the monumental task of creating a revised Septuagint by comparing it to other Greek and Hebrew versions of the Old Testament. The work took some 15 years to complete and is known as the Hexapla, meaning "sixfold," because it consisted of six texts written in parallel columns. In the first column was the Hebrew text that was considered standard by Palestinian Jews of the day (and that Origen believed was the version of the Hebrew

---

One of Origen's many books, Homilies on Genesis, Exodus, Leviticus, *is shown above as it appeared in manuscript in the 1480's. The illustrator, the Florentine Francesco Rosselli, included a portrait of Origen in the initial letter, inset.*

Bible that had been used by the Septuagint translators). The second column was a transliteration of the Hebrew words into Greek characters. Columns three and four were the Greek translations made by Aquila and Symmachus. In the fifth column was the Septuagint and in the sixth the Greek version translated by Theodotion. Up to three additional Greek translations were included in some sections of the Old Testament, making as many as nine columns.

Origen applied most of his labors to the fifth column, where he made revisions of the Septuagint. He wrote of his efforts, "When I was uncertain of the Septuagint reading because the various copies did not tally, I settled the issue by consulting the other versions and retaining what was in agreement with them. Some passages did not appear in the Hebrew; these I marked with an obelus [÷] . . . . Other passages I marked with an asterisk [*] to show that they were not in the Septuagint but that I had added them from the other versions in agreement with the Hebrew text. Whoever wishes may accept them; anyone who is offended by this procedure may accept or reject them as he chooses."

By any measure, the completed Hexapla was a mammoth accomplishment, running to an estimated 6,500 pages in 15 large volumes. Not surprisingly, it was never copied in full, although the column containing the revised Septuagint and individual sections such as the Psalms were copied and circulated. Unfortunately the original codex of Origen's work disappeared in the seventh century, one theory being that it was destroyed during the Muslim conquest of Palestine.

Copies of Origen's Hexapla, or even sections of it, are almost nonexistent today. The manuscript shown here is a palimpsest, or reused parchment. In the 13th or 14th century, a Greek text was written over a 10th-century copy of the Hexapla Psalms. Even though the Hexapla columns were scraped away before the parchment was reused, they can be seen through the later Greek writing.

Origen and the New Testament Canon Origen's interest in analyzing text applied to Christian writings as well. In his *Commentary on Matthew*, for instance, he noted the textual differences that existed in copies of the Gospels and epistles.

To Origen's mind, the main criterion for canonicity was how much an individual work was used by the churches. He fervently believed that Christian Scripture was divinely inspired. "The Scriptures were composed through the Spirit of God, and have both a meaning which is obvious and another which is hidden from most readers," he wrote. "The inspired meaning is not recognized by all—only by those who are gifted with the grace of the Holy Spirit in the word of wisdom and knowledge." ❖

Early Biblical Interpretation

CHRISTIANS SEARCHED THE SCRIPTURES FOR MEANINGS THAT COULD BE APPLIED TO THE LIFE OF THEIR COMMUNITIES.

For Jews and Christians alike, study of the Scriptures has often been an end in itself—a simple act of devotion. But from an early date, believers also began to scrutinize the Bible for what it had to say to their own generation and community. Such interpretation, or exegesis, was done for the purposes of preaching, pastoral care, formulating codes of behavior, and finding answers to theological or ethical questions not explicitly addressed by the text.

Inevitably, disagreements arose—over the significance of texts, their relative authority, how to account for inconsistencies or contradictions, and how to explain confusing stories. Guided interpretation developed, often based on a fairly definite set of rules or patterns.

Multiple Meanings Jews call biblical interpretation midrash, a word derived from the Hebrew for "to search." Some midrash occur in the Old Testament itself; for instance, the Deuteronomic legal codes are largely an expansion and commentary on Mosaic Law.

In the Gospels Jesus expounds on the meaning of Scripture, and many texts in the New Testament draw parallels between Old Testament prophecies and events and Jesus' life and teachings. Paul, for example, calls those who crossed the Red Sea "baptized" and says of the rock that gave them water that it "was Christ [1 Corinthians 10: 2–4]." Matthew is especially fond of pointing out events that took place in "accordance" with the prophets.

Second-century theologians, including Justin Martyr, Melito of Sardis, Irenaeus of Lyons, and Tertullian of Carthage, mined the Old Testament for evidence that Christ was foretold by the Hebrew prophets and that his coming was the fulfillment of God's covenant with Israel. The Old Testament thereby served as a "proof" of the Gospel.

The search of texts for hidden meanings or signs of future events was already known in the ancient world. The Jewish philosopher

The cleansing of the Temple, shown in a 14th-century fresco by Giotto, is given a variety of interpretations by Origen. It represents Jesus' work as the redeemer, his purging the church of corruption, his coming to each soul, and his arrival in the heavenly Jerusalem to deliver it from evil.

For Paul, the "first man, Adam," brought sin into the world, and Jesus, the "last Adam," redeemed mankind (1 Corinthians 15:45–49). The Fall is depicted on a bronze door panel of 1015.

Philo of Alexandria adopted the allegorical methods of earlier Greek philosophers to uncover the mystical significance behind Homer's works. Philo also searched the Hebrew Scriptures for the deeper meanings he felt enriched his own religious faith. He explained Abraham's journey from Ur to the Promised Land, for example, as an allegory of the soul's travels from ignorance to knowledge of God.

Levels of Meaning Christian exegetes of the second- and third-century Alexandrian school, such as Clement and Origen, followed Philo in the quest for hidden truths in the Scriptures, particularly in the Hebrew Bible. Origen discerned three levels of meaning in Scripture: allegory (the text's symbolic meaning and the highest level), typology (its moral significance), and literal, or historical, understanding (the lowest level of meaning). He based his scheme on the description in Paul's First Letter to the Thessalonians of the three aspects of the human being as "spirit and soul and body [1 Thessalonians 5:23]," corresponding to allegorical, typological, and literal interpretation. Sometimes Origen counted only two divisions, the "spirit" and the "letter." His system influenced other early Christian thinkers, particularly Gregory of Nyssa, Basil of Caesarea, and Gregory of Nazianzus in the East and Ambrose, Augustine, and Jerome in the West.

Some Christians, however, were wary of too free a use of allegorical interpretation, which to them often resembled personal mysticism. These conservative thinkers tended to look to the Scriptures for moral guidance or interpretations concerning Christ (the Christological approach). Some of Origen's severest critics emerged out of the school at Antioch, among them Theodore of Mopsuestia. The Antiochenes grounded their understanding of Scripture in the historical, restricting even Christological interpretation of much of the Old Testament.

Literal and allegorical approaches to the Bible sometimes arrived at a kind of balance, with the first staying anchored in the text and the second lending greater profundity to its interpretation. ❖

The early Christian thinkers Melito of Sardis and Justin Martyr drew parallels between "types," that is, events or personages, in the Old Testament and those in the New. One of these types was Isaac, because his father offered him up for sacrifice (shown in a 15th-century monochromatic painting by Andrea Mantegna). As Origen wrote, "Abraham offered to God his mortal son who did not die, and God gave up his immortal Son who died for all of us."

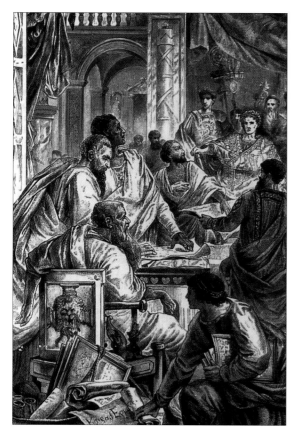

The emperor Constantine presided over the Council of Nicaea in 325. Although many debates over church doctrine continued long after the close of the council, there was also much agreement. Out of the council came the Nicene Creed, a statement of Christian belief accepted then—and still accepted today—by many churches.

Establishing the Christian Canon

WITH HIS SANCTION OF CHRISTIANITY, CONSTANTINE NOT ONLY LED THE EMPIRE BUT WAS HEAD OF THE CHURCH AS WELL. HE CALLED FOR UNITY WITHIN THE CHURCH AND AGREEMENT ON ITS SCRIPTURES.

The emperor Constantine's sanction of Christianity in 313 radically changed the fortunes of the church as persecution was replaced by the patronage of secular rulers. The emperor's support also prompted moves toward establishing a uniform doctrine within the church and toward centralizing political and religious authority.

Constantine introduced measures to promote harmony among Christians by resolving theological differences and establishing common definitions of the faith. For example, in 325 he summoned Christian bishops, theologians, and imperial advisers to a council in the city of Nicaea, Asia Minor, to settle controversies over the divinity of the Son of God, the nature of the Trinity, the calculation of the date of Easter, and other vexing problems. Two influential representatives there, Eusebius of Caesarea and Athanasius of Alexandria, who disagreed with each other over the question of the Son of God's divinity, were later instrumental in bringing about a common New Testament canon.

Eusebius of Caesarea Eusebius was probably born in Palestine, studied under Pamphilus—one of Origen's protégés—and was deeply influenced by Origen's work. During the rule of the emperor Diocletian, Eusebius was witness to the persecutions in Caesarea, but he was elevated to the position of bishop of Caesarea (Palestine's Roman capital) when Constantine signed an edict of toleration in 313,

Throughout his life Eusebius was deeply involved in the controversies of the fourth-century church and was a prolific, though not an eloquent, writer. Among his many works are a comprehensive *History of the Church*, a *Life of Constantine*, the *Preparation for the Gospel*—a treatise demonstrating the superiority of Jewish and Christian Scriptures over pagan myths and philosophy—and commentaries on Isaiah and

Eusebius of Caesarea, depicted above in a detail from a sixth-century book, the Rabbula Gospels, is known as the father of church history.

the Psalms. One of Eusebius' most important contributions to the church was his work toward establishing an accepted canon, which began at Constantine's behest.

As part of his program to standardize aspects of church life and practice, the emperor asked Eusebius to produce 50 Bibles for church use in Constantinople. To be able to perform the task, Eusebius first had to determine which Christian writings to include. Consequently he established three classes of Christian literature. The first group included texts that were already universally accepted as sacred. These were the four Gospels, Acts of the Apostles, 13 letters attributed to Paul, 1 John, and 1 Peter. Disputed or problematic texts went into the second category, which included seven books that are now generally regarded as canonical: James, 2 Peter, Jude, 2 and 3 John, Hebrews, and Revelation. In the third group were writings that—though perhaps viewed as sacred by some Christians—were rejected by Eusebius. Among the writings in this last group were the *Gospel of Peter, of Thomas,* and *of Matthias;* the *Acts of Andrew, of Paul,* and *of John;* the *Shepherd of Hermas;* the *Epistle of Barnabas;* the *Didache;* 1 and 2 Clement; and the *Apocalypse of Peter.*

Until the emperor Constantine embraced the church, Christians were persecuted by secular leaders, and their books were burned. The scene at right takes place on a morning in 303 in Nicomedia, Asia Minor—Diocletian's imperial headquarters. Roman soldiers have raided the church at right and are throwing books off the roof and onto a bonfire. One of the soldiers restrains a presbyter (identifiable by his blue-striped white tunic) to keep him from pulling books from the fire.

CANONICAL DEBATE FROM THE FIRST CENTURY TO THE FOURTH

For the first 300 years of Christianity, different Christian communities had distinct collections of New Testament books, and individual leaders expressed differing views as to what books should and should not be included in the canon. With the emperor Constantine's conversion to Christianity there was at last a central authority to demand a precise definition of the New Testament and a move toward a universally accepted closed canon. Essentially, the canon was closed in 367.

The chart below offers a simple overview of the debate over the canonicity of Christian writings during the course of three centuries.

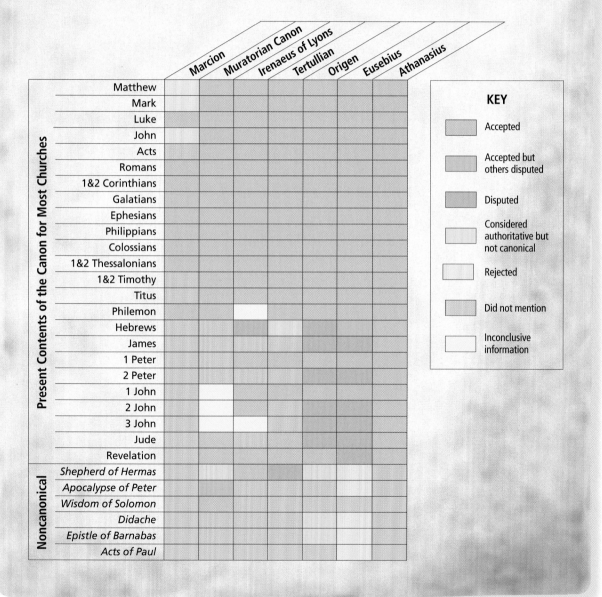

Columns: Marcion, Muratorian Canon, Irenaeus of Lyons, Tertullian, Origen, Eusebius, Athanasius

Present Contents of the Canon for Most Churches: Matthew, Mark, Luke, John, Acts, Romans, 1&2 Corinthians, Galatians, Ephesians, Philippians, Colossians, 1&2 Thessalonians, 1&2 Timothy, Titus, Philemon, Hebrews, James, 1 Peter, 2 Peter, 1 John, 2 John, 3 John, Jude, Revelation

Noncanonical: Shepherd of Hermas, Apocalypse of Peter, Wisdom of Solomon, Didache, Epistle of Barnabas, Acts of Paul

KEY
- Accepted
- Accepted but others disputed
- Disputed
- Considered authoritative but not canonical
- Rejected
- Did not mention
- Inconclusive information

Eusebius' reasons for classifying certain texts as questionable or spurious reveal the basic criteria for canonicity. Perhaps most important was a work's perceived apostolic authorship, though its antiquity and orthodoxy were also of consequence.

Athanasius of Alexandria Eusebius' selection undoubtedly influenced all future attempts at canonization because it was essentially endorsed by the emperor himself. But for all practical purposes, the canon was even more firmly settled in 367. At that time Athanasius, the bishop of Alexandria, wrote his Easter letter to the churches and monasteries of his diocese and identified the books they were to include in their New Testament Scripture. In doing so he agreed with Eusebius' choices as to what should be left out and supported the inclusion of the books in Eusebius' second category: James, 2 Peter, Jude, 2 and 3 John, Hebrews, and Revelation.

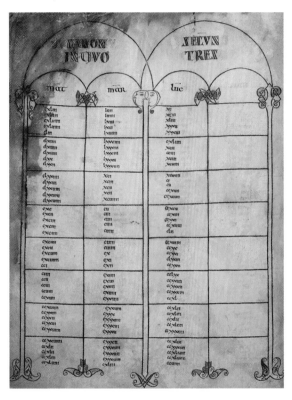

Athanasius' commentary on the Christian canon came toward the end of a long and stormy career. He was first made bishop of his native Alexandria in 328. However, his staunch defense of decisions made at Nicaea and his unwillingness to compromise with opponents (who at times included Eusebius) over controversial points of Christian doctrine caused him to be exiled from Alexandria on five occasions. It was after he returned from his last exile at the age of 72 that Athanasius composed his noted Easter letter.

He was in fact the first person to apply the term *canon* to the contents of the Bible, and he introduced the verb *canonize*, meaning "to give official sanction to" a written document. "These are the fountains of salvation, that they who thirst may be satisfied with the living words they contain," Athanasius wrote of the 27 New Testament books still recognized as the canon by most Catholic and Protestant Christians. He closed with the admonition: "In these alone is proclaimed the doctrine of godliness. Let no one add to or take anything from them."

Most churches agreed. Athanasius' canon had long been accepted by the church in Rome by the time it was confirmed by the pope in 405. In North Africa his canon was ratified by church leaders in Hippo Regius in 393 and in Carthage in 397. Carthage formally reaffirmed its acceptance of the canon in 419, reacting to the continuing debate regarding James, Jude, and Hebrews.

The churches had come a long way toward unity, but they would never be in absolute agreement on the New Testament canon. The Syrians used the *Diatessaron* as their canon for another half-century. And the Ethiopian church continues to recognize a book of Clement and several other books of church order. ❖

Eusebian canon tables, such as the eighth-century Anglo-Saxon example above, have appeared in many Gospel books. They are based on a system devised by Eusebius in his Evangelical Canons. Eusebius cross-referenced the four canonical Gospels with tables listing passages common to two or more of the Gospels. Such work helped scholars resolve seeming contradictions among the four texts.

Copying the Word

The period between the 4th century and the 15th was a remarkable time in the history of the Bible. During those years, knowledge of the Bible spread throughout Europe, and every place the Bible reached it was copied many times over. At least six alphabets were created so that the Scriptures could be written in languages as diverse as Armenian and Gothic.

Putting together a Bible was an arduous undertaking, as everything had to be done by hand. But scribes, artists, parchment makers, and bookbinders excelled. By the Middle Ages the Bibles that they so painstakingly produced were true works of art.

Scribes on a 10th-century carved ivory Bible cover

From the Completion of the Vulgate Bible to the Fall of the Byzantine Empire

PART FOUR TIMELINE *(Some of the dates below are based on scholarly speculation and are approximate.)*

| 4000 B.C. | 3000 B.C. | 2000 B.C. | 1000 B.C. | 1 B.C. A.D. 1 | A.D. 400 | A.D. 1455 | A.D. 2000 |

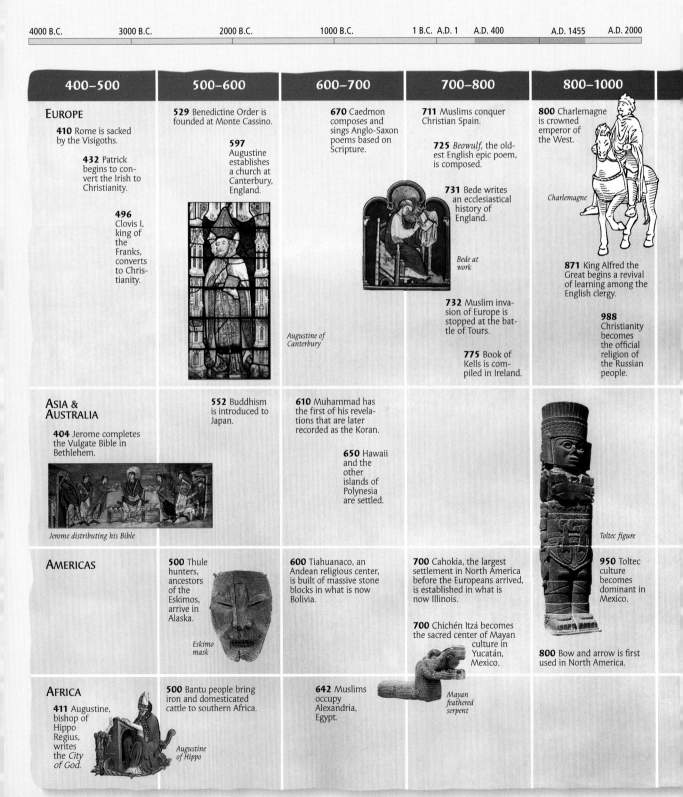

	400–500	**500–600**	**600–700**	**700–800**	**800–1000**
EUROPE	**410** Rome is sacked by the Visigoths. **432** Patrick begins to convert the Irish to Christianity. **496** Clovis I, king of the Franks, converts to Christianity.	**529** Benedictine Order is founded at Monte Cassino. **597** Augustine establishes a church at Canterbury, England. *Augustine of Canterbury*	**670** Caedmon composes and sings Anglo-Saxon poems based on Scripture.	**711** Muslims conquer Christian Spain. **725** *Beowulf,* the oldest English epic poem, is composed. **731** Bede writes an ecclesiastical history of England. *Bede at work* **732** Muslim invasion of Europe is stopped at the battle of Tours. **775** Book of Kells is compiled in Ireland.	**800** Charlemagne is crowned emperor of the West. *Charlemagne* **871** King Alfred the Great begins a revival of learning among the English clergy. **988** Christianity becomes the official religion of the Russian people.
ASIA & AUSTRALIA	**404** Jerome completes the Vulgate Bible in Bethlehem. *Jerome distributing his Bible*	**552** Buddhism is introduced to Japan.	**610** Muhammad has the first of his revelations that are later recorded as the Koran. **650** Hawaii and the other islands of Polynesia are settled.		*Toltec figure*
AMERICAS		**500** Thule hunters, ancestors of the Eskimos, arrive in Alaska. *Eskimo mask*	**600** Tiahuanaco, an Andean religious center, is built of massive stone blocks in what is now Bolivia.	**700** Cahokia, the largest settlement in North America before the Europeans arrived, is established in what is now Illinois. **700** Chichén Itzá becomes the sacred center of Mayan culture in Yucatán, Mexico.	**950** Toltec culture becomes dominant in Mexico. **800** Bow and arrow is first used in North America.
AFRICA	**411** Augustine, bishop of Hippo Regius, writes the *City of God.* *Augustine of Hippo*	**500** Bantu people bring iron and domesticated cattle to southern Africa.	**642** Muslims occupy Alexandria, Egypt. *Mayan feathered serpent*		

1000–1100	1100–1250	1250–1300	1300–1360	1360–1455

1000 Hungary, Scandinavia, Iceland, and Greenland are converted to Christianity.

1140 Gothic architectural style appears first at the church of St. Denis in France.

Church of St. Denis

1273 Thomas Aquinas completes his *Summa Theologica*.

Thomas Aquinas

1307 Dante Alighieri starts writing *The Divine Comedy*.

1384 John Wyclif inspires an English Bible translation.

John Wyclif

1054 Split between Orthodox and Roman churches is final.

1150 Muslims introduce papermaking to Europe.

1337 Hundred Years' War between England and France begins.

1387 Chaucer starts work on *The Canterbury Tales*.

1066 Normans defeat the Saxons at Hastings.

1348 Bubonic plague rages, killing a third of the population of Europe.

1431 Joan of Arc is burned at the stake.

Francis of Assisi preaching to the birds

1209 Francis of Assisi receives approval for his new order.

1290 Jews are expelled from England.

1453 Turks take Constantinople, marking the end of the Byzantine Empire.

1215 Dominican order is formed.

1298 Marco Polo publishes his account of Kublai Khan's China.

Bubonic plague in Europe

Easter Island sculptures

1095 Pope Urban II proclaims the First Crusade.

1233 Grand Inquisition is established.

1350 Firearms are first used in Europe.

1150 Angkor Wat, the largest worship center in the world, is built in Cambodia.

1290 Osman I establishes the Ottoman Empire.

1000 Giant stone sculptures are carved on Easter Island.

1211 Mongol Genghis Khan invades China.

1294 A Christian bishopric is established in Beijing.

1000 Chinese invent gunpowder.

1244 Jerusalem falls under Muslim control, where it remains for 700 years.

1040 Movable type is invented in China.

Genghis Khan

1000 Viking explorer Leif Ericsson lands on the North American coast.

1100 Anasazi people build cliff dwellings in southwestern North America.

1325 Aztecs settle and found their capital at Tenochtitlán, Mexico.

1440 Inca Empire in Peru begins its expansion.

Viking ship

Aztec calendar

1050 Islam spreads from North Africa to West Africa and up the Nile.

African sculpture of Portuguese soldier

1445 Portuguese explorers reach the mouth of the Congo River.

Jerome's Majestic Achievement

TO CREATE AN AUTHORITATIVE LATIN TRANSLATION OF THE SCRIPTURES, THE CHURCH NEEDED A SCHOLAR AND LINGUIST WHO WAS THICK-SKINNED ENOUGH TO WEATHER THE STORMS THAT IT WOULD PROVOKE.

Stubborn, obsessive, a madman—this was how some of his contemporaries described Jerome, the scholar who devoted his life to producing a Latin translation of the Bible. Later generations have been kinder, and by the Renaissance, Jerome was esteemed for his great learning and masterful prose style.

Eusebius Hieronymus, known in English as Jerome, was born about A.D. 346 at Stridon in Dalmatia. His wealthy Christian parents secured him a model Roman education, arranging for lessons in grammar, Latin, and Greek, and sending him to Rome to study under a famed grammarian. As he himself noted, "Almost from the very cradle I have spent my time among grammarians and rhetoricians and philosophers." The works he studied ranged from the structured orations of Cicero to the bawdy comedies of Plautus. Jerome built up his library by copying manuscripts.

Inspired by the ethic of the Christian ascetics, Jerome became a monk and lived for three or four years among a small community of like-minded Christians in Aquileia, Italy. Not long after the group disbanded, he experienced a transforming event: having fallen ill in Antioch, he dreamed of his judgment before God and a voice ringing out to accuse him, "You are a Ciceronian, not a Christian." Determined to prove his utter devotion to Christianity, he banished himself to the wilderness of the Chalcis desert, which is southeast of Antioch.

There Jerome lived in a cave, wore sackcloth, and filled his days with prayer and the study of Hebrew in an effort to conquer his worldly imagination. But, try as he might, he could give up neither his cherished library nor his great love of classical literature. "However much I did penance," he wrote, "I always ended up creeping back to Cicero or Plautus." He commented further on the copy of the Scriptures he had at his disposal: "Even if I suddenly pulled myself together and read the Bible . . . I would close it again, repelled by its clumsiness."

Jerome is a penitent hermit in this 15th-century portrait by Domenico di Michelino. In art Jerome is often shown with a lion, from whose paw he is supposed to have drawn a thorn, cardinal's garb (here a red hat), because of his service to Pope Damasus, and a stone for beating his breast.

In 379 Jerome left the desert and went to Antioch, then to Constantinople to study with leading theologians. He continued on to Rome, where Pope Damasus appointed him his secretary. The pope soon recognized Jerome's gifts as a biblical scholar and commissioned him to produce a new Latin revision of the Bible.

New Latin Bible By the early fourth century, a confusing variety of Scriptures in Latin and other languages were in circulation throughout the young church, many of them containing numerous inaccuracies. As Jerome later said, "There are almost as many forms of the text as there are copies." In undertaking his revised translation of the Gospels, he described his endeavor as one to "correct the mistakes by inaccurate translators and the blundering alterations of confident but ignorant critics, and further, all that has been inserted or changed by copyists more asleep than awake."

Jerome worked on his Gospel translation by comparing earlier, Old Latin versions to the original Greek. He completed it in a year's time and, apparently with the pope's approval, next turned his full attention to the Old Testament. (Scholars now believe he translated no other New Testament books.) As Jerome was in the midst of executing a translation of the Psalms, his great patron died, and he left Rome for Bethlehem. There he founded a religious community and,

OLD LATIN BIBLES

Though Greek remained the language of the Roman church until the mid-third century, Latin was used earlier in churches elsewhere in Europe and in North Africa from the late second century. These churches required Latin translations of the Scriptures.

Little is known about the origins of the Latin texts that predate Jerome. Surviving Old Latin manuscripts suggest they were translated from the Greek by different persons under various conditions.

So literal and unpolished are most of the texts—which made up the Bible of the Church Fathers—that Augustine was prompted to remark, "In the early days of the faith, every man who happened to gain possession of a Greek manuscript and who imagined that he had any faculty in both languages . . . dared to make a translation."

*P*ope Damasus restored the Roman catacombs, one of Jerome's youthful haunts, and revived the cult of the martyrs. A second-century catacomb is pictured below.

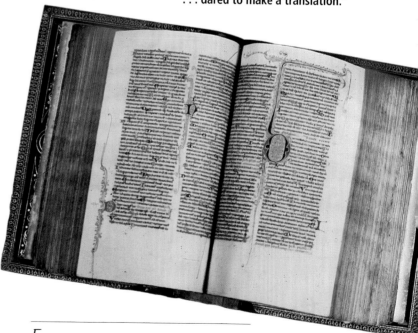

*E*ven in the 13th century, when this elegant Vulgate Bible was created in England, Bibles in Old Latin continued to be produced as well.

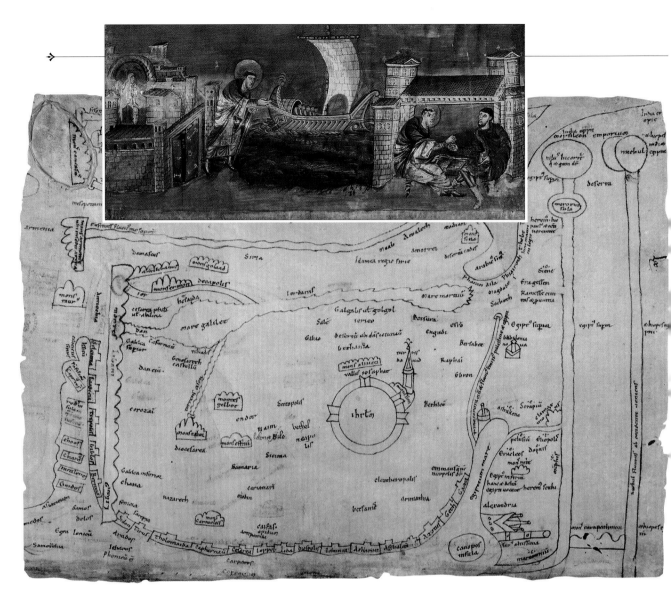

living as a monk, persisted in his life's work with the support of friends and an occasional private patron.

Jerome returned to his translation of the Book of Psalms (ultimately he created three versions) and went on to produce revised Latin versions of Job, the three books attributed to Solomon, and 1 and 2 Chronicles—basing his changes on the Greek Septuagint. But as he became practiced at the Hebrew language, he moved further away from the Greek text and relied instead on Hebrew and Aramaic manuscripts and the help of rabbinical scholars for a truer understanding of the original. He went so far in his quest for authenticity as to acquaint himself with Jewish oral tradition.

This scholarly approach to the Bible was risky since it challenged heartfelt Christian views about the sacredness of the received texts. Jerome wrote in his Gospel dedication: "Is there a man, learned or unlearned, who will not, when he . . . perceives that what he reads does not suit his settled tastes, break out immediately into violent language and call me a forger and a profane person for having the audacity to add anything to the ancient books?" He dealt with the sensitive issue by judiciously retaining those Old Latin terminologies and phrasings that reflected established church doctrine.

Soon Jerome discovered another discrepancy between the Septuagint and Old Latin translations and the Hebrew texts: the first two contained books that were not part of the Hebrew canon. The non-canonical works, said Jerome, were like "the crazy wanderings of a man whose senses have taken leave of him." Indeed, some of them he never translated at all. Labeling these books Apocrypha (for "hidden"), Jerome placed them outside the Christian canon as well.

As his eyesight began to fail, Jerome hired secretaries to read to him and, by listening to "the voice of the brethren," completed his work about 405. In addition to the previously mentioned biblical books, his translations included the five books of the Pentateuch, the prophetic books, Proverbs, Ecclesiastes, the Song of Solomon, Daniel (with Greek supplements), the Books of Samuel and Kings, Esdras (the combined Ezra-Nehemiah), Esther (with Greek supplements), Joshua, Judges, Ruth, Tobit, and Judith.

Jerome died in 420, having generated a body of work that counted 63 volumes of commentaries, including translations of Origen's biblical interpretations, some 100 sermons, and numerous and influential polemics, letters, and other writings.

Mixed Public Response While Jerome's Gospel translations were widely accepted from an early date, his Old Testament revisions were far from universally popular. They drew enthusiastic support from a small group within his own circle and fervent opposition from other scholars, some of whom were involved in ongoing debates with Jerome. Among congregants, a preference for the traditional text used in worship, which many of them knew by heart, long overshadowed an appreciation for Jerome's contribution. Sometimes the public response took a violent turn, as when, according to Augustine, a bishop set off a riot by reading passages of the revised Jonah to his parish.

Over time, Jerome's translation gained in popularity. In the mid-sixth century the scholar Cassiodorus prepared an edition of the Bible called the Codex Grandior that preserved much of the text. That Bible served in turn as the basis for the Codex Amiatinus, the earliest surviving Vulgate, or "common," text—a term that refers to Bibles composed largely of the books translated by Jerome. Also in the sixth century, Pope Gregory I made extensive use of the Vulgate Old Testament for his own commentaries. ❖

Jerome wrote that when he was under the "assault of desire" in the desert: "I threw myself in spirit at the feet of Jesus, watering them with my tears." A 15th-century book of hours illuminated by Simon Marmion shows Jerome kneeling before a vision of Jesus on the cross.

Ulfilas Among the Visigoths

A FOURTH-CENTURY BISHOP INVENTED AN ALPHABET IN ORDER TO BRING THE BIBLE TO EUROPE'S GERMANIC TRIBES.

D uring the early centuries A.D. Germanic tribes known as Goths, who made their home in Jutland and Scandinavia, swept southeastward across Europe to the Black Sea. In time, these conquerors from the north would storm and sack Rome and completely upend the ancient order of the Roman Empire. Ironically, the only literary trace of the Goths' early settlement in middle Europe was a Bible translated into their own tongue.

The Goths who settled in Dacia (present-day Romania) in the third century were known as Visigoths, meaning "West Goths." Born among them about 310 was Ulfilas (or Wulfila), the man who would translate the Bible from Greek into Gothic. Ulfilas' father may have been a Goth, but his mother was not. Her own parents probably were among the many Christians brought to Dacia as captives following Gothic raids in Asia Minor. By Ulfilas' time, the Visigoths were aware of Christianity not only because of their captives but also through the missionaries who had come to preach among them.

Bishop and Translator Ulfilas was able to learn Latin and Greek as well as Gothic and as a young man was a lector in Christian services. About 340 he traveled to Constantinople, where he was consecrated bishop of the Goths by Eusebius of Nicomedia, an influential proponent of Arianism. Arians were Christians who disputed the orthodox definition of the Trinity and did not accept that God the Father and God the Son were equal in every way.

Ulfilas made it his mission to spread Arian Christianity among the Visigoths. By 348, however, he and his followers left Dacia, probably driven out by persecution. They escaped to Nicopolis, in the area that is now Bulgaria, where Ulfilas served both as temporal and spiritual leader to his followers. A fifth-century writer described his power there as equal to that of a monarch.

It was in Nicopolis, perhaps about 350, that Ulfilas began to produce his Gothic Bible. His first obstacle was that Gothic existed only as a spoken language. Undeterred, he created a Gothic alphabet, doing so

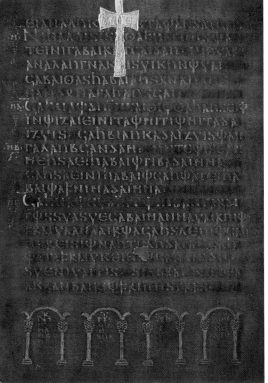

The Codex Argenteus, a page of which is shown above, is one of the most important extant copies of Ulfilas' Gothic Bible. It was written in silver ink on purple parchment. The Visigothic gold-and-jeweled votive crown, top, was made in Spain in the seventh century and was meant to hang in a church.

The Visigoths arrived in the area of the Black Sea in the third century. About 271 the Roman emperor conceded Dacia to them. In 410 the Visigoths sacked Rome. Within the next 100 years the Visigoths inhabited the Iberian Peninsula and reached the height of their power and influence.

by borrowing from Greek. Out of the 27 Gothic letters he devised, 18 or 19 were based on Greek letters, another 6 on Latin letters, and 2 on Gothic runes. Another problem Ulfilas had to overcome was linguistic, since he had to express Christian concepts such as the Holy Spirit and God the Father in a language that did not have words for those ideas. The task of translation is thought to have taken Ulfilas some 30 years.

Scholars disagree as to how much of the Bible Ulfilas actually translated. Greek sources claim that he completed the entire Old and New Testaments except for the Books of Samuel and Kings, which, according to tradition, he feared were too warlike for the flammable Goths. Nothing of Ulfilas' original manuscript survives, but fragments exist of fifth- and sixth-century copies of Ezra and Nehemiah, the Gospels, and the Pauline letters.

This Visigothic stone relief, showing Jesus between two angels, was carved for a church in Quintanilla de las Viñas, Spain, sometime in the seventh century.

Ulfilas' Influence

The Visigoths were still largely pagan when Ulfilas died about 382, but his work continued. His followers were responsible for the spread of Arian Christianity among the Germanic tribes between 382 and 395. Alaric, a Visigothic king, had converted to the faith before he sacked Rome in 410.

During the seventh century almost all traces of the Gothic language and Bible disappeared, due no doubt to the fierce reaction against Arianism, which had been pronounced heretical. King Reccared of Spain, where the Visigoths had settled early in the sixth century, ordered that all Arian books be collected and burned—books that included not only the Gothic Bible but other writings by Ulfilas. Nonetheless, Ulfilas' influence was profound. His missionary work was the first major step toward bringing Christianity into central Europe. His translation of the Bible and its spread throughout Europe remain one of the important links between the ancient and medieval worlds. ❖

Desert Fathers

DRAWING INSPIRATION FROM THE GOSPELS, SOME CHRISTIANS
SOUGHT SPIRITUAL FULFILLMENT THROUGH PHYSICAL DISCIPLINE.

As Christianity became established, and believers no longer
lived under the threat of persecution, martyrdom ceased
to be the ultimate expression of the faith. Consequently,
Christians endeavoring to attain spiritual perfection
began to withdraw from the world to take up a life of solitude, asceticism, and the contemplation of Scripture.

The Christian monastic movement originated in the late third
century A.D. in the desert regions of Egypt. By that time there already
existed a tradition of retreat to the desert by those seeking to escape
a variety of societal pressures, such as burdensome taxation, military
service, and debt. In fact, the practice had become so common that a
Greek word was coined for it—*anachoresis*, meaning "withdrawal."

The desert monastics were not so much running away as running
toward something that only the desert could provide: a release from
all obligation aside from a devotion to God's word as revealed in the
Scriptures. This yearning for the ascetic life was described in the highly

*Simeon the Elder of Syria (shown
in a 17th-century icon) followed in
the stylite monastic tradition. In
A.D. 423 he mounted a pillar and,
for nearly 40 years, preached from
his perch to visiting pilgrims.
Communal monasticism emerged as
hermits occupied adjacent cells in
the wilderness, such as the ones that
pockmark the volcanic hills of
Cappadocia in modern-day Turkey.*

influential *Life of Anthony*, written in the 350's by Athanasius of Alexandria about one of the founders of monasticism, Anthony of Egypt. The *Life* tells how, at age 20, Anthony was seized by an overwhelming emotion upon hearing the words of Jesus spoken in church: "If you wish to be perfect, go, sell your possessions, and give the money to the poor [Matthew 19:21]." Taking Jesus' message as a personal directive, Anthony left his village and eventually went to live for 20 years in the ruins of an abandoned fortress by the Red Sea.

Hermetic Life Others followed Anthony's example. Hermits, or anchorites, some of them women, took up residence in caves, ruins, or other rude dwellings. They shed all material possessions save those necessary for survival—a tunic, perhaps a pallet on which to sleep, and a container for trapping and carrying water. Alone in the desert they prayed, recited Scripture, worked, fasted, and maintained a constant vigil against the demonic spirits they believed to be all around them in the desert.

Knowledge itself was regarded as a form of vanity, and hermits rarely owned copies of the Scriptures. In fact, most were illiterate and knew the Scriptures only from hearing them read aloud. Of Anthony, Athanasius wrote: "In him memory took the place of books."

Common Life Stories and sayings of these "spiritual athletes" soon circulated, attracting followers and even tourists. Disciples made pilgrimages to the desert to speak to them or to become hermits themselves and remain close to the source of their inspiration. Thus, as loosely organized communities of monks grew up around charismatic elders, the solitary tradition began to yield to a cenobitic, or communal, way of life.

A native of Egypt named Pachomius established the first Christian monastic community in the early fourth century at Tabennisi in Upper Egypt. He is also credited with formulating the first monastic rule, consisting of 194 articles that outlined a schedule of shared meals, work, prayer, and discipline. The cenobitic monks modeled their communities on the ideal of the Apostles, whereby "all who believed were together and had all things in common [Acts 2: 44]."

Other rules of self-governance were established, collected, and distributed, leading to the further institutionalization of monastic life. The *Longer Rules* and *Shorter Rules* of Basil of Caesarea still guide Greek and Russian monks today. The most influential rule in the West was that of Benedict of Nursia (480–540). Benedict's dicta, which partially drew on the rules of Pachomius and Basil, eventually became the founding principles of Western monasticism. ❖

Anthony of Egypt prepares his disciple Paul for burial in this 15th-century work of the Spanish school. Paul had gone into the desert despite his advanced age and over Anthony's initial objections.

Pilgrimages

PILGRIMS JOURNEYED TO THE HOLY LAND TO WALK ON THE GROUND TROD BY THE FIGURES OF THE OLD TESTAMENT AND JESUS HIMSELF.

Mementos, such as this 6th-century oil flask from Palestine, above, were mass produced for the pilgrimage market. The relief on the flask shows the women at the tomb of Jesus and was meant to resemble the shrine of the Holy Sepulcher in Jerusalem. The Jordan River, shown crowded by pilgrims in a 19th-century lithograph, below, is mentioned more than 200 times in the Bible. As the place where Jesus was baptized, it is one of the most revered of all Christian sites.

For Christians, the practice of traveling to sites associated with Old and New Testament events and personages goes back to the mid-second century, when Melito, bishop of Sardis, went to Palestine probably in order to verify the authenticity of biblical data. Pilgrimage for devotional purposes was promoted at the time of Constantine, whose mother, Helena, had visited Jerusalem in 326 and identified the holiest of Christian places—the cave where Jesus was said to have been entombed. Constantine ordered that the Church of the Holy Sepulcher be erected on the site and commissioned the building of other churches in Jerusalem and Bethlehem.

Although some early Christian teachers, such as Augustine of Hippo, condemned pilgrimage for seemingly undermining church teachings on God's omnipresence, believers undertook the arduous trek to Palestine in ever greater numbers. Many felt with Jerome that it was "part of the faith to adore where His feet have stood."

Sacred Places A pilgrimage was a journey through time as well as space. Using the Scriptures as a guidebook, the pilgrim traveled to a succession of sacred places associated with the biblical events. Many set off from Mount Sinai and then followed the route of the Exodus. The pilgrim might visit the tombs of the Old Testament prophets, whose words were thought to foretell the coming of Jesus, then trace the peregrinations of Jesus, going from Bethlehem to Galilee, and

from Galilee to Jerusalem. Some pilgrims sought out the residences of the desert monastics in Egypt and Syria and the monuments dedicated to saints and martyrs, such as those of Peter and Paul in Rome.

But the most desired destination of pilgrimage remained the Holy Land. Marked by sacred places and crisscrossed by a network of pilgrimage routes, the Holy Land provided visible proof of God's plan and its fulfillment by Jesus. With every step the pilgrims took on their journey, they found the words of Holy Writ affirmed.

Guides for the Soul Written accounts of the Holy Land and early pilgrimages often served as supplementary guides for later pilgrims. Two such texts, both dating from the fourth century, were the list of biblical place names compiled by Eusebius and the itinerary written by the Bordeaux Pilgrim, which describes the anonymous author's route and his sojourns at 40 Old and New Testament sites.

Another fourth-century visitor, the woman Egeria, who probably hailed from southern Gaul, recorded a detailed itinerary of her tour to 63 Old Testament and 33 New Testament sites in Egypt, Palestine, and Asia Minor. Reenacting the Exodus, Egeria traversed the Sinai and carefully matched biblical text to place. "When you read the holy books of Moses," she noted, "you will clearly see everything that happened there." Egeria also made a pilgrimage to places associated with Jesus. She took in the Church of the Nativity, Lazarus' tomb in Bethany, the Apostle Thomas's tomb in Edessa, and, in Jerusalem, the churches on the sites of the Holy Sepulcher and the Mount of Olives.

By Egeria's time, pilgrims were a common feature of the Holy Land. The sites were maintained by monks, and monastic houses became hostels and rest stations. Monks doubled as guides, who explained the significance of the sites, prayed with pilgrims, and read aloud to them relevant passages from the Bible. Christian pilgrims often left Palestine with mementos from the sites, which they carried home as blessed keepsakes of their journey. ❖

FAITH OF ISLAM

With the Arab conquest of Jerusalem in 638, Palestine and its pilgrimage sites fell into the hands of the Muslims. The conquerors, who traced their ancestry to Abraham, venerated many of the Christian and Jewish sites in the Holy Land. But as Muslims, their chief pilgrimage obligation was to make a journey to Mecca. For it was there, according to the Islamic faith, that God revealed the Scriptures to Muhammad.

A devout man born into the ruling Arab tribe, Muhammad was meditating in the hills outside Mecca in the year 610 when he experienced a vision: The angel Gabriel appeared and ordered him to "Recite." The words Muhammad uttered that night and at intervals over the next 22 years were eventually compiled, recorded, and organized into the 114 chapters of the Islamic Scriptures, known as the Koran.

Varying Traditions

SOME PEOPLES LIVING IN THE NEAR EAST AND NORTH AFRICA HAVE BIBLE TRADITIONS
THAT MAY DATE AS EARLY AS THE LATE FIRST AND THE SECOND CENTURIES.

Among the earliest of the Christian translations of the Old and New Testaments are those made in Syriac, Coptic (a form of Egyptian), and Ethiopic.

Syriac Bible Traditions Syriac was an Aramaic dialect widely used in the Near East from the early Christian era through the Middle Ages. The earliest translation of the Old Testament into Syriac is thought to date from the late first or early second century. The translation was made from the Hebrew Bible and was later given the name Peshitta, meaning "simple" or "pure," to distinguish it from Syriac translations that were made from the Greek Septuagint.

The oldest translation of the New Testament in Syriac is a version of

Tatian's *Diatessaron* that dates from about 170. The *Diatessaron,* or "harmony of the Gospels," in which the four Gospels were combined into one, was extremely popular among Syriac-speaking Christians. Syrian bishops in fact had difficulty getting communicants to accept the Gospels as four separate books. In the fourth century the Syriac church introduced a manuscript called the Separated Gospels, which divided the four texts but retained some of the *Diatessaron's* wording. Syriac was eventually superseded by Arabic as the common language and survived only to be used in the liturgy.

Coptic Bibles Coptic was the language of Egypt from about the 3rd century to the 11th. Spoken Coptic was much like the language of ancient Egypt but with Greek words added to it. Until the Christian era the Egyptians had used a simplified form of hieroglyphs for their written language, but sometime in the early centuries after Jesus a Coptic alphabet closely related to Greek was developed.

There were at least five dialects in Coptic, and biblical translations were made from the Greek into all of them. The first was probably

The page from a seventh-century copy of the Peshitta, or Syriac translation of the Hebrew Bible, far left, is from the Book of Jeremiah. The illuminated page, from the sixth-century Syriac Rabbula Gospels, shows the Crucifixion and the women at the tomb.

Sahidic—the language of Upper Egypt—since the people there were the least familiar with the Greek language and could not read the Greek Bible. The Sahidic translation of the Old Testament is thought to have been begun as early as the year 200. The translation into Boharic, the dialect of the Delta region of Lower Egypt, was not made until somewhat later. Greek was a common language in the Delta, and the people's need for a vernacular Bible was less great. In time, Boharic became the major language of the Coptic Church.

What remains of Coptic biblical manuscripts is fragmentary. No complete Bible survives, nor does a complete New Testament. However, it is clear by the numbers of Coptic Christian papyri that the early church in Egypt was supported by an active and well-educated community of Christians. By the 17th century, Coptic was obsolete as a spoken language and was used only in the liturgy.

The 14th-century manuscript detail, above left, is inscribed in Coptic but has Arabic notes written above the boat. The 8th-century example of Coptic weaving, above, depicts the adoration of the Magi.

Ethiopic Bible Translations

The Old Testament is believed by some scholars to have been translated into Old Ethiopic, or Geᶜez, as early as the fourth century. Falashas, African Jews whose forebears migrated to Ethiopia during the time of Solomon, are credited with the work. It is not certain whether they based their translation on the Greek or Syriac Bibles.

The Geᶜez Old Testament canon is the largest of any Bible. It includes the Book of Enoch, Jubilees, and the apocryphal 3 Baruch. Ethiopic translations of the New Testament are thought to date sometime between the fourth and seventh centuries, but they show evidence of later revisions, with elements from both Coptic and Arabic texts.

Paul and Timothy are seen conversing on this page from a 15th-century copy of the Pauline epistles, written in Ethiopic.

The differences in the texts of the Ethiopic Bible, as well as its expanded Old Testament canon, make its study critical to scholars. The vernacular Ethiopian biblical texts have been referred to as the "end of the corridor," the repository for ancient material that was lost elsewhere. ❖

The Bible in the Eastern Churches

TRANSLATED BIBLES APPEARED IN ARMENIA AND GEORGIA IN THE FIFTH CENTURY
AND IN EASTERN AND CENTRAL EUROPE IN THE NINTH CENTURY.

The dispersion of the Bible throughout the Eastern churches was inextricably linked with the creation of individual alphabets and with the fostering of national consciousness.

Armenia has claim to being history's first Christian kingdom. Credit for its conversion is given to Gregory the Illuminator, an Armenian who was educated and ordained in the Roman town of Caesarea, Asia Minor, but who later returned to his native country. In the late third century Gregory converted his relative, Tiridates III, who was the king of Armenia, to Christianity. The rest of the nation converted to Christianity soon after.

The Bible in Armenia More than a century later the Bible was still not accessible to Armenians because few could understand Greek, Syriac, or Hebrew. But in the early fifth century, a monk known as Mesrop decided to translate the Bible into Armenian. About 404, with the blessings of Bishop Sahak, the head of the Armenian Church, and with the encouragement of the king, Mesrop created an alphabet of 36 letters using the Greek alphabet as his model.

Mesrop then set out to translate the Bible. Ultimately he succeeded in translating not only the Old and New Testaments into Armenian but also the

The Armenian alphabet was devised for the purpose of translating the Bible. The script appears above in a detail from a 1274 copy of the Gospels in Armenian.

liturgy, commentaries, and treatises by the Apostolic Fathers. Some scholars believe that Mesrop may have made part of his translation from the Syriac Bible and revised it in accordance with Greek manuscripts. The translation has been called "the queen of the versions" because of the role it played in unifying Armenians.

Mesrop also opened schools to teach people how to read and write Armenian. Through the bonds of a shared language and religion the people forged a national identity that has survived centuries. Pilgrims still flock to Mesrop's grave in Armenia to pay homage to the national saint, and his Bible continues to be used by Armenians wherever they are scattered.

The Bible in Georgia The history of Christianity in Georgia followed a similar pattern. The country's conversion to Christianity—which took place about 330—is credited to a pious slave woman who was brought as a captive to Georgia following a raid on Asia Minor, which was then under Roman rule. Known as St. Nino the Nun, she was so pious that she gained the attention of Georgia's King Mirian, whom she converted. The entire nation followed the king's example.

No one knows for sure when the first Georgian translation of the Bible was made, though it might

have been as early as the fifth century. The original Georgian translation may also have been based in part on the Syriac Bible and then revised to coincide with the Greek. Remarkably it was Mesrop who created the 38-letter alphabet that was used for translating the Bible and the liturgy into Georgian. During the years of his missionary work setting up schools, Mesrop spent some time in Georgia, where he devised the Georgian script, which was also based on the Greek alphabet. In the 420's, Mesrop traveled to Constantinople, but on his return journey he spent time in Caucasian Albania, where he created a third alphabet, which was used for the Albanian Scriptures.

The Georgian Bible is still in use in Georgia. There are, however, no remains of the Albanian Bible, which disappeared with the destruction of the Albanian church during the seventh-century Islamic wars.

The Bible in Eastern Europe Between the fourth and eighth centuries there was a growing estrangement between the Byzantine

Distinctive stone churches dating as early as the 7th century are found throughout Armenia. The Church of the Holy Cross, left, was built on the island of Aght'amar in Lake Van in the first quarter of the 10th century. The facade of the church is decorated with biblical reliefs. The detail below shows David ready to bring down Goliath with his sling.

Empire and the West over theological and cultural differences. The situation led to a schism in the church with Rome and the West on one side and Byzantium and the East on the other. As Islam became the reigning religion to the south and east of Byzantium, what would become known as the Orthodox, or Eastern, Church looked northward to gather new converts.

The Bible in Moravia For reasons both of faith and politics, Prince Rostislav of Moravia (Slovakia) wrote to the church in Constantinople in 862, saying in part: "Many Christians have arrived in our midst . . . we pray you to send us someone capable of teaching us the whole truth." Rostislav requested missionaries who would preach and conduct worship in Slavonic. He was sent the perfect candidates: a pair of highly educated Greek brothers named Constantine, or Cyril, and Methodius. Before the brothers set out for Moravia, Cyril devised a Slavonic alphabet drawing on Greek and Hebrew. (There are two early Slavonic alphabets—Cyrillic, named after Cyril, and Glagolitic—and it is unclear to scholars today which of the two he devised.)

In Moravia Cyril began to translate the Bible into Slavonic with the intention of training a native clergy. Though the work was lauded by the Slavs, it was vigorously opposed by Frankish missionaries, who, following Rome, held rigidly to the belief that liturgy could be performed only in Latin, Greek, or Hebrew. Continued opposition to their missionary work forced the brothers to travel to Rome to plead their case. Cyril presented an impassioned argument for the use of vernacular texts: "Have you no shame, to settle upon three languages only, and ordain that all other people, and all nations else, must be deaf and dumb forever?" After careful consideration, Pope Adrian II sided with the brothers and approved the use of their Slavonic liturgy.

In his moment of triumph Cyril was stricken with a grave illness. He died in Rome at the age of 42. Methodius returned to his mission among the Slavs and continued work on the Slavonic translation of the Bible. Despite the support of the pope, Methodius was opposed by

Georgian script appears above in a portion of an 11th-century menologion—the ecclesiastical calendar of the Eastern Church. Cyril and Methodius, who translated the Bible into Slavonic, are shown at right in an image from the 15th-century Radziwill Chronicle, *which records early Russian history.*

This Slavonic Gospel book was produced in Moldavia in 1429. The book is open to the Gospel According to Mark, where the evangelist is depicted at work writing his Gospel. The main script shown here is a form of Cyrillic called Bulgarian Church Slavonic. In the margin the corresponding text is written in Greek.

Frankish bishops, who had him arrested in 870. Three years later Pope John III ordered his release. After Methodius' death in 884, his followers were expelled from Moravia. Despite their failure there, Cyril and Methodius' work was not in vain—their disciples scattered throughout eastern Europe and their Slavonic translations were embraced in Bulgaria, Serbia, and Russia.

The Bible in Russia

Russia indeed proved to be the greatest missionary success for the Orthodox Church. In the late 10th century the brutal Prince Vladimir of Kiev agreed to convert to Orthodoxy when he married the sister of the Byzantine emperor. The effect of Christianity on Vladimir was miraculous. He built churches and monasteries and eschewed capital punishment. Orthodox Christianity became the official religion of the state.

It was in part due to Cyril and Methodius' translations of the Bible and the liturgy that the faith spread quickly throughout Russia. The Eastern Church believed strongly in proselytizing in the language of the people. In so doing Orthodoxy not only created a vernacular literature for the Slavic people but developed as a church with a strong national identity. ❖

Slavs adopted Christian iconography as well as Scripture. This detail from "Prayer in the Garden of Gethsemane" is from a 14th-century fresco at St. Clement's Church in Byzantine Macedonia.

The 12 Apostles gaze penetratingly from a 14th-century icon originating in Constantinople. In the first row are James, Peter, John, and Matthew.

This rare sixth-century icon on wood, picturing a nearly life-size image of Jesus, survived the eighth-century iconoclastic movement that destroyed many icons. It was found at the Monastery of St. Catherine at Sinai.

A tiny mosaic Annunciation reveals the deep spirituality of 14th-century Byzantine art.

Worshipers believed the image of archangel Michael (shown in a 10th-century icon) had healing powers.

This portable ivory triptych of the 10th century was used for private devotional purposes.

The worshiper, praying before this portable 15th-century Russian iconostasis (screen), would have sequentially invoked the names of the saints and appealed to them to intercede with God on his behalf.

The sophisticated rendering of Jesus and the mother of Christ and child on an ivory diptych, above, contrasts with the rustic character of the same subjects depicted on a tapestry panel, left. Both images date from about the sixth century. The ivory was probably made in Ravenna, and the tapestry most likely originated in Egypt.

Byzantine Icons

The icon, defined as a venerated image of sacred personages, attained a central place in the life of the Eastern church. Basil the Great praised religious imagery for its appeal to the eye, which he likened to the word's appeal to the ear. The eighth-century theologian John of Damascus defended icons, saying, "Since God has appeared in the flesh . . . I can represent what is visible in God."

As the cult of images grew and was tolerated by the church, basilicas became rich repositories for icons. Images of Jesus, the Virgin Mary, and the saints were displayed on church walls and eventually given a place of prominence on the iconostasis, a screen that divides the nave from the sanctuary.

But opposition to images mounted among Christians who regarded their use as a form of idolatry; and when, in 726, the Byzantine emperor Leo III proclaimed his hostility to icons, civil conflict broke out. Over the next 60 years, zealous iconoclasts (image breakers) removed and destroyed countless sacred images from the churches. An uneasy peace was reached in 787 when the orthodox Second Council of Nicaea proclaimed that the veneration paid to the icon is transferred to the person depicted in the image.

A Greek Psalter of 1066 depicts a group of iconoclasts removing an image of Jesus. Icon breakers often replaced icons with symbols.

The Vernacular Bible in Europe

BY THE END OF THE MIDDLE AGES, THE BIBLE HAD BEEN TRANSLATED INTO MANY EUROPEAN LANGUAGES—DESPITE ATTEMPTS TO FORBID THE PROCESS.

The manuscript detail shown here is taken from a six-volume German Bible known as the Wenzelsbibel, which was created about 1390 for King Wenceslas of Bohemia. The illumination is of the scene from Exodus in which Aaron's rod is turned into a snake.

At the start of the fifth century, when Jerome completed his Vulgate Bible, Latin was the literary language of Europe as well as the spoken language of urbanized European Christians. For a long time after Jerome, the Vulgate and earlier Latin translations of the Bible continued to be the preeminent texts for Christian worship, study, and preaching in Europe. But as Rome's influence lessened, and the movement and settlement of Germanic peoples throughout Europe continued, the use of Latin gradually faded. In order for the Bible to reach a new Christian population, it had to be delivered in vernacular languages.

Between the 7th century and the 15th, at least parts of the Bible were translated into most of the major European languages. However, translations of the entire Bible were rare throughout the Middle Ages and probably nonexistent before 1200. More often translating was confined to sections of the Bible—particularly the Gospels, the Psalter, and the historical books—and there were numerous summaries of the Old Testament in vernacular languages.

Initially, many translations took the form of glosses. In most glosses literal word-for-word transcriptions were written between the lines of the Latin manuscript, and explanatory notes were added, but there were variations. Notker Labeo, a German monk and teacher at the monastic school of St. Gall in the 10th and 11th centuries, translated both the Psalter and the Book of Job by writing a section in Latin verse and then its German equivalent, followed by his own commentary.

Early Texts By the 10th century, literary translations were being made in addition to literal ones. Poets and other writers often paraphrased stories from both the Old and New Testaments and gave public readings of these paraphrasings. Most of these works have been lost, but some fragments survive, including 337 lines of a rendition of Genesis and nearly 6,000 lines of the *Heliand* ("Saviour"), a versified Gospel based on Tatian's *Diatessaron*. Both of these epic poems date from the 9th century and were written in Old Saxon, a language of northern Germany. In France, Jesus' Passion was the subject of a narrative poem that originated in a convent in Cluny about the year 1000.

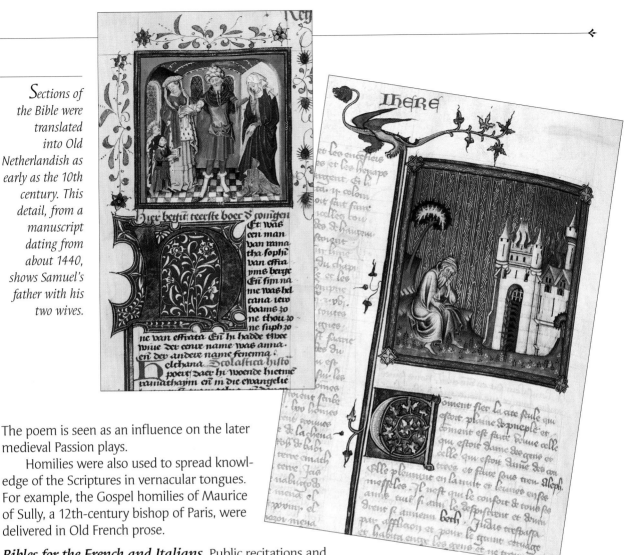

Sections of the Bible were translated into Old Netherlandish as early as the 10th century. This detail, from a manuscript dating from about 1440, shows Samuel's father with his two wives.

The poem is seen as an influence on the later medieval Passion plays.

Homilies were also used to spread knowledge of the Scriptures in vernacular tongues. For example, the Gospel homilies of Maurice of Sully, a 12th-century bishop of Paris, were delivered in Old French prose.

Bibles for the French and Italians

Public recitations and readings were not only popular but necessary as long as access to the Bible was limited mainly to the clergy. However, that situation began to change in the late 1100's when religious groups such as the Beghards and Beguines in the Low Countries and Germany and the Waldensians in France asked Christians to return to apostolic simplicity and pointed out interpretations of the Bible that differed from the church's. These groups encouraged the public to read the Bible and so the demand for vernacular religious texts soared. The end of the 12th century was an intense period for biblical translation.

In 1199 Pope Innocent III ordered an inquiry into the activity of translating the Bible. As a result he condemned heretical interpretation of the Bible but pronounced, "The desire to understand holy Scripture and the attempt to encourage others to live in accordance with its teachings . . . is indeed praiseworthy." However, a council of bishops who met in Toulouse, France, in 1229 to discuss the "heretical" activities of a group called the Albigensians forbade anyone who was not a member of the clergy to own a Bible in any language.

During the Middle Ages, books of the Bible were often combined with other texts in what were called History Bibles. For his 13th-century French Bible Historiale, Guyart des Moulins translated books and commentary from the Vulgate and added them to a Scholastic history written by Peter Comestor. A detail from a 14th-century copy of that work is shown above.

Although church authorities continued to forbid lay ownership of Bibles, vernacular translations continued to be made. Immediately after the pronouncements of the Council of Toulouse, in fact, King Louis IX commissioned a complete Bible written in French. Collections of translations were compiled in Paris or Picardy in the 13th century, and French texts were carried abroad, where they influenced translations into other European languages.

Italian translations of books of the Bible did not appear until the mid-13th century, and these early translations—particularly those of the Gospels, Revelation, and Psalms—were often based on earlier French and Provençal versions as well as on the Vulgate. Scholars believe that vernacular translations were not popularly produced in Italy until this relatively late date because early Italian dialects were similar to Latin, and for a long time even poorly educated Italians could understand Latin. However, when translation did begin, Tuscan and Venetian were the two dialects that were used most often in Italian Bibles.

German and Spanish Bibles

Meanwhile, during the 13th and 14th centuries, charges of heresy were leveled at many German translations of the Bible. An imperial edict in 1369 and a papal decree in 1375 prohibited the translation of religious books and Scriptures into German dialects, but these orders did not manage to prevent production. In 1370, for instance, Henry of Mügeln, a court poet, published a translation of the Psalter. His translation was so popular that 31 copies of the manuscript have survived.

Spain did not produce the number or variety of Bibles that other European countries produced. This may well have been because Spanish authorities kept a particularly strict eye on any activity that could be interpreted as heretical. Nevertheless, medieval Spain's history of Bible translation is a rich one.

As early as the 12th century, Jewish scholars were translating the Hebrew Bible into Spanish. By the 13th century, Spanish Jews were

The biblical Moses holds up the tablets of the Law, inscribed in Hebrew, in an illustration from the Alba Bible, Rabbi Moses Arragel's Spanish Old Testament.

Rabbi Moses Arragel, in the foreground, above, presents his translation of the Hebrew Bible to Don Luis de Guzmán in an illustration from the Alba Bible. The work was commissioned in 1422 and completed in 1433.

also contributing to the production of Christian Bibles by translating the Old Testament from the Hebrew Bible while Christians translated the New Testament from the Vulgate.

This was not the first time Jews had translated the Hebrew Bible into European languages. The very first full Old Testament in French, for instance, was made from the Hebrew Bible by Jews in Provence. However, the collaboration between Jews and Christians on Christian Bibles in Spain was unique, though not always appreciated. Reacting against Jewish-Christian translation in 1233, King James I of Aragon banned the production of vernacular Bibles. But, of course, the ban did not hold. One of James's own descendants, Alfonso III, was among those who reversed the order when he commissioned the translation of the Catalan Bible, which was probably made from the French.

Two Important Spanish Bibles One of the earliest and most important Spanish Bibles dates from the latter half of the 13th century and was sponsored by Alfonso X, the king of Castile and Leon. Alfonso the Wise, as he was known, was a great champion of education, literature, and the development of the Castilian language. Several works that drew on all the knowledge of the time—classical, Arabic, Christian, and Hebrew—were produced in his court. One of the works by Alfonso's scholars was a massive *Grande e General Estoria*, a five-volume history of the world that included a paraphrase of the Bible.

Another unique Bible was begun in 1422, when Don Luis de Guzmán, a nobleman, ordered Rabbi Moses Arragel of Guadalajara to make a new translation of the Old Testament. By that date, the Spanish translations that had been made from the Hebrew Bible in the 13th century were considered outmoded. The rabbi demurred, saying that as a Jew he would not be able to please a Christian lord. This answer infuriated Guzmán and he convinced the rabbi to take on the project with the understanding that a Franciscan and a Dominican friar would supervise his work. Thus began a remarkable collaboration that resulted in the Alba Bible, a work that is unlike any other medieval Bible in that it combines rabbinic wisdom with Christian interpretation. In his translation the rabbi provided readers with both Latin and Hebrew vernacular terms so that, "the Jew would not be startled by the Latin nor the Christian by the Hebrew words." ❖

The Bible in the British Isles

MONKS SPREAD CHRISTIANITY THROUGH IRELAND, SCOTLAND, AND ENGLAND AND PRESERVED SACRED SCRIPTURE.

Like the islands themselves that are often covered with clouds, the coming of Christianity—and the Bible—to the British Isles is shrouded in mystery. A legend claims that Joseph of Arimathea, who buried Jesus in his own tomb, brought Christianity to Britain (called Britannia by its Roman rulers), but there is no evidence to support it. The eighth-century historian Bede is probably closer to the truth. He claims that Christianity reached Britain in 156, when Lucius, a British king, wrote the bishop of Rome, "asking to be made a Christian."

Spreading the Good News By the fourth century, the British were dispatching evangelists to convert their neighbors. In the early fifth century Ninian, a Welshman, brought the Bible to the Picts in Scotland while Patrick in the footsteps of his predecessor, Palladius, was targeting the Celts and Druids in Ireland. Born in Britain, Patrick had been kidnapped and sold into slavery in Ireland. After escaping, he studied in a British monastery and returned to Ireland to preach the Gospel, baptizing thousands and establishing churches and monasteries.

While Christianity flourished in Ireland, it was under grave threat in the eastern parts of the British Isles. In the mid-fifth to early sixth centuries Germanic tribes—the Angles, Saxons, and Jutes—invaded, imposed their pagan beliefs on the populace, and laid siege to the church. In Ireland, however, the church went

Columba, a 6th-century monk, was dedicated to copying Scripture. He is shown, above left, wearing an abbot's vestments, in a 16th-century book of his life. Columba may have copied the Psalter shown above. One of the earliest of all surviving Irish manuscripts, it is called the Cathach, or "battler," because it was said to bring victory when carried three times around the battlefield.

Early Irish monks lived in clusters of beehive huts, such as the sixth-century dwelling shown at left, which is still standing on Great Skellig Island off the southwest coast of Ireland.

"WORK OF THE ANGELS"

During the more than three centuries that the monks of Ireland, Scotland, and northern England spent meticulously copying sacred Scripture, they became more and more elaborate in decorating their manuscripts. Of all the works they created, perhaps the most lavishly illustrated and most colorful was the Book of Kells. In fact, this book's illustrations and ornamentations are so rich in color and detail that a 12th-century commentator declared that they must be the work of angels rather than of men.

The Book of Kells is a collection of the four Gospels in which the work of at least four different artists can be distinguished. On nearly every text page there are ornate initial letters, often including convoluted beasts and human figures, which may have been influenced by Pictish art. Irish and northern English elements are also common. The text, unfortunately, is full of errors, but it too is beautiful, written in a fine ornamental hand.

The page shown above left, in part, is from the first Gospel. The text reads *"Tunc crucifixerant XRI cum eo duos latrones,"* which translates as "Then they crucified two bandits with him, the Christ [Matthew 27:38]."

Little is known of the origins of the Book of Kells, but it may have been created near the end of the eighth century at Iona, the monastery founded on an island off the coast of Scotland by Columba. The manuscript was probably moved to a new monastery at Kells, Ireland, in the ninth century after raiding Norsemen had overrun Iona.

from strength to strength, thanks largely to dedicated monks, who established monastic centers of spiritual and scholarly excellence. These Irish monasteries soon became magnets for scholars from England and the European Continent. With barbarian hordes laying waste to Europe and its great libraries, the Irish monks also took on the role of saviors of learning, copying not only Scriptures but Greek and Latin classics as well. In time, they began to export their learning by sending scholars to other lands. One of the first of these was Columba.

The Story of Columba Columba, whose name means "dove," was born in 521 in Garton, Donegal, into a princely family. He studied under some of the best scholars and developed an enduring love for Scripture. According to a popular legend, it was this love for Scripture that sealed his fate.

When Columba learned that his former master, Finnian, had the first copy of Jerome's Book of Psalms to reach Ireland, he copied it against Finian's wishes. When Finnian ordered Columba to return both the original and the copy, he refused, and the two went to King Diarmaid. Ruling in Finnian's favor, the king decided the world's first copyright case with the words: "To every cow her calf; to every book its copy." Later, when the king ordered that someone under Columba's protection be killed, the monk's clan attacked the king's forces, and 3,000 men were slain. As a consequence, Columba was exiled. For his penance he resolved to save at least 3,000 souls, the number he felt responsible for destroying in battle.

According to a seventh-century biography, in 563 Columba and 12 relatives set out in a fragile, leather-covered wicker boat into the treacherous North Channel between Ireland and Scotland. After landing on the tiny island of Iona, the band of clerics established a monastery that would eventually become famous around the world as a center of learning. In addition to converting the pagan Picts, Columba and his monks devoted their energies to copying the Scriptures.

Other Irish monks followed in Columba's wake to Scotland and Britain. Still others went to the European Continent, where they boldly brought the ancient learning, in the form of their hand-copied manuscripts, back to its place of origin. Ironically, the last part of western Europe to be converted to Christianity played a key role in preserving and reintroducing the faith—and the Scriptures.

Bede, known for his history of the English church and peoples, is shown at work in an eighth-century manuscript illumination. Bede was translating John's Gospel into English when he died in 735. The depiction of Joseph in his chariot, below, is from a copy of Ælfric's paraphrase of Genesis.

Return to England In an effort to convert England's new pagan rulers to Christianity, Pope Gregory sent a Roman prior, Augustine, to meet the Saxon ruler, Æthelbert, king of Kent. (Augustine probably did not realize that Æthelbert's Frankish wife, Bertha, was already a devout Christian.) In 597 Augustine and 40 monks arrived in England carrying a supply of books from the papal library, probably including the Latin Bible. Evidently the show of men and books impressed the pagan king, for he was subsequently baptized. This event opened the door for Augustine, the first archbishop of Canterbury, and his monks to convert thousands more Jutes, Angles, and Saxons in Britain.

a rode Iorep into phapaone · Jepæð tohim mnpæðep· Jmine
sebpoþpu · Jheopa pcep heopða · Jheopa hpyþep heopða · Jtalleþa
þing þehig agon comon ofchanaan lande· Jmihi rynd ongefren-
lande · Prod lice helæðþe hir fif gingran bpoðpu beþopan þonecyng

While Augustine's monks worked their way north and west, Irish monks ventured into Britain from the island of Lindisfarne in the northeast.

In the English Tongue For years Latin had been the language of the Bible. However, as more and more souls were converted to Christianity, the need arose for a Bible in a language the people and the large number of poorly educated priests understood. This need was partially met by adding Anglo-Saxon glosses, or translations, above the main texts of Latin Bibles, as can be seen in the 7th-century Lindisfarne Gospels. In addition, although the first complete English-language Bible did not appear until the 14th century, a number of earlier attempts were made to translate fully at least some of the Latin Scriptures into Old English dialects.

King Alfred the Great, who oversaw a revival of learning in the ninth century, is himself credited with translating portions of Exodus, the Acts of the Apostles, and the Psalms. A century later, Ælfric, the first abbot of a new abbey at Eynsham, near Oxford, translated the Old Testament books Genesis through Judges. Shortly thereafter, an anonymous literal translation of all the Gospels, known as the West Saxon Gospels, appeared in readable Old English.

The Bible and the Poets The Scriptures also provided inspiration to English poets. In the seventh century Cædmon, a cowherd at a monastery, composed and sang poems on biblical subjects. The only poem of his that remains, nine lines on the Creation, is the earliest surviving poem in English. In the ninth century Cynewulf wrote part of a poem about Christ and probably the poem "The Fates of the Apostles." There were also anonymous metrical versions of stories from Genesis, Exodus, Judith, and Daniel.

The most beautiful of all the Old English biblical poems is "Dream of the Rood," an anonymous dream vision in which the *rood* (an ancient word for "cross") speaks to the dreamer about Jesus' crucifixion. Jesus is represented as a typical Anglo-Saxon warrior hero who fights valiantly, and his disciples—and the cross itself—are described as his faithful retainers. The poem elegantly and emotionally re-creates the events that took place on Golgotha as reported in the Gospels. After the cross has concluded its emotional tale, the poem ends joyfully with a vision of Heaven, where the dreamer hopes one day to join his friends. ❖

The Cross Speaks

Part of the poem "Dream of the Rood" is inscribed with New Testament scenes on an eighth-century cross, left, at Ruthwell, Scotland. In the following modern prose excerpt, the cross speaks:

"Then the young hero—God Almighty—stripped himself. Firm and unflinching he mounted the high cross, brave in the sight of many, for he intended to redeem humanity. I trembled when the young hero clasped me, but dared not bow down to the earth. No, I would not fall to the ground; I knew full well I must stand firm. As I, the cross, was raised up, I bore aloft the mighty king, the Lord of Heaven— I dared not stoop. They pierced me with dark nails; the wounds can still be seen in me, gaping gashes of malice. I dared do nothing to seal them up, for they mocked us both together. I was drenched with the blood shed from the man's side after he had sent out his spirit. I endured many hard trials on the hill. I saw the God of hosts violently stretched out. Darkness with its clouds had covered the Lord's corpse, the fair radiance; a shadow moved in, dark beneath the heavens. All creation wept, all lamented the King's death. Christ was on the cross!"

Lindisfarne Gospels

One of the most admired manuscripts of all time, the Lindisfarne Gospels was the work of one man. The ornate Gospels were copied to commemorate the moving, in 698, of the body of Cuthbert, a former abbot of Lindisfarne, who was revered as a saint. Thanks to a colophon that was added about 250 years later, we know that Eadfrith copied and illuminated the Gospels, Æthelwald bound the manuscript, and Billfrith decorated the cover with gems and precious metals. (Eadfrith went on to become bishop of Lindisfarne and was succeeded as bishop by Æthelwald.) The colophon was written by Aldred, who also added Anglo-Saxon glosses above the text. The volume remained at Lindisfarne until 875, when it was taken away with the relics of Cuthbert for protection from raiding Vikings. According to a 12th-century story, the fleeing monks were caught in a terrible storm at sea in which three great waves swept over their ship and were turned to blood. The Gospels disappeared overboard but were found safely washed ashore after Cuthbert came to one of the monks in a dream and told him to search for the missing book.

Lindisfarne, an island off the northeast coast of England, is the site of the 7th-century Celtic abbey in which the Gospels were copied. Ruins of a later (12th-century) abbey on the same site are shown above. A local grave marker, left, is carved with the figures of Viking warriors, like the Norsemen who raided Lindisfarne in the late 8th century.

In the mid-19th century, this new, bejeweled cover was made for the ancient manuscript. All the decorative motifs for the cover were taken from the text.

A decorative carpet page faces the beginning of Mark's Gospel, left. To form the Gospel's opening word, IN, an I runs down the left side of the page and doubles as the left vertical stroke of the letter N. Mark's portrait is on a later page of the Gospel, below.

On the opening page of the Gospel According to Luke the illuminator let his fancy run free. Near the lower right corner of the page the head of a domesticated cat peers out, hungrily eyeing a parade of birds that march out along the bottom of the page from a flock of intertwined birds on the left.

Guardians of the Scriptures

GROUPS OF MEN SEEKING SALVATION AND GLORIFICATION OF GOD LIVED, PRAYED, AND WORKED TOGETHER. SOME OF THESE MONKS COPIED AND ILLUMINATED SCRIPTURE AS AN ACT OF DEVOTION.

Monks spent a good part of their day—and night—praying the Divine Office, a cycle of prayer that began before dawn and ended at bedtime. The illuminations shown on this page are from late medieval manuscripts. The monks below are chanting from their choir stalls.

Monastic life in Europe inexorably organized itself around the Rule devised by Benedict of Nursia, the monk who founded a monastery at Monte Cassino, in central Italy, about 525. Although Benedict greatly admired the desert hermits, he came to believe that the eremitic tradition was too demanding. Using elements of earlier rules, he developed a rule of moderation that stressed a proper balance between work and prayer that would enable each member of a community to strive for the goal of personal salvation. Free from the temptations and distractions of the outside world, the monks lived out their lives together in a monastery, pledging obedience to its abbot, or head monk, taking part in communal daily prayer, engaging in solitary contemplation of Scripture, and doing manual labor to contribute to the monastery's economic self-sufficiency,

Between the 6th and 11th centuries several thousand monasteries were founded in Europe. Among these houses, there was considerable variation in how the Rule was interpreted. The opinions of some monks as to the relative purity of the practices of others led to periodic reform movements, such as those that resulted in the creation of the separate Cistercian and Carthusian orders in the late 11th century.

The Divine Office Benedictines, known in early times as the black monks, for the color of their robes, believed that the essence of monastic life was daily worship, which Benedict called the *opus Dei* ("work of God"). This Divine Office consisted of communal prayer at eight canonical hours: matins and lauds (long before dawn), prime (early morning), tierce (mid-morning), sext (noon), none (midafternoon), vespers (evening), and compline (nightfall). Varying according to the time of the year and the observance of the house, each hour included psalms, silent prayer, a hymn, and readings from the

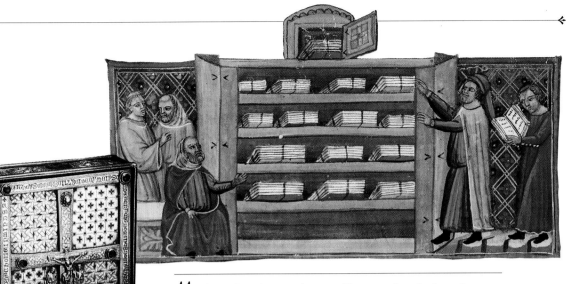

*M*onks and students gather at a library cupboard, above, in an illustration from a 15th-century French book. The ornate Irish book shrine at left was first crafted in the 12th century but later altered.

MONASTIC LIBRARIES

The barbarian invasions that swept across Europe in the third, fourth, and fifth centuries destroyed most of the great classical libraries, but in the sixth century libraries were built up in monasteries, where the monks were required to do spiritual reading.

Most monasteries had no more than a few hundred books, which were generally stored in different rooms, determined by whether they were used for prayer or study. If there was a separate room for a library, it was modestly furnished.

Books were stored flat in wall cupboards or sometimes in chests. Special books were kept in elaborate cases, called shrines. In late medieval libraries, *armora* (shelves for storing books upright) were built between arches, forming cells where the monks could read at long desks with one to three slanted shelves to hold more books. A librarian, who answered directly to the abbot, watched over the books and generally catalogued them.

Bible and the Church Fathers. At each hour the monks stopped whatever they were doing to pray together in church.

As cities and towns grew, the monks came to regard it as their duty to act as guardians of the spiritual welfare of these communities as well as agents of their own salvation. When they took it upon themselves to perform the prayerful and penitential obligations of the laity, the daily Office became longer and more complex, taking up more and more time. As institutionalized at the great monastery at Cluny, France, the Office became enormously ornate and time-consuming, and lay persons were employed to do much of the manual labor that was required by the Rule and needed for the order to survive.

The Scriptorium For most monks, manual labor meant farm work, but for a number of them it meant working with books. Although manuscripts could be copied almost anywhere in a monastery, some of the larger houses maintained a scriptorium, a specially protected room where scribes carried out the painstaking task of copying by hand the sacred texts of Christianity, which were essential to worship. In preserving and duplicating these sacred texts, the monks acted as the true guardians of the Scriptures. The rules of many houses contained complex, precisely delineated strictures regarding the care, protection, use, and loan of manuscripts, which were made available only under limited circumstances to other religious houses.

As part of their work, monks copied Bibles, Gospel books, breviaries, and psalters for use in their own monastery or other monasteries or on commission for patrons. They also copied biographies, histories, sermons, commentaries of the Church Fathers, and works of a secular nature. In those days before printing, books were often regarded as a monastery's most valuable treasures. ❖

The Monk as Scribe

FOR CENTURIES BEFORE THE PRINTING PRESS, MONKS PRODUCED MAGNIFICENT BIBLES COMPLETELY BY HAND.

Scrawled at the end of the text of a medieval Bible is a warning to thieves: "If anyone take away this book, let him die the death; let him be fried in a pan; let the falling sickness and fever seize him; let him be broken on the wheel and hanged." The writer of these threats was a monk, who had probably spent many years copying out texts, and though his sentiments could hardly be termed Christian, they are understandable. Because books were greatly cherished in the medieval world, they were not only painstakingly created but zealously preserved. Despite fires, thefts, and nibbling mice, more manuscripts have come down to us from the Middle Ages than any other type of artifact.

An Act of Devotion Book production was an important part of life in some monasteries; the very process of copying the Bible and other religious texts was an act of devotion. Indeed in recreating the texts of the Bible the monks were helping to insure its preservation and dissemination. The scribal monks might have likened themselves to the evangelists, who are frequently depicted as scribes, with pen poised over parchment, ready to set down the inspired words of Scripture.

The copyists were part of an elite group—less than 2 percent of Europe's population was literate during the Middle Ages. Even government business was largely conducted verbally: very few official written records exist from the time. The chief custodians of the written culture were priests and monks, whose main concern was the careful preservation of Scripture and other religious texts.

Manuscripts produced at monasteries often took a long time to complete since scribal monks had other duties—among them praying the Office up to eight times a day. The method of book production varied at monasteries. In some instances an individual who was both scribe and artist produced an entire manuscript by himself. In other

In the 1220 manuscript illustration above, monks are shown at work in a scriptorium—a room set aside for writing—in the tower of the Spanish monastery of Tábara.

cases a team of scribes and artists worked together on a single project. A magnificent 12th-century German Bible, known as the Worms Bible, for example, was produced by a group. Eleven people were involved in its creation, including four scribes, two of whom were also artists, and seven colorists, who were brought to the monastery to do the work.

In the early Middle Ages entire Bibles were rarely produced as single volumes. Because of the sheer length of the text (and the cost of copying it on parchment), it was far more practical to produce individual books of the Pentateuch, the Prophets, or the New Testament, for instance. Among the most highly valued and most frequently copied sections of the Bible were the four Gospels, which were often bound together as Gospel books. When whole Bibles were produced they might be oversized books designed for reading from a lectern rather than for individual study. To make it easier to read aloud at daily worship services, the manuscript was penned in black ink with accents judiciously placed throughout the text. By the 13th century, portable, compactly written Bibles were made in great number.

How the Books Were Produced At medieval monasteries even the most basic tools for book production—pen and ink—were usually made by the monks. To prepare his own quill pens, a scribe first chose the feathers—goose or swan feathers were considered the best, and they had to be dry and hardened before use. Using a knife, the scribe carefully cut the tip of the feather shaft into the proper shape. When completed it looked very much like the nib of a fountain pen: there was a sharp tip, the top of which was squared off, and a slit was cut up the center. As the scribe used the pen in his work, he had to resharpen it con-

ALCUIN AND THE FRANKS

During his reign as king of the Franks and emperor of the West, Charlemagne recruited scholars from all of Europe to bring culture to his court. Among the newcomers in 781 was the Anglo-Saxon monk Alcuin of York (inset above).

Alcuin introduced the Franks to Anglo-Saxon scholarship—considered the finest of the period. During his tenure he revised the liturgy of the Frankish church as well as producing a revised Vulgate.

In 796 Charlemagne made Alcuin abbot of the monastery of St. Martin in Tours, France. Under Alcuin's direction the scriptorium at Tours was one of the most productive in Europe. One of its achievements was the perfecting of a writing style called Carolingian minuscule, which could be written more rapidly than the earlier, larger letters. The example shown above is from the Moutiers Grandval Bible, produced at Tours between 834 and 843.

The Worms Bible of about 1148 was created by a team of 11 scribes and artists. In this detail from Hosea, the prophet forms one side of an historiated initial V, *the first letter of the word* Verbum. *The two lines above the* V *are rubricated, or written in red ink.*

A saintly monk is purchasing trimmed parchment from a parchment maker. The illustrated initial is one of a series from a 1255 German Bible that show scribes at their various tasks.

stantly. A 12th-century scholar reported that a scribe taking dictation had to have 60 to 100 quills ready for use in a day.

Once prepared, the quills were dipped into pots or horns containing ink. Black ink was made from a number of different recipes in the Middle Ages, but there were two distinct types. Carbon ink was made from charcoal or soot mixed with plant gum or sap. Metal-gall ink, used for many later medieval manuscripts, was made by combining iron sulfate with tannic acid. The tannic acid was drawn from oak galls, nutlike growths on the leaves or branches of oak trees that are cocoons for the larvae of gall wasps. When the larvae develop, they bore their way out of the oak galls. Once collected for use, the galls had to be pulverized and soaked for days in warm rainwater to remove the tannic acid.

Scribes are often pictured with two inkhorns, the second one usually containing vermilion ink. Made from ground cinnabar (mercuric sulfide), this red ink was used extensively for chapter headings, titles, initials, and other such "rubrics" (the term comes from the Latin word for red, *rubrica*). Red ink was also used sometimes in correcting

The pages of this 13th-century French psalter show ruled lines for the text and gold lines for the margins. In the inset, a saintly scribe trims parchment pages to size with a knife.

A monk might use a knife to sharpen his pen or to repair mistakes by scraping the ink off the parchment.

the text, which drew attention to the fact that the manuscript had been carefully checked.

While working, the scribe might bend over the manuscript or sit up straight at a table with a slanted top. (The slant helped keep the pen perpendicular to the parchment.) The exemplar, or master text, which the scribe was copying, was placed next to his own work. A weighted string was draped over the exemplar to mark the scribe's place.

Preparing the Pages If a monastery raised animals, the monks made their own parchment. Otherwise, they bought or traded for skins that had been prepared by an outside parchment maker.

Before beginning to write on fresh parchment, the scribe rubbed the sheet with pumice and smoothed it with chalk to remove any oil and to keep the ink from running. Then he ruled lines on the parchment to guide his hand in writing the text.

Initially ruling was done by scoring the parchment with a stylus or the back of a knife—a practice that sometimes resulted in cuts through the parchment. About the 12th century a pencil-like instrument was introduced for ruling, and from the 13th century on, lines were ruled in ink of various colors.

Visible ruled lines were not only expected in medieval manuscripts, they were preferred; unruled manuscripts were considered second-rate and unsightly. To ensure that the spacing between ruled lines matched from page to page, prickings, or small perforations, were punched through several sheets at the same time, usually in the margins of the page. In addition, if the manuscript was to be decorated, spaces for the illustrations were marked off before the copying began. All these preparatory steps were extremely time-consuming.

When the copyist finally was ready to write, it was a two-handed operation. In his right hand he held the quill pen. In his left hand he held a knife to sharpen his pen, smooth out rough sections of parchment, or scrape away any errors. He sometimes also used the knife rather than his own hand to hold down the page.

In this 11th-century German illustration, a monk in a cowled robe works on a text side by side with a lay artist in the cloister of a monastery.

Styles of Script For centuries, texts had been written in large capital letters called majuscules. Every letter stood separately, none touching the other, so the copyist had to lift his pen as he finished each letter. Writing in majuscules was slow work, and the letters, because of their size and spacing, took up a great deal of room on the valuable parchment. A simpler lowercase script, minuscule, which was originally used for documents and other texts, eventually was adopted for writing formal and sacred manuscripts as well.

Regional Variations Variations in writing styles evolved in different countries and even in particular monasteries. An Irish calligraphy developed known as insular majuscule ("insular" comes from the Latin word for island), a script that is brilliantly displayed in the *Book of Kells*. Insular majuscule eventually lost its popularity but it still remains the script of Gaelic.

Insular texts introduced an innovation in the seventh century when scribes in Ireland and England began to separate words to help the reader. In the old Roman style of writing, one word ran into the next without any space between them. The text had to be read aloud to be understood. This meant that scribes had to murmur to themselves as they read and copied the sacred texts and that the rule of silence in monasteries did not extend to the scriptorium in the early Middle Ages. By the second half of the 12th century, however, word separation was generally accepted throughout Europe, and scribes were required to work in complete silence. Monks nevertheless did make efforts to communicate. On occasion they wrote each other notes—informal scribblings that are preserved in the margins of some manuscripts.

This page from the Gospel According to Luke was written in Northumbria, England, at the start of the eighth century. As in other Anglo-Irish manuscripts of the day, space is allowed between the words.

Work Rules While at work on a manuscript, scribes were watched over carefully by the *armarius*, the monk in charge of the scriptorium. It was he, or the abbot, who decided what each scribe would copy for the day. Work rules were stringent. A ninth-century monastery in Constantinople meted out the following penalties. A scribe who neglected his copying would be placed on a bread and water diet. Dirty parchment earned the monk 130 penances. The punishment for taking someone else's parchment or for wasting glue was 50 penances. Breaking a pen in anger translated into 30 penances.

The work was carefully proofread and corrected, for if errors were introduced into the text, they would be copied over and over again.

Corrections are sometimes visible on manuscripts: Extra words are crossed out or underlined with dots. Longer sections to be deleted are marked with *va* at the beginning and *cat* at the end (*va cat* meaning that all the words between those syllables should be omitted).

Creating the Perfect Text In the search for master texts, there was a great deal of traveling between monasteries and much borrowing of books from one scriptorium to the next. Beautiful, error-free manuscripts were treasured. At the end of the Middle Ages the abbot of Sponheim waxed poetic about the scribes from the old days who were so well versed in their jobs "that a mere look at their pages was inducive to reading."

Copying the Scriptures was an arduous task. The monk spent days on end in intense concentration, holding his body in a cramped position, perhaps shivering with cold and squinting in the dim light. Fires to warm the copyists, and candles for light were prohibited near the flammable parchments. It was work that almost literally required the patience of a saint. ❖

Below the illumination on the dedication page of a 12th-century sacramentary are portraits of the craftsmen. On the left is the scribe, identified simply as "R." On the right is the painter, Hildebertus, and his assistant, Everwinus, who holds two pots of paint.

The Art of Illumination

ARTISTS LAVISHLY DECORATED AND ILLUSTRATED THE PAGES OF BIBLES AND OTHER BOOKS, TURNING THEM INTO TREASURES.

Artists kept their paints in separate open pots, as shown in this historiated initial C, which introduces an entry on color in a 14th-century English encyclopedia.

*A*urea testatur, "It is witnessed in gold," begins the dedicatory inscription in a Gospel book commissioned by the duke of Saxony and Bavaria in 1185. The words proclaim the sumptuousness of the volume. For several years a master illuminator—a monk named Herimann—labored over the illustrations. He created two dozen full-page paintings, including a coronation scene in which God placed a crown on the duke's head before a heavenly audience. It was one of the most beautiful books produced in the Middle Ages.

Illustrated medieval manuscripts are often referred to as illuminated. The term applies literally to illustrations that are lit up with details in gold and silver—yet the term has come to include all richly ornamented manuscripts. Similarly, individual manuscript illustrations, regardless of size, are called minia-

*I*nitial letters were various. At left Mary, holding a cross, forms the letter I and stands on top of a second letter I on a page from an 8th-century French manuscript. The V, above, from a 15th-century manuscript encloses the figure of St. Anthony, abbot.

tures—the word deriving from the Latin *miniare*, "to color with red," since originally these illustrations were all done in red.

Illuminated manuscripts contain various types of illustrations, from lavish full-page paintings to intricate border designs and decorated initial letters to start chapters. The use of highly elaborate initials developed in Irish and English monasteries in the seventh century and the practice spread to the Continent. Not only were these elaborate letters attractive, but they lent a strong organizing element to the page. In fact, initials of different sizes were sometimes used throughout a text for different purposes. The largest initial signaled the start of a manuscript; subsequent chapters and subdivisions were introduced with similar but smaller initials. Elaborate initials became an art form in themselves. Some were marvels of intricate design, interlaced with human and animal figures. The ones that depict events, or "histories," are called historiated.

The above page from an 11th-century Hexateuch shows the process of illustration. The figures are drawn and partially colored, but the page was never completed.

Carolingian Illumination

The illumination of manuscripts took a great artistic leap under the patronage of the emperor Charlemagne in the eighth and ninth centuries. Charlemagne bestowed generous grants on monasteries and invited foreign scholars to his court. The combined riches and foreign influences gave rise to the Carolingian style of illumination inspired by Anglo-Irish, Byzantine, and Roman traditions of painting. The books produced under the emperor's patronage were some of the most costly and luxurious manuscripts the world has seen, with lavish use of gold for lettering and paintings. Charlemagne gave precious volumes to allies, monasteries, and popes. With these books, art joined hands with religion and statecraft. By presenting a luxury book to a monastery, a ruler expected prayers for his cause. In turn, a monastery might present a fine book to the emperor in hope of receiving future patronage. Charlemagne quite deliberately used biblical iconography to suggest that his reign was divinely ordained. In the dedication to a volume of the Psalms that he presented to Pope Hadrian I, Charlemagne claimed that the Psalms are the golden words of King David and that he, Charlemagne, was David's successor. Similarly, Charlemagne's grandson Charles the Bald commissioned a Bible with a portrait of Solomon that is the very image of Charles the Bald.

Illuminations were often quite intricate, as seen in the detail at left from a 14th-century breviary. The elaborate, highly decorated, gold-embellished initial B, below, is from a 14th-century choir book. It encloses two painted scenes.

Ways of Working

Different styles of illumination evolved in different regions of Europe as well as in individual monasteries. And, as the demand for manuscripts increased throughout Europe during the medieval period, a hierarchy of artists evolved. The most skilled artist might draw the most important miniatures in the manuscript, while

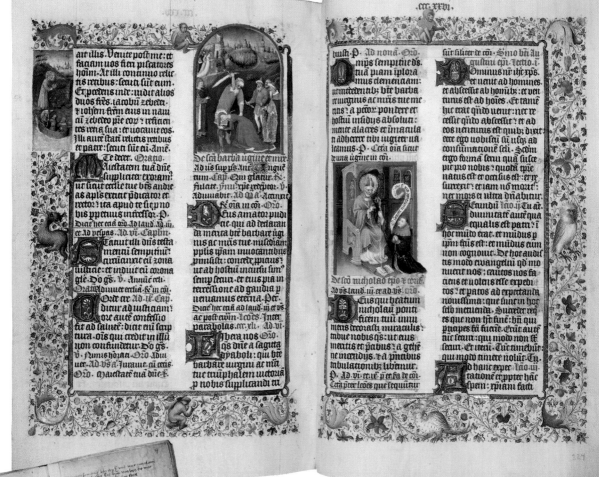

Artists often framed the text with elaborate borders that incorporated animals and foliage. The border in this 15th-century breviary from the Netherlands includes acanthus leaves similar to those in the illuminator's manual at left.

A 15th-century German illuminators' manual, shown above, describes how to color and shade an acanthus leaf.

an assistant might be entrusted with the less important drawings. In the latter medieval period, floral and geometric page borders were usually painted by border specialists, who would leave spaces in the design where the chief artist would later add figures.

Regardless of their level of expertise, most artists worked in the same general manner. After the page was laid out and appropriate spaces were left for illustrations, the text was written. Instructions for illuminators were sometimes noted in the margins and borders and in the spaces where the miniatures were to go. The instructions were frequently trimmed off during rebinding or were painted over, but some have inadvertently remained—oversights that have been critical in helping scholars understand the illumination process.

Putting the Picture on the Page Working within the designated spaces, the artist might rough out a design with a sharply pointed stylus of metal or bone or with a kind of graphite pencil. Then he went

WORKING WITH GOLD LEAF

The gold leaf used for embellishing the pages of illuminated manuscripts is actual gold that has been hammered into sheets so fine they are almost weightless. In some illustrations the details in gold appear to be no thicker than those in paint. In others, gold leaf provides a rich, three-dimensional effect because it was used on areas that had been built up with gesso (a sort of plaster).

Gold leaf was applied to the designated areas of an illustration after the scribe had finished with the page but before the painting was begun. The work was painstaking: gold flakes are apt to stick wherever a surface is moist or oily, and sheets will crinkle or blow away with the slightest breath of air. Craftsmen used several methods for applying gold leaf, one of which is described below.

1. Once the designated parts of the illustration had been built up with gesso or simply polished smooth, the artist prepared an adhesive called glair. He made it by whipping an egg white until it was stiff and then letting it stand until it reverted into a watery liquid. He sometimes added a touch of vinegar or realgar (sulfide of arsenic) to the glair as a preservative. He then brushed a thin coat of the mixture onto a portion of the illustration that would be receiving gold leaf.

2. After cutting a piece of gold leaf to the approximate size and shape of the prepared section, the artist picked it up with a flat brush or the moistened handle of a paint brush and carefully laid it into place. Gold leaf is so thin that it adheres instantly. The artist then repeated the process, slightly overlapping the individual pieces of gold leaf. He continued working in this way until the section was complete. Then he burnished the gold leaf with a tool made from a tooth or a glossy stone. Burnishing brought up the lustre of the gold and unified the individual layers.

3. Pieces of gold leaf that extended beyond the desired areas usually fell away during the burnishing. To complete the process, however, the artist outlined the gold areas with pen and ink to smooth out any ragged edges and redefine the original drawing. He then gave the page to another artist to add the color, or he colored it himself. The brilliant gold details would never tarnish or fade.

An artisan hammers coins into gold leaf, left, in an illustration from an Italian manuscript of about 1390. A writer of about the same time claimed that 145 leaves (probably a few inches square) could be made from a single coin.

Gold leaf was applied to a figure before the painting was done, as shown in the figure of Wisdom enthroned, top. After the gold leaf was applied, an artist added the color, as shown above in the scenes of Moses slaying the Egyptian. Both illustrations are from the 12th-century Winchester Bible.

259

over the outline with a thin ink, a process called crisping up. Next, he polished the areas to be painted to prepare them for decoration. Gold leaf was applied first because it had to be burnished, a process that could damage colors. In some cases, scribes indicated color selections with notes or letters. The letter *A* for instance indicated azure. In a 13th-century manuscript from a Cistercian monastery in France, a scribe wrote small letters in the margins to show what initial should be inserted in the text; next to each was a tiny daub of paint indicating what color the initial should be.

An artist usually developed the illustrations on many sheets of parchment simultaneously, so that the colors could dry on some while he was working on others. He added color layer by layer to create various tones and shadings. Finally, he highlighted the outline of the design with white penwork.

Originality was not necessarily the primary concern; just as the scribe tried to copy the master text precisely, so the artist often tried to recreate previous models. Miniature compositions were sometimes duplicated by tracing the image. The miniature could also be copied by pricking holes on a page along the outlines of the original drawing and then sprinkling charcoal dust over the pricked page, leaving an outline of the image on the fresh page that lay beneath it.

Artists wanted parchment of the highest quality for their art, but parchment was difficult to make and expensive to buy. It was not unknown for artists to paint miniatures on patches of parchment,

---

*F*ull-page illustrations and decorated initial letters were already used by Irish and English artists in the seventh century and can be seen in the eighth-century English psalter below.

WOMEN COPYISTS AND ILLUMINATORS

Throughout the Middle Ages, the tasks of copying manuscripts and illuminating the pages were largely in the hands of skillful monks and, later, professional laymen. But men were by no means the only practitioners of such arts. Just as monasteries were established as centers of learning as well as devotion, so were medieval convents, particularly the Benedictine ones.

Not all nuns became scholars, but many who did devoted their lives to writing original works or transcribing manuscripts. In fact, some of the finest medieval works of calligraphy are attributed to women. At times, nuns and monks worked jointly on books: in the 12th-century manuscript illustration above, the scribe Guta appears to the right of the central figure of Mary, and the artist, the canon Sintram, appears on the left.

Women, whether religious or lay artisans, worked less often as illuminators, but the profession was not unknown to them. From the 12th century on there are tantalizing examples of illustrations signed by women in both secular and religious manuscripts. Since few artists ever signed their work at all, there may be more illustrations by women than we know.

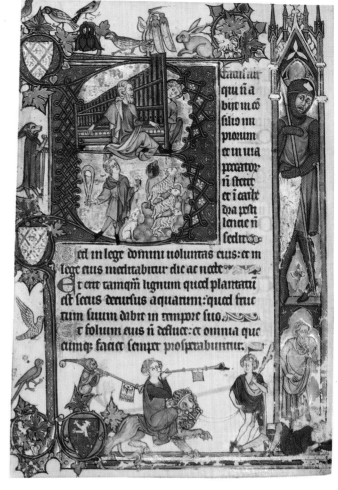

Scenes from David's life as a young man and as a king are used to illuminate the initial letter and borders of this page from a late 13th-century French psalter.

later gluing them into place on a page: in time many such miniatures became detached and were lost. In the later Middle Ages paintings were done on separate leaves and inserted into the manuscript, so that parchment of high quality was used only for the art.

Sources for Colors Pigments were derived from a variety of sources. Vermilion was obtained from grinding cinnabar—a highly poisonous compound made from mercury and sulfur. After red, the most common color used in medieval illumination was blue, which was made by grinding azurite stone. The most treasured blue of all was ultramarine from lapis lazuli, a semiprecious stone found only in Afghanistan. The color it yielded was so valued that when the wealthy duke of Berry drew up an inventory of his estate about 1400, he included two pots of ultramarine.

The pigment for green paint was obtained from the mineral malachite or from the verdigris that forms on oxidized copper. Yellow came from saffron or volcanic soil, and white from white lead. Artists bought the pigments from apothecaries, pounded them into powders, and then mixed them with egg or other binding substances.

A Near Ban on Illumination The very richness of manuscript illuminations provoked a reaction in the 12th century. Convinced that the joyously beautiful illustrations produced by the Cistercian monks were nothing more than devilish vanities, Bernard of Clairvaux, the head of the Cistercian order, abruptly banned excessive decoration in books—and in churches as well. However, some Cistercians simply ignored the decree and continued to produce manuscripts of exquisite artistry.

The monks' persistence might have been anticipated. Throughout the Middle Ages a pious love of beautiful Bibles, mass books, psalters, and other texts had been deeply ingrained in the hearts of monks, patrons, and princes alike. According to legend, when the tomb of Charlemagne was opened two centuries after his death, the emperor was found seated with a gold chain around his neck, a scepter in his hand, and an illuminated manuscript of the Gospels on his knees. ❖

The detail below is from a 14th-century breviary.

Medieval Bindings and Luxury Covers

Early Western techniques of bookbinding were based on Coptic precedents originating in fourth-century Egypt. The gatherings of a book were sewn through the folds with a linking stitch, and the ends of the thread were tied to boards covered with leather. In the Middle Ages large liturgical books came into use, and the techniques suitable for binding smaller Coptic books were superseded by a stronger sewn structure: a book's gatherings were sewn to cords and the cords were fastened to boards.

The plain outsides of these boards were embellished in a variety of ways. Books consulted frequently, such as those used in services, were usually covered in leather. The leather was sometimes decorated by stamping, leaving a raised design, or tooling, either without color (blind) or in gold leaf. Plaques—fashioned from silver, gold, or other precious materials and further adorned with cameos, jewels, enamelwork, or ivory relief—might be applied to the plain covers. Imperial donors often gave luxury volumes of this type to cathedrals and monasteries. These books were stored in church treasuries along with reliquaries and liturgical vessels and were removed only for use in the service.

This small seventh- or eighth-century Coptic Gospel cover, above, was made by mounting a leather cut-out pattern over gilded leather.

A scholar's prayer book of about 1400 illustrates the bookbinding techniques of the time. The binding consists of wooden boards covered in leather. Visible on the open front board are channels through which cords sewn to the gatherings were laced. In a practical touch, a space has been hollowed out for the owner's glasses.

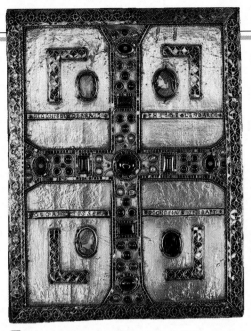

A palm-sized breviary copied by a friar in 1454 was bound as a girdle book to hang from the user's waist. Its leather cover is supplied with clasps and five raised brass bosses, or studs, to protect the contents from wear.

The seventh-century Lombard queen Theodolinda presented this large deluxe codex in a gold cover to the basilica in her chief city. It is one of the earliest metal covers made in the West.

This ninth-century Gospel boasts a lavish jewel-and-enamel-encrusted gold cover and finely wrought clasps. A combination of Christian and pagan images fills the central ivory relief.

A classical-style ivory cover of the fifth century features the lamb encircled by a wreath of victory and framed within a series of New Testament scenes, including the Nativity, top, and a rare early depiction of the Slaughter of the Innocents, bottom.

In the mid-15th-century French illustration above, the artist painted himself at work in his studio. Leading his visitors is the artist's patron, Jean Jouvenal des Ursins, the chancellor of France.

Books for Private Devotions

IN THE LATE MIDDLE AGES COMMERCIAL BOOKSELLERS PRODUCED DEVOTIONAL TEXTS AND OTHER VOLUMES FOR A GROWING PUBLIC.

By the 14th century, production of both religious and secular texts was largely in the hands of professional copyists and artists. The commercial book business grew up alongside cathedral schools and universities, and consequently it was towns with universities and cathedrals such as Oxford, Bologna, Rome, and Paris where the book trade was established. The demand for books increased along with literacy and the establishment of an affluent middle class. Paris alone in 1300 supported some 30 booksellers, or publishers. At long last, an ordinary person of means might be as likely to commission a book as a bishop or a prince.

Patron and Bookseller To commission a volume a patron visited the shop of a bookseller. In some instances a bookseller might himself be a scribe, but more often his purpose was to take the order, discussing details of style and content with the patron, and then subcontract the work to parchment makers, scribes, artists, and binders. Such artisans generally lived near one another in particular neighborhoods or quarters of a town, which simplified making arrangements for a book.

When the rich merchant Cosimo de' Medici decided to establish a library in Florence in the 15th century, he talked to the city's most famous bookseller, Vespasiano da Bisticci, who hired 45 scribes to reproduce 200 texts in less than two years. More typically a relatively fast scribe would spend six months copying a 400-page book.

Three main types of books were produced by secular booksellers in the late medieval period: prayer

In the background, at left, is a 15th-century book of hours by Simon Marmion showing the coronation of the Virgin. In the foreground is a detail from a 1475 Flemish illustration of Mary of Burgundy reading her book of hours.

books, including books of hours; scholarly texts; and literary volumes. The most common surviving books from that period are the books of hours, which were made for the private devotions of the public. If a medieval household possessed a book, it was usually a book of hours. Thousands of books of hours were commissioned and made in variations that range from humble to sumptuous. The ornateness of the volume generally reflected the patron's wealth or status. The subject matter of the illustrations could be determined by the patron, the bookseller, or the artist. The earliest surviving books of hours date from 13th-century Oxford, England, and from Germany, but by far the greatest number were produced in France and the Netherlands in the second half of the 13th century and later.

Private Devotions Although there is no single format to be found in all books of hours, they often open with a calendar of the church year, followed by quotations from the Gospels. The essential text is the hours of the Virgin, a series of prayers and texts devoted to the Virgin Mary meant to be read or sung at each of the canonical hours of the day. The hours are followed by psalms, prayers to particular saints who reflected the interests of the person who commissioned the book, and sometimes the office (a series of prayers) for the dead.

Books of hours were frequently commissioned as engagement and wedding gifts. Often, the illustrations in a book depict the donor or patron at his or her devotions. (The patron is often shown praying to Mary since the essential text is devoted to her.) Many books of hours were produced in a diminutive size to be carried in a woman's pocket or hung at her waist. A 14th-century poet described the middle-class wife as feeling incomplete unless she owned a book of hours, beautifully illuminated in gold and blue and secured with golden clasps. Children were often taught to read from the books; in fact, the word *primer* comes from "prime," one of the canonical hours. ❖

Books of hours usually open with a calendar of the liturgical year in which a page is devoted to each month. The example above is from the Très Riches Heures, *produced for the duke of Berry (brother of King Charles V) by the Limbourg brothers between 1411 and 1416.*

Hebrew Scribes and Illuminators

THE MIDDLE AGES SAW THE ESTABLISHMENT OF AN AUTHORITATIVE HEBREW TEXT OF THE BIBLE AND A FULL FLOWERING IN THE ART OF ILLUMINATING A VARIETY OF HEBREW RELIGIOUS TEXTS.

For some 500 years, from the 6th to the 11th century, the responsibility of sorting through manuscripts, compiling them, and copying an authoritative text of the Hebrew Bible was the task of dedicated scribes called Masoretes. This name was taken from the Hebrew word meaning "to hand down." The Masoretes followed in the tradition of the *Sopherim* (scribes) who, as far back as the last centuries B.C., worked to preserve the Scriptures. Because many rabbinic interpretations of biblical verses are based on details of spelling, it was imperative that a single, standardized biblical text be established.

The early 10th-century Aleppo Codex, considered by many scholars the most authoritative Masoretic text, was supplied with vowel and accent signs by the famous Masorete Aaron ben Asher.

Masoretic Notations Because the words of the Scriptures were considered inviolable, the Masoretes took great pains to ensure that the spelling and wording of the text did not change. Even obvious imperfections in the received text were replicated to the letter. But the scribes did make spelling corrections and supplied variant readings in the margins of the page.

The most common Masoretic notations concerned vowel sounds, the use of particles, and matters of syntax (word order). Such reading aids were necessary because the Hebrew language had fallen into disuse, and the ancient biblical script, which consisted solely of the consonants, was prone to misinterpretation. Scribes penned circles or other marks above words in the texts to refer readers to marginal notes on the occurrences of that word. Dots or lines above, below, and between the letters of text signified the vowels. Similarly, a system of accents indicated sectional divisions, pauses, stops, and other guides to chanting the text in the religious service.

Marginalia called the *qere* and the *kethibh* provided explanations for and alternate readings of particular words. One such *qere/kethibh*, for example, directed the scribe to write the word *God* by using the Hebrew consonants YHWH; it further informed the reader that "YHWH" should be understood as *Adonai*, the Hebrew for "Lord." The *qere* also served to update archaic formulations, fill in omitted portions of text, and correct errors or inconsistencies in meaning.

Different groups of scribes carried out this work over a long period of time and in different locales, resulting in variations even among

RULES FOR SCRIBES

According to the Talmud, every Jew had to write for himself a copy of the Torah; but because of the skill demanded for such work, an expert scribe was usually engaged to do most of the copying.

Such a scribe was required to follow strict rules with regard to such matters as the nature and handling of writing materials, the letter-for-letter replication of text, word spacing, and the application of decorative touches to letters. These rules appear in *The Tractate of the Scribes*, which was written in the eighth or ninth century.

Before he began work, the scribe purified himself in a ritual bath. He ruled a specially prepared parchment, made from a kosher animal, with a stylus and straight-edge for guide lines and spacing. The scribe used a reed pen and carbon-based ink to copy the text. He wrote the Hebrew letters meaning "God" only after pronouncing, "I am writing the name of God for the holiness of His name."

The oldest extant complete Hebrew Bible, the Leningrad Codex of 1008, conforms to the text of Aaron ben Asher. Passages from the Scriptures are woven into the design of this carpet page.

A 15th-century miniature from the Rothschild Miscellany *portrays a scribe writing in a book.*

the Masoretic texts. For example, the three major scribal schools—one centered in the Babylonian cities of Pumpedita and Sura and two others in the Palestinian city of Tiberias—developed autonomous systems for notating vowels and vocalizations.

Over the course of time, the methods of the masters at Tiberias, and of the ben Asher family in particular, came to be recognized as the standard for all subsequent texts. No less an authority than the great Jewish scholar Maimonides of Spain praised Aaron ben Moses ben Asher's Masoretic text in the 12th century. According to Maimonides, "Everyone relied on it . . . and I based myself on this for the Torah scroll that I wrote." Aaron ben Asher's text has become the basis for modern critical editions of the Hebrew Bible.

Art of the Hebrew Book Jewish law forbade decoration of the Torah scroll. However, surviving Hebrew books—codices were not used in the synagogue—testify to a rich tradition of illumination dating from at least the 10th century in Egypt. Hebrew illuminations of the 13th to

15th centuries are abundant, with especially sumptuous examples of medieval Haggadoth (the text used in the Passover service) and beautifully adorned Bibles, prayer books, and other religious texts.

Illuminated Hebrew manuscripts were produced over a wide geographic area stretching from Spain to Germany in the west and from northern Africa to Iran in the east. Scholars have delineated several artistic schools—known as Ashkenazi (Germany and northern France), Italian, Sephardic (Spain, North Africa, and Provence), Oriental, Byzantine, and Yemenite—which reflect distinct local traditions but nonetheless share some iconographic and stylistic elements.

In the 13th century, the ancient Hebrew iconography—imagery such as the implements of the sanctuary, the Ark of the Covenant, and the entrance to the Temple—was expanded to include other aspects of the Temple and its furnishings. Biblical events began to be depicted in German illustrations, and legends involving biblical figures appeared at about the same time in commentaries originating in various regions across Europe. Manuscripts from the Sephardic and Oriental traditions often featured carpet pages—pages decorated with intricate geometric patterns similar to the patterns found in Oriental carpets. In addition, decorative motifs of various kinds were used at the ends of biblical books and to demarcate other divisions in the text. In Hebrew iconography God is usually represented symbolically, by an outstretched hand or a ray of sunlight. ❖

A band of rabbits prepares to attack a wolf holed up in his fortified castle in a lively and original border illustration accompanying the grammatical compendium to the 1476 Kennicott Bible. With its 40 illuminated pages, this Bible is one of the most richly decorated examples of the Spanish school.

Because the Hebrew language contains no capital letters, entire initial words in manuscripts were illuminated, as seen in a 13th-century Haggadah.

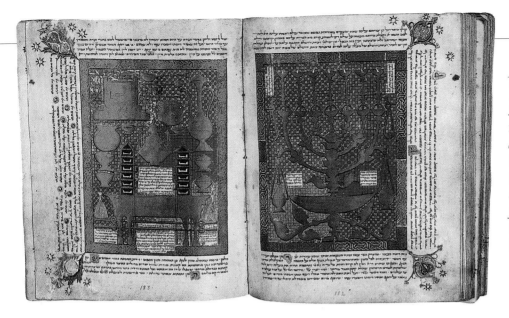

Typical of the Sephardic tradition, an array of Tabernacle implements extends over facing pages of the 14th-century Farhi Bible.

This Ashkenazi-style Haggadah of about 1300 avoids depicting human features by using bird heads. On the left Moses receives the Law, and on the right God's hands pass down the manna.

In many medieval Bibles, such as this 1469 copy of the Pentateuch from Yemen, the Masoretic notations are written in decorative micrography (tiny script).

New Ways of Studying Scripture

MONASTERIES GAVE RISE TO NEW WAYS OF FINDING MEANING IN THE SCRIPTURES—BY
SPIRITUAL COMMUNION WITH THE WORD AND, LATER ON, BY THE APPLICATION OF REASON.

The beginnings of medieval Christian interpretation of Scripture hark back to the Church Fathers, particularly Augustine of Hippo. As a young man, Augustine considered the stories of the Old Testament unrefined—until he was shown how to search the sacred texts for hidden meanings. Afterwards, Augustine's biblical commentaries were strongly tinged by allegorical interpretation, and they, in turn, influenced later Western biblical studies.

Threefold Meaning The sixth-century monk, theologian, and pope, Gregory the Great, held Augustine and his fellow theologians in high regard. Basing his scheme on that of Origen, Gregory described three levels of scriptural interpretation—literal or historical, allegorical,

In this 10th-century ivory Pope Gregory the Great writes, with the dove of the Holy Spirit at his ear, and scribes copy Gregory's text.

and moral—providing the foundation for subsequent Western exegesis. Eventually, a distinction was made between literal and historical meanings, and the two were separated, resulting in a fourfold scheme of reading Scripture.

Gregory believed that study of the Bible should be undertaken out of love for Christ and that the Bible's lessons in human frailty instructed the monk in obedience and humility. Thus Bible study was a key element in spiritual formation.

The devotional approach to Scripture—for the purpose of bringing the soul closer to union with Christ—dominated Bible study in the monasteries. The monk immersed himself in Scripture: he knew the words by heart, and those words set the rhythm of his days. By finding Christ in every word of Scripture, the monk, in effect, interpreted those words. Thus a 12th-century Cistercian monk, Bernard of Clairvaux, could say when reading the Old Testament prophets, "All . . . are mutes. Let me rather listen to Him of whom they speak."

Commentaries The question then arises as to which versions of the texts medieval monks were studying. While the interpreters of Augustine's time read and had access to an array of texts in Greek and Hebrew, most early medieval interpreters read neither language and knew the Scriptures only from Old Latin texts, the Vulgate translation, and, most important, through the teachings of the early Church Fathers. Thus early medieval interpretation was primarily based not on the original texts but on the biblical commentaries of such figures as Jerome, Ambrose, Augustine, and Gregory the Great.

In the seventh and eighth centuries, extracts from these commentaries were collected, arranged by topic, and called florilegia—from the Latin *flores*, for "flowers," and *legere*, meaning "to gather." Florilegia were sources of additional readings for church services and illuminated numerous topics and problems, helping to clarify dogmas, address moral questions, and bolster arguments in theological debates.

The gloss, in which the Scriptures were reproduced with commentaries written in the margins or between the lines of the text, first appeared in the 8th or 9th century. The 12th-century school of Anselm of Laon produced the *Glossa Ordinaria*, which gave interpretations by the Church Fathers for the whole of Scripture.

Scripture and Reason In the later Middle Ages, the foremost center of biblical interpretation in western Europe was the famous Abbey of St. Victor led by Hugh of St. Victor. Hugh developed a structured method for interpreting the Bible and wrote a student handbook that included a specific program of readings, plus tables, chronologies, and other guides to interpretation. Like the biblical analysis that issued from universities (new institutions of the time), Hugh's interpretation was based on reason and logic. Gradually this Scholastic method infiltrated other monastic schools, only to be eclipsed during the 14th century when, with a renewed interest in mysticism, the emphasis shifted again to a devotional approach to Scripture. ❖

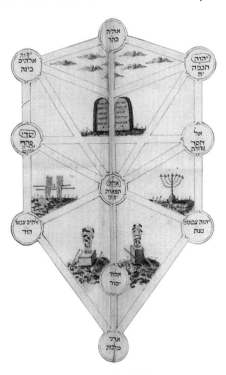

THE KABBALA

The ancient tradition of Jewish mystical thought, the Kabbala, began to flourish in southern France and Spain at the end of the 12th century. According to Kabbalistic philosophy, all truth is contained in the Hebrew Bible as it was revealed to the Patriarchs, prophets, and Jewish people. Scripture and the visible world are symbolic manifestations of the 10 *Sefirot*, or aspects of the Divine, which include concepts such as wisdom, love, power, and eternity.

In Kabbala manuscripts, the *Sefirot* are rendered as interconnecting patterns, as shown above in a detail from a 17th-century manuscript. All the laws of being and creation are said to be contained within the *Sefirot*. Kabbalists can interpret them and the patterns and relationships between them to understand the spiritual dimensions of the universe and find a path of spiritual growth.

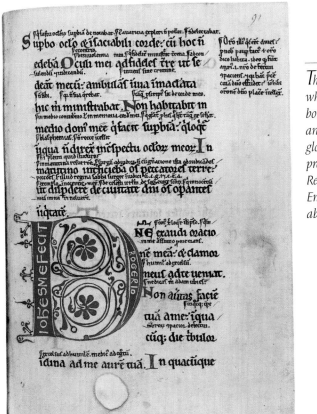

This Psalter, which features both interlinear and marginal glosses, was produced at Reading Abbey, England, about 1160.

Picture Bibles

THREE POPULAR TEXTS OF THE MIDDLE AGES USED ABUNDANT ILLUSTRATION TO IMPART THE LESSONS OF THE SCRIPTURES.

The majority of worshipers in the Middle Ages were unable to read. Even among the literate, few were proficient enough in Latin to read the long books of the Bible. Consequently, by the 13th century, a number of simplified, highly illustrated presentations of Bible events appeared in book form that were easily understood by unschooled worshipers. At the same time, lavishly illustrated biblical books were treasured by royalty.

Bible Moralisée The first of the sumptuous 13th-century *Bibles moralisées*, or moralized Bibles, is believed to have been produced for King Louis IX of France. Each page of the work contains two columns of text matched to four pairs of medallions—one picture taken from the biblical narratives, the other illustrating a commentary on that narrative. Louis IX's *Bible moralisée* contained 5,000 illuminations of biblical events and allegorical interpretations. The accompanying commentaries dispensed moral lessons gleaned from Scripture. Various versions of this manuscript were made for other royal patrons.

Bibles for the Poor in Spirit The *Biblia pauperum*, or Bible of the Poor, was designed for less exalted readers. Its illustrated Bible extracts and commentaries were probably developed as a teaching aid for preachers—the word *pauperum* referring to the Christian ideal of being poor in spirit. Surviving copies of the *Biblia pauperum* feature the same texts and illustrate the same subjects, suggesting that they were all based on one prototype.

Typically, a *Biblia pauperum* contains 34 or more full-page illustrations. In each, a scene depicting an event from the life of Jesus or Mary is set between representations of parallel Old Testament events or persons. The scene showing Jesus' entry into Jerusalem, for instance, is flanked by pictures of the Israelites greeting David after he slew Goliath and of Elisha

Paired scenes from a Bible moralisée *copied from the 13th-century original depict the creation of Eve from Adam's side and the church emerging from the wound in the crucified Christ's side. The accompanying text reads in part, "Adam's sleep is Christ's death."*

The saintly King Louis IX of France—the likely recipient of the first Bible moralisée—*is seen in an act of Christian humility, serving food to a monk, in a 14th-century miniature. Louis was a member of the Third (secular) Order founded by Francis of Assisi.*

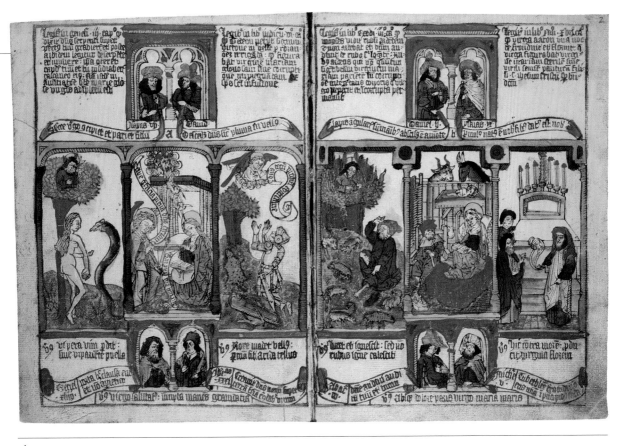

A 15th-century Biblia pauperum *blockbook depicts, on the left-hand page, the serpent tempting Eve, the Annunciation, and Gideon praying to God, with citations from Isaiah 7:14, Psalm 71:6, Ezekiel 44:2, and Jeremiah 31:22. The right-hand page shows Moses and the burning bush, the Nativity, and Aaron's blossoming rod, with citations from Daniel 2:45, Isaiah 9:6, Habakkuk 3:2, and Micah 5:2.*

ART OF THE BLOCKBOOK

In the 15th century, illustrated books such as the *Speculum humanae salvationis* and the *Biblia pauperum* began to be made by the woodblock printing method.

The technique involved carving images and text into a woodblock, inking the carved face of the block, laying a sheet of moistened paper on it, and rubbing the back of the paper with a burnisher to transfer the impression. The prints were sometimes hand-tinted, and then the blank reverse sides of the sheets were pasted together and gathered to form the blockbook.

Blockbooks were produced primarily in Germany and the Netherlands. Curiously, most were made after Johann Gutenberg invented movable type in the 1450's.

being hailed by the sons of the prophets. Brief Latin texts describe the Old Testament events and explain the significance of the illustrations. Four prophets are shown, two above and two below each central scene, along with scrolls bearing the words of their witness to Jesus.

The *Biblia pauperum* gave, then, vivid visual expression to a typological interpretation of the Bible, which presented Old Testament events and persons—called types—as foreshadowing the coming of Jesus. Image and text also reinforced church doctrine on matters such as the virgin birth of Jesus and the Trinity and helped combat heresy.

Mirror of Salvation A picture book that had the same purpose as the *Biblia pauperum* and used a similar technique was the *Speculum humanae salvationis* ("Mirror of Human Salvation"), attributed to Ludolph of Saxony in the early 14th century. The book was divided into 42 or 45 chapters, each illustrated by one New Testament event and three scenes anticipating that event. While the *Biblia pauperum* drew its images strictly from the Scriptures, the *Speculum* borrowed additionally from Christian legend and pagan history. For example, its pictures included the death of Codrus, king of Athens, and the ostrich delivering its young. The wide context implied that the whole of human history is the manifestation of God's plan. ❖

Medieval Worship

LAY CHRISTIANS CAME TO KNOW AND UNDERSTAND THE MEANING OF THE SCRIPTURES PRIMARILY BY WHAT THEY HEARD IN CHURCH.

Choral singing of standard prayers, including the Glory to God and the Nicene Creed, punctuated the Mass. The hymn below is the "Sursum corda" ("Lift up your hearts") from a missal of about 1200.

Though the Scriptures were the writings most medieval Christians knew best, only a small percentage of worshipers were educated enough actually to read them. Instead, a mostly illiterate congregation became versed in the Bible by hearing passages of Scripture read aloud to them in church and explained in the priest's homily. As early as the first century, Paul remarked, "So faith comes from what is heard [Romans 10:17]," and it is partially in recognition of this fact that churches devoted so much of the religious service to the spoken, and chanted, word.

Scripture and the Service A multiplicity of Christian liturgical traditions grew up in the Middle Ages in Europe, identified by scholars as Roman, Milanese, Spanish, Gallican, and Celtic. Indeed, the use of the Scripture on any given day varied from one congregation to the next. As the papacy gradually consolidated its doctrinal and governing authority, the liturgy itself became ever more regular, and a fixed schedule of scriptural readings for the liturgical year was ultimately established for the entire Western church.

Each day's service was organized around prayer, readings from the Scriptures, instruction, and the celebration of the Eucharist—the last of which became the focal point of the service in the late Middle Ages. The first part of the Mass, before the offering of the Eucharist, was attended by both the baptized faithful and the catechumens, or candidates for baptism. Usually after the intoning of psalms and other verses, a brief prayer service, and the procession of the clergy to the altar, the reading portion of the service began.

A lector, usually an educated cleric such as a deacon, stood on a platform facing the congregation and read from the Scriptures. Readings were generally devoted to two lessons (passages), one from the epistles, the Acts of the Apostles, or the Old Testament, and the other from the Gospels. The Old Testament lesson served to shed light on the Gospel reading by showing how Christ's coming was augured by the prophets and how his life was foreshadowed by earlier events. The New Testament readings—especially the Gospel lesson, which was the most

Devout Christians crowd into church as a priest celebrates the Eucharist in the 14th-century miniature at left. Celebrants often used rich, ornate liturgical vessels, such as the 10th-century onyx chalice from Constantinople, below, with its silver-gilt mounts, enamels, and pearls.

FEASTS OF OUR LORD

The celebration of the Resurrection on Easter, the Sunday after the last day of Passover, was established in the West by Constantine in the fourth century. Other feast days in the liturgical year were reckoned by the Easter date.

Lent, the 40-day penitential period before Easter, sprang from traditions based on the time of Jesus' fasting in the wilderness and the period of fasting that preceded the baptism of new converts at Easter. The joyous Pentecost season lasted for 50 days after Easter, with some churches giving special recognition to the first week in the season, its 40th day (the feast of the Ascension), or the last day.

Palm Sunday and the other Holy Week festivals originated with the descriptions in the Gospels of Matthew and John of Jesus' last days. December 25 was probably chosen as the day of Jesus' birth because it fell on, and would have replaced, a pagan holiday marking the "birth of the invincible sun."

important reading—were understood as messages that addressed the particular circumstances and problems of the attending congregation.

Next the priest delivered the homily, an articulation—either in Latin or the vernacular tongue—of the instruction the congregation should take from the day's readings. The priest might read a homily by one of the Church Fathers, or he himself might expound on the teachings from the Scriptures and speak further on the significance of other Christian writings, such as the letters of early church figures.

With the culmination of the liturgy of the word the faithful joined in the celebration of the Eucharist, consisting of the presentation of the offering for the priest's blessing and consecration, Communion, prayers, and the priest's dismissal of the people and final blessing.

Books Used in Worship Copies of entire Bibles were rare in the Middle Ages because such handwritten volumes would have been unwieldy and costly. Instead, the books of the Bible were divided into several volumes, with texts often rearranged for liturgical use. These included collections of the Gospels (usually the most lavishly decorated of all the books), lessons from the other New Testament books, and the Psalter. The Old Testament lesson usually appeared in the choir book on the page for that day. Sacramentaries contained the texts needed to administer the sacraments and lead the Eucharistic celebration (the Mass). Lectionaries included the Gospel and epistolary lessons. Antiphonaries reproduced sung texts. By the 10th century, missals had been introduced that combined the contents of lectionaries, sacramentaries, and antiphonaries. ❖

The Cathedral as Bible

The Gothic cathedrals that were built throughout Europe between the 12th century and the 15th are true embodiments of the Bible. A paramount example is the French Cathedral of Nôtre-Dame de Chartres, about 50 miles southwest of Paris, in which virtually every aspect of design has a symbolic significance that was not lost on parishioners and pilgrims—the elements can be read just as a book.

Most Gothic cathedrals are designed in the shape of a cross with the long part running east and west. The main altar is placed at the eastern end, toward the rising sun, a symbol of Jesus as the light of the world. The western end of the cathedral, where the main entrance is located, is associated with history, the passage from this world to the next, and the Last Judgment. The north side is associated with shadow, darkness, and the Old Testament, and the south with goodness, warmth, and the New Testament. The works of art—stained glass and stone sculpture—that are part of the architecture both inside and out follow those guidelines.

The detail of a stained-glass window, above, is from the south aisle of Chartres. It depicts events from the parable of the Good Samaritan as recorded in Luke 10:29-37.

The cathedral at Chartres, right, was begun in the 12th century and completed in the 16th. Figures sculpted into its north portal include, below, Isaiah, who points to the flowering branch of Jesse; Jeremiah, holding Jesus' halo; and Simeon, who holds the infant Jesus.

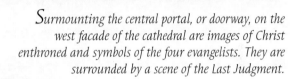

Surmounting the central portal, or doorway, on the west facade of the cathedral are images of Christ enthroned and symbols of the four evangelists. They are surrounded by a scene of the Last Judgment.

Chartres's lofty nave, above, and its jewel-like light create a celestial atmosphere.

The angel below is a detail from a stained-glass window depicting the Annunciation.

The north window, like other complex windows, is meant to be read from the bottom up. Anne holds the child Mary in the central lancet at the bottom, while above them, Mary holds Jesus at the center of the rose.

Biblical Drama

IN SOME PLACES, GOSPEL STORIES WERE ACTED OUT DURING WORSHIP SERVICES, AND THESE
REENACTMENTS WERE GRADUALLY EXPANDED INTO FULL PLAYS, GIVING BIRTH TO POPULAR THEATER.

Theater had no place in the early church, and by the late fifth century, no place in the Roman Empire. Church leaders had convinced the emperors to outlaw plays because they were associated with unsavory, bawdy, pagan spectacles.

Early Church Drama Ironically, when plays made a comeback, some 400 years later, they developed in church. Priests conducting Mass in Latin—a language unknown to most worshipers—started to dramatize the suffering of Jesus by using sights and sounds that transcended language: groans, sudden silence, and gestures, such as outstretched arms to suggest crucifixion. Worshipers were moved to excitement and tears when the priest finally raised the consecrated bread, the body of Christ.

Over the years, these simple amplifications grew into short dramas. The oldest known of these, *Quem quaeritis* (Latin for "Whom do you seek?"), dates from the 10th century and dramatizes the pivotal Christian event: the Resurrection. In it,

the three Marys talk with an angel at the tomb. The play was apparently sung inside the church, at Easter, with clergymen impersonating the women.

Believers must have delighted in this new approach to worship, for during the next 200 years church drama became popular through much of Western Europe. Soon plays were performed for other holy seasons, including Christmas and Pentecost, and the Easter story was expanded to include other characters, giving rise to the popular passion plays, which dramatized the life of Jesus.

By the 12th century, there was a wide variety of plays, and no longer were they necessarily tied to sacred days. Plays about Adam and Eve, Daniel in the lions' den, and the Antichrist were performed both inside the church and on church grounds, mainly in Latin. Clergymen played all the roles.

A Procession of Plays One event may have helped bring about major changes, for afterward religious plays began to venture beyond the church, adopt

King Belshazzar sits surrounded by his court, left, in the 12th-century church drama Daniel and the Lions. *The late-20th-century production shown here is performed by the Ensemble for Early Music in the Cathedral of St. John the Divine in New York City.*

Crowds close in around a pageant wagon to watch the biblical scene being presented. When the scene is finished, the wagon will be moved off and another will be rolled into place to present the following scene. The above drawing is a 19th-century reconstruction of a medieval performance of the Corpus Christi pageant at Coventry, England.

the language of the common folk, and use nonclergy actors. The event was the inauguration in 1264 of the feast of Corpus Christi, the "Body of Christ." In a procession through town and back to church, clergymen carried the Eucharistic bread and wine, rejoicing in the salvation provided by Christ's sacrifice. By the mid-1300's, most churches were observing this new feast day. Within a short period of time, in northern England, the procession started incorporating plays that were performed on high wagons that could be rolled from place to place.

Though the plays varied from town to town, the common intent was to entertain and educate the audience with Bible stories, from the Creation to the Last Judgment. The biblical characters were down to earth—in one play Noah was portrayed as henpecked—and the stories were lavishly embellished, sometimes with bawdy comedy.

For practical reasons the feast of Corpus Christi was an ideal time for presenting the plays, as it usually fell in the warm month of June on one of the longest days of the year. York, England, needed a long day, for it presented up to 57 short plays, each at a dozen locations around town, from first light to sunset. In other cities, the festivities ran several days. In either case, the plays mobilized much of the community. By law, no actor could portray more than one character in one play. As a result, the plays in York required 27 Christs.

Actors no longer came from the ranks of the clergy. Instead, business guilds staged the plays. When possible, guilds were linked to plays related to their craft—perhaps to showcase their wares. In York, shipwrights produced the play about Noah and the Flood, goldsmiths were assigned to the story of the Magi, and bakers staged the Last Supper.

Effect of the Plays Visitors flocked in from the countryside and neighboring hamlets, bringing money. As one city document of the time put it, the plays were performed "to the greater glory of God, and to the profit and increase of the city." These plays gave some people their only brush with Scripture. About 1644 an old Englishman recalled the day he learned all he knew of the story of Jesus: "I think I heard of that man you speak of once in a play at Kendall, called Corpus-Christ's play, where there was a man on a tree and blood run down."

In the late 16th century the Protestants prohibited these "popish" plays, which presented "idolatrous" scenes that lauded the Virgin Mary and used humans to portray God. Consequently biblical drama became rare, but plays on secular subjects thrived, reaching an apex at the turn of the century with the plays of William Shakespeare. ❖

Poverty Movements

AT A TIME WHEN MANY BISHOPS AND ABBOTS WERE LIVING IN SPLENDOR, VARIOUS GROUPS OF CHRISTIANS, INSPIRED BY THE GOSPELS, CHOSE TO RETURN TO THE *VITA APOSTOLICA*, THE AUSTERE LIFESTYLE OF THE APOSTLES AND OTHER EARLY CHRISTIANS.

By the late Middle Ages, the church was sadly in need of reform. Some bishops were living in splendor, ecclesiastical offices were being sold, and many priests were openly living with women. In the 11th and early 12th centuries, sporadic calls for reform were made by individual priests and monks and by Pope Gregory VII, but none had any lasting results.

Arnold and Waldes Beginning in the 1130's, Arnold, abbot of the Abbey of Brescia, Lombardy (in northern Italy), claimed that clerical vice resulted from the church's attempt to control the world. He asked the church to give over its property to the state and return to the poverty of the church's early days, when the Apostles and others shared their possessions. Arnold's call to the *vita apostolica*, or "life of the Apostles," was to be taken up independently by others in the years to come, but Arnold himself was banished by Pope Innocent II in 1139 and later executed for leading an open revolt against the pope.

One of the most successful of the men who sought to return to the *vita apostolica* was Waldes (or Valdès), a wealthy merchant from Lyons, France. Waldes's conversion started when he heard a troubadour singing a ballad about Alexis, a Roman patrician who gave up everything to lead the life of a virtuous pauper in hopes of enjoying rewards in the life to come. Inspired by this ballad, Waldes asked a priest how he might live like Christ. The

Waldes, an influential reformer, later known as Peter Waldo, died in 1197.

priest answered: "Go, sell your possessions, and give the money to the poor . . . then come, follow me [Matthew 19:21]." Waldes promptly provided for his wife and daughters, sold his remaining belongings, and gave the money to the poor. He had parts of the Bible translated into French and, after memorizing long passages, went about preaching that all people, not only monks, should imitate Christ by living in poverty.

The Poor in Spirit As Waldes attracted followers, known as the Poor in Spirit, he sent them out two by two, as Jesus had sent out his disciples, to teach and explain the Scriptures. In 1179 the archbishop of Lyons ordered Waldes to stop preaching, but he refused, saying, "We must obey God rather than any human authority [Acts 5:29]." Waldes and some followers went to Rome and asked Pope Alexander III to lift the ban. Although Alexander admired the lifestyle of the Poor in Spirit, he saw the vernacular Bible and the preaching of laymen as threats to ecclesiastical order. Consequently, he permitted Waldes and his followers to preach only if invited to do so by the local bishops—in effect, not at all.

Waldes defied the pope and continued sending men and women out to preach. His movement spread throughout France and into Italy. To Waldes, no teaching other than Christ's as outlined in the Bible was binding. At the Council of Verona in 1184 Pope Lucius III excommunicated Waldes's followers, but the movement continued. It divided into the Poor in Spirit, who took vows of poverty and lived and prayed together, and "friends," who remained in the church but supplied recruits and support for the former. In the 16th century Waldes's followers, the Waldensians, formed an independent church that still survives.

The Humiliati Also seeking a return to the *vita apostolica*, a group of pious men and women called the Humiliati espoused voluntary poverty and banded together to live a communal life of prayer and manual labor. Made up mostly of people from the upper levels of Lombard society, they were given the choice of living together in communities of celibate men or women or of being bound together in a fraternity with strict religious principles while living within their own families. They were a close-knit group, caring for their sick and engaging in community prayer.

All would have gone well except that they believed it was their evangelical duty to preach, though they were forbidden to do so. In 1184 the Council of Verona condemned them for preaching without authorization. However, in 1201, after investigating the group, Pope

Pope Innocent III, shown here in a fresco at a monastery in Subiaco, Italy, was a charitable man who provided care for the sick, the poor, the homeless, abandoned children, and penitent sinners. He approved of the reformers' wish to live simply, like the Apostles, but discouraged the laity from reading the Bible, which was best left to learned doctors of the church. The laity, he insisted, were like babies, who could digest only milk and not the solid food of sacred Scripture.

Jesus tells a rich young man to sell all he has, give it to the poor, and follow him in this illustration from a 14th-century German manuscript. This passage from Matthew, which had influenced the early Desert Fathers, prompted numerous reformers to seek simple lives. Waldes of Lyons and Francis of Assisi were among them.

Francis, "the little man of Assisi," loved Jesus so much and succeeded so well in imitating him that he was known as the "Other Christ."

Innocent III accepted the Humiliati back into the church, and sanctioned their way of life, which for their lay members was more austere than that of other laymen but not so severe as that of monks. The pope even gave the lay Humiliati permission to preach provided they avoided theological matters and dealt only with exhortations to the Christian life—an extraordinary privilege. The Humiliati went on for a while working within the church, even helping to curb heresy.

Francis of Assisi While the Waldensians and Humiliati were striving to imitate the Apostles, one extraordinary man went further still. Emphasizing Christ's humanity, Francis of Assisi strove to imitate the beloved person of Jesus himself as fully as humanly possible.

Like Waldes, Francis Bernardone was also taken with the songs of the troubadours. But in Francis's case it was the songs of gallant knights and their lady loves, not songs of saints, that appealed to the young man. Francis longed to be a knight in shining armor, but God had other plans for him: to transform the church by living a life of simplicity and poverty in imitation of the Gospels.

Francis was born in 1181 or 1182 in Assisi, a town nestled in the green hills of Umbria in central Italy. His father was a wealthy cloth merchant, but Francis, a fun-loving young man, was a poor businessman and squandered his father's money on himself and his friends.

When Francis was about 20 years old, he joined a war against the nearby town of Perugia. He was captured and imprisoned for a year, and he subsequently suffered a long illness. Upon recovery, Francis bought a horse and armor and went off to fight in the service of a famous knight, Walter de Brienne, hoping to emulate the knights in the troubadours' romances. But before reaching the battlefront, Francis was advised in a dream to turn back and to serve the master rather than the man. From that point on he led a more austere life. Once he traded places with a beggar. Another time he overcame a strong aversion and kissed a leper—who, according to some, was Jesus.

Voice From the Cross One day, while praying in the St. Damiano chapel, Francis heard a voice from the cross saying, "Repair my house." Not understanding the larger implications of this message, Francis set about making physical repairs to the building, selling his horse and some of his father's cloth to buy materials. When confronted by his angry father, Francis publicly stripped himself naked and disowned his worldly father in deference to his Heavenly Father. After hearing a reading of the same Gospel verse that had inspired Waldes, in which Jesus tells a rich young man to sell all he has and give it to the poor, Francis refused to own anything at all. He begged for food and shelter

While meditating on the suffering Jesus endured on the cross, Francis was visited by a crucified angel, who implanted the wounds of Jesus in Francis's body, as shown in a fresco, right, by the Italian master Giotto.

on a daily basis, and his love for chivalry was changed to love of poverty, which he lovingly referred to as his Lady Poverty. Francis modeled his life on the example of Jesus in the Gospels, and he was always joyful, paying homage to every animate and inanimate creature of God.

Three Franciscan Orders After attracting a dozen followers, Francis wrote a rule for these Friars Minor, based on Jesus' teachings. In 1209 Pope Innocent III approved the rule of this First Order. In 1212 Francis founded a Second Order, for women, now called the Poor Clares after their cofounder, Clare of Assisi. About 1221 he wrote a rule for a Third Order, for lay men and women, who were unable to live the communal life. The three orders spread quickly through the world.

Francis was so dedicated to the person of Jesus that he longed to experience all that Jesus felt. One day a winged seraph appeared and granted his wish to experience the sufferings of Jesus. Francis was left with the stigmata, the five wounds of Jesus, in his hands, feet, and side. Two years later, on October 3, 1226, Francis joyfully welcomed "Sister Death." Through the example of his holy life of simplicity and poverty, and without raising his voice in anger, Francis had succeeded, where others had failed, in helping repair, or reform, the church by bringing Christians back to Gospel teachings. ❖

DOMINIC AND HIS FRIARS PREACHERS

While Francis helped reform the church through the power of his example, Dominic, his contemporary, did so by preaching and fighting heresy. Dominic was born in Castile of noble parents, studied theology, and became a priest.

While in France in 1206, Dominic encountered a group called the Albigensians, who had revived an ancient heresy that claimed there were two supreme beings, one good and the other evil. Because the Albigensians believed that worldly possessions and pleasures came from the evil one, they lived in stark poverty.

Realizing that worldly preachers could not reach these people with the "true" gospel, Dominic and others went to them like the disciples in the Gospels, two by two, carrying no money, and begging their food. In this way, Dominic and the Order of Preachers he founded fought heresy through much of the Christian world.

Dominic, a man noted for his gentleness, placed great emphasis on study, particularly the study of Scripture, and he especially loved the Gospel of Matthew. The above 13th-century painting may be the earliest surviving likeness of him.

The Bible in the University

THE NEW MEDIEVAL INSTITUTION OF THE UNIVERSITY WAS THE FORUM FOR A FERTILE EXCHANGE
OF CHRISTIAN AND CLASSICAL IDEAS, GENERATING FRESH UNDERSTANDINGS OF SCRIPTURE.

In the early Middle Ages, formal education was the responsibility of monastic schools run primarily by and for monks. About 1100, cathedral schools appeared in the major urban centers, and in the early 13th century universities developed in Oxford, Cambridge, Paris, and Bologna. The cathedral schools and universities were directed by clerics and attracted both clerical and lay scholars.

Scholasticism At some of the universities a method of biblical study evolved that differed from the devotional approach favored by the monks. Called Scholasticism, it emphasized reason—rather than faith alone—in the search for theological truth.

A major influence on Scholasticism was the rediscovery of some of the major treatises of Aristotle and other all but forgotten ancient texts. These works were reintroduced to the West by Muslim and Jewish translations and commentaries. Aristotle's treatises on logic supplied some of the basic methods of Scholastic inquiry. Chief among these

was a classroom exercise called dialectics. This discipline involved the teacher's posing a question to students and then drawing on the Scriptures, biblical commentaries, and even papal decrees to provide doctrinal issues for debate. The object was to arrive at an answer based on reason.

Scholastic study of the Bible produced, among others, the works of Peter Abelard and Peter Lombard and the great treatise of the age, the *Summa Theologica* (1267-1273) by the Dominican friar Thomas Aquinas. In the *Summa*, Aquinas made a brilliant series of arguments that demonstrated a rational foundation for the profound mysteries set forth in the Bible. Aquinas' arguments, still models of philosophical reasoning, showed that faith and reason were harmonious, not contradictory, ways of understanding the world.

Return to the Ancient Languages Contemporaneous with Scholasticism there was a resurgent interest in the original biblical languages, provoked

Averroës, a medieval Arab philosopher, is shown at the feet of Aristotle in an illustration, left, from Averroës' highly influential commentaries on the works of the classical Greek philosopher.

in large part by the work of Jewish scholars, preeminently Moses Maimonides and Shlomo Yitzhagi, better known as Rashi. Maimonides' *Guide to the Perplexed,* written from 1185 to 1190 (before the *Summa Theologica*), attempted to reconcile Aristotelian philosophy with Jewish theology. Rashi favored the literal interpretation of the Hebrew Scriptures over the allegorical.

Three Franciscans produced major work in the field of ancient languages: the Greek scholar Robert Grosseteste, bishop of Lincoln and founder of the Franciscan school at Oxford; the celebrated Oxford professor and Hebraist Roger Bacon; and the Hebraist Nicholas of Lyra, author of a volume of commentaries published in 1339 that became a standard text for theological studies. Nicholas' literal approach to the Scriptures was informed by the writings of Rashi, under whose influence Nicholas went so far as to reject readings that found prophecies of Christ in the Old Testament. So important did study of the ancient languages become that in the early 14th century chairs in Greek and Semitic languages were established in all universities.

Bible References In addition to offering new methods of interpretation, scholars at the universities made other important contributions to Bible study. The division of the books of Scripture into chapters is credited to Stephen Langton, a lecturer on the Bible in Paris and later archbishop of Canterbury and one of the authors of the Magna Carta.

A wide array of companion volumes to the Bible—including Holy Land geographies and glossaries of biblical words, events, plants, and animals—

also came from universities. In 1230 Hugo of St. Cher assembled the first concordance to the Latin Vulgate translation. The concordance listed alphabetically thousands of key words found in the Scriptures and thus served as a valuable reference source. ❖

In this 14th-century fresco Thomas Aquinas is elevated to a throne above the figure of Averroës, to whom the Dominican was indebted for many of his ideas concerning Aristotle.

Students listen intently to a lecture (shown on a 14th-century relief from Bologna). The universities of Bologna and Paris are the oldest in Europe.

Wyclif and the Lollards

JOHN WYCLIF BELIEVED THAT THE BIBLE CONTAINS THE WHOLE TRUTH. THE CHURCH CONDEMNED HIS IDEAS BUT HE INSPIRED OTHERS TO TRANSLATE THE BIBLE AND CARRY HIS TEACHINGS FORWARD.

The preaching of John Wyclif, an eminent 14th-century scholar and theologian, inspired the first complete translation of the Scriptures into English. Wyclif's belief in the need for an English Bible grew in part from his displeasure with the established church, which suffered from corruption and schism. He was convinced that the church should hold no wealth and wield no power and that its hierarchical structure was wrong. To him, God's law was found not in the decrees of the pope but in the authority of Scripture. To obey God, Wyclif felt, everyone, including the common people, must be able to read the Bible in his own language.

Wyclif spent nearly his entire career at Oxford University, where he was a devoted Bible scholar and preacher. Beginning about 1374 he wrote a series of treatises, most notably *On the Truth of Sacred Scripture*, which won him a loyal following. His writings articulated the concept that each person is immediately responsible to God and must obey his law. Wyclif's ideas became associated by some with social reform and were seen as a cause of a peasants' revolt in 1382. Soon after the revolt, a council convened by the archbishop of Canterbury condemned Wyclif's doctrines and his criticisms of the pope and church. Forced to leave Oxford, Wyclif retreated to the parish of Lutterworth, where he continued his radical writings until his death in 1384.

The Lollards Wyclif's followers were given the derogatory name of Lollards, meaning "mutterers." Like Wyclif they believed that the body and blood of the Eucharist were symbolic rather than actual and that Christ's presence in the Eucharist is spiritual.

Wyclif was called to trial by the bishop of London in 1377, but the proceedings ended in a riot. He is shown at the trial in this detail from a 20th-century mural.

REFORM IN BOHEMIA

In 1390 the writings of John Wyclif were taken to Bohemia, where they had a decisive influence on a young theologian, Jan Hus. A scholar and preacher who had been born among the peasantry, Hus shared Wyclif's desire to reform a corrupt church and his belief that the Scriptures should be the supreme authority for Christians.

Hus's anticlerical message and vigorous preaching of the Gospels in the Czech language attracted a large nationalist following—the Hussites—some of whom adopted the communal life of poverty led by members of the early church.

In 1415 at a council convened in Constance, Germany, Hus refused to pledge obedience to the pope and acknowledge the hierarchy of the church and was burned at the stake for heresy. A period illustration showing his death and the removal of his ashes appears above. His martyrdom incited years of strife among the Hussites and other religious factions in Bohemia.

They opposed the hierarchy of the church and the luxurious living of its bishops. They also continued to strive for an English Bible and English prayers. The church viewed their beliefs as heresy, and their movement was forced underground.

The "Wyclif" Bible Wyclif did not translate the Bible himself, but the two earliest English translations of the full Bible were done by Lollard followers and are known by Wyclif's name. Both were made from the Latin Vulgate. The first, done in the early 1380's and attributed to Nicholas of Hereford and others, painstakingly preserved the Latin word order, which sometimes obscured the meaning in English. The second, completed about 1395 by Wyclif's friend and secretary, John Purvey, resulted in a more idiomatic and readable text.

Although the Lollards sometimes added commentaries to the translations, nothing in the actual texts was overtly contrary to church interpretation. Yet the emphasis on an English Bible by the Lollards made the English church hostile to the very idea of such a thing. In 1408 a council convened at Oxford specifically forbade translations of the Scriptures into English and held that the possession of an English Bible must be approved by diocesan authorities.

Despite the church's attempts to burn and destroy them, Wyclif Bibles were widely used by noblemen, clergy, and—most significantly—common people. Nearly 200 manuscripts of the two versions have survived. The popularity of these translations clearly demonstrated the lasting appeal of Wyclif's central doctrine—"Every Christian ought to study this book because it is the whole truth." ❖

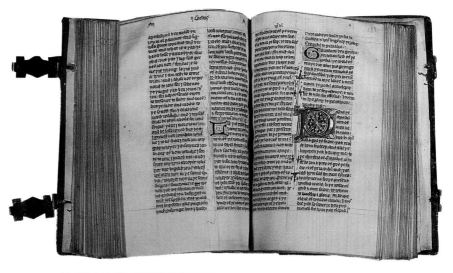

Although each copy had to be hand-written, the Wyclif Bible—particularly the second version—was immensely popular among English readers. The edition above dates from 1440.

The Printed Word

*I*n about 1456 the Bible was printed with movable type, revolutionizing the copying of Scripture and making it possible to reproduce and distribute it far and wide. By 1500, printers at work in more than 250 European towns had printed more than 90 editions of the Bible. Hundreds of editions have appeared since then in every size and price range, in virtually every language, and in every region of the globe, no matter how remote. Today computer technology is being teamed with printing, promising even greater accessibility to the Bible in the future.

A shelf of Bibles printed over the past four centuries

From the Gutenberg Bible to the End of the Second Millennium

PART FIVE TIMELINE *(A few of the dates below are based on scholarly speculation and are approximate.)*

4000 BC — 3000 BC — 2000 BC — 1000 BC — 0 — AD 1000 — AD 1455 — AD 2000

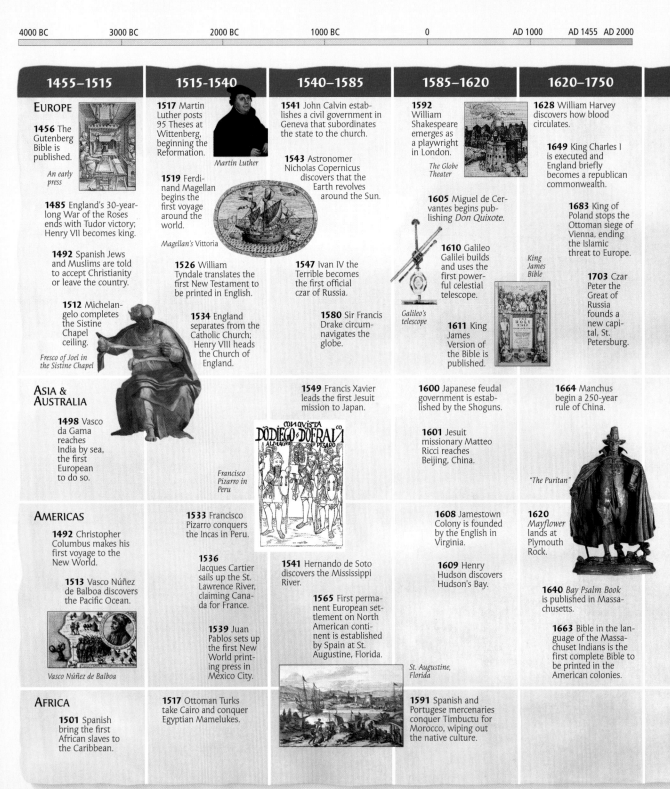

1455–1515

EUROPE

1456 The Gutenberg Bible is published.

An early press

1485 England's 30-year-long War of the Roses ends with Tudor victory; Henry VII becomes king.

1492 Spanish Jews and Muslims are told to accept Christianity or leave the country.

1512 Michelangelo completes the Sistine Chapel ceiling.

Fresco of Joel in the Sistine Chapel

ASIA & AUSTRALIA

1498 Vasco da Gama reaches India by sea, the first European to do so.

AMERICAS

1492 Christopher Columbus makes his first voyage to the New World.

1513 Vasco Núñez de Balboa discovers the Pacific Ocean.

Vasco Núñez de Balboa

AFRICA

1501 Spanish bring the first African slaves to the Caribbean.

1515–1540

1517 Martin Luther posts 95 Theses at Wittenberg, beginning the Reformation.

Martin Luther

1519 Ferdinand Magellan begins the first voyage around the world.

Magellan's Vittoria

1526 William Tyndale translates the first New Testament to be printed in English.

1534 England separates from the Catholic Church; Henry VIII heads the Church of England.

Francisco Pizarro in Peru

1533 Francisco Pizarro conquers the Incas in Peru.

1536 Jacques Cartier sails up the St. Lawrence River, claiming Canada for France.

1539 Juan Pablos sets up the first New World printing press in Mexico City.

1517 Ottoman Turks take Cairo and conquer Egyptian Mamelukes.

1540–1585

1541 John Calvin establishes a civil government in Geneva that subordinates the state to the church.

1543 Astronomer Nicholas Copernicus discovers that the Earth revolves around the Sun.

1547 Ivan IV the Terrible becomes the first official czar of Russia.

1580 Sir Francis Drake circumnavigates the globe.

1549 Francis Xavier leads the first Jesuit mission to Japan.

1541 Hernando de Soto discovers the Mississippi River.

1565 First permanent European settlement on North American continent is established by Spain at St. Augustine, Florida.

St. Augustine, Florida

1585–1620

1592 William Shakespeare emerges as a playwright in London.

The Globe Theater

1605 Miguel de Cervantes begins publishing *Don Quixote*.

1610 Galileo Galilei builds and uses the first powerful celestial telescope.

Galileo's telescope

1611 King James Version of the Bible is published.

1600 Japanese feudal government is established by the Shoguns.

1601 Jesuit missionary Matteo Ricci reaches Beijing, China.

1608 Jamestown Colony is founded by the English in Virginia.

1609 Henry Hudson discovers Hudson's Bay.

1591 Spanish and Portugese mercenaries conquer Timbuctu for Morocco, wiping out the native culture.

1620–1750

1628 William Harvey discovers how blood circulates.

1649 King Charles I is executed and England briefly becomes a republican commonwealth.

1683 King of Poland stops the Ottoman siege of Vienna, ending the Islamic threat to Europe.

King James Bible

1703 Czar Peter the Great of Russia founds a new capital, St. Petersburg.

1664 Manchus begin a 250-year rule of China.

"The Puritan"

1620 *Mayflower* lands at Plymouth Rock.

1640 *Bay Psalm Book* is published in Massachusetts.

1663 Bible in the language of the Massachuset Indians is the first complete Bible to be printed in the American colonies.

1750–1800	1800–1850	1850–1900	1900–1950	1950–2000

1782 James Watt patents a new steam engine, opening the way for the Industrial Revolution.

Watt's steam engine

1789 Paris mob storms the Bastille, launching the French Revolution.

1796 Edward Jenner demonstrates a safe innoculation against smallpox.

1770 James Cook discovers New Zealand and Australia.

Captain Cook in New Zealand

1776 Continental Congress adopts the Declaration of Independence.

1777 Robert Aitken publishes the first English-language Bible in America.

1787 United States adopts the world's first constitution.

1769 Egypt declares its independence from the Ottomon Empire.

1806 Holy Roman Empire ends with the Confederation of the Rhine.

1815 Napoleon is defeated at Waterloo.

Napoleon Bonaparte

1827 World's first photograph is produced by the physicist Joseph Niepce.

Early camera

1848 *Communist Manifesto* is published.

1803 Louisiana Purchase doubles the size of the United States.

1817 Simón Bolívar and José de San Martín begin efforts to liberate South America from the Spanish.

1848 Mexican-American War ends and U.S. gains Texas, New Mexico, and California.

1822 Liberia is founded as a colony for freed American slaves.

1859 Charles Darwin publishes *On the Origin of Species*.

1862 Louis Pasteur's "Germ Theory" locates the source of infections.

U.S. marines at Iwo Jima

1853 Crimean War begins.

Civil War

1861 American Civil War begins.

1865 U.S. President Abraham Lincoln is assassinated.

1876 Alexander Graham Bell invents the telephone.

Alexander Graham Bell

1869 Suez Canal is opened in Egypt.

1914 World War I erupts when Austrian Archduke Franz-Ferdinand is assassinated in Sarajevo.

1917 Bolshevik Revolution begins in Russia.

Lenin

1939 World War II begins with the Nazi invasion of Poland.

1945 World War II ends.

1948 Independent State of Israel is established.

1949 Mao Tsetung establishes the People's Republic of China.

1903 Orville and Wilbur Wright make the first heavier-than-air flight at Kitty Hawk.

1914 Panama Canal opens.

1920 Women win the right to vote in U.S. elections.

Suffragist banner

1929 Great Depression begins.

Nelson Mandela

1957 Soviet Union launches Sputnik I.

1991 Soviet Union is dissolved with the fall of the Communist government.

Statue of Lenin toppled.

1992 Civil war erupts in Yugoslavia.

Israeli flag

1950 Korean War begins.

1952 Revised Standard Version of the Bible is published.

1963 U.S. President John F. Kennedy is assassinated.

1969 U.S. astronaut Neil Armstrong walks on the moon.

1999 Panama assumes control of the Panama Canal.

1980 African continent becomes free of European control.

1994 Free elections bring Nelson Mandela to power in South Africa.

The Age of Gutenberg

THE DISSEMINATION OF THE BIBLE—INDEED, OF ALL KNOWLEDGE—
WAS REVOLUTIONIZED WHEN A GERMAN CRAFTSMAN MADE MASS
PRODUCTION OF THE WRITTEN WORD A REALITY.

An 18th-century engraving portrays Gutenberg in a pensive mood as he looks over the first pages printed on his press. There are 11 surviving, generally intact Gutenberg Bibles printed on vellum, including the example above from the Pierpont Morgan Library collection. This copy was probably given its luxuriant foliage design and gold leaf initial letters at Bruges. It is open to the Book of Daniel.

Books were "printed" even before Gutenberg invented movable type. They were made by the time-consuming process of engraving woodblocks, inking them, pressing paper over the inked surface, and lifting off rather crude page prints. The potential for introducing mistakes in carving the block was great, and corrections had to be patched in. Gutenberg's movable-type technique allowed the printer to make any number of changes as he set a page, and the type could be reused time and again to print other pages or works or to duplicate the first printing at a later time.

Surprisingly little is known about the background of the originator of this ingenious printing method. Johann Gutenberg was born about 1390, the son of a patrician family in Mainz, Germany. He was trained as a goldsmith and in the 1430's moved to Strasbourg to work

PAPERMAKING

Papermaking was invented in China about A.D. 105. But for nearly 650 years, the technique remained an Eastern secret—until Chinese prisoners of war revealed it to their Arab captors. Paper use spread rapidly in the Arab world and traveled to Europe by way of the Moors. The first recorded uses of paper in Europe were in 950 in Spain and 1102 in Sicily.

Some Europeans greeted paper with skepticism, owing in part to the church's objections to its Muslim origins and also for the practical reason that locally made paper was poor in quality. But paper use increased and about 1150 the first European paper mill was constructed at Jativa, Spain.

Papermaking changed little for centuries. As shown above in a 16th-century woodcut, a mold was dipped into a vat filled with water and rag pulp and drained of excess liquid. The resulting sheet was placed in a screw press to squeeze out more liquid, lifted off the press, and hung up to dry.

for a manufacturer of polished stones and mirrors that were sold to pilgrims who stopped at the cathedral in Aachen.

Gutenberg returned to Mainz sometime in the 1440's. By that time, he must have been deeply involved in experimentation with printing; for in 1454, having borrowed substantial sums of money from the lawyer Johann Fust, he printed his first known publication: a papal indulgence—that is, a document that certified the bearer had asked for and received from the church some remission of time in Purgatory. Most likely, Gutenberg published many papal indulgences, along with other bread-and-butter items, such as calendars and Latin textbooks, to help keep his printing enterprise afloat.

Printer's Art To establish and operate a printing press was an expensive proposition, requiring an initial outlay of money for work space, tools, materials, such as fine vellum and metals, and hiring the services of numerous specialists required by the printer's art. Typesetting for Gutenberg's press may have been done by several compositors working on two or three presses at once.

No description of Gutenberg's press survives, but scholars believe that it was based on the press used by papermakers to squeeze water out of the sheets of rag pulp. More is known about Gutenberg's type. It was made by first striking a hard metal die in the mirror image of the letter against soft metal. The resulting impression, or matrix, was filled with a

Continued on page 296

Revered as the first printed book, the Gutenberg Bible is also a great work of printer's art, as this detail from the first page of Genesis demonstrates. The ink Gutenberg used, close in quality to oil-based paint, has never lost its luster.

INSIDE A 15TH-CENTURY PRINT SHOP

Little is known for certain about Gutenberg's shop or those of his successors. But much can be surmised from 16th-century depictions of presses and surviving presses of the 17th century, because printing techniques remained virtually unchanged for centuries.

In this imagined scene, a compositor sits at his type case—a tray with compartments for each character—and arranges lines of text on a hand-held composing stick. As he completes each line of type, he will wedge it into a type form, or metal frame, to create a mirror image of a four-page printed sheet. An apprentice, after placing a composed form on the press bed (far right) and inking it with a leather pad (shown on the press crossbeam), has clamped a sheet of damp paper into a frisket, or holder, folded it over the form, and slid the entire apparatus under the platen, or plate attached to the press screw. He is seen lowering the platen to press the paper against the type. The master printer is checking a completed sheet before hanging it up to dry. After the reverse sides of the sheets are printed and corrected, the pages are folded, collated (background), and readied for the binder.

After Gutenberg's former partner, Johann Fust, won his suit against the printer, he seized the press and type and, with the assistance of Peter Schoffer, issued an exquisite edition of the Psalter in 1457. The book's red initial letter and capitals, blue background and scrollwork, and black typeface were produced by the three-color printing method. A page from the Psalter appears above, alongside a recreation of a plate that could have been used to print it.

molten alloy—probably lead, bismuth, and antimony. When it hardened, it formed a piece of type. To make a page of type, the letters were set into a plate, locked in, inked, and pressed against paper.

Gutenberg caused great excitement in the fall of 1454 by exhibiting sample pages of his Bible at the Frankfurt trade fair. An Italian visitor (the future Pope Pius II) praised the Bible's lettering, which he said could be read without glasses. He further reported that all of the 180 or so copies of the Bible in production had found buyers.

In November 1455, about the time the print run on his Bible wound down, Gutenberg had a falling out with Johann Fust, who sued him. Fust was awarded ownership of Gutenberg's printing equipment, and he and his future son-in-law, Peter Schoffer, finished production on the Bible themselves. Thus remuneration for Gutenberg's masterpiece went not to its creator but to his creditors.

Gutenberg's Bible There are 48 surviving copies of Gutenberg's 42-line Bible, so-called because most of its pages are composed of 42 lines of text arranged in a double column. Eleven of the surviving copies are printed on vellum and 37 are on paper. The text is the revised Vulgate translation produced in the early 13th century at the University of Paris and considered the best version at the time. It also included Jerome's prologue to the translation. The Bible was printed in the folio format used for Bibles for public readings: each set of four book pages was created from a single large sheet folded over once. It was usually bound in two volumes.

The Gutenberg Bible has no title page, page numbers, or any other feature to distinguish it from a manuscript edition. Gutenberg affected a hand-copied look in other ways as well. For example, he made multiple casts of certain letters—eight variations of the lower-case letter *a* alone—in the effort to imitate the quirks of script and disguise the machine-made origins of his lettering. He cast a total of about 270 Gothic-style letters, including capitals, lower-case letters, connected letters (such as the ligatures *æ* and *œ*), and also 125 symbols for common abbreviations, such as the ampersand (&).

Gutenberg also adapted the width of a letter's metal support to the width of the letter itself. Thus, an *i* stood on a slender strip and an *m* on a broad one, avoiding the uncalligraphic and unsightly problem of spaces between letters. He also designed type for use in specific trouble spots, such as places where a right-leaning letter butted against a left-leaning one.

Printing Revolution Gutenberg's invention of mass-quantity printing caused a revolution in the European publishing world. Printers trained in Mainz set up their own shops in other parts of Germany, and printing presses began to appear throughout Europe. Italy soon rivaled Germany as the leading center of printing, and by the 1470's Venetian editions had glutted the book market. So brisk was the trade in books in Latin that many printers in England gave up printing books they could import to concentrate instead on English-language editions. By the end of the 15th century, printing shops operated in some 250 cities and towns across Europe.

The advent of the printing press greatly accelerated distribution of the Bible, and by 1500 more than 90 editions of the Vulgate had been published. Bibles in vernacular languages were printed as well: The second-known printed Bible, published in Strasbourg in 1466, is a German translation. The first printed example of the Scriptures in Hebrew was a 1477 edition of the Psalms from Bologna.

Scholars once thought Fust's suit had ruined Gutenberg, but it is now believed that he carried on his work at another shop. Gutenberg died in Mainz in 1468, too early to witness the religious upheaval his invention helped foment. Thanks to the printing press, the Bible became so widely available that the church could no longer prevent its being read directly by the laity without the intermediary of the clergy. The new accessibility of the Scriptures added fuel to the Protestant Reformation, which insisted on the primacy of the Scriptures over their interpretation by the church. ❖

By the late Middle Ages, printed books were sold in many venues, including trade fairs, stationer's shops, and bookstores. Below, purchasers line up inside a shop to buy a law book from the author.

A page from a copy of the first printed Bible in Italian is shown below. The book was printed in Venice in 1471 by Vindelinus de Spira and illustrated by the anonymous Master of the Putti.

One of the earliest printed editions of a Latin Bible, above, was published in 1472 by Bernhard Richel of Basel. It includes hand-colored rubrications and initial letters.

Printed by Heinrich Quentell in 1478, the lushly illustrated Cologne Bible, left, greatly influenced later editions of the Scriptures.

Printed Bible Decoration

Gutenberg left the decoration of his 42-line Bible up to the discretion of the buyer. But in the decades after the appearance of Gutenberg's Bible, books began to be published in decorated editions. These featured a variety of design elements, from simple rubrication—the use of a different color, usually red, for titles and other headings—to engraved initials, marginal details, and full illustrations. Two-color printing in red and black was also popular and widely used for liturgical and law books. The process, more costly than single-color printing, required the sheets of paper or vellum to be run through the press twice.

The first illustrated printed Bible, published by Gunther Zainer of Augsburg about 1475, included woodcut initials and illustrations that could be hand-colored after purchase. The next advance was illustrated printed books in which the decoration was printed from the same plate as the type. These illustrations were of high aesthetic merit and did not need to be amplified or colored by hand. At the end of the 15th century, printing came to dominate book publishing, and illumination in printed books died out.

The first complete printed Hebrew Bible was produced by Joshua Solomon in 1488. Its intricate scrollwork and delicate Hebrew lettering can be seen above in the opening page of the Book of Judges.

A handsome Bible printed by Anton Koberger in 1483 features woodcut illustrations, including this one of the story of Noah, which is complete with a mermaid and merman.

The Impact of Humanism

BETWEEN THE 14TH AND 16TH CENTURIES NEW SCHOLARSHIP RESULTED IN CORRECTIONS TO THE STANDARD BIBLICAL TEXTS.

During the Renaissance, which began in Italy in the 14th century, scholars expanded greatly on what had been started at the universities in the Middle Ages. To such existing subjects as logic, metaphysics, and natural science, they added classical literature and languages, history, poetry, moral philosophy, and other humane studies. This new branch of learning became known as humanism and its scholars as humanists.

Back to the Sources As humanist ideas spread northward, knowledge of ancient languages and culture was applied to the study of Christianity. "Back to the sources" was the humanists' watchword as they searched early texts in order to understand the Bible's true meaning. Humanists believed the lack of knowledge of Hebrew and Greek had led to distortions of meaning and hence of belief. For many theologians this view was an attack on Christian tradition and it implied a theological revolution.

The Italian Lorenzo Valla was the first of the humanists to attempt a correction of the Vulgate—the Bible accepted by the

The greatest scholar of northern humanism was Desiderius Erasmus of Rotterdam, Holland, portrayed above by Hans Holbein.

In his 1516 New Testament, right, Erasmus included both the Vulgate translation of the text and his own edition of the original Greek text. The work was published in Basel, Switzerland, by Johann Froben.

Robert Estienne, a French scholar and printer, published an important edition of the New Testament in Geneva in 1551. His name apears on the title page of the book in its Latin form, Roberti Stephani.

THE COUNCIL OF TRENT

In late 1545 a church council convened in the Italian city of Trent to formulate the church's response to the Reform movement.

On April 8, 1546, the council issued two decrees. One delineated the official, Catholic Old and New Testament canons. The other declared the Vulgate to be the authoritative text in matters of faith and morals. However, the council implicitly acknowledged the Vulgate's imperfections by calling for a new edition "in the most correct manner possible."

Church scholars labored on a corrected version for almost four decades, until Pope Sixtus V pushed the work to its completion. The Sistine Vulgate was issued in March 1590, along with a papal bull threatening excommunication to anyone who modified future editions. Yet within one week of Sixtus' death that same year, the church, troubled by many of his interpretations, suspended sales. Under the direction of Gregory XIV and then Clement VIII, a new edition was issued in 1592.

Though the Clementine Vulgate remains the church's official text, the question of textual accuracy is still important. Work continues on a new edition, which will set forth the Latin text "in the most correct manner possible."

church. Valla was an historian, a philosopher, and a student of ancient languages. In 1455 he wrote *Annotations on the New Testament*, a major work correcting the Vulgate's Latin on the basis of the Greek original. Although it was attacked by traditionalists, some of the greatest scholars of the time recognized that Valla's work showed how the original meaning of the New Testament might be recovered.

Erasmus' New Testament

In 1504 the Dutch scholar Desiderius Erasmus discovered a manuscript of Valla's *Annotations*. Reading Valla's work intensified Erasmus' intention to dedicate his life to the restoration of New Testament theology. He began by publishing the *Annotations* for the first time in Paris in 1505. In 1516 he published the first Greek edition of the New Testament, basing it on a comparison of several Greek manuscripts. For its time it was an exceptional achievement and was enthusiastically received. Included in the first edition was Erasmus' corrected version of the Vulgate. In the second edition, in 1518, he replaced the Vulgate with his own Latin translation and only included the Vulgate again in 1527 because his own translation was criticized.

Although Erasmus' work was influential, champions of the Vulgate still feared that scrutinizing biblical texts, as Erasmus had done, exposed the authority of the Scriptures and of the church to question. Such critics were not mollified by Erasmus' assertions that the faith could only be made stronger by the restoration of a truer, more accurate text of its sacred literature.

Other humanists experienced similar resistance. The scholar and printer Robert Estienne worked in Paris from 1528 to 1551, when opposition from Catholic theologians at the Sorbonne (the University of Paris) who objected to the notes Estienne included in his Bibles made him fear for his safety. He fled to the more tolerant atmosphere of Geneva, Switzerland, where he continued his scholarship.

Estienne produced complete Bibles and Old and New Testaments in Hebrew, Greek, and Latin. For the most important of his Greek New Testaments, published in 1550, he drew on more Greek manuscripts than Erasmus had done for his editions. Estienne's 1551 Greek and Latin New Testaments introduced the division of chapters into verses that remains the standard. ❖

Polyglot Bibles

IN THE 16TH AND 17TH CENTURIES, SCHOLARS FURTHERED STUDY
OF THE BIBLE BY PUBLISHING MULTILINGUAL EDITIONS.

The debate over establishing the true text of the Bible was of vast importance to 16th-century humanist scholars, and it led to the publication of polyglot Bibles. In these Bibles, translations of the Old and New Testament texts in several languages were printed along with the original languages in parallel columns. Their purpose was to facilitate comparison of early biblical texts in order to reach a truer understanding of the origins, language, and meaning of the Scriptures. Polyglot Bibles were scholarly labors of immense magnitude as well as monumental achievements in printing.

The Earliest Polyglot The earliest polyglot Bible is the Complutensian, compiled by a team of scholars led by the archbishop of Toledo, Francisco Jimenez de Cisneros, between 1514 and 1517. The scholars assembled to do the editing at a university that Cisneros had established in Alcalá de Henares, Spain. The term *Complutensian* comes from Complutum, the Latin name for Alcalá. The Complutensian's Old Testament includes the Hebrew Masoretic text, an Aramaic paraphrase (Targum) of the Pentateuch, the Vulgate, and the Greek Septuagint. The New Testament consists of the Greek text and the Vulgate.

Despite the assertion in the Complutensian's prologue that Scripture is "filled with . . . insights which cannot become known from any other sources than from the very fountain of the original language," many traditionalists were dis-

The scholarly Archbishop Cisneros, inset, initiated the compilation of the Complutensian polyglot. This page from Exodus gives the Hebrew, Latin, and Greek versions in three columns. Below them is the Aramaic paraphrase and its Latin translation.

302

The title page from Christophe Plantin's polyglot Bible appears at left. Plantin and his son are depicted at right in a 1591 painting by Jacob de Backer. In the background of the painting St. Christopher can be seen carrying the boy Jesus on his shoulders.

turbed by the humanist perspective inherent in such a Bible. Not only did the church fear that lay Bible study might lead to heresy, but growing anti-Semitism in Spain promoted a fear of the Hebrew language and Bible. Several scholars who contributed to the Complutensian were persecuted by the Inquisition.

Later Polyglots Between 1569 and 1572, the French printer Christophe Plantin brought out a beautifully designed and printed eight-volume polyglot. Because it was sponsored by King Philip II of Spain, Plantin's version is known as the Royal polyglot of Antwerp. Edited by the Spaniard Benedictus Montanus, it owed a great deal to the scholars of Alcalá but also added the Syriac version of the New Testament.

The next important edition, the 10-volume polyglot of Paris, appeared between 1629 and 1645. Although less successful than the Antwerp polyglot in its design, it included Syriac and Arabic translations as well as the first complete printed Samaritan Pentateuch. Even so, the Paris polyglot was soon overshadowed by the 6-volume London polyglot, which was published between 1654 and 1657. This last of the great polyglot Bibles was also the first such Protestant edition. Prepared under the direction of the English scholar Brian Walton, it presented nine languages—Hebrew, Aramaic, Samaritan, Greek, Latin, Ethiopic, Syriac, Arabic, and Persian. In scholarly scope and design, the London polyglot is regarded by many as the greatest of all the multilingual editions of the Bible. ❖

In Plantin's polyglot Bible the Latin text of the New Testament is given on the left side of the page and the original Greek on the right, as in this opening page of Matthew's Gospel.

CHRISTOPHE PLANTIN

Only one printer was prepared to undertake a project as ambitious as the Antwerp polyglot. He was Christophe Plantin, a Frenchman who in 1549 settled in Antwerp, a center of European publishing.

Plantin began his career as a binder and seller of books, but in 1555 he established himself as a printer. He secured the patronage of Philip II of Spain, who granted him a monopoly on the printing of all liturgical books distributed in Spain's dominions. Within a short time, Plantin had more than 20 presses, making his shop the largest of its kind in Europe.

Plantin's greatest achievement, the Antwerp polyglot, was produced between 1568 and 1572 despite formidable obstacles. For one thing Philip's promised support was slow in coming, which left Plantin near financial ruin. In addition, members of the Inquisition found the work troublesome. Only in 1580 was the Antwerp polyglot allowed to circulate.

Luther's Bible

BY TRANSLATING THE BIBLE INTO EVERYDAY GERMAN, LUTHER
CREATED THE CENTRAL TEXT OF THE PROTESTANT REFORMATION.

*This portrait of young Martin
Luther is one of many painted by
Lucas Cranach, who also published
some of Luther's writings and led
the workshop that illustrated them.
The picture below was reproduced in
a 1517 reformist pamphlet against
the preacher of indulgences Johann
Tetzel, whose excesses in explaining
indulgences led to charges that he
and others were selling them. Tetzel
is said to have delivered a sermon
with the jingle: "As soon as the coin
in the coffer rings, the soul from
purgatory springs."*

The German monk, priest, and theologian Martin Luther is best
known for posting his Ninety-five Theses on the door of All
Saints Church in Wittenberg, Germany, on October 31, 1517. The
propositions attacked certain church beliefs and practices, including the granting of indulgences—freeing a soul from punishment for
sins that have already been forgiven—and struck a blow to the authority of the church. The Ninety-five Theses were only the first of an
extraordinary number of works in which Luther expressed his ideas
concerning church reform and theology.

Luther's most radical act took indirect aim at the church: his translation of the Bible into German. Other German translations were
already in circulation, to be sure, but Luther's represented a departure
from these in several respects. It was first
of all a scholarly translation based on
close study of the Greek and Hebrew texts
and consultation with numerous scholars. More important for the ordinary
person, the translation was written in
vigorous, idiomatic German prose by a
master of popular expression. As
Luther himself described his
approach, "We must not . . .

ask the Latin letters how we are to speak German; but we must ask the mother in the home, the children on the street, the common man in the marketplace about this, and look them in the mouth to see how they speak, and afterwards do our translating."

Education of a Reformer Luther's background prepared him well for his dual roles as theologian and biblical scholar. In 1505, after taking his B.A. and M.A. degrees, he began the study of the law, only to abandon it after a month to join the strict Augustinian order of monks at Erfurt. Two years later he was ordained a priest and, after receiving his doctorate in 1512, was appointed professor of theology at the University of Wittenberg.

At Wittenberg, Luther entered a period of profound spiritual anxiety over his salvation. He found special solace in Paul's words that "a person is justified by faith apart from works [Romans 3:28]." He interpreted these words to mean that there is nothing a believer can do, neither penitence nor good works, to gain salvation; God's grace is freely granted to the one who has faith. This conviction led to the declarations against indulgences in the Ninety-five Theses.

In upholding the doctrine of justification by faith alone, Luther, in effect, nullified the priesthood and the papacy. This doctrine was heresy, and the church's response was swift. The Ninety-five Theses were condemned in a papal bull. When Luther refused to recant, writing other inflammatory tracts, the papacy issued a bull of excommunication.

In 1521 Luther was summoned to the Diet of Worms, a council of the Holy Roman Empire. When granted the opportunity to disavow his writings, he refused, answering with the famous words: "I do not accept the authority of popes and councils . . . my conscience is captive to the Word of God. I cannot and I will not recant anything. . . . Here I stand, I cannot do otherwise." Made an outlaw by the imposition of the ban of the empire, Luther was whisked away by his prince, Frederick of Saxony, to the safety of the ancient castle of the Wartburg.

Bulla contra errores Martini Lutheri z sequacium.

Luther nails his Ninety-five Theses on the door of All Saints Church, shown in a modern print. The theses read in part, "[The pope] would do better to sell St. Peter's and give the money to the poor folk who are being fleeced by the hawkers of indulgences." Three years later a bull of excommunication, above, was issued against Luther.

There in solitude he set about translating the Scriptures, moved by his passionate belief that the Word of God should be available to "the priesthood of all believers" in their own language.

"God in Every Syllable" Luther began with the New Testament, using Erasmus' emended Greek text as his standard. He painstakingly labored over every detail in recognition that "God is in every syllable. No iota is in vain." He tried to determine the authenticity and grammatical accuracy of the texts and to capture every nuance of meaning. For example, to verify the references in Revelation 21 to certain precious stones, he asked a friend to "get permission from court to let us have the loan of some to see what they are like."

Unlike other biblical scholars, Luther showed little interest in apparent inconsistencies in the Scriptures. What did it matter that the versions of Jesus' birth in Matthew and Luke differ, "if we have the right understanding of Scripture"? However, he did attempt to establish the relative values of

A 16th-century engraving depicts Nuremberg, one of the major German publishing centers. Usually, Luther's pamphlets were first printed in Wittenberg and then published in other German cities, including Nuremberg, Leipzig, and Augsburg.

various canonical books. His criterion for books of both the Old and New Testament was based on whether, in his opinion, the texts proclaimed Christ. Thus he judged as inferior books the Epistle to the Hebrews, those of James and Jude, and the Book of Revelation.

In January 1522, less than a month into his work on the translation, Luther feared that "the task far exceeds my powers. Only now am I discovering what translating really means and why no one has thus far dared associate his name with an undertaking of this kind." Nevertheless, he completed a first draft in two and a half months. Luther took the translation to Wittenberg on March 6, 1522, and put it through revisions with the help of the eminent Greek scholar Philipp

A magnificent edition of Luther's translation was released in 1541 in Wittenberg. A contemporary of Luther's said that his New Testament was "multiplied by the printers in a most wonderful degree, so that even shoemakers and women and every lay person . . . read it greedily."

Melanchthon. The initial printing of 3,000 copies was carried out in secrecy beginning in May, and Das Neue Testament Deutzsch appeared the following September. Priced at about a carpenter's weekly wage, it sold out within three months. During Luther's lifetime, more than 100,000 copies of his German New Testament were sold.

Even as the New Testament was being printed, Luther turned to the far more arduous task of translating the Old Testament. His approach to the Hebrew Scriptures was colored by the Christian view of Jesus as the fulfillment of the Old Testament. Thus, for example, Luther shows his Christian bias in translating the Hebrew phrase that literally means "deliverer of Israel," as "Savior."

Luther translated the Old Testament from a variety of Hebrew texts. Not a strong Hebraist himself, he relied on the advice of the scholar Matthaus Aurogallus, and a council of experts made further revisions. The translation took 12 years to complete and was published in several parts. In 1534 the entire Bible appeared in a six-part edition, the first of 11 complete editions before Luther's death in 1546.

Luther reworked his translation ceaselessly. For example, he made hundreds of emendations for the second printing of the New Testament, and he revised the Psalter in 1531 with the help of a team of scholars. He said, "Translating . . . requires a right pious faithful, diligent, God-fearing, experienced and practised heart." ❖

The Path Toward an Authorized English Bible

DURING THE REIGN OF THE TUDORS, ENGLISH TRANSLATIONS OF THE BIBLE WERE ALTERNATELY CONDEMNED OR ENDORSED ACCORDING TO A VOLATILE POLITICAL AND RELIGIOUS CLIMATE.

Some of the most resonant phrases in the English language—such as "fight the good fight" and "the spirit is willing but the flesh is weak"—were coined by William Tyndale, the first Englishman to translate the Bible from its original languages. Tyndale's translation was the basis of all subsequent English Bibles, including the famous Authorized, or King James, Version. Remarkably, Tyndale carried out his work over a mere dozen years, while constantly evading persecution from the church.

Born about 1494, Tyndale studied at Oxford and Cambridge, eventually taking holy orders. Like Wyclif, Tyndale believed that the Bible—not the church hierarchy—was the instrument of salvation. Deeply convinced that Scripture must be available to everyone, he traveled to London in 1523 seeking permission from Bishop Cuthbert Tunstall to translate the Bible into English. Tunstall denied the request and Tyndale left England for the European Continent the following spring. While he was on the Continent, his work was subsidized by a layman

friend, Humphrey Monmouth, and by some other London merchants.

By August of 1525, Tyndale and his assistant, William Roye, had finished translating Erasmus' Greek New Testament into English. Publication of the manuscript was interrupted by authorities in Cologne, but Tyndale and Roye managed to flee, taking their work with them. Early the next year Tyndale succeeded in publishing the complete New Testament and began sending copies to England. In October 1526 many of these were burned in London; Bishop Tunstall purchased the New Testaments solely to destroy them. Tyndale was condemned for what were perceived as his Lutheran leanings, and efforts to suppress the translation were dramatically effective; only two of Tyndale's original New Testaments now survive. (Revised editions were published in 1534 and 1535.)

About 1529 Tyndale learned Hebrew, mastering it sufficiently to produce outstanding translations of the Pentateuch—the first five books of the Bible. He also completed translations of nine other Old Testa-

The portrait of William Tyndale, above, was painted in the 16th century. Its inscription names Tyndale as a martyr. The verse painted under his hand translates as: "To scatter Roman darkness by this light, The loss of land and life I'll reckon slight."

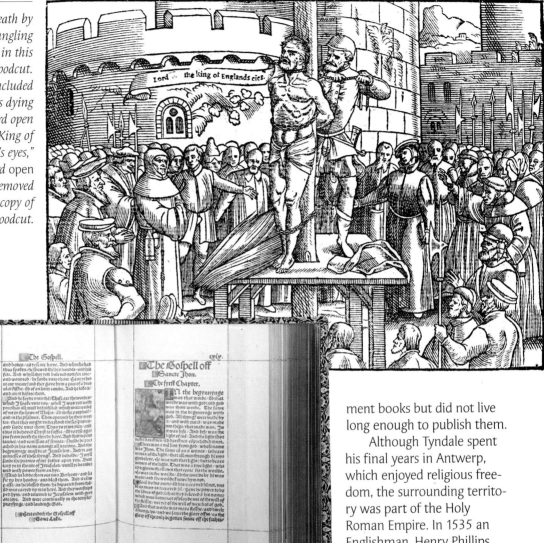

Although Tyndale's Bible did not present the complete text of the Old and New Testaments, it was the first English Bible to appear in printed form. This facsimile of Tyndale's 1526 Bible is open to the Gospel According to John.

ment books but did not live long enough to publish them.

Although Tyndale spent his final years in Antwerp, which enjoyed religious freedom, the surrounding territory was part of the Holy Roman Empire. In 1535 an Englishman, Henry Phillips, acting for an unknown agent, lured Tyndale from the safety of his house. He was seized by the emperor's men and made a prisoner of the state. Tyndale was tried for heresy, condemned, and, on October 6, 1536, strangled. His body was burned at the stake.

Tyndale's dying words were, "Lord, open the King of England's eyes." Sadly, he was unaware that Henry VIII's eyes were already opening. For more than a year a complete English translation of the Bible had been circulating in England. The Coverdale Bible had appeared with the king's permission, if not his blessing.

Coverdale's Bible Miles Coverdale was a student at Cambridge University when he became attracted to Luther's ideas. In 1528 Coverdale left England for the Continent, where, between 1529 and 1535, he

Miles Coverdale appears at top right in a portrait engraving. Coverdale's Bible, published in Marburg, Germany, in 1535, was the first complete Bible to be printed in the English language. A copy of the first edition, above, is open to the beginning of the Book of Genesis. Six woodcut engravings depict the days of creation. A total of 168 woodcuts enlivened the Coverdale Bible. The second edition was the first Bible actually printed in England.

worked with Tyndale on translations of the Old Testament in Hamburg and Antwerp.

Coverdale published the first edition of his Bible in October 1535. Hoping to gain the king's approval, he included in the volume a long dedication to Henry VIII and Queen Anne (Anne Boleyn). His timing was good. In 1534 Thomas Cranmer, the archbishop of Canterbury, had asked his bishops to begin work on an authorized version. Little had been done on this project when Coverdale's Bible was printed, and probably this fact, more than the florid dedication, won Henry's verbal approval for the translation. Coverdale's Bible was never formally accepted as authoritative, however, because its prologue and notes suggested Luther's reforms, and the translation was too far from the original texts.

Although Coverdale knew Latin and German, he lacked the scholarship to translate the Bible from its original languages. In his dedication he states that he relied heavily on the work of five translations. These included Tyndale's, the Vulgate, Luther's German translation, a Swiss-German Bible, and a Latin translation by a Dominican priest.

Coverdale was the first English translator to introduce chapter summaries and to separate the Apocrypha from other Old Testament books. Only some of his phrasing survives in modern Bibles.

Matthew's Bible The Bible whose influence far exceeded that of Coverdale's translation was Matthew's Bible, which was printed in 1537, probably in Antwerp. Though its title page credits "Thomas Matthew," this Bible was most likely edited by John Rogers, a scholar and friend of Tyndale's. Rogers's work is a composite, consisting of Tyndale's New Testament of 1535 and as much of the Old Testament as Tyndale had translated before his death (the Pentateuch and Joshua through 2 Chronicles). The remaining Old Testament books (Ezra through Malachi) and the Apocrypha were from Coverdale.

By 1537, the time was ripe for obtaining Henry VIII's formal approval, and his chancellor, Thomas Cromwell, secured "the kinges most gracyous lycence" for the Matthew Bible. Yet, because of Rogers's use of notes from Tyndale and other Protestants, it also was not acceptable, and so, with royal support, Cromwell gave Coverdale the task of revising Matthew's Bible to make it suitable.

For this first authorized version of the English Bible, Coverdale drew on the best Hebrew and Greek texts, as well as Tyndale's Bible. The result was the Great Bible (named for its size), first published in 1539 with financing provided by Cromwell. A further revision of the Great Bible was published in 1540, becoming the standard text, and by 1541 seven editions had been issued, numbering about 21,000 copies. In St. Paul's Cathedral in London, where copies of the translation were set up and read aloud, crowds of worshipers listened. They were so loudly enthusiastic that the bishop of London issued a prohibition against Bible reading during the sermon.

In one of history's ironies, the third and fifth editions of the Great Bible note that they have been "overseen and perused" by Bishop Tunstall. Tunstall knew he was authorizing a Bible that relied heavily on Tyndale's translations, yet under King Henry's command he was forced to sanction the work he had once tried so hard to abolish.

THOMAS CROMWELL

The man who did the most to ensure that the English had access to the Bible in their own language was Thomas Cromwell, Henry VIII's chancellor from 1533 to 1540. Cromwell (portrayed by Hans Holbein above) was the spirit behind an injunction requiring that a copy of the English Bible be placed in every parish church.

Published in September 1538, the injunction ordered the clergy to provide "one book of the whole Bible of the largest volume in English" and place it where "your parishioners may most commodiously resort to the same and read it." The "largest volume" referred to the Great Bible, then being printed in Paris at Cromwell's expense.

The Great Bible was finally published in April of 1539. Its appearance—and the permission it conferred on the public to read and discuss Scripture freely—was greeted with great enthusiasm by many and with hostility by the more conservative churchmen.

After falling out of favor with the king, Cromwell was executed in 1540. In 1543 an Act of Parliament restricted reading of the English Bible to the upper classes.

The engraving on the title page of the 1539 Great Bible is ascribed to Hans Holbein. At the top, God appears from the clouds to bless Henry VIII. Henry is handing copies of the Bible to the archbishop of Canterbury, Thomas Cranmer, on his left, and to Thomas Cromwell on his right. They in turn pass Bibles along to the populace.

311

Bible of the Geneva Exiles When Mary Tudor became queen of England in 1553, she was determined to roll back the Reformation and reinstate Catholicism in her country. She wed the Catholic Philip II of Spain and induced Parliament to recognize papal authority. The persecution of Protestants followed and, with it, a rush of exiles to Geneva, where work on the Geneva Bible commenced.

The Geneva translators produced a revised New Testament in English in 1557 that was essentially a revision of Tyndale's 1534 edition, with changes based on the Latin translation executed by the French theologian Theodore Beza. Much of the work was done by William Whittingham, brother-in-law of John Calvin, the French theologian and reformer who stressed the doctrine of predestination.

The Geneva New Testament was barely off the press when work began on a revision of the entire Bible, a process that took more than two years. Whittingham again acted as translator and probably had the assistance of two fellow exiles, Anthony Gilby and Thomas Sampson. The New Testament was a revision of Whittingham's 1557 version, with greater attention paid to Beza's work and the Greek text. The Old Testament drew on the Great Bible edition of 1550, altering it in light of available Hebrew and Latin texts and of a French version being prepared in Geneva at the same time. The translators strove to give their translation a Hebrew flavor and so, as they noted, "reserved the Hebrew phrases notwithstanding that they may seem somewhat hard in their ears that are not well practised."

Queen Mary, depicted in a 1554 portrait, earned the name Bloody Mary because of her harsh persecution of Protestants. The engraving below shows an incident of 1555, when a group of Protestant martyrs was publicly burned at Canterbury.

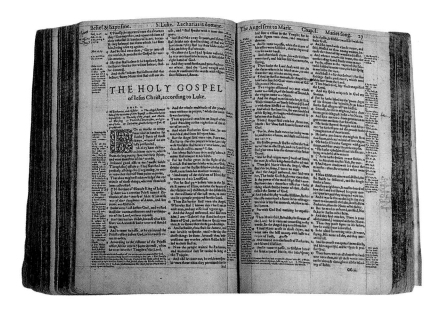

In 1560 a complete revised Bible was published in Geneva, "translated according to the Ebrue and Greke, and conferred with the best translations in divers languages." The Geneva Bible was printed in England only after the death, in 1575, of Archbishop Matthew Parker, editor of the Bishops' Bible.

Shakespeare and the Geneva Bible

The Geneva Bible was the edition in general use in England during Shakespeare's time, and much of the language of his plays and sonnets echoes its wording and themes. In particular, echoes of the Geneva translation of the Book of Job can be heard in *Othello*, *Richard II*, and *As You Like It* and in Hamlet's most famous soliloquy. The opening of the soliloquy, below, is printed side by side with Job 6:2-4, 7:21, 6:8-9, and 7:13. (The excerpts from Job have been arranged to correspond to the sequence of the soliloquy.)

Hamlet, Act III. Scene 1.	*Book of Job*
To be, or not to be, that is the Question:	*Oh that my grief were wel weighed,. . .*
Whether 'tis Nobler in the minde to suffer	*For it wolde be now heavyer than the sand of the sea:*
The Slings and Arrowes of outragious Fortune,	*therefore my wordes are swallowed up.*
Or to take Armes against a Sea of troubles,	*For the arowes of the Almightie are in me . . .*
And by opposing end them:	*& the terrours of God fight against me.*
To dye, to sleepe,	*now shal I slepe in the dust,*
No more; and by a Sleepe, to say we end	*and if thou sekest me in the morning,*
The Heart-ake, and the thousand Naturall shockes	*I shal not be founde.*
That Flesh is heyre to?	
'Tis a consummation	*Oh that I might have my desire, & that*
Devoutly to be wish'd. To dye, to sleepe,	*God wolde graunt me the thing that I long for!*
	That is, that God wolde destroye me:
To sleepe, perchance to Dreame; I, there's the rub,	*When I say, My couche shal relieve me,*
For in that sleepe of death, what dreames may come,	*& my bed shal bring comfort in my meditation,*
When we have shuffl'd off this mortall coile,	*Then fearest thou me with dreames,*
Must give us pawse. . . .	*and astonishest me with visions.*

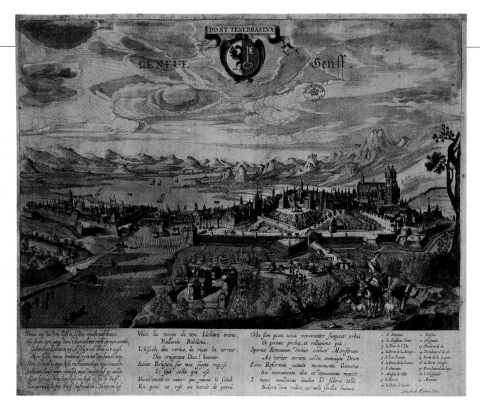

An engraving of about 1650 shows the Calvinist city of Geneva, a vital center of biblical scholarship once called by Geneva Bible translator William Whittingham "the store of heavenly learning and judgment."

The first edition of the Geneva Bible, published in that city in 1560, was dedicated to Queen Elizabeth I. Crowned in 1558, Elizabeth once again turned England in a Protestant direction.

The Geneva Bible was instantly popular. At least 140 editions were printed, and for 40 years after the King James Version was published, the Geneva continued to be the Bible of the home. In 1643 extracts from it were printed in the *Soldier's Pocket Bible* issued to the army of the Puritan leader Oliver Cromwell.

Many of the commentaries written in the margin of the Geneva Bible expressed general Protestant beliefs, such as justification by faith alone. Some, like the commentary on Psalm 147:2, imparted Calvinist teachings on subjects such as predestination: "God's just judgment . . . appointed the reprobate to eternal damnation." The commentaries also offered alternative translations. Some of the later editions included strongly worded condemnations of the Roman Catholic Church. One note went so far as to identify the pope as the Book of Revelation's "beast that cometh out of the bottomless pit [Revelation 11:7]."

Bishops' Bible In 1559 Queen Elizabeth ordered that a copy "of the whole Bible of the largest volume in English" be placed in every parish church. The Great Bible was reprinted, but Archbishop of Canterbury Matthew Parker wished to have a new translation suited for reading aloud in church. In 1566 he assigned sections of the Great Bible to a team of revisers, most of them bishops. The group was to depart from the Great Bible only to correct inaccuracies or clean up offensive language and to mark dull passages, such as lengthy genealogies, so that readers could bypass them. The revision was completed in 1568.

NOT-QUITE-RIGHT BIBLES

Numerous Bibles have nicknames stemming from their archaic vocabulary. The Geneva Bible has been called the Breeches Bible because it states that Adam and Eve "sewed figge-tree leaves together, and made themselves breeches." The Coverdale Bible is dubbed the Bug Bible because it advises, "Thou shalt not nede to be afrayed for eny bugges by night."

Various printings of Bibles are named for the typographic errors that appear in their texts. The so-called Murderers' Bible misprints "murderers" for "murmurers" in Jude 16. The Printers' Bible, an edition of the King James, laments that "printers" (not "princes") "have persecuted me without cause." The Wife-Hater Bible warns of the consequences "If any man come to me, and hate not his father . . . yea, and his own wife also"—instead of his "life." The Adulterer's Bible leaves out an essential "not" and commands, "Thou shalt commit adultery."

Though approved by the Convocation of Canterbury, the Bishops' Bible apparently did not receive Elizabeth's authorization. It was a conservative and dignified translation, less radical in its language and tone than the Geneva Bible but borrowing from it at various points. The notes retain a Protestant flavor but avoid harsh comments on the Roman Catholic Church and hierarchy. As the Bible of the Church of England, the Bishops' Bible went through 20 editions in 42 years and served as the official basis for the King James Version, which took from it a number of well-known phrasings.

Douay-Rheims Bible The need for preachers to give adequate translations of the Latin Bible in English—and the desire of the Catholic Church for a sacred text that would answer Protestant translations—resulted in the first English Bible for Catholic worshipers.

Because of persecution under Elizabeth, some English Catholics fled across the Channel to Douay in northern France. There in 1568 they established a Catholic college that was later moved to Rheims. The Catholic translation was begun in Rheims in 1578 by Gregory Martin, an Oxford scholar and a lecturer in Hebrew and the Bible. Martin translated at a rate of two chapters a day, submitting the text to two colleagues for editing. The New Testament was issued in 1582. The Old Testament, delayed by lack of funds, appeared in 1609–10, by which time the college had returned to Douay.

Though a portrait of Elizabeth I adorned the title page of the Bishops' Bible, the queen apparently never officially endorsed it.

The title page to the Rheims New Testament states it is "translated faithfully into English out of the authentical Latin, according to the best corrected copies of the same."

The Douay-Rheims translation, proclaimed the official Catholic version at the Council of Trent in 1546, is a literal rendering of the Latin Vulgate Bible. However, Martin and his editors also consulted the Hebrew and Greek, and other translations, with an eye toward accuracy and grammatical usage. In an effort to preserve the Latin tone of the Vulgate, the translators coined Latin-English terms, such as "supersubstantial bread" (for "daily bread" in the Lord's Prayer). At the end of the New Testament they provided a glossary of 58 obscure renderings, among them, "acquisition," "adulterate," and "victim." Many of these no longer sound strange to the English speaker.

The translation, along with its annotations, strongly defends the Catholic faith and indicts "the absurd translation" of other English Bibles, with their use of "'congregation' for 'church,' 'elder' for 'priest,' 'image' for 'idol' . . . and such like, to what other end . . . but to conceal and obscure the name of the Church." While the New Testament produced in Rheims was a source for the King James Version, the Douay Old Testament was published too late to influence it. ❖

King James Version

ENGLAND'S AUTHORIZED VERSION OF THE BIBLE, SEVEN YEARS IN THE MAKING,
REMAINS ONE OF THE MOST BELOVED REVISIONS.

Early 17th-century England enjoyed an era of creative ferment. At the same time that Shakespeare was writing *Macbeth*, a new English-language Bible was produced that combined rigorous scholarship and elegant language. Called the Authorized, or King James, Version, this translation, published in 1611, became the most influential rendering of the Bible in English.

Need for a New Bible When James I became king of England in 1603, there were two translations of the Bible in use; the Geneva was the most popular, and the Bishops' was used for reading in church. King James frowned on the Geneva version because of its Calvinist commentary, which he viewed as "very partial, untrue, seditious, and savouring too much of dangerous and traitorous conceits." He disliked, for instance, notes that seemed to him "to allow disobedience to kings." A marginal note for Exodus 1: 9 indicated that the Hebrew midwives were correct in disobeying the Egyptian king's orders, and a note for 2 Chronicles 15:16 said that King Asa should have had his mother executed and not merely deposed for the crime of worshiping a false idol.

At a conference with bishops and theologians at Hampton Court Palace in 1604, the king listened to a suggestion by the moderate Puritan scholar Dr. John Reynolds that a new translation of the Bible was needed. James agreed. Three years earlier in

Scotland he had proposed the same thing himself. Though one conference member, Richard Bancroft, the bishop of London (and later archbishop of Canterbury), groused, "If every man's humour were followed, there would be no end of translating," the king was enthusiastic. He remained a moving force in organizing the enterprise.

Planning the Work The project was meticulously planned and executed. In 1604 a total of 47 of England's foremost Bible scholars and linguists were chosen to serve on six panels; two of them met at Oxford, two at Cambridge, and two at Westminster. Each panel was assigned particular books of the Bible to translate. Once each of the groups had made its translation, the work was reviewed by a committee of 12, made up of 2 scholars from each of the six panels.

An elaborate set of guidelines was drawn up to ensure that eccentricities and partisan leanings were eliminated in the new version. The names of biblical characters were to retain the traditional English spellings; some old ecclesiastical words were to be used ("church," for instance, instead of "congregation"); marginal notes were to be used only to clarify Hebrew and Greek words and to point out parallel passages in the text. The Bishops' Bible was declared the basis for the translation, but earlier translations were to be used if it was judged that they agreed better with the original text. The parti-

King James, above, championed a uniform translation of the Bible and helped initiate the project .

The Evolution of a Psalm

The opening lines of Psalm 23 in the King James Version are familiar to many. As these comparisons demonstrate, the poetry of the verse in English had been evolving for some time before 1611.

The Lorde is my shepherde, I can wante nothinge.
He fedeth me in a grene pasture, and ledeth me to a
fresh water. He quickeneth my soule, & bringeth me
forth in the waye of rightuousnes for his names
sake. Though I shulde walke now in the
valley of the shadowe of death, yet I feare no evell,
for thou art with me:
thy staffe & thy shepehoke comforte me.
Coverdale Bible, 1535

God is my sheephearde, therfore I can lacke nothyng:
he wyll cause me to repose my selfe in pasture
full of grasse, and he wyll leade me unto calme
waters. He wyll convert my soule: he wyll bring me
foorth into the pathes of righteousnesse for his
name sake. Yea though I walke through the valley of
the shadowe of death, I wyll feare no evyll: for thou
art with me, thy rodde and thy staffe be the
thynges that do comfort me.
Bishops' Bible, 1568

The Lord is my shepherd, I shal not want.
He maketh me to rest in grene pasture & leadeth me
by the stil waters. He restoreth my soule, & leadeth
me in the paths of righteousnes for his Names sake.
Yea, thogh I shulde walke through the valley of the
shadow of death, I wil feare no evil: for thou art
with me: thy rod and thy staffe, they comfort me.
Geneva Bible, 1560

The Lord is my shepheard, I shall not want.
He maketh me to lie downe in greene pastures:
he leadeth me beside the still waters. He restoreth
my soule: he leadeth me in the pathes of
righteousness, for his names sake. Yea though
I walke through the valley of the shadowe of death,
I will feare no evill: for thou art with me,
thy rod and thy staffe, they comfort me.
King James Version, 1611

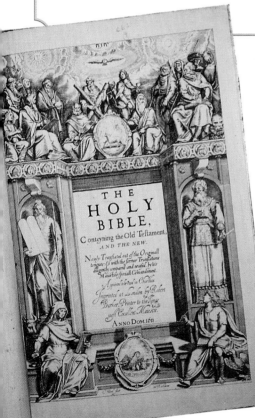

The title page of the 1611 Authorized Version, left, does not mention King James by name. The inscription indicates that the translation was to be read in churches.

cipants were not, strictly speaking, supposed to create a new translation "but to make a good one better, or out of many good ones one principal good one."

A Mellifluous Text Because the text of the King James Version was to be used at church services, the translators worked hard to make it suitable for reading aloud—its punctuation indicated emphasis and its rhythmic prose could be used to great effect. The translators noted in the preface that they made a deliberate attempt not to be restricted "to an uniformity of phrasing, or to an identity of words." The very freedom and richness of the language lend the translation freshness. The text's oral quality can also be traced to the translation process. Since each translator had to read his version aloud to the others, his work was written as language to be spoken.

The actual work of translating took the panels roughly three years; another three years were spent in reviewing the translations and an additional nine months in preparing it for press. It was published in London in 1611 in a black-letter folio edition measuring 16" x 10 1/2". Three editions appeared that year, the first one known as "the great HE edition," and the other two known as "the great SHE editions," because of a variation among the Hebrew manuscripts in the closing words of Ruth 3:15. The first edition translates the passage "he went into the city," while the subsequent editions read "she went into the city."

A New Standard The translators dedicated their work "to the most high and mighty prince James," and while it is referred to as authorized, it was never officially recognized by the king or mandated as the only permissible church text. Nonetheless, it immediately replaced the Bishops' Bible as the standard in churches, and within 40 years it supplanted the Geneva Bible as the most popular text for private use.

Though the King James Version was widely embraced by all factions of the church in England—even by the Puritans—it was not without its detractors. An esteemed scholar, Dr. Hugh Broughton, perhaps miffed that he had not been chosen as one of the translators, dashed off a strongly worded letter to the royal court condemning the King James Version when it first appeared. "The late Bible . . . bred in me a sadness that will grieve me while I breathe, it is so ill done," he wrote. "Tell His Majesty that I had rather be rent in pieces with wild horses, than any such translation by my consent should be urged upon poor churches. . . . The new edition crosseth me. I require it to be burnt." Fortunately, Broughton's suggestion was ignored.

The literary quality of the King James Version—the strength and nobility of its language combined with its openness to a variety of interpretations—has earned it an indisputable authority. It took more than 250 years before any large-scale revision of the text was attempted. Then the editors of the English Revised Version, respectful of the original King James Version, had this to say of the 17th-century translation. "We have had to study this great Version carefully and minutely, line by line; and the longer we have been engaged upon it the more we have learned to admire its simplicity, its dignity, its power, its happy turns of expression, its general accuracy, and, we must not fail to add, the music of its cadences, and the felicities of its rhythm." ❖

King James I and his court attend a service in the courtyard of the old St. Paul's Cathedral in London. The king is seen sitting in the balcony and wearing a plumed hat.

TEXTS LEADING TO AND FROM THE KING JAMES VERSION

DATE	WORK	DESCRIPTION
10th century B.C. to 1st century A.D.	Hebrew Scriptures (Old Testament)	Known today as the Masoretic text
282 B.C. to 1st century B.C.	Septuagint	Greek translation of Hebrew Scriptures
1st century A.D.	New Testament	Written in Greek
405 A.D.	Vulgate	Latin translation. Old Testament translated from Hebrew and Septuagint. New Testament Gospels translated from Greek
1382	Wyclif Bible	First translation of full Bible into English. An almost word-for-word equivalent of the Vulgate translation made by followers of John Wyclif
1516	Erasmus' New Testament	Edition of New Testament in Greek with Latin translation—both by Desiderius Erasmus
1526	Tyndale Bible	First printed New Testament in English. Translation made by William Tyndale. New Testament translation made from Erasmus' Greek. Pentateuch and Jonah translated from Hebrew in 1530 and 1531
1534	Luther's Bible	Translation into German by Martin Luther. New Testament based on Erasmus' Greek edition, Old Testament translated from Hebrew
1535	Coverdale Bible	First complete printed English Bible. Translation by Miles Coverdale relying heavily on Tyndale Bible, as well as Vulgate and other Latin translations, Luther's German translation, and a Swiss-German Bible
1537	Matthew Bible	Edited by John Rogers. New Testament relying on Tyndale translation; Old Testament using existing Tyndale books, supplemented with books from Coverdale
1539	Great Bible	Revised version of Matthew Bible made by Miles Coverdale. Based on Tyndale Bible as well as Greek and Hebrew texts
1560	Geneva Bible	Translation made by William Whittingham and others. New Testament a revision of Tyndale's text. Old Testament based on Great Bible as well as Hebrew, Latin, and French texts
1568	Bishops' Bible	Translation by committee consisting largely of English bishops. Revised version of the Great Bible
1609–1610	Douay/Rheims Bible	Catholic Bible begun by Gregory Martin. A literal rendering of the Vulgate Bible
1611	King James Version	Translation made by committees of scholars. Based primarily on Bishops' Bible. Also based on Tyndale, Matthew, Coverdale, Great, and Geneva Bibles, and Douay-Rheims New Testament
1881–1885	English Revised Version	Revision of King James Version made by 50 scholars. Revisions based on an improved edition of Greek text
1901	American Standard Version	Variant of the English Revised Version including phrasing preferences of American scholars
1952	Revised Standard Version	Revision of American Standard Version made by an international ecumenical committee
1989	New Revised Standard Version	Revision of Revised Standard Version made by a continuing ecumenical committee

Taking the Bible to the Far East

THE INTREPID MISSIONARIES WHO TOOK CHRISTIANITY TO ASIA WERE CHANGED BY THE CULTURES THEY ENCOUNTERED.

T hough Christian missionaries traveled to the Orient beginning as early as the second century, concerted efforts to propagate and establish the faith in these distant lands came more than a thousand years later, with the opening of trade routes between East and West. Wherever marketplaces grew up in Asia—a continent rich in the precious metals, gems, silks, and spices that the West coveted— missionaries were sure to follow. In their zeal to spread the Gospel and their willingness to endure almost any hardship to do so, the Christian evangelists were every bit the equals of the celebrated merchants of the day.

Even among such dauntless souls, certain individuals stand out. The Spanish Jesuit Francis Xavier, called Apostle to the Indies and to Japan, was later declared a saint for his missionary work. He was born Francisco de Yasu y Xavier in 1506, the fifth and youngest child in an aristocratic Spanish-Basque family. While a student at the University of Paris, he forged a friendship with a fellow Spaniard, Ignatius of Loyola, and on August 15, 1534, Loyola, Xavier, and five companions gathered in a chapel in Paris to vow obedience to the pope and pledge their lives to serving others.

The oath formed the basis of the Society of Jesus, or Jesuits. In 1537 Xavier and Loyola were ordained priests. One year later they made a pilgrimage to Rome, where, in 1540, Pope Paul III formally recognized the Jesuits.

Mary, Jesus, and Mary's mother, Anne, are given Asian features and dress in an 18th-century Indian painting, above. Below, a 17th-century map of Goa, the Portuguese base in India, includes a vignette of Francis Xavier kneeling before the local bishop.

Forays Into India and Japan In April 1541 Xavier embarked from the Portuguese capital of Lisbon on the arduous sea journey to Goa, Portugal's colonial stronghold in India. He was not the first Christian missionary to reach India, however. A small but flourishing community

of Christians in the southwestern part of the country worshiped in the Syriac language and traced its origins back to the Apostle Thomas.

Xavier turned his attentions to the Paravas, a lowly caste of fishermen and pearl divers living along the southernmost tip of the Indian subcontinent and on the island of Ceylon (Sri Lanka). Less than a decade earlier, the Paravas had converted to Christianity in exchange for promises of church protection from their enemies. But without the benefit of clergy to lead them or provide instruction in the Bible, the converts had failed to embrace the faith fully. Xavier undertook to teach them, keeping by his side the catechism he had translated into the native language of Tamil. He exerted the full force of his personality in bringing the Word to the Paravas and was enormously successful. So tirelessly did he labor, administering the sacrament of baptism, that at the end of particularly strenuous days he sometimes found he could not move his arms.

After working for three years in India, Xavier moved on to the Malay Peninsula, the Moluccas, and, in 1549, to the island nation of Japan, where the Portuguese had begun to trade seven years before. There he taught using a catechism translated into Japanese. Exceeding all expectations, he made great strides among the native population. By the 1590's, when Christianity began to be suppressed in Japan, some 300,000 Japanese called themselves Christians.

Francis Xavier was tireless in his efforts to take the Gospel to the Orient, and there are countless stories of his work and of miracles associated with him. According to the story depicted in the above print, his ship ran out of drinking water during the long voyage to Japan in 1549. To solve the problem, some of the ship's crew lowered the holy man overboard and where his feet touched the salt sea, it was miraculously turned into fresh drinking water.

During his stay in Japan, Xavier had become aware of China's powerful influence over neighboring cultures, and he grew determined to take the Bible to that most inaccessible of Far Eastern kingdoms. But he was unable to find a boat to the Chinese mainland, and late in 1552 he fell ill and died on a small island off the coast.

Taking the Scriptures to China Xavier's mission in China was fulfilled by another Jesuit, the Italian cleric Matteo Ricci, an erudite and versatile man of scientific bent, who preached to the Chinese by appealing to their love of learning. Ricci sought out the most educated and influential members of Chinese society. If they could be won over, he knew, the larger public would follow.

Clad as a Buddhist monk, Ricci established himself in the city of Chaoking in 1583. Six years later, having adopted the dress of a Confucian scholar, he won fame as the "Doctor from the Great West Ocean." Ricci's home became a showcase for the most innovative and impressive artifacts of European culture and science, including books and paintings; prisms, clocks, and other scientific gadgets; and the "Great Map of Ten Thousand Countries," made by Ricci himself. In 1601 his renown gained him admittance to the imperial city of Beijing, and in the nine years before his death, he gained some 2,000 Chinese adherents, many of them officials of the court.

To reach the Japanese, Jesuit missionaries, shown on a late-16th-century painted screen, had to argue philosophy with Zen priests and adopt such local customs as ritual tea drinking and public bathing. In 1597, at Nagasaki, the Great Martyrdom began, followed by decades of widespread persecution of Christians.

Ricci's greatest legacy was his success in working with, and adapting his teachings for, a people of a totally different culture from his own. He acquired a deep understanding of Chinese values and virtues and used this knowledge to bring the Chinese people to his own faith. By steeping himself in the local culture he found common ground between Christian and Chinese belief systems. For example, in the Chinese notion of *Shang-ti*, meaning "lord on high" or "supreme ruler," he discerned a predisposition to belief in a single God. Ricci learned several Chinese dialects and translated the Ten Commandments and a catechism into Chinese. He also allowed converts to maintain certain traditional practices, such as ancestor worship and the veneration of Confucius.

Ricci's immediate successor in China, a Belgian Jesuit named Nicholas Trigault, went so far as to request papal permission to allow Chinese church services to be conducted in the vernacular rather than Latin. Ultimately Ricci's open-mindedness to foreign influences led to a debate that raged within the Catholic Church for more than a century: How should missionaries properly approach non-Westerners?

Bible Translation in Asia In 1744 the papacy sided with Ricci's opponents, maintaining that church practice and instruction should not be altered to fit the traditions of another culture. But for the next wave of missionaries in the Orient—who were Protestant—the wisdom of one aspect of Ricci's work was clear: the translating of the tenets of Christian faith into native languages.

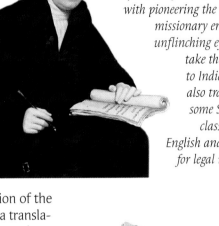

William Carey, shown in a portrait of 1812, is credited with pioneering the modern missionary era by his unflinching efforts to take the Gospel to India. Carey also translated some Sanskrit classics into English and fought for legal reforms.

The 19th century was something of a golden age of Bible translation in Asia. For the first time published translations of the Scriptures reached dozens of Asian peoples. No one pursued the activity of translating more energetically than the English Baptist missionary William Carey. In 1801, while posted in India, Carey produced the first translation of the New Testament into Bengali. Eight years later, he completed a translation of the entire Bible. With the help of local assistants, Carey and two colleagues—known as the Serampore trio—directed the translation of the Bible into as many as 44 Indian languages and dialects.

The earliest prominent American missionary was the Baptist clergyman Adoniram Judson, who survived imprisonment in squalid jails, a bout of malaria, and his wife's death, to oversee missionary activity in Burma. His work attracted some 7,000 converts. Judson also mastered the difficult Burmese language and, by the time of his death in 1850, had translated the Bible into Burmese and had finished work on a grammar and most of an English-Burmese dictionary.

The Scottish missionary Robert Morrison translated the Bible into Chinese in 1823. In 1837 Karl Gutzlaff of Prussia rendered the Gospel of John in Japanese, the oldest extant translation in that language. In 1800 the Bible, or portions of it, had been translated into 13 Asian languages. By 1830, that number had increased to 43. ❖

Grace Irwin, a missionary in China, sets out—by wheelbarrow, no less—to reach the local people. She is accompanied by a "Bible woman," a local person who helped missionaries cope with the local language and customs.

አካን ሰሎም በስምን-ሰብግዝ*ተ፡ መ፡ብሳ፡ ባ፡ ፡ ንዳ፡ በፈ፡

A 20th-century miniature portrays the meeting of Solomon and the Queen of Sheba, from whom the Ethiopian royal dynasty claims descent. At the end of the 18th century a complete Bible in the Ge‘ez language of Ethiopia became available, and in 1824 the books of Scripture began to be printed in Amharic.

The Bible in Africa

CATHOLIC AND PROTESTANT MISSIONARIES SET UP STATIONS ALONG THE COAST OF AFRICA AND GRADUALLY MOVED INTO THE INTERIOR.

With the rise of Islam in the seventh and eighth centuries, the early Christian centers in North Africa were largely swept away. The remaining Christians were mostly in Egypt and Ethiopia.

A second phase of Christianity began in Africa at the end of the 15th century, when Portuguese explorers arrived, followed by Catholic missionaries. In the Kingdom of Kongo (now in Angola and Zaïre) the king was baptized and his son became a bishop. Other Christian enclaves grew up in the Niger delta Kingdom of Warri, on the west African coast, and among the peoples of the Zambezi River, which stretches from present-day Zambia to Mozambique. By the mid-18th century, British, Dutch, and Danish traders had set up 30 forts along the Gold Coast, and Protestant missionary initiatives were taken up by the Moravians and the Society for the Propagation of the Gospel.

Slave Trade Some early missionaries denounced the lucrative slave trade that had grown up in Africa, and the Catholic Church issued an

This carving of a missionary was done in 1930 in Nigeria, home to more than 3 million speakers of Yoruba. The first complete Yoruba Bible was translated by a committee made up mostly of Africans.

Robert Moffat, shown above, had a total of 10,000 copies of the Old Testament printed at his missionary station in Kuruman on a press that had been hauled many miles in an ox wagon.

A 17th-century staff from the Kongo, right, pictures a praying Christ figure. The region was made famous in 1877 by Sir Henry Morton Stanley's navigation of the Congo River.

official statement condemning the traffic in human beings in 1686. Nevertheless, the nefarious slave trade continued unabated. By the end of the 18th century, opposition to slavery, combined with mounting evangelical fervor, created a new era of missionary activity in Africa. Evangelical missions, such as the British Baptist Missionary Society, converted thousands of local Africans as well as freed slaves who had returned to Africa. Like David Livingstone, the intrepid Scottish missionary and explorer, these missionaries believed that fair trade would replace the slave trade.

African Languages Missionaries penetrated to the interior of the African continent in the hope of propagating the Word among remote populations. Often they faced tremendous odds because few of the local languages had ever been written. Generally they had to teach converts to read the Bible in a European tongue or else invent an alphabet and painstakingly translate the Scriptures into the language of the people.

In addition, Africans often had no experience of many basic Christian concepts, and they lacked the words to express them. How, for instance, should "Holy Spirit" be translated for a people who understood "spirit" primarily in the sense of spirits of the dead? Translators who were familiar with local tradition sometimes incorporated native elements in their renditions. For example, the Gospel of John in the Luo language of East Africa opens: "From long long ago there was News, News was with the Hunchback Spirit, News was the Hunchback Spirit." The term "Hunchback Spirit" is the literal translation of the name for God in that language.

Several 19th-century missionaries devoted their lives to translating the Scriptures into the languages of Africa. Robert Moffat, father-in-law of David Livingstone, produced a Bible in the South African tongue of Tswana in 1857. In the 1850's and 1860's Samuel A. Crowther, a Nigerian who had been rescued from a slave ship and raised a Christian, translated most of the New Testament into Yoruba. The German missionary Jonathan Ludwig Krapf spent the 1870's translating Scripture into the Galla language of Ethiopia. In 1857 John William Colenso, the Anglican bishop of Natal, completed a Gospel harmony in Zulu, followed in the late 19th century by the American Bible Society's rendering of an entire Zulu Bible. ❖

A Dominican friar appeals to the Aztecs to abandon human sacrifice, cannibalism, and polygamy. The scene is depicted in a 1698 painting, above, by Miguel Gonzalez. The 17th-century Mexican crucifix at right is decorated with Indian carvings.

Taking the Gospel to the New World

THE SUCCESS OF THOSE WHO CARRIED THE GOSPEL TO THE NEW WORLD RIVALED THAT OF THE APOSTLES.

B etween Christopher Columbus' voyage of discovery in 1492 and the nearly total liberation of the Western Hemisphere from European control in 1825, zealous Europeans brought much of the New World into the fold of Christianity. This awesome accomplishment began with the priests who carried the cross while the soldiers wielded the sword. When Columbus sailed west, Queen Isabella of Spain, who sponsored him, was so consumed with piety that she decreed that any lands Columbus encountered would be Christianized. Columbus named the island on which he landed San Salvador ("Holy Savior"), and, believing he had reached the Indies, he called the inhabitants Indians. On his second voyage, in 1493, Columbus brought along a Benedictine monk and five priests to evangelize the natives.

Champions of the Indians Columbus wrote that the Indians on Hispaniola "could better be freed and converted to our Holy Faith by love than by force." In 1493 Pope Alexander VI proclaimed that the Spanish rulers should Christianize the Indians peacefully. But the thirst for profit subverted these noble goals. The Spanish soon instituted a system that granted settlers Indian tribute and labor— in practice, slavery—in exchange for Christian instruction.

Right-thinking Christians raised their voices in protest. At a Christmas Mass in 1511 a mainly slave-owning congregation heard their priest denounce the forced-labor policy in his sermon: "In order to make your sins against the Indians known to you, I have come up on this pulpit, I who am a voice of Christ crying in the wilderness. You are in mortal sin for the cruelty and tyranny you use in dealing with these innocent people. By what right do you keep these Indians in such cruel and horrible servitude?" This plea by the Dominican friar António de Montesinos, commonly known as Fray Antón, was the first effort by a religious figure to redress the wrongs committed by Spaniards against Indians.

In Cuba the Dominican friar Bartolomé de las Casas, a former slaveowner and the first priest ordained in the Americas, also came to believe that the Indians were being abused. In 1514 he launched a long crusade for the native population of the New World. Pope Paul III affirmed his cause by issuing a bull in 1537 stating that "the Indians are truly men," deserving of baptism. When the "New Laws" forbidding Indian slavery were passed in 1542 and approved by Emperor Charles V, De las Casas was instrumental in enforcing them.

The Conquest of Mexico In 1519 Hernán Cortés sailed to Mexico, where he announced the principles of the church to the Aztecs and ordered them to accept Spanish rule and the supremacy of the pope. He even tried to convert the emperor, Montezuma, explaining that Christians worshiped "one true and only God named Jesus Christ, who suffered death for the salvation of the whole human race." The Aztecs refused to submit, and their empire of 20 million was defeated by fewer than 1,000 Spaniards. Cortés felt justified: "It is war and warriors that persuade the Indians to give up their idols and their bloody sacrifices; thus they more quickly believe our preachers and accept the Gospel and baptism."

Between 1493 and 1825 European missionaries poured into the New World to convert the Indians of North and South America, paying heed to the Gospel message, "Go therefore and make disciples of all nations [Matthew 28:19]." Some of the major missions and Christian settlements of colonial times are shown on the map of North America, below, and on the map of South America on the following page.

CARIBBEAN
SEA

Cartagena
Darién

Quito

Orinoco River

Amazon River

ATLANTIC
OCEAN

VICEROYALTY
OF PERU

Lima
Ayacucho
Arequipa
Cuzco
Lake
Titicaca
La Paz
Potosí

BRAZIL

Olinda

São Salvador

TREATY OF TORDESILLAS 1494

Ouro Prêto
Rio de Janeiro
São Paulo
São Vicente

ANDES MOUNTAINS

Paraná River

Asunción

PACIFIC
OCEAN

Santiago

Buenos
Aires

La Plata
River

Straits of
Magellan

Three years after the conquest,
the conversion of the Aztecs began in
earnest. In 1524 a group of Franciscans
called the Twelve Apostles arrived and within
five decades established nearly 400 missions in
central Mexico and, eventually, some 12,000
churches. The friars worked tirelessly. Bernardino de
Sahagún learned the Indian language and studied the
local history and customs. Pedro de Gante founded the
first Mexican school and the first art academy in the Western world and claimed some 14,000 baptisms in a single day. In
1539, under the patronage of Juan de Zumárraga, a Franciscan who
became Mexico's first bishop, a printer from Spain set up shop and
published primers, catechisms, and other texts. It was probably the
first printing press in the New World.

Bishop Zumárraga may also have witnessed the first miracle in the
New World. In 1531 an Indian, Juan Diego, encountered "a woman
clothed with the sun, with the moon under her feet, and on her head
a crown of twelve stars [Revelation 12:1]." To authenticate his claim,
Diego gave the bishop a serape on which an image of the lady had
mysteriously appeared. The bishop's successor founded a basilica honoring the lady, Our Lady of Guadalupe, as patroness of Mexico.

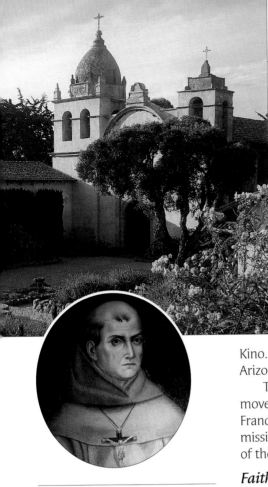

North America
Other Spaniards explored the New World: In 1513 Ponce de León became the first European to stand on land that is now part of the United States. In 1541 Francisco Vásquez de Coronado and six Franciscans planted a cross on the banks of the Kansas River and Hernando de Soto reached the Mississippi River. Over the next century, Jesuits, Dominicans, and Franciscans established missions in Florida, Texas, and the Southwest.

New Mexico was founded in 1598, and Franciscan missionaries fanned out among the pueblos, converting some 34,000 Indians. Then in 1680 an Indian revolt resulted in the deaths of 21 missionaries and—according to reports of the time—some 400 settlers. The Spaniards fled, but by 1692 they were back, taking up their missionary work again. Dedicated Jesuits labored farther to the west, notably Eusebio Francisco Kino. Between 1687 and 1711, Kino founded a chain of missions in Arizona, Mexico, and California.

Toward the end of the colonial era, as Russian Orthodox traders moved southward from Alaska into California, the Spanish sent the Franciscan Junípero Serra to protect their claims. Serra founded nine missions between San Diego and Sonoma, and during the half century of the missions' existence, some 90,000 Indians were baptized.

Francisco Junípero Serra, a Spanish Franciscan friar and professor of philosophy, did extensive missionary work in Mexico and then in 1769 went to California, where he founded a total of nine missions. He is buried in Carmel at the mission basilica of San Carlos Borromeo, above, which was his headquarters.

Faith and the Incas
It took Francisco Pizarro and his 167 conquistadors two years (1531 to 1533) fully to overpower the Incas of Peru, but the empire's 6 million inhabitants were really defeated in a mere half hour, when Vicente de Valverde, a Spanish Dominican, approached the Incan emperor, Atahualpa, and some 5,000 unarmed attendants in the town square of Cajamarca. Using an interpreter—and with soldiers lying in wait—Valverde commanded the Incas to submit. When Atahualpa asked the friar for evidence of his authority, Valverde handed him a Bible. Atahualpa threw the book down, unaware of its significance. With the war cry "St. James!" the Spaniards viciously attacked the Incas, massacring most of them within minutes.

Various religious orders contributed to the life of the colony in Peru. In 1551 the Dominicans founded the first university in the Americas, San Marcos in Lima, and Domingo de Santo Tomás prepared a catechism in one of the Incan languages. Franciscans went to Lima in the mid-1500's to establish the Province of the Twelve Apostles, which had jurisdiction over all the native parishes of South America for a decade, and later built mission colleges.

When the Jesuits arrived in 1568, they faced nearly insurmountable obstacles involving geogra-

The image of Jesus from Chimayo, New Mexico, right, is an Indian bulto, *a carved figure made of painted wood and human hair.*

The conquistador Pizarro kneels before Peru's emperor, Atahualpa, in this book illustration from about 1600. After capturing Atahualpa, the Spanish baptized him, gave him the last rites, and "humanely" strangled him.

Jean de Brébeuf, a French Jesuit, lived among the Huron Indians in what is now Ontario, Canada, for a total of 15 years. In 1649, after leaving his Mission of Sainte-Marie Among the Hurons, shown below in a reconstruction, he was captured, cruelly tortured, and killed by invading Iroquois Indians.

phy, climate, a lack of workers, language differences, and the interference of slave-owning colonists. Nevertheless, they learned the local languages and organized the Indians in disciplined Christian villages. Their goal to convert and civilize their charges was most successfully realized in Paraguay, where they baptized more than 700,000 natives. However, because of their hold on economic power in Spanish America, the Jesuits incurred the Crown's hostility. In 1767 they were banned from Spanish territory. Their missions fell into ruin, and their Indian charges set adrift.

Portuguese Brazil In 1494 the Treaty of Tordesillas gave control of the vast eastern part of South America, later known as Brazil, to Portugal. The Portuguese first visited there in 1500 and established their first settlement 32 years later. In 1549 six Jesuits arrived. Their leader, Manoel da Nóbrega, established schools and sent his men into the hostile interior to found missions. These missionaries encountered a vast, unexplored land, sparsely populated by often cannibalistic native people and threatened by roving slavers. Working tirelessly, even in the steaming Amazon jungles, the missionaries baptized and taught thousands and were regarded as the natives' greatest protectors.

Two men stand out. José de Anchieta labored for 44 years to learn the Tupí language, create an alphabet for it, and write a dictionary and grammar of the language, turning it into the common tongue of the diverse tribes. He also established schools, preached the Gospel, and defended the natives against their enemies. Antônio Vieira ran dangerous missions in Amazonia and delivered powerful sermons against slavery. In 1759, as a result of anticlerical factions in Portugal, the Jesuits were expelled from the colonies. Left without guidance, some of the indigenous people and African slaves eventually transformed Catholicism in some areas of Brazil into Macumba, a combination of Christianity and East African religion.

French Catholic Canada Christianity reached the land now known as Canada in 1534, when Jacques Cartier erected a cross on the Gaspé Peninsula, claiming the land for France. But France paid little heed to her New World possession until 1608, when Samuel de Champlain established a settlement at Québec and the French made a greater effort to convert the Indians.

First to arrive in 1615 were four missionaries of the Récollets Order, but, refusing to live with "savages," they were forced to admit defeat within a decade. The less fastidious Jesuits, or Blackrobes as the Indians called them, arrived in 1625 and devoted themselves to teaching the Indians the Gospel and converting and baptizing them.

Trying their best to serve Indian interests, the Jesuits lived in the Indian villages and shared some of their hardships. The priests discerned commonalities between Indian and Catholic beliefs. In their own way, both religions acknowledged the power of prayer, believed in an afterlife, revered ritual and ceremony, and followed a moral

René-Robert Cavelier de La Salle erects a cross on the banks of the Mississippi River on April 9, 1682, claiming for France the entire river valley, an immense 900,000-square-mile region the French called Louisiana. The scene is recreated in a mid-19th-century painting by the American George Catlin.

code. But the Indians did not believe there was only one God or that the sacraments could benefit the soul's afterlife. They believed, instead, that religious practice improves only one's earthly life.

The Indians soon perceived Christian rituals as threats. When disease broke out, they blamed the Blackrobes because they administered the sacraments to the dying and refused baptism to healthy Indians whose conversion they felt was not genuine. Eventually, six missionaries and two lay helpers were tortured and killed by the Iroquois.

Other missionaries ventured into the interior of North America. Notably, in 1673, the Jesuit Jacques Marquette sailed down the Mississippi River and founded missions among the Illinois Indians. In 1682 René-Robert Cavelier de La Salle transported a small group to the mouth of the Mississippi. Like all the other missionaries of the colonial period, these men braved the American wilderness in the name of God to "declare his glory among the nations [1 Chronicles 16:24]." ❖

Apostles to the Indians

BETWEEN 1658 AND THE BEGINNING OF THE 20TH CENTURY THE SCRIPTURES WERE TRANSLATED INTO MOST OF THE NORTH AMERICAN INDIAN LANGUAGES.

It was a most exotic gift. Charles II of England was presented with a Bible published under the strange title *Mamuse Wunneetapanatamwe Up-Biblum God.* This first complete Bible printed in the English colonies, in 1663, was a translation into Massachuset, the hitherto unwritten dialect spoken by the Massachusetts Bay Indians.

The Bible was a step toward fulfilling one of the stated purposes of English colonization in North America, as described in the charter of Massachusetts Bay: to "wynn and incite the Natives of [the] Country to the Knowledg and Obedience of the onlie true God . . . and the Christian Fayth."

The prevailing attitude of the English colonists was that their own culture was superior to the Indians' and that the Indians must attain, in the words of the Puritan missionary John Eliot, "visible civility before they can rightly injoy visible sanctitie." Thus, for example, Eliot fined his Indian charges for failing to cut their hair "comely, as the English do."

In 1650 Eliot persuaded some of the Massachuset Indians to move to a "praying town" he founded at Natick. There the seminomadic hunters and gatherers tended gardens, raised cattle, built houses in the English style, and were a captive audience for the missionary's message. In return, the Indians received food, clothing, and other gifts; for Eliot hoped their prosperity would be a sign to other potential converts that conversion would be beneficial to them. He established 14 such towns, which even at the height of their success in 1675 were probably inhabited by less than one-tenth of the area's native population.

Eliot's work stirred keen interest in England and inspired the formation there in 1649 of the Corporation for Promoting and Propagating the Gospel of Jesus Christ in New England. Later known as the New England Company, it helped purchase land for Eliot's towns and subsidized a translation of the Bible into Massachuset, a dialect of Algonquin. This, his greatest achievement, was a daunting task because of the difficulty of translating for a vastly different culture. As a result, Eliot's Bible contains some linguistic oddities. For instance, because the Indians held chastity to be a virtue required of men rather than women, the parable of the 10 virgins, as translated in the King James Version, was rendered as

---

The seal adopted by the Company of Massachusetts Bay features an Indian saying, "Come over and help us," echoing the plea of the Macedonians in Paul's vision as told in Acts of the Apostles 16:9.

The Reverend John Eliot appears in a portrait by an unknown artist. In addition to his Bible, below right, Eliot printed a dictionary and grammar, a catechism, and religious tracts, all in the Massachuset language.

the parable of the "ten chaste men" in Eliot's translation of Matthew 25:1-12.

Eliot's Bible In both the translation and the printing of the Bible Eliot was ably assisted by an Indian whose English name was James Printer. "We have but one man," the minister wrote of James, "that is able to compose the sheets and correct the press with understanding." The New England Company furnished the publisher, Samuel Green, with a new press, an ample supply of type and paper, and the skills of an experienced English typographer, Marmaduke Johnson. But the publication was stalled when Johnson, a married man, fell in love with one of Green's daughters. Eventually the men worked out their differences. The Massachuset New Testament appeared in 1661 and a complete Bible in 1663. Fifteen hundred copies of the New Testament were printed, 200 of which went to Indians. The other copies were shipped to England, to be distributed to current and prospective patrons.

The good relationship Eliot had cultivated with the Indians was shattered in 1675 by the outbreak of King Philip's War, which pitted colonists against Indians. Most praying Indians refused to fight and became the targets of both white and Indian attacks. In October 1675 the government rounded up the praying Indians and imprisoned them in internment camps, where they endured a bitter winter. Eliot protested vehemently but to no avail, and many Indians died.

The praying towns were devastated and the faith of survivors was deeply shaken. Eliot attempted to revive his missionary work, preparing a new edition of the Bible in 1685. He died in 1690, and only 40 years later the number of full communicants belonging to the church in Natick had dwindled to three.

The Cherokee Sikwayi, known as Sequoya, is shown in a portrait (copied after an earlier lithograph) with a chart of his syllabary on the wall behind him. Sequoya's phonic system enabled the Cherokees to establish a press and the first dual Indian-English-language newspaper.

Other Apostles Thomas Mayhew achieved more durable missionary success among the Wampanoags on Martha's Vineyard and Nantucket. Mayhew acquired the islands in 1641 and, proclaiming himself "Lord of the Manor of Tisbury," set up a kind of manorial regime there. His son, also named Thomas, learned the Massachuset dialect and preached to the Indians. Thus began a family ministry that spanned five generations. The Mayhews converted most of the local Indians, and by 1670 the first Indian church was organized on the islands, serving some 3,000 Christians.

The 18th and early 19th centuries produced several noteworthy missionaries who worked with Indians in the northeast. The Congregationalist minister John Sergeant spent about 14 years among the Housatonic Mahican Indians in western Massachusetts and persuaded the colonial legislature to set aside six square miles of land for Indian habitation, a meeting house, and a school. Thus was born the "Stockbridge Nation." Sergeant translated prayers, a catechism, and Bible lessons into the Indian tongue.

David Brainerd worked for four years among the Indians of Connecticut, New York, New Jersey, and Pennsylvania until he died of tuberculosis in 1747. Brainerd's fame rests on his journal, which became an inspirational guidebook for other missionaries.

The Mohawk chief Joseph Brant collaborated with the Anglican clergyman John Stuart on a translation of the Gospel of Mark, which was published in 1787. The Gospel of John was translated into Mohawk by Captain John Norton, another chief, and printed in London in 1804.

Perhaps the most famous native linguist was Sequoya, who, about 1820, created an 86-character alphabet for the Cherokees of the southern Allegheny and Great Smoky Mountains. Sequoya deeply respected the written word: "If I could make things fast on paper," he said, "it would be like catching a wild animal and taming it." The American Bible Society issued a Cherokee edition of the New Testament using Sequoya's alphabet in 1857.

In the 1830's the Methodist missionary James Evans developed a written language for the Crees. He used scrap material to build the first printing press in the Canadian northwest and published Cree editions of hymns, prayers, and Scriptures. His phonetic writing system was successfully transferred to other Indian and Inuit languages.

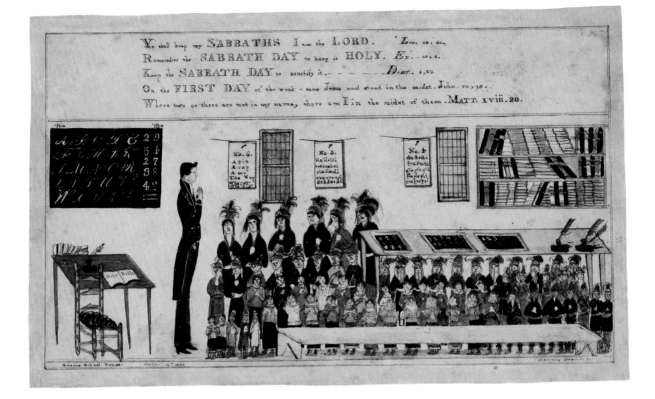

In the second half of the 19th century, the American Bible Society translated the Scriptures into a number of Indian languages, among them Choctaw, Muskogee, and Dakota. A Dakota Bible was printed in 1879—the first complete Bible in an Indian tongue since Eliot's.

Beyond the Rockies The Reverend Jason Lee answered the call to go West and live among the Indians of Oregon in 1834. Lee expressed his zeal for the job, saying, "Oh that I could address the Indians in their own language! My ardent soul longs to be sounding salvation in the ears of these red men." His pioneering efforts in the Pacific Northwest were furthered by others. But the harsh realities of bringing the Word to an alien culture are exemplified by the story of Marcus and Narcissa Whitman. The Whitmans made the grueling overland journey to Oregon by wagon and established a mission among the Cayuses. The Indians initially welcomed them, but as more immigrant families settled in the area, encroaching on native land, hostility toward missionary activity grew. In 1847, following several disturbances at their station, the Whitman family and 14 other whites were murdered.

Nevertheless, missionary work continued, and for some Indians the power of the Bible's message survived the crisis in Indian-white relations. In the words of an elderly chief of the Mohaves: "When you read out of that Book I know it is God's Book, for it pulls my heart." ❖

An 1821 watercolor entitled "Keep the Sabbath" by Dennis Cusick, son of a Tuscarora chief, portrays the missionary James Young leading a class of Indians in prayer on the Buffalo Creek Reservation. Various English lessons hang on the classroom wall.

Bibles for a New Nation

THE WORDS OF THE BIBLE HELPED SHAPE THE VERY NATURE OF THE COLONIES AND SUSTAINED AMERICANS DURING THE DIFFICULT FORMATIVE YEARS OF THE YOUNG UNITED STATES.

Richard Mather, right, patriarch of the Massachusetts family that included Increase and Cotton, was one of the translators of the Bay Psalm Book. *The translators' rendering of Psalm 23— quite different from the King James version—appears at the bottom of the left page above. It begins: "The Lord to mee a shepheard is, want therefore shall not I."*

The religious refugees who left England in the 17th century for the New World set their sights on a lofty goal: to build a "city upon a hill," a community based on the Scriptures that found in the Word of God the answer to every question, moral or social.

For the Pilgrims, who arrived at Plymouth in 1620, the Scriptures meant the Geneva Bible produced by English exiles in Calvinist Switzerland. By 1630, when the Puritans anchored in Massachusetts Bay, the King James, or Authorized, Version had overtaken the Geneva Bible as the Scripture for virtually all English-speaking Protestants. John Cotton, whose ringing sermon had sent them on their way, had read to them from the Authorized Version of the Bible: "I will appoint a place for my people Israel, and I will plant them, that they may dwell in a place of their own and move no more [1 Chronicles 17:9]."

Bay Psalm Book Many of the Puritans who settled the Massachusetts Bay colony were university educated, and one of their first acts, in 1636, was to establish Harvard College. In addition, because the community leaders were aware of the power of the printed word in confirming and extending the authority of church and state, they set up a printing press in Harvard Yard—the first in the English colonies.

The operation was chiefly financed by a wealthy clergyman, Jose Glover, who retained the locksmith Stephen Day to install and repair the equipment. Day was barely literate, so his son Matthew, who had

JEFFERSON'S BIBLE

Thomas Jefferson (shown above in a portrait bust of about 1789) was a devout man who believed that the teachings of Jesus represented the highest moral truth and who valued worship for the civic good it could produce.

About 1803 Jefferson, then President, began work on a Gospel abstract. The manuscript, entitled *The Life and Morals of Jesus of Nazareth*, included those parts of the four Gospels that he felt expressed the true message of Jesus. As Jefferson explained in a letter to John Adams, "I have performed this operation for my own use, by cutting verse by verse out of the printed book, and by arranging the matter which is evidently [Jesus'] and which is as distinguishable as diamonds in a dunghill."

The manuscript—arranged in four text columns of English, Greek, Latin, and French—was completed about 1820. It was not printed until 1904, when Congress authorized a limited edition.

apprenticed as a printer in England, ran the press. The first book printed by the Days was *The Whole Booke of Psalmes Faithfully Translated into English Metre*, better known as the *Bay Psalm Book* of 1640.

The psalms had been translated from the Hebrew by the clergymen Richard Mather, John Eliot, and Thomas Weld. In the preface, Mather acknowledged the shortcomings of the translation as a literary work but stated that his purpose was "Conscience rather than Elegance, fidelity rather than poetry."

Non-English Bibles The crown claimed a copyright on the King James Bible, and the printing of that version was a privilege accorded exclusively to the King's Printer and the Universities of Oxford and Cambridge. Hence, the first complete Bibles published in the English colonies appeared in languages other than English, these being John Eliot's 1663 translation in a tongue of the Massachusetts Bay Indians and an edition 80 years later of Luther's German translation.

The Luther Bible was printed in Germantown, outside Philadelphia, by a German immigrant named Christopher Sauer (or Sower). A man of many trades—farmer, tailor, clock maker, and manufacturer of cast-iron stoves—Sauer also imported Bibles from his homeland and then he set up a printing press in 1738 with funds provided by a group of German Baptists. Guided by the motto, "To the Glory of God and the Good of Mankind," Sauer and his German employees worked for three years on their Bible. The edition was ready in 1743 and was sold at 18 shillings. But some paid nothing at all: "To the poor and needy," Sauer explained, "we have no price."

English-Language Bibles
In his 1810 book entitled *The History of Printing in America*, Isaiah Thomas of Worcester, Massachusetts, tells of an English-language Bible that was available in the colonies by 1752. It was supposedly printed in Boston by the Kneeland and Green establishment. To avoid prosecution the firm used the imprint, "London: Printed by Mark Baskett, Printer to

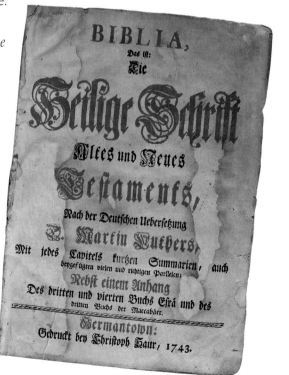

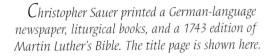

Christopher Sauer printed a German-language newspaper, liturgical books, and a 1743 edition of Martin Luther's Bible. The title page is shown here.

This sketch, dated about 1800, depicts the lively scene at a Lutheran church service in York, Pennsylvania. While the pastor delivers his sermon, congregants greet one another, someone tends the stove, and the sexton shoos a stray dog.

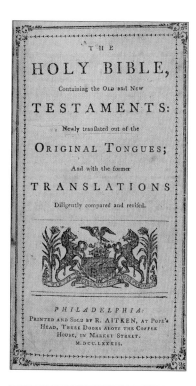

THE

HOLY BIBLE,

Containing the OLD and NEW

TESTAMENTS:

Newly tranflated out of the

ORIGINAL TONGUES;

And with the former

TRANSLATIONS

Diligently compared and revifed.

PHILADELPHIA:
PRINTED AND SOLD BY R. AITKEN, AT POPE's HEAD, THREE DOORS ABOVE THE COFFEE HOUSE, IN MARKET STREET.
M.DCC.LXXXII.

The Presbyterian Synod of Philadelphia attempted to lend Robert Aitken financial help by ordering its parishes to buy only his Bible, shown above, for distribution among the poor.

the King's Most Excellent Majesty." No copy of the "Baskett Bible" survives, however, and it is possible that it never existed at all.

After the outbreak of the American Revolution, colonial presses began to publish the King James Bible openly. First came Robert Aitken's edition of the New Testament, printed in Philadelphia in 1777 against great odds. Not only was the work done on poor equipment, but on one occasion Aitken had to save his type and printing materials from destruction by the red coats by spiriting them out of town and hiding them under a barn.

The New Testament edition went through several printings, and then, in 1782, Aitken published a complete Bible. The Philadelphia *Freeman's Journal* praised it as "purely American," saying that the Bible "has risen, like the fabled Phoenix, from the ashes of that pile in which our enemies supposed they had consumed the liberties of America." It was also the only Bible ever to be sanctioned by Congress. But praise came more easily than profits. At the end of the war, cheaper imports became available, and Aitken's finances crumbled.

THE WOMAN'S BIBLE

At the end of the 19th century, some 20 women's-rights activists undertook to study the Bible from a woman's perspective. They hoped that by subjecting Scripture to the scrutiny of women "quick to see the real purport of the Bible as regards their sex," they would prevent men from using the Word of God to discriminate against them.

The group wrote and edited *The Woman's Bible* under the direction of Elizabeth Cady Stanton, a women's-rights leader. The book consists of Bible excerpts and commentaries expressing the view that, though the Scriptures contain universal truths, they were recorded by fallible human beings. A commentary on the two accounts of Eve's creation in Genesis 1 and 2–3, for example, suggests that the first, with its "declaration of the feminine element in the Godhead, equal in power and glory with the masculine" is "more worthy of an intelligent woman's acceptance."

Still, other publishers forged ahead with their own editions of the Scriptures. Isaiah Thomas became the leading publisher of the era and its most prolific Bible purveyor. He published two King James Bibles in 1791: a costly edition with 50 full-page engravings by American artists and a second that he agreed to sell at a discount price supplemented by "Wheat, Rye, Indian Corn, Butter or Pork."

In 1790 Dublin-born Mathew Carey published the Douay-Rheims Bible, the first Catholic version printed in the United States. Despite the limited market for the Bible—there were only 471 subscribers—Carey went ahead with his plans, producing what is now the scarcest of all North American Bibles.

Unusual Bibles The lexicographer Noah Webster single-handedly revised the King James Version in 1833. Webster updated the language and substituted euphemisms for "language which cannot be uttered in company without a violation of decorum." Thus, "they bruised the teats of their virginity [Ezekiel 23:3]," became "they were first corrupted." Webster considered this Bible the crowning achievement of his career, but his bowdlerized King James had little long-term impact on the history of the Bible.

Rufus Davenport, a Boston businessman who lost his fortune through some bad deals, published *The Right-Aim School Bible* in 1834, to which he appended a petition to the government concerning debt laws. The New York Asylum for the Blind printed a New Testament with raised letters in 1836, a full 17 years before the development of braille. Other specialized Bibles included the *Soldier's Pocket Bible*, distributed by local Bible societies to American troops as they marched south to fight in the Mexican War. During the Civil War the American Tract Society distributed 24-page Bible selections to the Union troops. Meanwhile, the South suffered such acute Bible shortages that a black market in Bibles sprang up, and Confederate guards paid their prisoners as much as $15 for a copy. The Confederate States Bible Society succeeded in slipping English Bibles past the Union blockade, providing much needed spiritual solace to their side in the war. ❖

A portrait of Anna Gould Crane and her granddaughter by the folk artist Sheldon Peck, dating about 1845, shows them posed next to the family Bible, evidently a revered possession.

The Bible and the Family

"With Adam's fall we sinned all," begins many a primer from the 18th century. In some households and schools the Bible was used to teach children to read, but its stories formed the basis of early schoolbooks as well. Similarly, when girls went to school in the 18th and early 19th centuries, they often practiced needlework by cross-stitching prayers or verses from Scripture and used scenes from the Old and New Testaments as the subjects of their silk-embroidered or watercolor pictures. The finished pictures were hung up at home by proud parents.

The Bible and its themes, in fact, figured in family life in a variety of ways. Children marched animals two by two onto Noah's ark toys or played with other Scripture playthings, known as Sunday toys because they were considered acceptable for quiet play on the Sabbath. Adults graced their dining tables with pitchers and sugarbowls decorated with molded images of the Apostles or Bible scenes, such as Rebecca at the well. Colorful pottery figures of Old Testament scenes decorated mantels. Reading the Bible together was an evening pastime in many households, and the Bible itself was often used as a repository of family records.

The Atwood family of New Hampshire posed with their Bibles, top, when Henry Darby painted the family portrait in 1845. The opening page of the 1727 New England primer, above, starts with A for Adam and B for the Bible.

Noah's ark toys, popular since the 17th century, often were made in the form of houses on boats. The ark at right, made of painted wood, includes 62 animals.

Jonah puts money into the whale's mouth, above, on a 19th-century American mechanical bank.

The return from Egypt, left, was among a number of 19th-century biblical figural groups from Staffordshire, England.

Bible stories are told in picture puzzles, or rebuses, "for the amusement of youth" in the "Hieroglyphick" Bible, top, published in Hartford, Connecticut, in 1825.

Ann Johnson, not the best speller, entitled her watercolor "Baptisam of Our Saviour." It is thought to have been painted in New York State about 1840.

Rebecca Morris, an English girl, included verses of Ecclesiasticus 28:1-7 and Romans 12:9-16 when she cross-stitched her sampler in 1787.

The Hebrew Bible in America

THE FIRST HEBREW BIBLE PUBLISHED IN AMERICA APPEARED IN 1814. THE FIRST ENGLISH TRANSLATION
OF THE HEBREW SCRIPTURES BY JEWS IN AMERICA APPEARED SOME 40 YEARS LATER.

Many of the Jews who fled Spain and Portugal as a result of the Inquisition in the 16th century settled in Holland and in England. When Dutch and English ships sailed for the New World in the 17th century, Jews sailed with them. Among the most significant early Jewish colonial settlements were those at Recife in eastern Brazil, Curaçao, Surinam, Guyana, Barbados, and Jamaica. Small numbers of Jews also settled in North America, particularly in the Dutch city of New Amsterdam (later New York) and Newport, Rhode Island.

North America By 1730 or so, Jews with roots in Central and Eastern Europe had begun to outnumber those from Spain and Portugal in the colonies. However, the colonial Jewish population remained slight during the 18th century, perhaps never more than 2,000 to 2,500 people.

Initially the Jews gathered in private homes or rented quarters to pray. North America's first synagogue was built in New York in 1729. Some 30 years later a second synagogue was built in Newport. This historic structure, still in use today, is evidence that if the Jewish population was small, it was of substance in Newport. By 1800, other Jewish congregations had formed in Savannah (1733), Philadelphia (1740 and 1800), Charleston (1749), and Richmond (1789).

The Hebrew Bible Colonial synagogues housed Torah scrolls brought from Europe, but there were few full Bibles. At the time of the Revolution there were still no rabbis in the British colonies and most

*H*arry Lieberman, who emigrated from Poland in 1906, painted "The Blessing and the Curse," left. In it Moses instructs the elders of Israel to set up 12 stones on Mt. Ebal and to write down the laws.

of the Jews neither read nor spoke Hebrew. Jonas Horwitz, a scholarly physician who about 1812 proposed to publish the first American edition of the Hebrew Bible, estimated that at that time there were fewer than 12 complete Hebrew Bibles available for purchase in the United States. They were primarily used by Christian scholars.

The farsighted Horwitz had brought Hebrew type with him when he emigrated from Europe to Philadelphia. He gained the support of a dozen Christian clergymen for his proposed project but ultimately transferred the rights, along with the work he had completed, to the printer Thomas Dobson. The so-called Dobson Bible, which appeared in 1814, was the first Hebrew Bible produced in the United States.

Biblical Scholarship The start of biblical scholarship among Jews in the United States is often credited to a Jewish rabbi named Isaac Leeser, who emigrated from Germany in 1824. Leeser founded the American Jewish Publication Society in Philadelphia and was responsible for producing the country's first Hebrew primer and textbooks for use in Jewish schools, an English translation of the Hebrew prayer book, and, in 1845, a translation of the Pentateuch. Leeser's most important contribution, however, was the first complete Hebrew Bible in English, published in 1853.

Beginning in the 1870's, Eastern European Jews were emigrating to America in ever greater numbers. By the 1880's, there were about a quarter of a million Jews in the country and English was quickly becoming their common language. By that date, biblical scholarship had come a long way from its start in Leeser's day, and scholars deemed it was time for a new translation of the Hebrew Bible. Finally, in 1895, a team of American Jewish scholars under the auspices of the Jewish Publication Society of America set to work on the project. It took them more than 20 years.

Published in 1917, the translation was hailed as a significant accomplishment for world Jewry. As the editors explained, "We have applied ourselves to the sacred task of preparing a new translation of the Bible into the English language, which, unless all signs fail, is to become the current speech of the majority of the children of Israel."

The prominence of the English language among Jews, as well as continuing strides made in biblical scholarship, prompted another translation of the Hebrew Bible, completed in 1982, by the Jewish Publication Society. The new edition, rendered in up-to-date idiomatic English, was not only a great achievement for its scholars, but its timing was perfect. It arrived as American Jews were experiencing a cultural reawakening to their traditions and to their Bible. ❖

*N*ewport's historic synagogue, top, was established in 1759 as Yeshuat Israel *but was later named for the Touro family. One family member was a rabbi there in the 18th century; two others restored the structure in the 19th. The 1814 Dobson Bible was the first Hebrew Bible printed in the United States.*

Slavery and the Bible

THE BIBLE WAS USED AS A MEANS TO JUSTIFY SLAVERY AT THE SAME TIME IT PROVIDED SLAVES WITH HOPE FOR THEIR SALVATION.

The Bible has been subject to a wealth of interpretations. Perhaps the distance between them was never greater than during the United States' crisis over slavery. The Bible was used by slaveholders, abolitionists, and slaves alike as justification for their respective and opposing positions. Supporters of slavery cited biblical passages that they claimed upheld the South's "peculiar institution." In particular, they pointed out that some Old Testament patriarchs, Abraham among them, held slaves and that slavery existed in Judea during Jesus' time, yet there is no record of Jesus ever preaching against it. They also cited a New Testament passage in which Paul supposedly advises a runaway slave to return to his master (Philemon 1: 10-18).

Antislavery advocates found such arguments insupportable. Slavery in their view was an abomination and incompatible

A shackled slave holding the Bible, above, illustrates a flyer for an 1837 meeting of the Massachusetts Antislavery Society. An unknown Southern folk artist carved the preacher with his Bible, below left, about 1870. The quilt, below, made by Harriet Powers, a former slave, about 1898, is appliquéd with Old and New Testament scenes.

with the message of the Gospels. The duty of all Christians, the antislavery advocates believed, was to work toward the abolition of slavery, both in the United States and throughout the world.

The Slaves' View of Scripture Because the Bible was used with such conviction as a means of keeping slaves in bondage, the slaves might understandably have viewed the Bible negatively. Instead, they found solace in it, particularly the Old Testament. It helped ease the pain of the present and provided hope for their future. For the slaves who became Christians there was no question of the meaning of God's Word: they had its promise of salvation.

Many slaveholders were reluctant to allow slaves instruction in Christianity for fear that it might make them less submissive. Moreover, the offering of Christian instruction was implicit recognition that slaves were humans, not merely a species of property.

Yet the slaves' faith in the Bible's teachings was also useful to slaveholders as a means of appeasing their own conscience. Thus many slaves were offered a limited education in the Bible. They were usually made to attend church services with their masters or under supervision, so that they could hear appropriately selected Bible texts and sermons—those that seemed to uphold the prevailing social order. Few slaves, however, were allowed to learn to read the Bible, or anything else, for fear that access to knowledge might lead to more assertive behavior.

Their Own Services and Preaching Nonetheless, the slaves managed to practice Christianity in ways that were partially independent of their masters. On weekday nights or after Sunday services, slaves often gathered at one of the cabins or at a safe place out-of-doors to conduct their own services. Then they could hear preaching from one of their own, perhaps a slave who had managed to obtain some rudiments of literacy and religious education. They mastered the Bible orally, as had the early Christians, and derived special relevance to their own situation from its lessons and tales. They identified particularly with the plight of the Israelites in Exodus and saw Moses as their great biblical hero. Those who, in time, helped the slaves to their own freedom—leaders such as Harriet Tubman, who helped people flee from slavery on the Underground Railroad, Abraham Lincoln, and General Ulysses S. Grant—were sometimes likened to Moses.

The slaves awaited salvation and the day of jubilee on which they would all be freed. And they translated the tales and lessons they learned from the Bible into music—spirituals that remain among the most beautiful and enduring portions of America's cultural heritage. Indeed, these songs, which both instruct and inspire, embody a folk consciousness that has powerfully informed the African American awareness of tradition. ❖

SISTERS AGAINST SLAVERY

Two of America's most outspoken abolitionists were a pair of sisters from South Carolina. Angelina Grimké, above left, and her sister Sarah, above, were raised in a well-to-do slaveholding family. As young women in the 1820's, however, they left home and later went to work for the abolitionist cause.

Both sisters had letters published in the abolitionist magazine *The Liberator* and wrote antislavery pamphlets. Angelina was the author of an *Appeal to the Christian Women in the South*. Sarah wrote an *Epistle to the Clergy of the Southern States*.

The Grimkés also took the very unusual step of speaking on the lecture circuit—unusual because women simply did not lecture before mixed (male and female) audiences in the 1830's. Their appearance on the circuit was widely condemned, but they also drew large crowds and moved many people with the earnestness of their message. In order to win over their most hardened opponents on the circuit, the Grimkés were always careful to use Scripture as the basis of their appeal.

Joseph Smith and "The Book of Mormon"

IN A QUIET CORNER OF NEW YORK STATE, A YOUNG MAN RECEIVED NEW REVELATIONS, WHICH HE FELT SHOULD BE MADE PART OF CHRISTIAN SCRIPTURE.

Joseph Smith receives the gold plates containing the text of The Book of Mormon *from the angel Moroni in a detail from a 1966 oil painting by Kenneth Riley. The text on the plates was written in what Smith called Reformed Egyptian.*

At the time that 14-year-old Joseph Smith was experiencing his first vision of God, in 1820, revival fires were starting to sweep his home region of western New York so furiously that evangelists would come to call the district "burned over." Feeding the flames were impassioned sermons about the imminent return of Jesus. Out of this fervor came widely diverse interpretations of the Bible, even among established denominations, and experiments in Christianity, including celibate communities and a group of "Bible communists" that gained notoriety by practicing "complex marriage," encouraging sex among all their members.

Looking for a Church Amid this "tumult of opinions," as he later reported it, Joseph Smith prayed about what church to join. Suddenly, hovering above him, stood God the Father and Jesus Christ. They told him to join no church, saying all were wrong. Three years later Smith was visited by the angel Moroni, a resurrected human who had buried gold plates in a nearby hill some 1,400 years ago. On these plates was inscribed the story of a group of Hebrews who had left Jerusalem shortly before the Babylonians destroyed it in 586 B.C. and sailed to the Americas. In the New World they saw visions about the future ministry of Jesus and followed his teachings centuries before his birth. These Hebrews eventually split into two groups, Nephites and Lamanites. Many were destroyed in natural disasters that occurred at the time of Jesus' crucifixion. Jesus later visited the righteous remnants of the two groups and there was a period of peace. After A.D. 400, wars resulted in the annihilation of the Nephites but not before a prophet named Mormon compiled the history and his son, Moroni, buried it.

In 1827 Moroni entrusted Smith with the plates long enough for him to translate them "through the mercy of God, by the power of

God." The translation was published as *The Book of Mormon* in 1830. Soon after, Smith founded The Church of Jesus Christ of Latter-day Saints.

Mormon Scriptures

The Book of Mormon, later subtitled *Another Testament of Jesus Christ,* convinced some Christians that the canon for Scripture remained open, and *The Book of Mormon* was supplemented by two later books. *The Doctrine and Covenants* reveals the way of salvation in the latter days (before the Second Coming) and gives instruction for the government of the church, warning individuals and nations of impending destruction if they do not repent. *The Pearl of Great Price* contains selected translations, pronouncements, and revelations to Joseph Smith. All three books joined the Bible as Mormon Scripture. The Bible alone, Smith said, is "the word of God as far as it is translated correctly," but it is insufficient because over the ages it has been distorted by "ignorant translators, careless transcribers, or designing and corrupt priests."

Smith's followers hailed him as a prophet equal in status to those in the Bible and fully able to restore the true teachings of God. Smith retained the King James Version of the Bible but started to revise the text, making changes in some 3,000 verses. He expanded the first six chapters of Genesis from 151 verses to 356. To 1 John 4:12, which says, "No man hath seen God at any time," Smith added, "except them who believe." Parts of his translation appear in *The Pearl of Great Price.* In 1979 the Mormons published an edition of the King James Bible with cross-references to the other Mormon Scriptures.

Moving On

Persecution and bloodshed dogged the Mormons as they sought to establish a headquarters in Ohio, then in Missouri, and then in Illinois. Many Americans regarded Smith's teachings—especially his belief that his followers should practice polygamy—as unorthodox. Nevertheless, Smith announced his candidacy for president of the United States in 1844. When some disgruntled Mormons launched a newspaper to attack him, he issued an order to destroy the press, and he was arrested and put in jail. A few weeks later, on June 27, 1844, a mob stormed the jailhouse and shot him to death. Again the Mormons had to pack up and leave. Most followed Brigham Young, president of the church's council of 12 Apostles, to Utah, where The Church of Jesus Christ of Latter-day Saints finally found a place where they could stay. ❖

Egbert Grandin of Palmyra, New York, printed 5,000 copies of The Book of Mormon *on this press in 1830. The volume, which numbered more than 500 pages, was the first edition of the new scriptural work.*

The Bible in the South Seas

MISSIONARIES, USUALLY MARRIED COUPLES, TRAVELED AROUND THE GLOBE TO TAKE THE WORD TO THE PEOPLE OF THE SOUTH SEAS.

Hiram Bingham and his wife, above, met a mere three weeks before sailing to Hawaii. Only married missionaries were sent to the islands because husband and wife could help each other as well as demonstrate to the islanders the virtues of Christian family life. Hiram is shown preaching, below, while Queen Kaahumanu looks on.

Captain William Bligh and the mutineers on the *Bounty* captivated the preacher Thomas Haweis with their colorful tales of the South Seas. As a result, Haweis helped start the London Missionary Society in 1795 to take the Gospel to South Sea islanders, who were seen as cannibalistic and sexually promiscuous. Partly because the *Bounty* mutineers had drawn up a local vocabulary, Haweis chose Tahiti as the first field of service. The society chartered a ship, the *Duff,* and sent out 39 missionaries. Four were ordained; the others were artisans: tailor, shoemaker, carpenter.

Tahiti and New Zealand Once in Tahiti, the missionaries found the *Bounty* dictionary woefully inadequate. Using phonetics, they developed a written language and began translating the Bible. The bricklayer Henry Nott was the principal translator. Two other missionaries and King Pomare II helped. Though the Bible was not completed until 1835, parts of it were published earlier, as a work in progress, with the help of the missionary William Ellis, a printer who had brought along a press.

Father Jean Velghe painted biblical and other religious scenes on the walls of St. Benedict's Church, on the big island of Hawaii, to help bring the Scriptures to life.

The missionaries encountered opposition but brought about change. The king was baptized and he enforced scriptural laws. Biblical speech patterns entered the language, and European customs were adopted.

Meanwhile, in Australia, Samuel Marsden, chaplain to the settlement of British convicts in New South Wales, decided to take the Gospel to the Aborigines in New Zealand, 1,200 miles to the east. When he failed to convince the Church Missionary Society to send him, he hired a ship himself, and on Christmas Day 1814 he preached New Zealand's first Christian sermon. He later bought land for a mission station and helped nurture the work in return visits. By the mid-1800's, there were missionary stations throughout the North Island.

Hawaiian Bible In 1819 the American Board of Commissioners of Foreign Missions sent a group of missionaries, led by Hiram Bingham, to Hawaii. When they arrived the king allowed them to stay, partly because he saw the value of the missionary doctor who was among them and perhaps because he was searching for a religion to replace the local practice of human sacrifice that he had recently outlawed. His haughty queen, Kaahumanu, refused to give the missionaries any more than a little finger to touch in greeting. But after she became ill and Bingham's wife nursed her to health, she converted to Christianity. Chiefs and their subjects followed her lead.

As in Tahiti, the missionaries created a written language, translated and printed the Bible, and taught the people to read. One chief was so excited about the prospects of literacy that he forbade his people to marry until they could read and write. By 1831, some 52,000 Hawaiians were enrolled in missionary schools that taught reading, writing, and religion. Supplies were so limited that in some places eager students used cut-up surfboards to write on. Within 20 years, the missionaries had fulfilled their assignment to learn the language of the people and to give them the Bible and the skill to read it. ❖

CATHOLICS IN HAWAII

The quest for souls was not always a cooperative effort. In Hawaii it was characterized by Protestant-Catholic tension. By the time the first Catholic missionaries arrived from France in 1827, the Protestants were already firmly established and they considered the coming of the Catholics an intrusion. Hiram Bingham and other Protestant missionaries preached against Catholic idolatry, and the Hawaiian chiefs outlawed Catholicism. In 1831 two Catholic priests were deported to California and Hawaiian Catholics were imprisoned or sentenced to hard labor. In 1839, under political pressure from France, Catholicism was legalized in Hawaii and Catholics were given equal rights with Protestants. In time, all Christians came to work together to bring the Good News to the Hawaiians.

On August 10, 1796, the Duff embarked from England on a seven-month-long, 17,000-mile journey with 39 missionaries aboard. It sailed around the southern tip of Africa, east toward Australia, then 3,500 miles beyond, dropping anchor along the black sand beaches of Matavai Bay, Tahiti.

The Rise of Bible Societies

For almost 200 years Bible societies have been making the Scriptures available in hundreds of languages to readers around the globe.

In 1802 Thomas Charles, a prominent figure in the Welsh evangelical movement, went to a London meeting of the Religious Tract Society seeking inexpensive Bibles in Welsh. The society could not fill his request, but members concluded that there ought to be a society formed "for the wider distribution of the Scriptures without note or comment." If the Welsh needed Bibles that they could afford and read, certainly there were others who would welcome the Scriptures if they could obtain them in their own language.

Within two years the British and Foreign Bible Society was formed. Its declared purpose was to produce and circulate the Scriptures in the world's many languages. In its first year the society pub-lished the Gospel of John in Mohawk, and in 1807 it funded a Chinese translation of the Bible.

Britain did not monopolize Bible distribution for long. In 1808 the Philadelphia Bible Society was formed in the United States. Similar societies were organized in New York, New Jersey, Maine, Massa-chusetts, and Connecticut the following year—each received a financial gift from the British and Foreign Bible Society.

By 1814, there were 69 societies distributing Bibles within their communities in the United States, but there were none reaching the rural areas of the South and West. That shortfall was alleviated in 1816 when the interdenominational American Bible Society set up headquarters in New York City.

Throughout the 19th century, missionaries carried the Scriptures to people around the world, as the engraving at far left suggests. Local and national Bible and tract societies in Europe and North America worked hard to spread the Word.

Using funds contributed by members, the American Bible Society issued more than 6,000 Bibles its first year and launched what would become a world-wide missionary effort. In its second year the society began a tradition of supplying Scriptures to the armed forces when it gave Bibles to the crew of the U.S.S. *John Adams.* That same year it began a foreign-language publication program when it produced a small number of New Testaments in Spanish.

Success of the Societies The British and Foreign Bible Society and the American Bible Society were neither the first nor the only groups to make the spread of the Bible their focus, but they were particularly successful in their efforts. Their determination to publish the Scriptures "without note or comment" allowed many denominations to support the societies' goals. The two societies also made inexpensive editions of the Bible available and hired colporteurs, or agents, to sell them.

Colporteur Samuel Benson posed in Niagara, New York, after walking across the state selling Bibles in spite of snowstorms in the 1920's.

Members of the Church Army Flying Squadron pose with their bicycles, left, in 1911. These missionaries distributed Bibles for England's Anglican Church. An American Bible Society representative, below, traveling in a mobile office on the Mexican border in 1932, shows the Bible in Spanish to young and old readers.

In its early decades the American Bible Society depended on the persuasive abilities of its colporteurs and local auxiliaries to distribute Bibles and New Testaments. They did heroic work in four major campaigns, or "re-supplies." The first was begun in 1829 when the society announced that it intended to supply every family in the country with a Bible. Those families who could were expected to pay; the poor would be given Bibles. At that time the total population of the United States was under 13 million. The second campaign began in 1856 when the country's population had doubled. The third, launched in 1866, lasted a decade. During that time 5,454,788 families were visited and 376,257 households were supplied with Bibles. The fourth campaign began in 1882 and continued until 1890. This time 6,309,628 families were visited and 473,804 Bible-less homes were supplied.

Special Programs Meanwhile, many other programs were

351

The distribution of Bibles by the thousands called for efficient production. At left, workers bind Bibles at a Tapley, New Jersey, plant.

developed. In 1827 an American missionary based in India appealed to the American Bible Society for Bibles—not only for the people he served but for American missionaries everywhere. The society agreed and before long most missionaries abroad used it as a source for copies of the Scriptures.

In 1835 programs that allowed the blind to read the Scriptures were begun. The first grant aided Dr. Samuel Howe, who pioneered a system of raised letters. Scriptures for the blind have been published ever since, though now they are in braille.

Immigrants to the United States were greeted with a copy of the Scriptures in their own languages when they stepped off the boat. Some New Testaments were printed with a column of text in German, Italian, Dutch, or Norwegian next to the corresponding passage in English and thus served as English-language primers. Bibles in French and German were printed in New York. To reach other immigrants the society imported Bibles, Testaments, and Gospels in Welsh, Italian, Swedish, Danish, Dutch, and Portuguese.

Much of the various Bible societies' work in the distribution of Scriptures was done door to door. A representative from the Agency for Colored People, above, sells a Bible to a Southern woman in the 1930's.

Dispute Over the Apocrypha Both the American and British Bible societies experienced some intense internal debates in their formative years. The question of what to do with the Apocrypha dominated many meetings in the early history of the two societies. Since Catholics and several Protestant denominations believed these books should be included in the Bible, the British society supported the publication of inclusive editions where they would be appropriate. But in 1826 Scottish auxiliaries insisted that the Apocryhpa did not belong in any Bible published by the British and Foreign Bible Society. A year later the American Bible Society adopted a similar stance. Today, however, the books of the Apocrypha are included in some editions.

Bibles and the Civil War During the years of the Civil War, the American Bible Society had to rally its efforts in order to overcome the difficulties of getting Bibles to the battlefront. By the end of the war, it had managed to distribute some 3 million New Testaments and Bibles to both Union and Confederate soldiers, escaped slaves, and freed-

THE GIDEONS INTERNATIONAL

When John Nicholson tried to check into the Central Hotel in Boscobel, Wisconsin, one night in 1898, he was told that there were no vacancies, and he had to share a room with a stranger. Later that night Nicholson asked his roommate's permission to leave the lamp lit while he read the Bible. The roommate, a fellow salesman named Samuel Hill, agreed and asked Nicholson to read aloud, as he too was "a Christian man."

Within a year the two men were not only good friends but had organized an association of Christian travelers. They named their association after Gideon, an Old Testament leader (Judges 6:1–8:33) and began efforts to convert others by encouraging Bible reading.

In 1908 the Gideons decided to do more than encourage Bible reading—they would distribute Bibles to the places their members were likely to spend evenings on the road. The first gift—25 copies of the King James Bible—went to the Superior Hotel in Iron Mountain, Montana. Subsequently the Gideons placed more than 40 million Bibles and New Testaments in hotel, motel, and hospital rooms in 172 countries. The Bible above dates from about 1915.

Bibles were sold wherever people gathered. Agent Harry Bacherat sold Bibles and Testaments "in all languages" at Coney Island.

men, as well as to civilians. "Providence has plainly ordained that we shall be one people, with one government, one civilization, one Bible," the society stated in a report after the war's conclusion.

In the years since then, the American Bible Society has furthered its original mission—the distribution of the Scriptures without note or comment. In 1946 the society's directors voted to join with 13 other societies to form the United Bible Societies, which now includes more than 100 national societies. They are responsible for distributing the Scriptures in more than 200 languages—more than 500 million Bibles, New Testaments, and selections from Scripture a year. ❖

Translating Scripture Today

THERE ARE HUNDREDS OF TRANSLATIONS OF THE BIBLE, AND NEW ONES CONTINUE TO BE MADE.

Translation it is that opens the window, to let in the light; that breaks the shell, that we might eat the kernel; that puts aside the curtain that we may look into the most holy place; that removes the cover of the well, that we may come by the water." So wrote the scholars who produced the King James Bible, whose text has been called "the noblest monument of English prose." More than 250 years elapsed before a full revision of the King James Version was undertaken, but the number of revisions and translations has soared since then, particularly in the latter half of the 20th century.

There are a number of reasons for the recent outpouring. Archeological discoveries in the 19th and 20th centuries—including the discovery of ancient texts—provided important help and created a better understanding of daily life in biblical times. The study of linguistics has developed considerably in the past hundred years, giving us a deeper understanding of the complexities of language. And the principles of translation have changed dramatically.

Translating Styles There has always been a division of opinion about priorities in translating. A translator must decide whether it is more important to reflect the literal form and linguistic structure of the original language or to represent the concept and spirit of the original text, even if that means losing some of the language structure. For example, ancient Hebrew's unique rhythms and extensive use of repetition and wordplay cannot easily be replicated in modern languages. Martin Luther wrestled with the problem when he made his 1534 translation of the Bible, writing, "Whoever would speak German must not use Hebrew style. Rather he must see to it—once he understands the Hebrew author—that he concentrates on the sense of the text."

The translation principle that stresses meaning over structure has

Translations produced by the American Bible Society include the versions above in Japanese, Korean, Lao, Navajo, Polish, Portuguese, Russian, Ukrainian, and Tagalog.

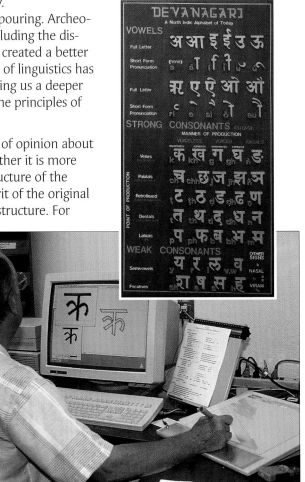

A Comparison of Modern Translations

The differences among modern translations of the Bible can be subtle or great. The versions of Matthew 6:9–13 below demonstrate the various ways that phrases and words can be interpreted.

New International Version, 1973

"This, then, is how you should pray:
'Our Father in heaven, hallowed be your name,
your kingdom come, your will be done
on earth as it is in heaven.
Give us today our daily bread.
Forgive us our debts, as we also have forgiven
our debtors. And lead us not into temptation,
but deliver us from the evil one.'"

New Revised Standard Version, 1989

"Pray then in this way:
Our Father in heaven, hallowed be your name.
Your kingdom come. Your will be done,
on earth as it is in heaven.
Give us this day our daily bread. And forgive us our
debts, as we also have forgiven our debtors.
And do not bring us to the time of trial,
but rescue us from the evil one."

New American Bible, 1986

"This is how you are to pray:
Our Father in heaven, hallowed be your name,
your kingdom come, your will be done, on earth
as in heaven. Give us today our daily bread;
and forgive us our debts, as we forgive our debtors;
and do not subject us to the final test,
but deliver us from the evil one."

The Contemporary English Version, 1995

"You should pray like this:
Our Father in heaven, help us to honor your name.
Come and set up your kingdom, so that everyone on
earth will obey you, as you are obeyed in heaven.
Give us our food for today. Forgive us our
doing wrong, as we forgive others. Keep us from
being tempted and protect us from evil."

The specialist at left is creating a digital version of the Devanagari (Indian) alphabet so that translators can compose the Bible text on the computer. The complete Devanagari alphabet is shown in the inset.

taken hold particularly since World War II and has challenged the dominance of traditional texts—the King James Version, the Douay-Rheims Version, and most of their revisions—which were firmly in the camp of literal translations. However, there have also been new versions and translations that have maintained the literal tradition and have gained immense followings. "As literal as possible, as free as necessary" were the guiding words of the scholars who prepared the New Revised Standard Version, which was published in 1989. When the editors of the New International Version began their translation in 1965, they returned to the original texts, seeking the "accuracy of the translation and its fidelity to the thought of the biblical writers." At the same time, they simplified the language of the Bible and made it more contemporary. In contrast, the translator Everett Fox in The Five Books of Moses (1996), the first volume of the Schocken Bible, attempted to "draw the reader into the world of the Hebrew Bible" by evoking the exotic rythmns, repetitions, and patterns of the original text.

Revising the Language A poll conducted for the American Bible Society in the 1990's revealed that more than two-thirds of the country's Bible owners wanted the old-fashioned language and complex grammar of the King James Version to be simplified. "The truth can't set you free if you can't understand it" was the campaign slogan for the easy-to-read 1995 Contemporary English Version from the American Bible Society. Words not readily understood were changed—thus, Noah's "ark" became a "boat," the "manger" a "bed of hay," and swords were beaten not into "plowshares" but into "rakes and shovels." The Contemporary English Version is only one of the many Bible revisions and translations that are now available in modern English.

The computer program demonstrated at right allows translators to see the intonation of a language. Such tools can be helpful when translating the Bible for a culture that previously had no written language.

In correcting and modernizing the language of recent versions, many translators have made an effort to make the language inclusive, eliminating gender bias. In earlier translations, the original meaning of the text is sometimes obscured by gender assumptions. For instance, the words *he* or *him* are often used even when the original text does not indicate whether someone is male or female. The elimination of gender bias is evident in the New Revised Standard Version. The Contemporary English Version, the earlier Good News Bible, and the Revised English Bible also use inclusive language.

Translations Around the World The Christian missionary impulse to take the Bible to the farthest corners of the earth fueled much of the translation work that took place in the 19th and 20th centuries. Using familiar words and idioms is essential in making the Bible's message comprehensible to cultures so different from those portrayed in the Scriptures. Certain words have no meaning for some people—a landlocked desert tribe in Africa might be baffled by such phrases as "anchor of the soul" [Hebrews 6: 19] or "shipwreck in the faith" [1 Timothy 1: 19]. "Your sins . . . shall be like snow" [Isaiah 1: 18] has been translated as "white as an egret's feather" and "white as cotton," reflecting regional equivalents.

Other translating dilemmas involve specificity in languages—for instance, the Zulu language has 120 ways to say "walking," and Nupé, one of the languages of Nigeria and Niger, has 100 words for "greatness." The art of translation is to understand and to make use of the

STANDARD TEXTS FOR OLD AND NEW TESTAMENTS

Over the centuries many variations in Bible translations—and disagreements over the correctness of those translations—have depended on the translators' choice of Hebrew and Greek texts to work from. Scholars today, however, are largely in agreement as to which texts should be used as the basis of modern translations.

The most widely accepted text of the Hebrew Bible, or Old Testament, is the 1990 *Biblia Hebraica Stuttgartensis*—a revision of a text edited some 60 years earlier. Both are based on the Leningrad Codex of 1008, which is generally regarded as the best surviving manuscript of the complete Hebrew Bible.

The version of the New Testament that is considered the best for Bible translators is the Greek New Testament (fourth edition, 1993). It draws from all the important papyrus and parchment manuscripts of early Christian writings as well as early New Testament texts in Latin, Syriac, Coptic, Armenian, Georgian, and Old Church Slavonic. Wherever relevant, citations from the early Fathers of the Church are included as well.

In a Yamai village workroom in Papua New Guinea, right, members of a Wycliffe translating team work with native speakers on producing a version of the Gospel According to Mark in the Awad Bing language.

nuances of local dialects and customs, thereby avoiding the problems that can result from too literal a translation. For example, one word-for-word translation of Acts 9:1 referred to Paul as "breathing out threatenings and death," leading local people to believe that Paul was a sorcerer.

The Pace of Translation The translation of the Bible into various tongues proceeds at a rapid pace. It is estimated that by 1804, parts of the Bible had been translated into as many as 70 different languages. By the end of 1995, at least one book of the Bible had been translated into more than 2,100 languages.

Since World War II most of the translations have been done by Protestant missionary societies, such as the Wycliffe Bible Translators, an organization founded in 1934 that takes its name from the 14th-century Bible translator. By 1995, Wycliffe translators had rendered the New Testament into more than 400 different languages. Many of the ongoing translating projects involve languages that do not have a written form, are spoken by fewer than 10,000 people, and are in danger of disappearing forever. Armed with up-to-date computer equipment and linguistic training, the translators establish themselves within a community and then work closely with local people to translate the Scriptures into their language. Despite great advances in technology, however, translation of the Bible is still a painstaking process requiring highly specialized knowledge and a sensitivity to the needs of the people for whom the translation is being made. ❖

The missionary above is testing his translation of the Gospel According to Mark on the Machiguenga Indians of Peru.

Today's Bibles

BIBLES AND RELATED TEXTS, GAMES, TOYS, WORKBOOKS, AND VIDEO AND AUDIO CASSETTES ARE
NOW AVAILABLE TO SUIT THE NEEDS OF EVERYONE FROM CHILDREN TO SENIORS.

Displays in Bible bookshops reveal the growing demand for Bibles tailored to the interests of niche markets. There are storybook Bibles for parents to read to their children and devotional Bibles with inspiring articles for adults. For readers interested in cultural and historical background there are thick volumes such as the HarperCollins Study Bible, which is 60 percent Scripture and 40 percent notes, with updated information based on recent study of the Dead Sea Scrolls and archeological discoveries. The selection of Bibles and related materials is so daunting that many shoppers turn to Bible guidebooks to direct them through the maze and to their niche. Booksellers even have a Bible hotline available to them.

Bibles for Adults Among the most popular Bibles are those designed for use in private devotions. The text is typically accompanied by short articles that tell readers how to apply specific Bible teachings to their lives. Other Bibles highlight issues pertinent to women, to men, to young couples, and to people in recovery programs. People who commute to work can listen to the Bible being read on audiotapes. For those who like to read Scripture wherever they may be, there is a loose-leaf Bible with pages that fit into a pocket calendar notebook. And for sports fans there is a Bible with pictures of Christian athletes and their testimonials about Bible verses that they find meaningful.

The style of study Bibles has developed as they have become increasingly popular. Study Bibles always combined such features as a verse-by-verse commentary, an atlas, and a condensed concordance, but they have become more diverse. The Quest Study Bible features some 6,500 questions and answers. "Why did Jesus walk on water?" it queries. Answer: To strengthen the disciples' trust when they were disap-

pointed by his refusal to be made king the day before. The Word in Life Study Bible resembles and reads like a newspaper with boxed features and explanatory notes. Other study Bibles target small groups by providing thought-provoking questions for discussion.

Supplementing the many Bibles are such works as Bible encyclopedias, dictionaries, atlases, concordances, commentaries, and books that focus on specific topics such as Bible plants and animals. For readers who do not know Greek and Hebrew but are interested in the sources of English translations, there are Bibles that include the original words and their definitions. There are also condensed Bibles.

Bibles for Children Coloring-book Bibles, pop-up books and comic books of Bible stories, and picture Bibles with photographs of Bible scenes that were reenacted on location are among the many offerings for young readers. There are Bible and video cassettes for toddlers, and there are Bible activity books that encourage children to do such things as draw a map as they read about Abraham's journey. Other illustrated books range from titles such as *My First 100 Hebrew Words*, to the *Awesome Book of Bible Facts*. The fact book asks, "Was Goliath taller than a National Basketball Association star?" The answer (found in Samuel 17:4) is that he was over nine feet tall. Cartoon Bible videos and even Nintendo video games present the drama of the Bible in a multimedia approach that has the potential of interesting even those children who wouldn't think of curling up with a good book.

The Bible remains America's best-selling book. An estimated 9 out of 10 households have at least one copy of it, and 75 percent have more. With current efforts to package the Bible to meet the spiritual needs of every segment of the population, it is probably one of the best-read books as well as the best-selling. ❖

Bible products on the market today include miniature Bibles, special-interest Bibles, color-coded study Bibles, translations into contemporary or simple English, Bibles with multiple versions of the texts, crossword puzzles, games such as Bibleopoly, children's Bibles and jigsaw puzzles, language builders, question-and-answer trivia books, audio cassettes, video cassettes, and comic books.

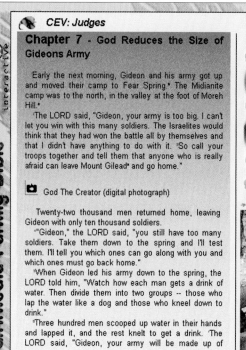

CEV: Judges

Chapter 7 - God Reduces the Size of Gideons Army

Early the next morning, Gideon and his army got up and moved their camp to Fear Spring.* The Midianite camp was to the north, in the valley at the foot of Moreh Hill.*

The LORD said, "Gideon, your army is too big. I can't let you win with this many soldiers. The Israelites would think that they had won the battle all by themselves and that I didn't have anything to do with it. *So call your troops together and tell them that anyone who is really afraid can leave Mount Gilead* and go home."

📷 God The Creator (digital photograph)

Twenty-two thousand men returned home, leaving Gideon with only ten thousand soldiers.

*"Gideon," the LORD said, "you still have too many soldiers. Take them down to the spring and I'll test them. I'll tell you which ones can go along with you and which ones must go back home."

*When Gideon led his army down to the spring, the LORD told him, "Watch how each man gets a drink of water. Then divide them into two groups -- those who lap the water like a dog and those who kneel down to drink."

*Three hundred men scooped up water in their hands and lapped it, and the rest knelt to get a drink. *The LORD said, "Gideon, your army will be made up of

Judges 4
-Deborah and Barak
-Defeat of Sisera
Judges 5
-Sing for the Lord
-Victory Is Retold
-Jael Is Praised
Judges 6
-Midian Steals from Israel
-The Lord Chooses Gideon
-Gideon Tears Down Altar
-Gideon Gathers an Army
-Gideon Defeats Midianites
Judges 7

outline
search
index

God the Creator by Michelangelo

Interactive video programs allow study of the Bible through a variety of media. The example at right allows the user to read and compare up to four translations of a biblical passage and to explore the same passage through related art work, animation, and video film.

Complete Bibles and concordances are available in pocket- and book-size computers that can be carried anywhere. With some models, users can insert cartridges with different translations or study guides.

Computers and the Bible

THE LATEST COMPUTER TECHNOLOGY HAS TURNED OUT TO BE SURPRISINGLY USEFUL FOR BIBLE STUDY.

Computers have revolutionized aspects of Bible study both for lay readers and for scholars. Today's software programs provide access to research materials that were previously unavailable to many people, and they make the cross-referencing of study materials easier. With the right software, for instance, someone reading about the Crucifixion in Matthew 27 could type in a command on the computer keyboard and read a Bible scholar's commentary on the passage. With another couple of keystrokes the user might compare the passage with the corresponding accounts in the other Gospels or view a map of ancient Jerusalem showing what is traditionally believed was Jesus' route to Calvary.

A Computer Library The size of a computerized Bible program can range anywhere from a single translation of the Bible to a collection of the major translations, as well as the Hebrew and Greek texts. Many computerized Bibles double as concordances that can search for and display a desired verse or phrase in seconds. If the user wants to know how often and where a term is found in the Bible or in a particular part of the Bible, the program will show that information. Someone who wants to find a verse that describes Jesus as a sacrificial lamb, for instance, might command the program to search for the words *lamb* and *slaughter* in the New International Version. The computer would then search the 31,173 verses of Scripture and display the 6 in which the two words appear together. Some programs also allow the user to print out the 6 quotations together for future reference.

There are also pocket-size electronic Bibles that include concordances. These mini-computers also feature search programs, though their tiny display screens can show only a few lines of text at a time. They have the added advantage of being able to be used anywhere because they operate on batteries.

Programs for Home Study Some computer products include study programs that allow users to write their own notes and commentaries alongside the biblical passages they are studying and to keep their notes with the text when they print the notes out. Teaching programs provide students of Hebrew and Greek with language drills and the fonts for writing in those languages. Other software includes Bible games for children, outlines of books, atlases, and hundreds of research texts, including the six-volume *Anchor Bible Dictionary.* Multimedia Bibles link passages of Scripture to music, photography, works of art, and videos. There are also a great variety of Bible-computing books and magazines available to guide people through an ever expanding maze of products.

Through computer programs known as hypertexts, biblical passages are linked with related reference materials. Whenever readers have a question about a passage, they can immediately find out what the various encyclopedias, grammars, dictionaries, and other reference works have to say about a specific phrase or verse. If the reader is concerned with comparing the texts of various translations of the Bible, there are programs that show parallel portions of several translations on the same screen. The parallel texts can be scrolled through simultaneously for line-by-line comparison of word usage and meaning. New computer tools and research programs are appearing continuously to help ease and deepen biblical study. ❖

*I*nternet software programs, as described in the book at left, allow users access to Bible libraries, study programs, and other resources throughout the country.

*S*oftware for home use includes interactive videos, adult study programs, and reference packages combining text, concordance, dictionary, and more.

Modern Biblical Scholarship

BIBLE SCHOLARSHIP IS A FIELD WHERE SPACE-AGE TECHNOLOGY MEETS
ANCIENT WRITINGS TO SOLVE LONG-STANDING MYSTERIES.

Advanced infrared imaging retrieves invisible words from a
fragment of parchment. Statistical analysis shows correlations and discrepancies in the phrasing of the Pentateuch.
Breakthroughs in DNA research make it possible to trace
the lineage of recovered manuscripts to the animals whose skins were
used to make them.

The late 19th and 20th centuries have witnessed major biblical
documentary finds at St. Catherine's monastery in the Sinai, the Cairo
genizah in Egypt, and among university collections. But the most
important discovery—and for the past half-century a laboratory for
cutting-edge technologies—has been the Dead Sea Scrolls, some of the

*The Dead Sea Scrolls are mostly
housed in the Shrine of the Book
and the Rockefeller Museum in
Jerusalem. The scrolls are now
recorded on microfiche, and
computerized data bases will soon
allow complete access to the texts.
The scrollery in the Palestine
Archaeological Museum is shown
below in a 1958 photograph.*

CAIRO GENIZAH

Since Jewish law forbids the destruction of sacred texts, when such items suffer damage they are often stored in a room in the synagogue called the genizah (literally, "storage"). The immense value of one genizah was recognized in the late 19th century.

In 1896, two learned Scottish twins, Margaret Dunlop Gibson and Agnes Smith Lewis, bought some manuscript pages from a Cairo dealer. They took their purchase to Solomon Schechter of Cambridge University, who identified one text as part of the long-lost Hebrew original of the Book of Ecclesiasticus. Suspecting that the documents had come from the ninth-century Ben-Ezra Synagogue in Cairo, Schechter set off to "empty" the synagogue's genizah.

Schechter swallowed "the dust of centuries" as he removed more than 100,000 fragments dating from as early as the sixth century. Among the fragments were biblical and talmudic texts, liturgical and legal documents, and letters, including one by Maimonides.

Perhaps the most exciting finds were two incomplete and overlapping copies of a text now known as the Damascus Document. Schechter dated these manuscripts to the 10th and 12th centuries and, because they used biblical Hebrew, dated the text on which they were based to before the destruction of the Temple in A.D. 70. References to the "Teacher of Righteousness" and the "Man of Scoffing" led Schechter to believe that the manuscripts described a religious sect. When fragments of the Damascus Document were also found among the Dead Sea Scrolls, Schechter's manuscripts were identified with the Qumran sect.

*B*elow, Solomon Schechter works amid crateloads of fragments recovered from the Cairo genizah and taken for study to Cambridge University. The Damascus Document, right, has been called the first Dead Sea Scroll.

oldest known biblical manuscripts (see pp. 122–129). The remains of some 800 of these scrolls are currently being probed, digitized, analyzed—paleographically, statistically, genetically, and chemically—and meticulously pieced together.

A Complex Puzzle Before scholars can begin to study the contents of badly fragmented Dead Sea Scrolls, they must sort out which pieces belong to the same documents. In assembling like fragments, researchers look at the type of material used to make the scroll, whether papyrus or parchment, and at the relative thickness and color of fragments. They also match up the guide lines, or scorings, used by the scribe to write his text evenly, and consider the relationship of script to lines. Experts in scripts, called paleographers, can often assist in matching pieces by distinguishing the hands of individual scribes.

The computer's ability to amass and provide rapid access to huge amounts of data has proved extremely useful in several areas of biblical study. Computers can compare script styles and fragment shapes and identify and chart linguistic formulations, such as repetitions of words, grammatical constructions, punctuation, and sentence and syllable lengths. In addition, computer-generated concordances allow

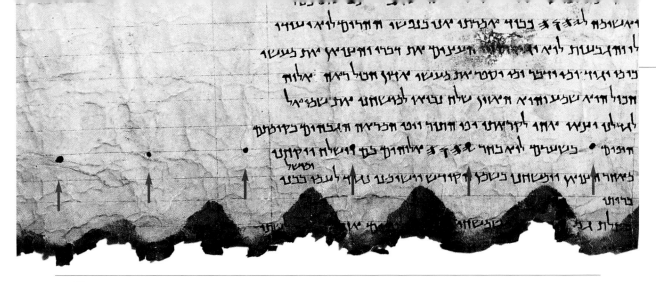

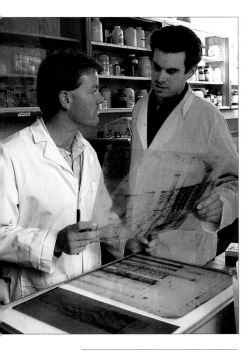

The damage to the Psalms scroll indicated by the row of arrows was caused by a worm eating through the rolled manuscript. The increasing distance between the points indicates that the scroll was rolled up from left to right. Such damage patterns help scholars match up more severely fragmented scroll pieces.

Scott Woodward and his colleague Joel Myers examine a film strip taken of the results of a DNA test performed on a fragment of Dead Sea Scroll.

scholars to do searches for specific words and thereby make close comparisons of the use and context of those words in the various biblical manuscripts. Many of the scrolls, however, are nonbiblical, and scholars must match fragments only on the basis of similarities in their physical characteristics, subject matter, and the pattern of the damage they have sustained.

Genetic Clues Genetic research provides further physical evidence. When the microbiologist Scott Woodward was asked about the likelihood of extracting DNA—the genetic building blocks of all living things—from the animal skins used in the scrolls, he called the procedure a "pretty safe bet." After all, he reasoned, scientists had recovered DNA from the remains of Egyptian mummies and woolly mammoths. With the scrolls, "We're only talking about 2,000 years."

Beginning in 1994 Woodward and scholars at Hebrew University isolated the DNA in minute samples of various scrolls. After multiplying the DNA and examining several key genes, the team identified the sample skins as mostly goat. Further research should reveal the animal herd—even the very animal—used to make a parchment. Moreover, by checking the DNA against genetic material taken from animal bones at other sites in the area, scholars hope to establish the geographic origins of the herds and, extrapolating from that information, of the document itself. "We can nail down where they were written," says Woodward. DNA testing may resolve another issue: whether all of the scrolls came from the Qumran community, or if the caves served as a repository for documents originating in other parts of Palestine.

Bringing a Text to Light Biblical scholarship now benefits from technology developed by the National Aeronautics and Space Administration (NASA). Whereas the human eye sees only a limited portion of the light spectrum, the use of infrared photography extends the visible range. When Dead Sea Scroll fragments are photographed with infrared-sensitive film, written words appear to be darker and backgrounds are blanched out. Technologies pioneered by NASA for the space program—including advanced infrared techniques for the remote sensing of the earth's surface—discern even longer wavelengths in the light spectrum than does infrared photography.

In the summer of 1994 researchers from the Ancient Biblical Manuscript Center, Hebrew University, and NASA's Jet Propulsion Laboratory were able to make substantial gains over all earlier efforts to read a number of the most damaged Dead Sea Scrolls. The fragments had been recorded with an instrument called an imaging spectrometer, which picks up slight variations in light, and the resulting digitalized picture had been fed into a computer. The image was then "tuned" on the computer screen, highlighting and defining features of the text and bringing out more of the previously obscured words.

Dating Ancient Manuscripts Some biblical scholars are especially interested in obtaining precise dates for the sectarian Dead Sea Scrolls. They believe that the dates may shed further light on Judaism and the origins of Christianity.

Dates obtained by paleographers can now be compared to the results of radiocarbon dating, a procedure that indicates the amount of carbon-14 isotope—a class of atomic element—present in a formerly living material. Carbon-14 decays at a known rate in certain substances; so that, by measuring the rate of decay of carbon-14 in a given artifact, it is possible to determine a range of dates for that artifact. In 1995 fragments from 18 Qumran documents were examined by a team of University of Arizona scientists and Israeli scholars. These and earlier carbon dating tests tended to confirm the results reached independently by paleographers, that the scrolls fall largely within the period of the second century B.C. to the first century A.D., a time when many sects of Judaism were in conflict, including the first Christians.

Time-honored methods of scholarship still raise intriguing questions. In 1995 Carsten Thiede of Germany asserted that papyrus fragments from a copy of the Gospel of Matthew at Oxford University are the remains of the oldest known New Testament document. The handwriting style, he noted, along with the appearance on one fragment of an early Christian abbreviation for divinity, suggest a date from the mid-first century A.D. In the unlikely event that it is validated, this highly disputed claim would upset the prevailing theory of the dates and order of the Gospels' composition. ❖

*R*adiocarbon dating, such as that performed at the University of Arizona, involves burning the sample to release carbon dioxide for processing and measurement.

A tiny fragment of Dead Sea Scroll, seen in visible light on the left, when photographed with infrared-sensitive film, right, reveals the phrase: "He wrote the words of Noah."

*P*apyrus fragments from a copy of the Gospel of Matthew are written in a Greek uncial script that, according to one scholar's theory, was rarely used after the mid-first century A.D.

Glossary

allegory Method of biblical interpretation that seeks symbolic meaning in the Scriptures.

anchorite (from the Greek *anachoresis* meaning "withdrawal") Person who lives in solitary contemplation of God.

antiphonary Volume containing the sung portion of the Divine Office.

Apocalypse (from the Greek for "revelation") The Revelation to John.

apocalyptic Type of writing, such as Revelation, revealing that history unfolds in accordance with a divine plan.

Apocrypha (from the Greek for "hidden") Writings, such as Judith and Tobit, that are included in some Christian Old Testament canons but not in the Hebrew canon.

apologetics Studies that deal with defending the Christian faith.

Apostolic Fathers Figures who wrote nonbiblical Christian works during the first and second centuries.

Arians Followers of Arius, who believed that the Son was not of the same substance as the Father. Arianism was condemned in A.D. 325 at the Council of Nicea.

Ark of the Covenant Chest in which the tablets of the Law were carried and that was later housed in Solomon's Temple; by extension, the cabinet in which the Torah is kept in a synagogue.

Ashkenazim Jews who trace their ancestry to Eastern Europe.

Bible moralisée Illustrated book of the 13th century containing Bible excerpts with commentary.

Biblia pauperum (Latin for "Bible of the poor") Illustrated book of the 13th to 15th centuries, drawing parallels between Old and New Testament passages.

Book of the Dead Ancient Egyptian text believed to be used by the deceased in the afterworld.

book of hours Book of private devotion containing prayers for use throughout the day.

breviary Volume of texts used for praying the Divine Office.

bulla Clay pouch for holding and transporting trade tokens in the Near East.

canon (from Greek for "standard") List of books of Holy Scripture deemed authoritative.

Carolingian Frankish dynasty founded in the seventh century by Pepin of Landen. It reached the height of its power and artistic achievement under Charlemagne (emperor 800–814).

catacomb Early Christian subterranean cemetery.

catechism Text providing instruction in the Christian faith.

catechumen Person receiving instruction in church teachings in preparation for baptism.

cenobites Monks living a communal life in accordance with a rule.

Christologic interpretation School of biblical interpretation that seeks prefigurings of Christ in the Old Testament.

Chronicler Name given to the putative author of 1 and 2 Chronicles and Ezra-Nehemiah

codex (plural, codices) Book form, still in use, consisting of gatherings, or groups, of pages sewn through the folds along one edge and bound together.

colophon Inscription at the end of a book giving information about its production, sometimes including the date and place of publication and the name of the scribe, printer, or publisher.

composing stick Small metal holder used by typesetters in arranging lines of type for printing.

Copts Members of the Christian church in Egypt.

Covenant Code (or Book of the Covenant) Portion of the Book of Exodus containing the Law.

cuneiform System of wedge-shaped writing developed in the area of the Tigris and Euphrates river valleys in the fourth millennium B.C.

D source One of the four literary sources of the Pentateuch. Called D because it consists mainly of the Book of Deuteronomy.

Dead Sea Scrolls Name given to the documents found in caves near the ruins of the Dead Sea community of Qumran.

Decalogue The Ten Commandments.

Deuteronomic Code Laws of the Torah set forth in the Book of Deuteronomy concerning the centralization of worship and defining prophecy, kingship, and holy war.

Deuteronomic History Account of history given in the Old Testament books of Deuteronomy through 2 Kings.

Diaspora Dispersion of Jews from the land of Israel and their resettlement in other lands.

Diatessaron Harmonization of the Gospels into a single work done by Tatian in the second century.

Didache Manual of church life that contains some of the earliest known instructions for the celebration of Christian sacraments. It is included among the writings of the Apostolic Fathers.

diptych Two-leaved hinged tablet or altarpiece, sometimes portable.

Divine Office Prayer cycle chanted and recited during the traditional canonical hours of the day: matins and lauds, prime, terce, sext, none, vespers, and compline.

Documentary Hypothesis Prevailing theory that the Pentateuch resulted from the weaving together of four separate accounts—known as J, E, D, and P.

doublet Story told twice in the Pentateuch. For example, the Creation is described in both Genesis 1:1-2:3 and Genesis 2:4-25.

E source One of the four literary sources of the Pentateuch, believed to have originated in northern Israel. Called E because of the author's frequent use of the name *Elohim* for God.

epistle In the strict sense, letter addressed to a community; often used to mean any letter.

eremite (from the Greek for "desert") Person who goes alone to the desert; hermit.

eschatology Branch of theology concerned with final events, such as the Last Judgment.

Essenes Jewish religious order often associated with the Qumran community of the Dead Sea Scrolls.

exegesis Interpretation of texts, particularly of Scripture.

exemplar Original text from which a copy is made.

exordium Portion of a formal letter in New Testament times that extends thanksgiving, intercession, and praise.

florilegium Volume of biblical commentaries arranged by topic, popular in the Middle Ages.

folio Sheet of paper or parchment folded once to create four pages; large book made up of folios.

fresco Wall painting made by applying pigment to wet plaster.

frisket In printing, holder that is folded over the paper and type and put through the press.

gathering Set of sheets folded inside one another. Gatherings are bound together to form a codex, or book.

Gemara Rabbinical writings on the Jewish Law and related topics. These writings were eventually combined with earlier commentaries, the Mishnah, to form a collection known as the Talmud.

genizah Storage space connected to a synagogue for housing old or damaged holy texts and objects.

Gentile Non-Jewish person.

gloss Commentary on text and explanations of words and phrases written between the lines of a text or in its margins.

gnosticism (from the Greek for "knowledge") Religious philosophy asserting that divine order is disclosed only to select persons.

God-fearer Non-Jewish believer in the God of the Hebrew Bible.

Gospel (from the Old English word *godspel*, meaning "good tale") The good news brought by Jesus that the kingdom of God is at hand and, by extension, a book about Jesus' life and message.

Haggadah Text used in the Passover service.

Hasmonean Jewish dynasty under John Hyrcanus and his successors, lasting from 134 to 63 B.C. and described in 1 and 2 Maccabees.

Hebrews Abraham's clan and their descendants. Called Israelites from the time of Jacob.

Hellenists Jews who were immersed in Greek culture.

Hexapla Work by the early Christian scholar Origen that compares the Hebrew and Greek texts of the Old Testament in six columns.

Hexateuch First six books of the Bible.

hieroglyphic System of pictographic writing used in ancient Egypt.

historiated initial First letter of a part of a manuscript enclosing a depiction of figures or a scene.

Holiness Code Laws found in Leviticus 18–26, presenting moral and religious tenets of Judaism.

Holy of Holies Inner sanctuary in the Temple in Jerusalem housing the Ark of the Covenant and accessible only to the high priest.

humanism Renaissance system of study characterized by the revival of classical learning.

Humiliati Medieval poverty movement originating in Lombardy.

Hyksos (from Egyptian for "rulers of foreign lands") Invaders from Asia who ruled Egypt from about 1710 to 1550 B.C.

icon Image of a revered person, prominent in Byzantine tradition.

iconography Tradition of imagery associated with a particular event or theme.

iconostasis Screen covered with icons dividing the sanctuary from the nave in a Byzantine church.

illumination Strictly, the use of gold or other precious metals to decorate a manuscript. Commonly, any hand-painted decoration of a manuscript.

Incipit Opening words of a text.

indulgence Pardon granted by the church for sins, canceling punishment a person may have had to endure in Purgatory for those sins. Luther attacked the doctrine of indulgences.

Israelites Originally, descendants of Jacob (renamed Israel by God).

J source Probably the earliest of the four literary sources of the Pentateuch, believed to originate in Judea. Called J because of the author's frequent use of the name *Jahveh* (Yahweh) for God.

Johannine Concerning the Apostle John or the books of the New Testament traditionally ascribed to him.

Judah Southern half of the divided kingdom, of which Israel was the northern half.

Judea Roman province ruled by Herod; in a more limited sense, one of the divisions of the province (with Samaria and Galilee).

Kabbala Mystical Jewish system of interpreting Scripture.

ketibh/qere Notations made by Hebrew scribes in copying Scripture.

Koran Sacred Scriptures of Islam, believed by Muslims to have been revealed to Muhammed.

LXX Abbreviation for the Septuagint, Roman numerals referring to the roughly 70 elders who are said to have made the translation.

leaf Unit of a book comprising the front and back of a sheet.

lectionary Volume with Bible readings used during a church service.

lector Reader of the scriptural lesson in a church service.

liturgy (from the Greek word *leitourgia*, meaning "service") Rites performed in the course of a church service.

Lollards Followers of the medieval English reformer John Wyclif.

lunellum Knife used in the preparation of parchment.

majuscule Script composed entirely of capital letters.

manuscript Hand-written text.

Masoretes Jewish scribes who, beginning about A.D. 500, copied the authoritative text of the Hebrew Bible, the Masoretic text.

matrix In printing, a metal die from which a letter of type is cast.

membrana Sheet of parchment used to make a scroll.

Menorah Seven-branched candelabrum originally placed in the Temple sanctuary; an eight-branched menorah is used in the celebration of Hanukkah.

Messiah (derived from the Hebrew for "anointed") One sent by God to restore Israel and reign over humankind; Christians believe Jesus is the Messiah prophesied in the Old Testament.

micrography Tiny script used in Hebrew manuscripts and sometimes arranged in decorative patterns.

Midrash (derived from the Hebrew for "to search") Jewish biblical interpretation.

miniature Illustration that forms a distinct unit within the decorative scheme of a manuscript page.

minuscule Script characterized by small letters that are written in a cursive style.

Mishnah Collection of commentary on the Jewish Law, completed about A.D. 200.

missal Volume of the prayers and rites used at Mass for every day of the year.

Montanist Follower of Montanus, who believed that divine revelation was continuing.

Mosaic Law Written law received by Moses from God on Mount Sinai and set forth in the Torah.

mystery play Theatrical reenactments of biblical events performed in medieval Europe.

oracle Message from God, as in a dream or received by a prophet.

oral law Rabbinic law composed primarily of interpretations of the written law and believed to have been orally transmitted to Moses by God on Mount Sinai.

orant Image of praying figure with arms outstretched.

ostracon Pottery fragment used as a writing surface.

P source One of the four literary sources of the Pentateuch. It is called P because of the central role played by priests.

paleography Study of the history of ancient hand-writing styles.

Palestine Roman province that included the land of Israel.

palimpsest Writing surface that was reused after the original text had been erased.

papyrus Writing surface made from the pith of the papyrus plant.

parable Teaching that takes the form of an extended metaphor, expressed in a few words, or of a full-length story.

parchment Writing surface made from prepared animal skin.

Parousia (from the Greek for "arrival") Coming of Christ at the end of time.

Patriarch One of the three founding fathers of Israel: Abraham, Isaac, and Jacob.

Pentateuch First five books of the Bible: Genesis, Exodus, Leviticus, Numbers, and Deuteronomy.

percamenarius Parchment maker.

peroration In a formal letter of the first century, the reiteration and expansion of an appeal.

Peshitta Syriac text of the Bible, dating from the early fifth century.

Pharisees Jewish group that, in contrast to the Sadducees, accepted the Prophets and the Writings as Scripture and advocated the oral law as well as the written law.

phylactery (in Hebrew, *tefillah*) Tiny case containing Scripture, worn by men on the arm and forehead during morning prayer.

pictograph Early form of writing in which a picture was used to represent a word.

platen In printing, a heavy, flat plate that is pressed against type and paper to produce printed text.

polyglot Multilingual edition of the Bible including the texts in their original languages alongside translations into other languages.

poverty movement Religious movement espousing a life of voluntary poverty and modeled on the *vita apostolica*, or life of early Christians at the time of the Apostles.

Priestly Code Laws of the Torah not contained in the Covenant, Deuteronomic, or Holiness codes; associated with the P source.

proof In a formal letter of the first century, an appeal for action.

Prophets In the Hebrew Bible, writings classified as the Former Prophets (Joshua, Judges, Samuel, and Kings) and the Latter Prophets (Isaiah, Jeremiah, Ezekiel, and the 12 Minor Prophets).

proverb Saying that sums up a particular truth or observation. Proverbs are found in both the Old and New Testaments.

Psalter Book containing the biblical psalms, often used in worship.

Pseudepigrapha Group of about 65 Jewish and Christian religious writings that are in neither the Hebrew nor the Christian Bible.

Q (from the German *Quelle*, meaning "source") Hypothetical source of material found in Matthew and Luke but absent from Mark.

quire Group of sheets folded together and collated to make a book.

rabbi (Hebrew for "great") Title designating a teacher.

received text The standard edition of a biblical text that has been passed down to the present day.

redactor Person or group of persons believed responsible for compiling and editing the four sources of the Pentateuch.

rubric (from *rubrica*, Latin for "red") Title, heading, or other writing in a book, such as directions for the rite, that is not part of the main text, usually written in red.

ruling Guide lines used by a scribe to help him write the text evenly.

runes Letters of an alphabet used by ancient Germanic peoples, including the Anglo Saxons.

sacramentary Volume containing the prayers spoken or intoned by the celebrant during a sung Mass.

Sadducees Jewish group connected with the high priesthood, which rejected the oral law.

Sanhedrin High court of Jewish law active in Jesus' time.

Scholasticism Medieval philosophical movement that proves the doctrines of faith by reason.

scriptorium Room set aside for writing or copying manuscripts, usually in a church or monastery.

scroll Writing material made by attaching sheets of parchment or papyrus end to end and rolling them into the shape of a cylinder.

Semites (from the name *Shem*, eldest son of Noah) Various peoples, including Canaanites, Arabs, Hebrews, Aramaeans, Assyrians, Babylonians, and Phoenicians.

Sephardim Jews who trace their ancestry to Spain, Portugal, or North Africa.

Septuagint Greek translation of the Hebrew Bible begun in the third century B.C. in Alexandria, Egypt.

signs source Hypothetical document listing the signs, or miracles, performed by Jesus and believed to have been used as a source by the author of the Gospel of John.

Sopherim Hebrew for "scribes."

Speculum humanae salvationis (in Latin, "Mirror of Human Salvation") Picture book of the 14th century, demonstrating parallels between the New and Old Testaments and nonbiblical events.

stele Stone pillar inscribed in commemoration of an event.

stylites Monks who spent their lives in contemplation atop a pillar; exemplified by Simeon.

stylus Pointed instrument for writing on a wax tablet.

synagogue (from the Greek for "assembly of people") Gathering of worshipers or the building in which they congregate.

Synoptic Gospels First three canonical Gospels—Matthew, Mark, and Luke—which present the life, death, and resurrection of Jesus in a similar fashion.

Talmud Collection of rabbinical and scholarly interpretations of and commentaries on Jewish Law and ethics as set forth in the Bible.

Tannaim Scholars of the oral law.

Targum Translation of the Hebrew biblical texts into Aramaic.

Testament Original meaning, a covenant between man and God. Thus "New Testament" refers to a new covenant with God.

Torah First five books of the Bible, also called the Pentateuch: Genesis, Exodus, Leviticus, Numbers, and Deuteronomy. Also refers to God's instruction to the Israelites.

transmission Manner in which the text of the Bible or other writing is passed down through the ages.

triptych Three-leaved hinged tablet or altarpiece.

type case Printer's tray for holding unassembled type. It is divided into compartments to separate the letters in their various forms as well as punctuation marks and other pieces of type.

type form Metal frame holding letters of type arranged to produce several pages of printed text.

typology Method of biblical interpretation that seeks parallels between Old and New Testament events and finds prefigurings of Jesus in the Old Testament.

uncial Script characterized by a distinct separation of block letters. It was common from the fourth to the eighth centuries.

vellum Fine writing material made of calf skin.

vita apostolica (Latin for "life of the Apostles") an ideal of living based on the austere and communal lives of the Apostles and other early Christians.

Vulgate Latin text of the Bible made up mainly of Jerome's translations.

Writings Books of the Hebrew Bible not included in the Torah or in the group of writings classified as the Prophets. The Writings comprise Psalms, Job, Proverbs, Ruth, the Song of Solomon, Ecclesiastes, Lamentations, Esther, Daniel, Ezra–Nehemiah, and Chronicles.

Yahweh Christian pronunciation of the Hebrew designation of *YHWH* for God.

Zealots First-century Jewish nationalists who resisted Roman rule.

Credits

Illustrations, Maps, and Charts

Karin Kretschmann 16, 41, 54, 55, 87, 132, 133, 189, 218, 259
Ivan Lapper 18–19, 124–125, 213
John A. Lytle 28

Chris Maggadini 106–107
Alan Parry 82–83
Rodica Prato 22–23, 50, 72, 94, 95, 123, 135, 144–145, 179, 196–197, 225, 327, 328

Reineck & Reineck 33
Paul Shaw 70
Dahl Taylor 34–35, 62–63, 294–295

Photographs

Abbreviations

AAA	Ancient Art & Architecture Collection, Ronald Sheridan's Photo Library, London
ABS	Courtesy of The American Bible Society, New York City
AI	Alinari, Rome
AM	Arxiu MAS, Barcelona
AR	Art Resource, New York City
BAL	The Bridgeman Art Library, London
BAV	Biblioteca Apostolica Vaticana, Vatican City
BL	By Permission of The British Library, London
BM	©British Museum, London
BN	Bibliothèque Nationale, Paris
BPK	Bildarchiv Preussicher Kulturbesitz, Berlin
CNMHS	Caisse Nationale des Monuments Historiques et des Sites, ©Arch. Phot., Paris
CUL	Cambridge University Library, England
DH	David Harris, Jerusalem
EL	Photography by Erich Lessing
GC	The Granger Collection, New York City
GDO	G. Dagli Orti, Paris
Gi	Giraudon, Paris
IAA	Courtesy of The Israel Antiquities Authority, Jerusalem
IM	Israel Museum, Jerusalem
J-LC	Jean-Loup Charmet, Paris
JTS	Courtesy of The Library of The Jewish Theological Seminary of America, New York City
MMA	The Metropolitan Museum of Art, New York City
NGS	National Geographic Society, Washington, D.C.
NYPL	The New York Public Library, Astor, Lenox and Tilden Foundations
PAH	Photothèque André Held, Ecublens, Switzerland
PML	The Pierpont Morgan Library, New York City
RMN	Réunion des Musées Nationaux Agence Photographique, Paris
Sc	Scala, Rome
SH	Sonia Halliday Photographs, Weston Turville, England
V & A	The Victoria & Albert Museum, London
WFA	The Werner Forman Archive, London
ZR	Zev Radovan, Jerusalem

Pages: 1, 3 *(detail)* Kunsthistorisches Museum, Vienna, EL/AR. **2** GC. **11** *Top (detail)* BN, Ms Lat.1, fol.3v. *Bottom* St. Martinskirche, Memmingen, Germany, photo: Lala Aufsberg. **12** *(detail)* Cathedral, Gerona, Spain, EL/AR. **13** *(detail)* S. Francesco, Montefalco, Italy, AI/AR. **14–15** Galleria Doria Pamphili, Rome, Sc/AR. **16** *4000-3400 (Top)* George Gerster/Comstock, Inc. *Bottom* Courtesy of The Oriental Institute Museum, University of Chicago. *3400-3100 Top* Louvre, RMN. *Center (detail)* Louvre, GDO. *3100-2600 Top* Louvre, RMN. *Bottom* Courtesy of The Oriental Institute Museum, University of Chicago. *2600-2350* Spectrum Colour Library. *2350-1950 Top* Joseph J. Scherschel, ©NGS. *Center* Victor R. Boswell Jr., ©NGS. *Bottom* Comstock, Inc. **17** *1950-1600 Top* Louvre, RMN. *Bottom* Archaeological Museum, Heraklion, Crete, EL/AR. *1600-1400 Top (detail)* Egyptian Expedition of MMA, Rogers Fund, 1930. *Center* Jehangir Gazdar/Woodfin Camp & Associates. *Bottom (detail)* National Museum of Art, Athens, GDO. *1400-1292* Egyptian Museum, Cairo, GDO. *1292-1190 Top* Engraving by Gustave Doré, "The Holy Bible" c.1866. *Center* Academia Sinica Collection, photo: Wan-go H.C. Weng. *Bottom* Paul Breeden, ©NGS. **19** DH. **20** *Top* Nik Wheeler/Black Star. *Center* Archaeological Museum, Damascus, Hirmer Verlag, Munich. *Bottom* AAA. **21** *Center-right (detail)* Iraq Museum, Baghdad, Sc/AR. *Center-left* Ashmolean Museum, Oxford University. **24** Jewish

Museum, AR. **25** Daniel Blatt. **26** *Center-left* Louvre, photo: ©Michael Holford. *Center-right* Louvre, EL/AR. **27** National Museum, Aleppo, Syria, EL/AR. **29** Werner Braun. **31** *Top* BM. *Bottom* Louvre, RMN. **32** *Top-left* Robert Harding Picture Library. *Top-right* ©1996 John McGrail. *Center* Louvre, EL/AR. **33** *Top* Dimitri Kessel, Life Magazine, ©Time Inc. *Center* Pierre Boulat, Life Magazine, ©Time Inc. *(both)* BM. **36** Alain Choisnet/The Image Bank. **37** GC. **38** *Top* AAA. *Bottom* Egyptian Expedition of MMA, Rogers Fund, 1930. **38–39** BM. **40** *Top-left* Egyptian Museum, Cairo, GDO. *Top-right* ZR. *Bottom-left* AAA. *Inset* GDO. **41** *Top-foreground* Louvre, RMN. *Top-background* BM. *Center* Louvre, RMN. **42** *Top* BN, J-LC. *Bottom* Oriental Division, NYPL. **43** *Top* Garo Nalbandian/ASAP. **44** *Center* Brian Brake/Photo Researchers, Inc. *Bottom* Will & Deni McIntyre/Photo Researchers, Inc. **45** Victor Boswell, ©NGS. **46** Engraving by Gustave Doré. **47** CUL, Ms Or. 233. **48** *Left* Louvre, RMN. *Right* Nathan Benn/Woodfin Camp & Associates. **50** *Right* Egyptian Museum, Cairo, GDO. **51** *(detail)* PML, Ms M. 638, fol.12v/AR. **52–53** IAA, photo: IM. **54** *1010-960 Top* Duomo, Cividale del Friuli, Italy (Udine) Sc/AR. *800-650 Top* BM, 124772/AR. *Center* Palazzo Vecchio, Florence, Sc/AR. *Bottom* Lee Boltin. *650-560* GC. *560-500, Top BM. Center, Bottom (both) (detail)* Louvre, EL/AR. **55** *500-400 Top* AAA. *Center* Oldrich Karasek/Tony Stone Images. *Bottom* Justin Kerr. *400-325* Musei Capitolini, Rome, AI/AR. *325-200* IM, EL/AR. *200-150* BM, GC. *150-65* Yigael Yadin Estate. **56** *Top* ZR. **57** *Bottom (both) (details)* PML, Ms M. 638, fol.29/AR. **58** *(detail)* JTS. **60** ZR. **61** Palace School, Aachen, RMN. **64** *Top* ZR. *Center* JTS. **65** JTS, photo: Suzanne Kaufman. **66** *(detail)* BL, Add. Ms 11639, fol.116a, BAL/AR. **67** Cathedral, Strasbourg, EL/AR. **68** Photo: ©Michael Holford. **69** Austrian National Library, Vienna, Cod.s.n. 2701, fol.252. **71** *Top* Archaeological Museum, Istanbul, EL/AR. *Bottom* The Jewish Museum, Gift of Evelyn and Bob Roberts, AR. **72** ZR. **73** *Top* ZR. *Bottom* V & A, photo: ©Michael Holford. **74** *Top* Engraving by Gustave Doré. *Bottom* JTS, photo: Suzanne Kaufman. **75** *Left & right* BM, photo: ©Michael Holford. **76** St. Bavo Cathedral, Ghent, Gi/AR. **77** *Top* Arena Chapel (Scrovegni Chapel), Padua, Sc/AR. *Center* Archaeological Museum, Istanbul, EL/AR. *Bottom* CNMHS/SPADEM **78** St. Martinskirche, Memmingen, Germany, photo: Lala Aufsberg. **79** *(detail)* Musée de Cluny, RMN. **80** *Top* Hirmer Verlag, Munich. *Bottom* Courtesy, School of Theology at Claremont, photo: ©John C. Trever. **81** *(detail)* BN, Ms Grec. 1208, fol.162. **83** *Top* IM. *Bottom* IAA. **84** *Center* ZR. *Bottom* IAA, photo: IM. **85** *Top-right* ZR. *Top-left* ZR. *Center* IAA, photo: IM. **86** *(all)* ZR. **87** *Center* David Dorning. *Right* BAV. **88** Vorderasiatische Museum, Berlin, photo: Gian Berto Vanni/AR. **89** *Top* BM. *Bottom* BM, EL/AR. **90** Winchester Cathedral, BAL/AR. **91** ZR. **92** *(detail)* Biblioteca Estense, Modena, Sc/AR. **93** *(detail)* Cathedral, Gerona, Spain, EL/AR. **98** S. Eulalia, Parades de Nava, Spain, Sc/AR. **99** *Top* BL, Add. Ms 18856, fol.211. *Bottom* BM. **100** BL, Royal 19 D.111, fol.181. **101** *Top* Courtesy of The Hispanic Society of America. *Center* DH, IM. **102** AAA. **103** *Top* Mead Art Museum, Amherst College, Gift of Herbert W. Plimpton: The Hollis W. Plimpton, Class of 1915, Memorial Collection 1973.91. *Center (detail)* Museo Civico, Brescia, AR. **104** BM. **105** *Top* BAV. *Bottom* J-LC. **106** AAA. **108** BAV. **109** John Rylands University Library of Manchester. **110, 111** *(both)* DH. **112** Foto Stadtarchiv, Worms. **113** PML, Ms M. 644, fol.238v/AR. **114** *Center* ZR. *Bottom* Jewish Museum, London. **115** *Left* DH. *Right* BL, Oriental and India Collections. **116** Instituto da Biblioteca Nacional e do Livro, Lisbon. **117** *Top* DH. *Center* Juedisches Museum der Schweiz, Basel, EL/AR. **118** Piazza della Signoria, Florence, Sc/AR. **119** *Top* Bargello, Florence, Sc/AR. *Bottom* PAH. **120** AAA. **121** *Left* Musée Condé, Chantilly, Gi/AR. *Right* IM, EL/AR. **122** *Top-left* Richard T. Nowitz. *Top-right* Albatross Aerial Photography. **126** DH. **127** MMA, Purchase, Joseph Pulitzer Bequest, 1963. (63.40). photo: Schecter Lee. **128** *Top-left* IAA. *Top-right* IM, The Shrine of the Book, D. Samuel and Jeane Gottesman Center for Biblical Manuscripts. *Center* ZR. *Bottom-left* Yigael Yadin Estate. *Bottom-right* IAA. **129** *Center-far left* Yigael Yadin Estate. *Center-left & right* Yigael Yadin Estate, Hebrew University of Jerusalem. *Bottom* Werner Braun. **130–131** EL/AR. **132** *65-40 B.C. Center* Vatican Museum, EL/AR. *Bottom* National Maritime Museum, Haifa, EL/AR. *40 B.C.-A.D. 1 (detail)* PML, Ms M.

69, fol.60/AR. *A.D. 1-35 Top (detail)* PML, Ms M.855 fol.111/AR. 35-70 *Center (detail)* BL, Harley Ms 1527, fol.97. *70-90* Diaspora Museum, Tel Aviv, photo: Richard T. Nowitz. **133** *90-120 Bottom (detail)* Musée Condé, Chantilly, Gi/AR. *120-175 Top-right* IM, EL/AR. *Top-left* MMA, Rogers Fund. *Center* Reuters, The Bettmann Archive. *175-250 Top* Musée Cantonal d'Archeologie et d'Historie, Lausanne, Gi/AR. *Center* Church of the Multiplication, Tabgah, Israel, AR. *Bottom* Fowler Museum of Cultural History, UCLA, photo: Richard Todd. *325-400 Center* Richard Todd. **136** *Top-left & center (all)* GC. *Top-right* Louvre, RMN. **137** Werner Braun. **138** *Top* DH. *Bottom* Pinacoteca di Brera, Milan, Superstock. **139** Bibliothèque des Arts Décoratifs, J-LC. **140** Lee Boltin. **141** Sc/AR. **142** Fitzwilliam Museum, Cambridge University, BAL. **143** Kavaler/AR. **144** Museum of Catalan Art, Barcelona, AM. **146** *(detail)* Grotte Vaticane, Vatican City, EL/AR. **147** *Top (detail)* BL, Harley Ms 1527, fol.23. *Bottom* Chiesa del Carmine, Florence, Sc/AR. **148** *Top* AAA. *Center* BM. **150** Christie's, London, Superstock. **151** Jane Taylor/SH. **152** *Top* Harlan Hatcher Graduate Library, University of Michigan. *Bottom* BL, Harley Ms 1527, fol.97. **153** SH. **154** Staatsgalerie, Stuttgart, Superstock. **155** F.H.C. Birch/SH. **156, 157** *(both)* V & A, AR. **158** *(detail)* MMA, Gift of John D. Rockefeller, Jr., The Cloisters Collection, 1937. **159** SH. **160** *Top* Duomo, Siena, Sc/AR. *Bottom* Carrand Collection, Bargello, Florence, Sc/AR. **161** The Institute For Antiquity and Christianity, Claremont, Calif. **162** *Top* Arena Chapel, (Scrovegni Chapel), Padua, Superstock. *Center* ZR. *Bottom* MMA, Gift of Junius S. Morgan, 1919. 19.73.179. **163** MMA, Gift of Mrs. Henry Goldman, 1944 44.114.1. **164** Musée Ville de Strasbourg. **165** *(detail)* Koninklijk Museum voor Schone Kunsten, Antwerp. **166** *Left (detail)* PML, Ms M. 728, fol.63v/AR. *Right (detail)* Al/AR. **167** MMA, Robert Lehman Collection, 1975. **168** *Top (detail)* Al/AR. *Center* National Gallery, Prague, Gi/AR. **169** MMA, Jules Bache Collection, 1949. **170** *Left (detail)* Manuscript Library of The Armenian Patriarch of Jerusalem, DH. *Right (detail)* Al/AR. **171** Bibliothèque municipale de Besançon. **172** *Top* Uffizi, Florence, Sc/AR. *Bottom* Museo Cristiano, Brescia, Mauro Pucciarelli, Rome. **174** *Top (detail)* Al/AR. *Bottom* BN, Ms Lat. 8850, fol.180v. **175** Germanisches Nationalmuseum, Nürnberg. **176** BL, Royal Ms 28.VII, fol.168v. **177** IAA, photo: IM. **178** Musée des Tapisseries, Angers, photo: Caroline Rose, CNMHS/SPADEM. **179** *(detail)* Musée Condé, Chantilly, Gi/AR. **180** V & A, C.M. Dixon. **181** PML, Ms M. 644, fol.112/AR. **182** Richard T. Nowitz. **183** Rare Books & Manuscripts Division, NYPL. **184** BL, Or. Ms 1404, fol.15A. **185** *Left* IAA, photo: IM. *Center* IM. **186** *Top* PML Ms M. 654.1/AR. *Bottom* John Rylands University Library of Manchester. **187** *Top* BL, Add. Ms 33270. *Right* AAA. *Center* BAV. **188** Duomo, Rossano, Italy, Sc/AR. **189** *Top* BL, Angelo Hornak. *Bottom* BL, Mss. 43725. **190** *(detail)* S. Clemente, Rome, Sc/AR. **191** *Top* Reproduced by kind permission of the Trustees of the Chester Beatty Library, Dublin. *Bottom (detail)* Madeline Grimoldi Archives, BAV, Ms Greco, 1613, fol.258. **192** SS. Giovanni e Paolo, Rome, Sc/AR. **193** *Left* Museo Nationale delle Terme, Rome, EL/AR. *Right* Wadsworth Atheneum, Gift of J. Pierpont Morgan. **194** *Top* AM. *Center* SH. **195** Al/AR. **196** Musei Capitolini, Rome, Sc/AR. **198** *Top (both)* Sc/AR. *Center* Nardini Editore, Florence. *Bottom (detail)* Basilica Aquileia, Italy, Sc/AR. **199** *Top* Mausoleum of Galla Placidia, Ravenna, Sc/AR. *Center* BM. *Bottom* Grotte Vaticane, Vatican City, EL/AR. **200** Accademia, Florence, Sc/AR. **201** *Top* Coptic Museum, Old Cairo, photo: Jean Doresse, 1949/Institute for Antiquity and Christianity, Claremont, Calif. *Bottom* Mauro Pucciarelli, Rome. **202** Church of the Chora, Istanbul, photo: Ara Güler. **203** Beinecke Library, Yale University. **204** Sfax Musée, PAH. **205** *Center* Musée de Brignoles, PAH. *Bottom (detail)* Mausoleum of Galla Placidia, Ravenna, Sc/AR. **206** *Top* PAH. *Bottom* BM, EMG. dc 18. **207** Jewish National and University Library. **208** *(both)* Biblioteca Estense, Modena, Ms Lat. 458, photo: Roncaglia. **209** Biblioteca Ambrosiana, Milan, Dr. Bruce Metzger. **210** Arena Chapel (Scrovegni Chapel), Padua, Sc/AR. **211** *Top* Cathedral, Hildesheim, Germany, EL/AR. *Center* Kunsthistorisches Museum, Vienna, EL/AR. **212** Stock Montage, Inc. **213** *Top (detail)* Biblioteca Laurenziana, Florence, photo: Alberto Scardigli. **215** BL, Royal Ms 1.B.VII, fol.10v. **216-217** Kuntsthistorisches Museum, Vienna, EL/AR. **218** *400-500 Center* BN. *Bottom* Bibliothèque St. Geneviève, Paris, Ms 218, J-LC. *500-600 Top* SH. *Bottom* National Museum of Man, Canada. *600-700 Bottom* Yucatan Regional Museum of Anthropology, Merida. *700-800 Top* BL, Add Ms 39943, fol.2. *800-1000, Top* Cathedral, Metz, Gi/AR. *Bottom* ©Michael Holford. **219** *1000-1100 Center* SEF/AR. *Bottom* GC. *1100-1250 Top* Sc/AR. *Center* Santa Croce, Florence, Sc/AR. *Bottom* GC. *1250-1300 Top* GC. *1300-1360 Top* Prints Division, NYPL. *Bottom* Dirck Halstead. *1360-1455 Top* GC. *Bottom* ©Michael Holford. **220** Musée des Beaux-Arts de Montréal. **221** *Left* Catacomb of Priscilla, Rome, Sc/AR. *Right* ABS, photo: Richard Berenson. **222** *Top (detail)* BN, Ms Lat. 1, fol.3v. *Center* BL, Add. Ms 10049, fol.64v. **223** BL, Add. Ms 38126, fols.227v-228. **224** *Top* AAA. *Center* Uppsala University Library, fol.30r. **225** Archivo Oronoz/Artephot. **226** *Top* Fridmar Damm/Leo deWys, Inc. *Inset (detail)* Attrib. to Yusuf al-Musawwir, Coll. Abou Adal #92, PAH. **227** *(detail)* Painting by Pascual Ortoneda, Barcelona Museum, Inv. 65783, PAH. **228** *Top* Dumbarton Oaks, acc. no. 48.18. *Bottom* "Immersion of Pilgrims" by David Roberts L.641(4)1920 Courtesy of the Trustees of the V & A. **229** *Left (detail)* "Stories of the True Cross" by Piero della Francesca, S. Francesco, Arezzo, Italy, Sc/AR. *Right* Museum of Turkish & Islamic Art, Istanbul. **230** *Left* Biblioteca Ambrosiana, Milan. *Right* Biblioteca Laurenziana, Florence, Sc/AR. **231** *Top-left (detail)* BN, Ms Copte 13, fol.21v. *Top-right* AAA. *Bottom* Courtesy, Institute of Ethiopian Studies, Addis Ababa, photo: Malcolm Varon, N.Y.C. ©1995. **232** *(detail)* PML, Ms M. 740, fol.6v/AR. **233** *Top* Tbilissi Museum of Fine Art, PAH. *Bottom* M. & J. Lynch/AAA. *Inset* GC. **234** *Left* Bodleian Library, Oxford University, Ms Georg. B1, fol.2. *Bottom* Academy of Science, St. Petersburg, EL/AR. **235** *Top* Bodleian Library, Oxford University, Ms Canon. Gr. 122, fols.89v-90r. *Bottom* EL/AR. **236** *Top-left* Pushkin Museum, Moscow, Sc/AR. *Top-right* from EKDOTIKE ATHENON S. A. *Sinai, The Treasures of the Monastery. Center-left* BM, WFA/ AR. *Center* V & A, AR. *Center-right* Treasury of St. Mark's, Venice, Sc/AR. *Bottom* The Walters Art Gallery, Baltimore. **237** *Top-left* "Icon of the Virgin," Tapestry weave, wool, 178x110 cm. Egypt, Byzantine period, 6th c. ©The Cleveland Museum of Art, 1995, Leonard C. Hanna, Jr. Bequest, 67.144. *Top-right* State Museums of Berlin, Museum for Late Antique and Byzantine Art, photo: Liepe/BPK. *Bottom (detail)* BL, Add. Ms 19352, fol.27v. **238** Austrian National Library, Cod. 2759, fol.56. **239** *Left (detail)* BL, Add. Ms 15410, fol.177b. *Right* Collection of the J. Paul Getty Museum. **240, 241** *(both)* AM. **242** *Top-left* The Bodleian Library, Oxford University, Ms Rawl. B.514, fol.iii(v). *Top-right* Royal Irish Academy, fol.48. *Bottom* Kevin Schafer/Tony Stone Images, Inc. **243** Trinity College, Dublin. **244** *Top* BL, Add. Ms 39943, fol.2, 4T26. *Bottom* BL, Cotton Ms Claudius B. IV, fol.68. **245** AAA. **246** *Top* Ian Berry/Magnum Photos, Inc. *Center* English Heritage. *Bottom* BL, Smith, Nicholson & Co. **247** *Top* BL, Cotton Ms Nero D IV, fol.94v-95. *Center* BL, Cotton Ms Nero D IV, fol.936. *Bottom* BL, Cotton Ms Nero D IV, fol.139. **248** *Top (detail)* BN, Ms Lat. 1176, fol.132, SH. *Bottom (detail)* BL, Cotton Ms Domitian A XVII, fol.122v. **249** *Left* Shrine of the Book of Dimma, Trinity College, Dublin, photo: Lee Boltin. *Right (detail)* BN, Ms Fr. 782, fol.2v. **250** *(detail)* PML, Ms M. 429, fol.183/AR. **251** *Top* BL, Add. Ms 10546, fols.5v-6. *Inset (detail)* Staatsbibliothek, Bamberg, Msc. Bibl. 1, fol.5v. *Bottom (detail)* BL, Harley Ms 2803, fol.264. **252** *Top, bottom,* and **253** *Top* Royal Library, Copenhagen, details from Ms 4, 2°, fols.183v, 195r, 124v. **252** *Bottom-left* PML, Ms M. 730, fols.129v-130/AR. **253** *Center* Staats- und Universitätsbibliothek Bremen, Ms b.21, fol.124v, photo: ©Dr. Ludwig Reichert Verlag Wiesbaden. **254** BN, Ms Lat. 9389, fol.116r. **255** *Top (detail)* By permission of the President and Fellows of Corpus Christi College, Oxford University, Ms CCC 1, fol.251. *Bottom* Royal Library, Stockholm, Ms A144, fol.34. **256** *Top* BL, Royal 6E.VI, fol.329 *(detail) Bottom-left* BN, Ms Lat. 12048, fol.1v. *Bottom-right (detail)* V & A, AR. **257** *Top (detail)* BL, Cotton Ms Claudius B IV, fol.63v. *Center (detail)* Hradcany Castle, Prague, EL/AR. *Bottom (detail)* PML, M. 653, fol.2/AR. **258** *Top* PML, Ms M. 87, fols.323v-324/AR. *Center* Staats- und Universitätsbibliothek, Göttingen, Ms Uffenb. 51, fols.3v-4r. **259** *Top* PML, *(detail)* Ms M. 1056, verso. *Center (details) Winchester Bible,* fols.21v & 278v, *(both)* Winchester Cathedral. **260** *Top* Bibliothèque du Grand Seminaire de Strasbourg, Codex 37, fol.4. *Bottom* BL, Cotton Ms Vespasian A I, fols.30v-31. **261** *Top* PML, Ms M. 729, fol.16/AR. *Bottom (detail)* Hradcany Castle, Prague, EL/AR. **262** *Top* PML, Ms M. 569FC/AR. *Bottom* Bibliothèque Cantonale et Universitaire, Fribourg, Switzerland, M. L64, photo: Jean Mülhauser. **263** *Top-left* Duomo, Monza, Italy, Sc/AR. *Top-right (both):* Spencer Collection, NYPL, photos: Jonathan Wallen from *Treasures of the New York Public Library* by Davidson and McTigue, pub. Harry N. Abrams, N.Y. *Bottom-left* BN, Ms Lat. 9383, *Bottom-right* Duomo, Milan, EL/AR. **264** *Top (detail)* BN, Ms Lat. 4915, fol.1. *Center* V & A/E.T. Archive. London. *Bottom (detail)* Austrian National Library, Vienna, Codex 1857, fol.14v°. **265** *Top* PML, Ms M. 944, fols.52v-53/AR. *Center* Musée Condé, Chantilly, Ms 65/1284, fol.2r°, Gi. **266** Ben Zvi Institute, Jerusalem, DH. **267** *Top* DH. *Bottom* Photo: Bruce and Kenneth Zuckerman, West Semitic Research, in collaboration with the Ancient Biblical Manuscript Center, courtesy, Russian National Library (Saltykov-Shchedrin), Leningrad Codex, fol.474a. **268** *Top* Bodleian Library, Oxford University, Ms Kennicott 1, fol.442. *Bottom* State Library of Berlin, Hamilton 288, fol.15, photo: Kössel/BPK. **269** *Top* ZR. *Center* IM. *Bottom* BL, Ms Or. 2348, fol.38v. **270** Kunsthistorisches Museum, Vienna, EL/AR. **271** *Top* Etz Haim, Amsterdam. *Bottom* Bodleian Library, Oxford University, Ms Auct. D.4.6, fol.91. **272** *Top (detail)* Austrian National Library. Vienna, Codex 2554, fol.1*v. *Bottom (detail)* BN, Ms Fr. 2813, fol.265. **273** Christie's, N.Y. **274** AAA. **275** *Top (detail)* PML, Ms M. 716.4/AR. *Center* Treasury of St. Mark's, Venice, WFA/AR. **276** *Top* SH and Laura Lushington. *Bottom (both)* SH. **277** *Top-left* G. Guittot/DIAF. *Top-right* and *Bottom-left* Kumasegawa/Artephot. *Bottom-right* Fabbri/Artephot. **278** New York Ensemble for Early Music. **279** The Beinecke Rare Book and Manuscript Library, Yale University. **280** Culver Pictures, Inc. **281** *Top* Sc/AR. *Bottom* Episcopal General Vicarate, Diocese of Trier, Germany, photo: Franz Ronig. **282** Museo Francescano, Rome, Al/AR. **283** *Top* Courtesy of the Fogg Art Museum, Harvard University Art Museums, Hervey E. Wetzel Bequest Fund. *Bottom* S. Croce, Florence, Sc/AR. **284** *(detail)* PML, 21194/AR. **285** *Top (detail)* S. Maria Novella, Florence, Sc/AR. *Bottom* Museo Civico Medievale di Bologna. **286** *(detail)* City of Manchester Town Hall, by permission. **287** *Top* Rosgartenmuseum, Konstanz, Germany, Hs1, fol.58a. *Bottom* ABS, photo: Richard Berenson. **288-289** ABS, photo: Robert D. Rubic, N.Y.C. **290** *1455-1515 Top* The Bettmann Archive. *Center* Sc/AR. *Bottom GC. 1515-1540 Top* Hubert Josse/AR. *Center GC. Bottom* The Lundoff Collection. *1540-1585 Bottom* GC. *1585-1620 Top* AAA. *Center* G. Tortoli/AAA. *Bottom* ABS, photo: Richard Berenson. *1620-1750 Bottom* Sculpture by Augustus Saint-Gaudens, MMA, Bequest of Jacob Ruppert, 1939. **291** *1750-1800 Top* GC. *Center* Artist: John Webber, National Maritime Museum, London. *1800-1850 Top* Sc/AR. *Center* Science Museum, Science & Society Picture Library, London. *1850-1900 (both)* The Lundoff Collection. *1900-1950 Top* Sc/AR. *Center-right* Michael Tamborrino/ The Stock Market. *Center-left* Christian Michaels/FPG International. *Bottom* Museum of Connecticut History. *1950-2000 Top* The Bettmann Archive. *Bottom* John Parkin/AP/Wide World Photos. **292** *Top* PML, 818, Vol.II, fol.131v-132/AR. *Inset* AKG Photo. **293** *Top* The American Museum of Papermaking, Institute of Paper Science Technology, Atlanta. *Bottom* BAL/AR. **296** *(both)* Gutenberg Museum, Mainz. **297** Mediatheque Municipale de Cambrai, Ms 620, fol.1. **298** *Top* ABS, photo: Richard Berenson. *Center* PML, 26983/AR. *Bottom* CUL, BFBS.229.A78. **299** *Top* BL, G. 1804. *Center* PML, 21590(CHL 1349)/AR. *Bottom* ABS, photo: Robert D. Rubic, N.Y.C. **300** *Top* Louvre, Sc/AR. *Bottom* ABS, photo: Randall States. **301** BL, 675c5. **302** *Top* Museum Plantin-Moretus, Antwerp. *Inset* Cathedral, Toledo, Spain, AM. *Bottom* Rare Books and Manuscripts Division, NYPL. **303** *Top* Cathedral, Antwerp, Dienst Kunstpatrimonium. *Bottom* Museum Plantin-Moretus, Antwerp. **304** *Top* Nuremberg National Museum/AR. *Bottom* AAA. **305** *Left* German Information Center, N.Y.C. *Right* GC. **306** AAA. **307** BL, 679I15. **308** With permission of the Principal, Fellows and Scholars of Hertford College, Oxford University. **309** *Top* BL, C37h2. *Center* ABS, photo: Randall States. **310** *Left* ABS, photo: Richard Berenson. *Right* Engraving by J. Brain, NYPL Picture Collection. **311** *Top* The Frick Collection. *Bottom* BL, C18 d1. **312** *Center* Society of Antiquaries, London, BAL/AR. *Bottom* GC. **313** *Top* ABS, photo: Richard Berenson. **314** BL, BAL/AR. **315** *Top* The Bettmann Archive. *Center* BL, 218c13. **316** By courtesy of the National Portrait Gallery, London. **317** ABS, photo: Richard Berenson. **318** "The Preaching at St. Paul" by John Gipkyn, Private Collection. **320** *Top* The Free Library of Philadelphia, photo: Joan Broderick. *Bottom* Museu Nacional de Arte Antiga, photo: ©Michael Holford. **321** Naval Museum, Lisbon, GDO. **322** Lisbon Museum of Art, GDO. **323** *Top* GC. *Center* ABS. *Bottom* Overseas Missionary Fellowship International, Canada. **324** Private Collection, Paris, Gi/AR. **325** *Top* BM, WFA/AR. *Center* Portrait by George Baxter, National Portrait Gallery, London. *Bottom* Musée Royal Afrique Centrale, Tervuren, Belgium, WFA/AR. **326** *Top* Avchivo Oronoz/Artephot. *Center* Museo del Palacio de Bellas Artes, Mexico City, Gi/AR. **329** *Top* ©1995 James Blank/Shangle Photographics. *Inset* Portrait by T.G. Mosqueda, Santa Barbara Mission Archive Library. *Bottom* Taylor Museum Collection, Colorado Springs Fine Arts Center. **330** *Top* BL, AC442L.16.371. *Bottom* Bill Ivy. **331** Paul Mellon Collection, National Gallery of Art, Washington, D.C. **332** Courtesy, American Antiquarian Society. **333** *Top* The Henry E. Huntington Library and Art Gallery. *Bottom* Courtesy of The John Carter Brown Library at Brown University. **334** Portrait by Robert Lindneux, Woolaroc Museum, Bartlesville, Okla. **335** Private Collection, photo: Bob Mates. **336** *Top* Courtesy of The John Carter Brown Library at Brown University. *Inset* Courtesy, American Antiquarian Society. **337** *Top* Bust by Jean-Antoine Houdon. George Nixon Black Fund, Courtesy, The Museum of Fine Arts, Boston. *Bottom* ABS, photo: Robert D. Rubic, N.Y.C. **338** *Left* Courtesy of The John Carter Brown Library at Brown University. *Right* Sketch by Lewis Miller, Courtesy of The Historical Society of York County, Pa. **339** Courtesy of The Museum of Folk Art, N.Y.C. **340** *Top* Gift of Maxim Karolik to the M. and M. Karolik Collection of American Paintings, courtesy, Museum of Fine Arts, Boston. *Inset* Rare Books and Manuscripts Division, NYPL, photo: Robert D. Rubic. N.Y.C. *Bottom* Shelburne Museum, Shelburne, Vt., photo: Ken Burris. **341** *Top-left* Courtesy, American Antiquarian Society. *Top-right* Rendering by Rose Campbell-Gerke, Index of American Design, ©1995 Board of Trustees, National Gallery of Art, Washington D.C. watercolor, gouache, and graphite on paperboard, photo: Dean Beasom. *Center-left* Stoke Museum, England, E.T. Archive, London. *Center-right* Shelburne Museum, Shelburne, Vt., photo: Ken Burris. *Bottom* Abby Aldrich Rockefeller Folk Art Center, Williamsburg, Va. **342** Collection Frank J. Miele Gallery, N.Y.C., courtesy of The Museum of American Folk Art, N.Y.C., photo: John Parnell. **343** *Top* John T. Hopf, courtesy, Friends of Touro Synagogue. *Inset* American Jewish Historical Society, Waltham, Mass., photo: Julian Brown. **344** *Top* Sophia Smith Collection, Smith College. *Bottom-left* Abby Aldrich Rockefeller Folk Art Center, Williamsburg, Va. *Bottom-right* Bequest of Maxim Karolik, courtesy, Museum of Fine Arts, Boston. **345** *(both)* ©The Church of Jesus Christ of Latter-day Saints, used by permission. **347** *Top* Photo: Weldon C. Andersen, ©The Church of Jesus Christ of Latter-day Saints, used by permission. *Center* Photo: Don O. Thorpe, ©The Church of Jesus Christ of Latter-day Saints, used by permission. **348** *Top* Portraits by Samuel Finley Breese Morse, Yale University Art Gallery, Gift of Hiram Bingham, B.A. 1898. *Bottom* Allan Seiden, The Hawaiian Legacy Archive. **349** *Top* ©Douglas Peebles. *Bottom* Alexander Turnbull Library, Wellington, New Zealand. **350** Church Army, London. **351** *(both)* ABS Historical Archives. **352** *(both)* ABS Historical Archives. **353** *Top* Courtesy, The Gideons International. *Bottom* ABS Historical Archives. **354** *Top* ABS. *Center* Courtesy, Museum of the Alphabet, JAARS Center, Waxhaw, N.C. *Bottom* Courtesy, Wycliffe Bible Translators Inc., Summer Institute of Linguistics, photo: Barb Alvarez. **356** Courtesy, JAARS Center, Waxhaw, N.C., photo: Bud Speck. **357** *Top* Photo: Don Hesse. *Bottom* Photo: Kirk Franklin, *(both)* Courtesy, Wycliffe Bible Translators, Inc. **358** *Bibleopoly*, Late for the Sky Production Co., Cincinnati, Ohio. *Jesus and Zaccheus*, ©1995 by The Standard Publishing Co., used by permission. *Good News Bible, Teach Yourself New Testament Greek, The Explorer's Bible,* and *The Promise (all)* Produced by Thomas Nelson, Inc. *The Parenting Bible,* ©1994 by The Zondervan Corporation and *The Student's Complete Vocabulary Guide to the Greek New Testament* by Warren C. Trenchard, ©1992 by Warren C. Trenchard, *(both)* used by permission of Zondervan Publishing House. **359** *Top* Videos, courtesy, The Reader's Digest Association, Inc. *The Precise Parallel New Testament,* ed. John R. Kohlenberger III, Oxford University Press. *The Preschoolers Bible,* ©1994 by Educational Publishing Concepts, Inc., Text ©1994 by V. Gilbert Beers, published by Victor Books, used by permission. *The Complete Book of Bible Trivia,* published by Tyndale House Publishers, Inc. *The Life of Christ; The Easter Story,*™ and ©1993, 1995 Marvel Characters, Inc. All rights reserved. *Bible Crosswords Collections #4,* published by Barbour & Company, Inc., P.O. Box 719, Uhrichsville, Ohio. *The Tiny Bible,* World Publishing Co., Grand Rapids, Mich. *Discovering the Whole Story* (cassette) by Verna Dozier, Cowley Publications, Boston, Mass. *The Rainbow Study Bible* (opened), ©1981, 1986, 1989, and 1992 by Rainbow Studies, Inc. All Rights Reserved. Photo Montage: Steven Mays. **360** *Top* ©Grolier Electronic Publishing, Inc., Thomas Nelson and DS2 Interactive. *Center* Courtesy, Franklin Electronic Publishers, Inc. **361** *Top Internet for Christians* by Dr. Quentin Schultze, published by Gospel Films, Inc./Gospel Communications Network, Muskegon, Mich. *Center-left The Lion PC Bible Handbook,* reproduced courtesy of Lion Publishing, Oxford, England, distributed in U.S.A. by Logos Information Systems. *Center-right Read With Me Bible* CD-ROM ©1993 by The Zondervan Corporation, used by permission of Zondervan Publishing House. *Bottom-left* Software design *The Holy Scriptures,* used by permission, Christian Technologies, Inc., Independence, Mo. *Bottom-center The Dead Sea Scrolls,* published by Pixel Multimedia and Aaron Witkin Assoc., under exclusive license of IAA. Marketed worldwide exclusively by Logos Research Systems, Inc., Oak Harbor, Wa. *Bottom-right The New Family Bible,* reprinted with permission by Time Warner Interactive Group. Photo Montage: Steven Mays. **362** J. Baylor Roberts, ©NGS. **363** *Top* Taylor-Schechter Collection, CUL, Cambridge, England T-S 10 K.6. *Center* JTS. **364** *Top* DH, IM. *Center* Brigham Young University, Provo, Utah. **365** *Top* University of Arizona, Tuscon, photo: Janet McCoy. *Center* Photo: Bruce & Kenneth Zuckerman, West Semetic Research. *Bottom* By permission of the President and Fellows of Magdalen College, Oxford University, Ms Gk.17.

Acknowledgments

Staff of Art Resource, New York City

Staff of The British Library Photographic Services, London

Staff of Photographic Services, The Israel Museum, Jerusalem

The Church of Jesus Christ of Latter-day Saints

Seth Jerchower of Special Collections, and the Staff of the Graphics Collection Room, Jewish Theological Seminary of America Library, New York City

Edward Kasinec, Chief, and the Staff of the Slavic and Baltic Division, The New York Public Library

Kate Lewin, Photo Research, Paris

Irene Lewitt, Photo Research, Jerusalem

Dr. Liana Lupas and Maria Deptula, The American Bible Society, N.Y.

Jach Rushing, Wycliffe Bible Translators, Huntington Beach, California

Index

Page numbers in **bold** type refer to illustrations.